KILLER IMAGES

Nonfictions is dedicated to expanding and deepening
the range of contemporary documentary studies.
It aims to engage in the theoretical conversation
about documentaries, open new areas of scholarship,
and recover lost or marginalised histories.

General Editor, Brian Winston

Other titles in the **Nonfictions** series:

Direct Cinema: Observational Documentary and the Politics of the Sixties
by Dave Saunders

Projecting Migration: Transcultural Documentary Practice
edited by Alan Grossman and Aine O'Brien

The Image and the Witness: Trauma, Memory and Visual Culture
edited by Frances Guerin and Roger Hallas

Films of Fact: A History of Science in Documentary Films and Television
by Timothy Boon

Building Bridges: The Cinema of Jean Rouch
edited by Joram ten Brink

Vision On: Film, Television and the Arts in Britain
by John Wyver

Chavez: The Revolution Will Not Be Televised – A Case Study of Politics and the Media
by Rod Stoneman

Documentary Display: Re-Viewing Nonfiction Film and Video
by Keith Beattie

The Personal Camera: Subjective Cinema and the Essay Film
by Laura Rascaroli

The Cinema of Me: The Self and Subjectivity in First Person Documentary
by Alisa Lebow

KILLER IMAGES

Documentary Film, Memory and the Performance of Violence

EDITED BY
JORAM TEN BRINK & JOSHUA OPPENHEIMER

WALLFLOWER PRESS
LONDON & NEW YORK

Arts & Humanities
Research Council

A Wallflower Press Book
Published by
Columbia University Press
Publishers Since 1893
New York · Chichester, West Sussex
cup.columbia.edu

A complete CIP record is available from the Library of Congress

ISBN 978-0-231-16334-7 (cloth) ISBN
978-0-231-16335-4 (pbk.) ISBN
978-0-231-85024-7 (e-book)

Design by Elsa Mathern

CONTENTS

BATTLE FOR HISTORY: APPROPRIATING THE PAST IN THE PRESENT

PERFORMING VIOLENCE

ACKNOWLEDGEMENTS

The genesis of this volume is the UK Arts and Humanities Research Council-supported research project 'Genocide and Genre', awarded to us through the University of Westminster. At the core of the project was the making of the film *The Act of Killing* (2012) which, alongside the present volume, examines cinema's unique position in exploring both the routines of violence as well as the rhetoric and imagination that begets violence. The film and the critical reflections in turn grew out of the explorations of the filmmaking collective Vision Machine Film Project. To Vision Machine collaborators Christine Cynn, Andrea Zimmerman and Michael Uwemedimo, words cannot express our debt. Also, deserving special mention is *The Act of Killing*'s lead producer, Signe Byrge Sørensen.

At the University of Westminster, special thanks must be offered to Rosie Thomas and Peter Goodwin who have been a reliable source of encouragement and guidance throughout.

We owe special gratitude to Alisa Lebow, who, in addition to contributing to this volume, offered numerous useful suggestions about its form.

We are grateful to innumerable colleagues – academics and filmmakers – for their support, inspiration and advice over the three years we have been preparing this book. We would also like to thank the Goethe Institute in London and Birkbeck College of the University of London for hosting several of the events that contributed to the production of this volume.

We cannot praise enough the hard work and dedication of Lia Na'ama ten Brink in transcribing and editing the interviews in this volume through the different stages of the book's development. She offered endlessly inspiring and wise insights throughout the process. It is fair to say there would be no book without her help. We would also like to thank the tireless efforts of Yoram Allon and Jodie Taylor of Wallflower Press in bringing this book to print. And, of course, last but not least, to all the contributors to this volume, for their insight, original research and patience, a very, very special thank you.

Joram ten Brink & Joshua Oppenheimer
September 2012

NOTES ON CONTRIBUTORS

BENEDICT ANDERSON, Aaron Binenkorb Professor of International Studies, Emeritus, Cornell University. Citizen of Ireland. Specialist on the history and politics of Indonesia, Thailand and the Philippines. Banned from Indonesia between 1972 to 1999. Author of *Java in a Time of Revolution* (1972), *Imagined Communities* (1983), *Language and Power* (1992), *The Spectre of Comparisons* (1998), *Under Three Flags* (2005), among other works. Founder and long-time editor of the journal *Indonesia*.

JORAM TEN BRINK is a filmmaker and Professor of Film at the University of Westminster, London, where he is also director of Doc West, the Centre for Production and Research of Documentary Film. His films have been broadcast and theatrically released internationally, and his work has been screened at the Berlin and Rotterdam film festivals and at MoMA in New York. His previous publications include, as editor, *Building Bridges: The Cinema of Jean Rouch* (2007).

STÉPHANIE BENZAQUEN is an art historian and curator. She is currently a PhD candidate at the Centre for Historical Culture, Faculty of History and Arts, Erasmus University Rotterdam. She gained her MA in Art History at the Sorbonne University in Paris. Since 1999, she has organised projects and exhibitions in Israel, Central and Eastern Europe, Russia, France and Thailand.

MICHAEL CHANAN is a documentarist, author of numerous books on both film and music, and Professor of Film & Video at the University of Roehampton, London. In the 1980s, he shot a number of films in Cuba and Latin America, most of them for Channel Four, and published the first edition of his history of Cuban Cinema. He first became involved in Latin American cinema when he curated a retrospective of new Chilean cinema in London in 1976, and recently renewed his interest in that country with 'Three Short Films About Chile', shot in 2011. He blogs as Putney Debater.

ARIEL HERYANTO is Associate Professor of Indonesian Studies and Head of Southeast Asia Centre, The Australian National University. He is the author of *State Terrorism and Political Identity In Indonesia: Fatally Belonging* (2007), and editor of *Popular Culture in Indonesia: Fluid Identities in Post-Authoritarian Politics* (2008).

THOMAS KEENAN teaches literature and human rights at Bard College, New York, where he directs the Human Rights Project. He is the author of *Fables of Responsibility* (1997), co-editor of *New Media, Old Media* (2005) with Wendy Chun, and co-author, with Eyal Weizman, of *Mengele's Skull* (2012).

ALISA LEBOW is a Reader in Film Studies at the University of Sussex. Her research is generally concerned with issues related to documentary film, recently to do with questions of the political in documentary. Her books *Cinema of Me* (2012) and *First Person Jewish* (2008) explore aspects of the representation of self and subjectivity in first person film. She is also a filmmaker whose films include *Outlaw* (1994), *Treyf* (1998), and *For the Record: The World Tribunal on Iraq* (2007).

ADAM LOWENSTEIN is Associate Professor of English and Film Studies at the University of Pittsburgh. He is the author of *Shocking Representation: Historical Trauma, National Cinema, and the Modern Horror Film* (2005) as well as essays that have appeared in *Cinema Journal, Critical Quarterly, Film Quarterly, Post Script, Representations, boundary 2,* and numerous anthologies.

DANIEL MORGAN is an Assistant Professor of Film Studies in the Department of English at the University of Pittsburgh. He is author of *Late Godard and the Possibilities of Cinema* (2012) as well as many articles on topics in film theory and aesthetics.

JOSHUA OPPENHEIMER is a filmmaker based in London and Copenhagen. His most recent film is *The Act of Killing* (2012). He is a founding member of the filmmaking collaboration Vision Machine, with whom he worked for over a decade with militias, death squads and their victims to explore the relationship between political violence and the public imagination. He was a senior researcher on the AHRC-funded 'Genocide and Genre' project at the University of Westminster, and is the co-editor, with Helena Reckitt, of *Acting on AIDS: Sex, Drugs and Politics* (1997).

GARRETT STEWART, James O. Freedman Professor of Letters at the University of Iowa, is the author of several books on prose fiction as well as *Between Film and Screen: Modernism's Photo Synthesis* and *Framed Time: Toward a Postfilmic Cinema* (2007). His novel *Violence: A Narratography of Victorian Fiction* was awarded the 2011 Barbara and George Perkins Prize from the International Society for the Study of Narrative. He was elected in 2010 to the American Academy of Arts and Sciences.

MICHAEL UWEMEDIMO is a filmmaker, writer and curator, and a founding member of the filmmaking collaboration, Vision Machine. With Vision Machine he developed a performance-based historiography of political violence. Through a series of long-running film projects with survivors and perpetrators of state-sponsored violence, he has been developing a working process in which the production methods and forms of fiction can be combined with the techniques and engagements of documentary. For the past three years Michael has been living and working in Port Harcourt, Nigeria. Michael is also a Lecturer in Film at Roehampton University and Project Director, Collaborative Media Advocacy Platform (CMAP).

BRIAN WINSTON, Professor of Communications and Lincoln Chair at the University of Lincoln, started his career in 1963 on Granada TV's long-running news documentary film series *World in Action*. In 1985, he won an Emmy for Episode 8 of WNET's *Civilization and the Jews*, 'Out of the Ashes'. He is the author of many books and articles on the documentary, inlcuding *Claiming the Real II: Grierson and Beyond* (2008), and is general editor of the *Nonfictions* series from Wallflower Press, of which this volume is a part.

INTRODUCTION

In 1914, Mexican bandit turned revolutionary, Pancho Villa, starred in an action movie called *The Life of General Villa*. The Mutual Film Corporation offered Villa $25,000 and 50 per cent of the film's profits. Villa accepted, eager for the additional finance it brought to his campaign against the armies of Porfirio Diaz. The deal required that Pancho Villa fight his battles by daylight and in front of Mutual's rolling cameras, and that he re-enact them if more footage was needed. In the words of the Mutual Film Corporation president, Villa agreed 'to run his part of the insurrection for moving pictures, taking a prominent part himself'.[1] The film's co-star was silent movie actor and future Hollywood director Raoul Walsh, who consequently had numerous cameos in several historic battles of the Mexican Revolution. (And although *The Life of General Villa* was the first and last movie that the film's supervising producer, D. W. Griffith, would make with the Mexican revolutionary, the very next year Griffith would cast Walsh as Lincoln's assassin in *Birth of a Nation*.) *The Life of General Villa* opened in New York City within two months of the last battle Villa staged for the cameras.

Cinema has long shaped not only how political violence, from torture to warfare to genocide, is perceived, but also how it is performed. Today, when media coverage is central to terror campaigns, and newscasters serve as embedded journalists in the 'war on terror''s televisual front, understanding how the moving image is implicated in the imagination and actions of perpetrators and survivors of mass violence is all the more urgent.

The cinematic image and mass violence on huge scales are two defining features of modernity. The possibilities and limits of that image in nonfiction film – as 'witness' to and 'evidence' of collective violence – have been central concerns of such filmmakers as Marcel Ophüls, Claude Lanzmann and Rithy Panh, as well as the theoretical reflections on 'post-traumatic cinema' that their work has catalysed (for example, Joshua Hirsch, Malin Wahlberg, Thomas Elsaesser, Janet Walker, E. Ann Kaplan, Tony Haggith and Joanna Newman). Lanzmann's film work, in particular, is marked by the conviction that the horror of such violence lies beyond cinematic imagination. However, one consequence of imagining the trauma of genocide as inevitably exceeding the cinematic image is to neglect the implication of that image in genocide itself. Often a cinematic imagination is directly implicated in the machinery of annihilation. The Nazi interdiction on any photographic trace of the extermination programme is as revealing of a cinematic consciousness attendant to genocide as their production of a false cinematic record to disguise the 'final solution' (consider, for instance, the propaganda film 'documenting' the contented life of Theresienstadt concentration camp prisoners, *The Führer Gives a Village to the Jews* (1944)).

In the first Liberian civil war, warlord Joshua Milton Blahyi (better known as 'General Butt Naked') would screen action movies to the young children he abducted to be soldiers. He showed actors getting killed in one film, and appearing again in another film. He told the children that when they kill people, they come alive again in another movie; that made it easier for the kids to kill.[2] In Sierra Leone, *Rambo* (1982) was a canonical text for Revolutionary United Front rebels, who borrowed their *noms-de-guerre* directly from Hollywood action films. As recently as 2002, Guantánamo torturers developing their 'enhanced interrogation techniques' looked no further than prime-time television for inspiration: Jack Bauer offered a treasure trove of techniques in his weekly torture of terrorists.[3] And in North Sumatra, Indonesia, the army recruited its death squads during the 1965–66 'extermination of the communists' from the ranks of self-described 'movie theatre gangsters' – thugs who controlled a black market in movie tickets, and who used the cinemas as a base for more serious criminal activity. The army chose these men because they had a proven capacity for violence, and because they already hated the leftists for boycotting American films (the most popular, and profitable, in the cinemas). These killers explicitly fashioned themselves – and their methods of murder – after the Hollywood stars who were projected on the screens that provided their livelihood. Coming out of the midnight show, they describe feeling 'just like gangsters who stepped off the screen'. In this heady mood, they strolled across the boulevard to their office and killed their nightly quota of prisoners, using techniques borrowed directly from movies. (This particular intersection of cinema and mass-murder is the territory explored by Joshua Oppenheimer's film, *The Act of Killing* (2012), discussed in two contributions to this volume.)

Cinema is often directly implicated in the imagination and machinery of mass-violence. Thus, if the cinematic image and mass violence are two defining features of modernity, the former is significantly implicated in the latter. The nature of this implication is this volume's central focus. If the book's chapters share a common starting point, it is that cinema offers unique opportunities to explore both the routines of violence as well as the rhetoric and imagination that begets violence. The contributions here engage with film and video projects that explore the perspectives of both perpetrators and survivors. They investigate cinema both as a tool for articulating histories of political violence, while at the same time analysing how cinema itself can operate as an actor in these histories. This latter exploration may itself be divided into two broad areas.

First, there are chapters that explore how the moving image, as for Pancho Villa and Indonesia's movie-theatre gangsters, may play a direct role in the execution of political violence. These consider, of course, the deployment of moving images in the execution of the violence itself. This is not limited to the direct use of moving images as components of high-tech weaponry, as propaganda or as instrument of political mobilisation; it also includes how the cinematic inflection of perpetrators' imaginations can become a crucial resource in the execution of violence (as it was for Indonesia's movie-theatre gangsters). As urgently, these essays explore the impact of narrative – cinematic, historical, as well as those generated by the broadcast media – on the imaginations of key bystanders who might intervene to reduce violence, including the 'international community' and the general public.

Second, in a logical development of Jean-Luc Godard's insight that 'forgetting extermination is part of extermination',[4] there are contributions that examine the contemporary consequences of historical remembrance, specifically the cinematic recovery of violent pasts. These chapters examine cinema as a set of diverse practices that can intervene in how historical accounts of violent pasts function in the present. They explore how perpetrators' accounts (including official histories by victorious and unchallenged perpetrators) may function as crucial elements of a regime of terror and repression. Specifically, they interrogate how violence may originally be staged as spectacle, one whose 'theatre of operations' was to be symbolically rehearsed again and again in official histories and their fictive projections in works of cinema. Here, the smooth functioning of such regimes may be disrupted by filmmaking projects that either exploit inconsistencies within perpetrators' accounts, or that frame such accounts with the responses of those subjects they exclude – survivors. These contributions ask how such methods might enable communities of survivors to respond to, recover and redeem a history that sought to physically and symbolically annihilate them?

Several contributors interrogate the tension between cinema's potential to document violence and the cinematic impulse to stylise historical rendition – most fruitfully by deconstructing the deceptively transparent genres of authentic testimony and historical realism.

This book's focus is decidedly not the ethical, aesthetic or political consequences of the representation of violence in cinema in nonfiction film. Neither it is a study of the history of screen violence or the genres of film violence (a developed area of Film Studies). Rather, this volume focuses on cinema's engagement with the performance of violence. Although most chapters are studies of nonfiction film projects, Adam Lowenstein and Daniel Morgan use fiction films (Japanese horror and late Godard, respectively) to analyse how cinematic space may be structured (and ruptured) by repressed or traumatic histories.

This anthology offers scholarly contributions from academics, as well as insightful discussions by filmmakers about their own practice (Harun Farocki, Avi Mograbi, Errol Morris, Joshua Oppenheimer, David Polonsky and Rithy Panh). The contributions from filmmakers are offered in the hope that their direct experience working in theatres of violence, from Iraq to the US military's training machine, from Lebanon to Israel to Palestine, and Indonesia to Cambodia, will offer important insights into the cutting-edge possibilities of cinematic intervention in contexts of mass violence.

It is divided into four main sections. The first, *(De)activating Empathy*, investigates the gulf between the declared intention and actual effects of the moving images that emanate from the world's conflict zones. Under what conditions does media attention to political violence generate (or fail to generate) the political will for constructive intervention? Under what conditions do images desensitise us to violence? Under what conditions do they create sympathy, and what are the effects of that sympathy? The book opens with a detailed study of the use (and misuse) of broadcast news images of the siege of Sarajevo. What difference did these images have in stopping ethnic cleansing? The answers are surprising, and demand a radical rethinking of Enlightenment assumptions of a public sphere, in which knowledge begets empathy begets constructive action. Here, it appears that the political stories we tell with violent images are, ultimately, far more important than the poignancy of the images themselves in determining their consequences. The imperative for specifically 'humanitarian' action that accompanies decontextualised, depoliticised images of suffering may, in numerous ways, prove counterproductive.

This is followed by an exploration of two video interventions in zones of violent conflict: the feature-length documentary, *Burma VJ* (2008), which presents the work of Burma's video journalists, and the video projects of the Israeli human rights NGO, B'Tselem. Both projects involve activists using video cameras to document conflict. The chapter offers a detailed analysis of each project's goals and strategies, and concludes by questioning their methods, impact and unspoken ideological commitments. Specifically, the chapter questions whether suffering, turned into a marketable narrative, hinders critical understanding or political action.

Harun Farocki's recent project, *Immersion* (2009), documents the use of VR by the US Army as a therapeutic tool to help soldiers recover from post-traumatic stress upon their return from the battlefields of Iraq and Afghanistan. Soldiers' memories of what they experienced in the theatre of war (the violence they lived through) is re-staged with the help of a VR console game. In this form of exposure therapy, the soldiers are visually *immersed* in their experiences of violence and combat. Yet in a sinister twist, the identical mise-en-scène is used to desensitise pre-combat soldiers to the potentially traumatic impact of violence prior to their deployment. That the same moving images used to help individuals forget the trauma of war is *also* used to make soldiers more effective fighting machines is, again, an ironic corollary to Godard's proposition that forgetting violence may be, in this case quite literally, part of the apparatus of violence.

'Violent elements typical of Brazilian films are means of provoking the public out of its alienation', proclaimed the filmmaker Glauber Rocha in 1965. Closing the first section of the book, we revisit his essay on the aesthetics of hunger in its attempt to make manifest the structural causes of violence. Rocha proposed an equation between hunger and violence, as violence is a direct response of Latin America's poor to the conditions of their deprivation. Set against the background of 1960s Latin American cinema, a detailed analysis of Rocha's manifesto is presented here – and the conclusions are contrary to those of the previous three contributions. Here, the aesthetics of violence is marshalled for the revolutionary purpose of provoking viewers out of alienation and into action with the intention of subverting and, ultimately, destroying the material causes of poverty.

The second section, *Memory of Violence: Visualising Trauma*, discusses major strategies used by nonfiction filmmakers over the past fifty years to deal with traumatic effects of violence. It opens with a reflective analysis of efforts to visualise the trauma of the Holocaust from the 1950s to today. Because there exists only 1'59" of moving images of the mass execution of Jews in Eastern Europe (along with fragmentary moving images photographed in the days following the liberation of the death camps), there are considerable challenges for generations of documentary filmmakers seeking to address the trauma of the Holocaust. Claude Lanzmann's nine-hour film, *Shoah* (1985), effectively sums up the strategies available for the realist Holocaust documentary (in the absence of archive footage) – and exposes its shortcomings. Is the Holocaust beyond the reach of documentary? Perhaps not, suggests this contribution, as it surveys other modes open to nonfiction filmmaking (the films of Péter Forgács, Joram ten Brink and, especially, Orly Yadin and Sylvie Bringas's animated film, *Silence*). The chapter argues that these filmic modes create the degree of *ostranenie* (de-familiarisation) needed to overcome the over-familiarity of the narrative of the Holocaust (and its iconography) after more than fifty years of realist visual treatment.

The next three chapters further develop this exploration of animation as a tool for projecting the ruptured psychic tissue of memory (including its lacunae, blindspots and wormholes) in the aftermath of traumatic violence – in this case the September 1982 massacre of several thousand civilians at the Sabra and Shatila Palestinian refugee camps in Lebanon. Here, the film work in question is the world's first animated feature-length documentary film, *Waltz with Bashir* (2008). The first of these chapters addresses the question of the psychic adequacy of documentary images, and examines the possibilities of creating a 'screen memory' – 'a psychic topography' of the soldiers' mind. This is followed by an interview with the film's art director on the visual strategies deployed in creating the film.

The next chapter explores how fictional cinematic space may be structured by repressed historical violence. Examining the horror films of Japanese filmmaker Kiyoshi Kurosawa, this contribution argues that the horror genre's 'elasticity' allows Kurosawa to explore repressed traumatic history. Here, traumatic violence (the atom bomb attacks on Hiroshima and Nagasaki, the firebombing of virtually every major Japanese city, military aggression followed by defeat) once repressed, becomes spectral and haunts the surface of Kurosawa's films, while structuring their cinematic and imaginative spaces. Repressed nonfiction trauma conditions the very space of fictive imagining.

The following chapter closes this section with a similar exploration of how fictive language is structured by (and in response to) historical violence and political trauma. This time, however, the focus is on Jean-Luc Godard's *Allemagne 90 neuf zero* (1991). In his films and videos since the late 1980s, Godard's project has been to develop aesthetic resources for facing and grappling with the legacy of a century marked by violence. Here, stuttering, silence and disruption is often more important than understanding. His work is founded on the conviction that film is implicated in the historical events it seeks to analyse. In *Allemagne 90 neuf zero*, Godard makes a case for cinema as uniquely capable for addressing history in a way that other media and modes of analysis cannot, resulting in historical understanding and knowledge made possible by innovations in film form.

The third section of the book, *Battle for History: Appropriating the Past in the*

Present, explores how narratives of the past are used and implicated in contemporary settings. It opens with an interview with the Israeli director Avi Mograbi, on his use of film to subvert the narratives of official histories (which are invariably written by history's 'winners', and therefore, most often, by perpetrators). The focus of the interview is Mograbi's sardonic essay film, *Avenge But One of My Two Eyes* (2005). Mograbi's cinematic style as provocateur from behind the camera changes the dynamics of the events that he documents at Israeli Army checkpoints in the West Bank. This allows him to highlight moments of violence and humiliation that otherwise would remain invisible. Here is proposed a central mission of nonfiction cinema: to document, on a regular basis, a 'way of life' for both victims and perpetrators of violence, and thereby to make present for our understanding the mechanisms of violence, the way that violence that we wish would be unimaginable is not only imagined, but far too easily performed. The chapter explores, too, the ethical implications of Mograbi's unusually pronounced self-reflexivity (one that many filmmakers avoid) in his documentation of systemic violence.

The next two chapters in this section explore re-enactment as another cinematic strategy to confront the violent past: here, re-enactment as a strategy of performing the past in order to reveal its implication in the present. Under the guise of excavating and manifesting (in the present) authentic details of the past, many re-enactment projects (and the re-enactors themselves), knowingly or not, are interested in the past for its significance in the present. In this sense, re-enactments are always interventions in the present. The first of these chapters discusses Peter Watkins' films *Culloden* (1964) and *La Commune* (2000). While re-enactment (and in the case of films like *Punishment Park* (1971) and *The War Game* (1965), re-enactment of hypothetical histories and 'pre-enactments') has been a core filmmaking strategy for Watkins, the chapter explores how the re-enactment process deployed in *Culloden* and *La Commune* constituted a platform not only for an in-depth historical analysis of the battles being re-enacted, but, and even more so, for an articulation of parallels between the past and the present. In that sense, like Rocha's violent imagery, these films open new possibilities for analysis and action *in the present*. Walter Benjamin's understanding of the historian as one who summons the past (and in particular the tradition of the oppressed) into the present, so that it 'flashes up at the instant it can be recognized', is very close indeed.[5]

The second chapter on re-enactment discusses the contemporary politics involved in Jeremy Deller's massive re-enactment of the Battle of Orgreave between the police and striking English miners in 1984. The re-enactment was performed in 2001 as a major live performance, and documented for a feature-length documentary, *The Battle of Orgreave* (2001), by film director Mike Figgis. The chapter explores Deller's fascination with 'living history' and using re-enactment as a critical tool to look at the past's implication in the presence. By seeking to elicit conflicting narratives of the violence at Orgreave, Deller seeks to undermine the authoritative official history of the events, and to re-ignite the radical imagination of the striking miners in 2001 Britain.

The next chapter, 'Remediating Genocidal Images into Artworks: The Case of the Tuol Sleng Mug Shots' investigates the appropriation by visual artists of mug shots of political prisoners at the Khmer Rouge's Tuol Sleng political prison (also known as S21) in Phnom Penh. The inmates in Tuol Sleng were photographed as soon as they arrived at the prison. Their picture was attached to the 'confessions' extracted (or fabricated) by their jailers; after the prisoner 'confessed', he or she was invariably murdered at the killing fields outside Phnom Penh. When Tuol Sleng was turned into the Tuol Sleng Genocide Museum in 1980, these photographs were enlarged and put on display. The mug shots have become icons of the Cambodian Genocide. While the chapter recalls the first section's investigation of the use of iconic images of violence as tools for the activation of empathy, as well as Deller's notion of 'living history', it focuses on the visual and material strategies by which artists struggle to articulate and respond to mass violence. In particular, the chapter explores how artists attempt to subvert the Khmer Rouge's 'monocular' way of seeing (in which the camera became a component in a murder machine), and thereby create less tainted forms in which iconic images of suffering may yet bear witness to a past that must not be forgotten.

Closing this section is a chapter on a struggle elsewhere in South East Asia to deal with a legacy of genocide, in this case the 1965–66 massacre of between 500,00 and two million alleged communists by the Indonesian military and its paramilitary death squads. 'Screening the 1965 Violence' discusses cinema's role in creating and maintaining an official history that erases the genocide from *public* discussion. (When the official history, compelled by logic, is forced to acknowledge at least some anti-communist violence, it is invariably described as the heroic 'extermination' (*penumpasan*) of communist traitors.) For the final fifteen years of Indonesia's military dictatorship, a four-hour propaganda film, *The Treason of the September 30th Movement of the Indonesian Communist Party* (1984), was mandatory yearly viewing for all Indonesian students from primary school to university. The chapter analyses this film as the overarching framework for any discussion, fantasy or allusion to the genocide ever since. It proceeds to discuss the difficulties faced by contemporary Indonesian documentary filmmakers who seek to challenge ideological matrix of this history. Here, film is implicated in the machinery of annihilation, and in any potential historical recovery.

The fourth and final section, *Performing Violence*, builds upon the second section's exploration of the potential of post-traumatic cinema to recover repressed memories of the violent past and translate these to the screen, and the third section's concern with re-enactment as intervention in the present. Here, through explorations of the *ontology* of the performances that constitute re-enactments, as well as the *epistemological* limits on our analysis of these performances, we encounter the difficulties, perhaps even the impossibility, of distinguishing between performance and remembrance. 'Authenticity' and 'authentic remembrance' become thorny concepts indeed. Here, the (mis)use of the camera as a tool in the performance of violence itself, as well as its use in documenting re-enactments of violence for the purpose of historical recovery, becomes ethically and politically fraught as never before.

The Cambodian filmmaker Rithy Panh, in his film *S21: The Khmer Rouge Killing Machine* (2003), uses re-enactment as a means to recover the embodied memory of guards at the Tuol Sleng prison in Phnom Penh, specifically gestures and motions that were part of the machinery of killing. In the first chapter of this section, Panh discusses in detail his use of re-enactment as a tool for the precise excavation of perpetrators' bodily memory. He discusses, too, his surprising methods of securing the cooperation of the perpetrators, motivated by his conviction that testifying is the only way by which perpetrators of crimes against humanity can regain their own humanity.

This contribution is followed by a second interview with Avi Mograbi. Here, Mograbi discusses the innovative use of a digital mask in his film *Z32* (2008). In this film, the mask is constructed to conceal the identity of a perpetrator – an Israeli soldier who has murdered an elderly Palestinian civilian. Here, the soldier, code-named Z32, confronts his actions and his memories, including a visit to the site of the killing. Through the film, the soldier seeks absolution for his actions, yet does not have the courage to apologise publicly (as many of his fellow soldiers have done). Mograbi reflects upon his own responsibility as a filmmaker in eliciting performances from a perpetrator of violence in exchange for anonymity. Specifically, Mograbi highlights the ethical dilemma faced by viewers of a cinematic performance that is used as a tool to recover and expose a murder, but simultaneously to help the murderer find redemption.

Benedict Anderson then investigates the historical and political context around Joshua Oppenheimer's films, *The Act of Killing* and *Snake River* (2012). In both films, Oppenheimer films elaborate re-enactments staged by the victorious perpetrators of Indonesia's 1965–66 genocide. Here, seemingly unrepentant and boastful perpetrators draw on their cinematic fantasies to dramatise their roles in the killings, suggesting genres, writing scripts and directing scenes. Through this disturbing dramatic space, *The Act of Killing* investigates the routines of violence, and analyses the rhetoric and imagination of the killing machine. The chapter analyses the function of the perpetrators' on-screen boasting, the impunity that it performatively asserts and the history of the political system of which it is symptomatic. Anderson argues that impunity is fundamentally a performative state, achieved through reiteration of explicitly or implicitly boastful performances by the perpetrators of past violence before different audiences. The circuit is completed when survivors accept their powerlessness, and a 'general public' accepts that perpetrators are to be respected and even revered as heroes. Oppenheimer's

all aspects of the production
camera in *Snake River*) shorts
rson goes on to interrogate the
irector, who invites them to re-
how triumphant and boastful
into history.
ading of performances by two
n his film project on the Indo-
to declaim their past for the
their accounts using whatever
rviews to large-scale re-enact-
ir 'redemption'), Oppenheimer
ng perpetrators' historical ac-
ose accounts. These cinematic
self-imagining out from under

The book's final chapter is a discussion with Errol Morris about his film *Standard Operating Procedure* (2008). Here, we continue the discussion of perpetrators using cameras to stage their actions, but the focus is now on the photographs of torture and abuse taken by the guards at Abu Ghraib prison in Baghdad. The film's investigative premise is that the photographs are not what they appear to be: they are neither evidence of the 'few bad apples' the military claimed, nor of guards so sadistic that they are happy for their friends to see them delight in humiliating others (a story the public might simultaneously deplore and relish, with a fascination not unrelated to the emotions inferred from the guards' smiles). The posing soldiers are usually not even the perpetrators: their smiles and 'thumbs up' would suggest the violence was staged for the photographs, yet the key violence (a homicide) happened off camera, and the perpetrator appears in none of the photographs. Furthermore, the photographs' quality of being staged *may itself have been staged* as an elaborate cover for the photographer's project of documenting and, ultimately, exposing the abuse. Yet the very fact that posing for a snapshot while smiling next to a murder victim could be an efficient cover speaks volumes about the climate at the prison, and above all its 'standard operating procedures'. Morris's discussion (and film) not only questions the violence that went on inside the prison's walls and the soldiers' use of photography, but how we see ourselves through the stories we tell about images of violence.

And that, surely, is the central concern of this volume.

NOTES

1 N. Brandt (1964) 'Pancho Villa: The making of a modern legend', *The Americas*, 21, 2, 146–62. See also, R. Walsh (1974) *Each Man In His Time: The Life Story of a Director*. New York: Farrar, Straus and Giroux.
2 Testimony by Blahyi included in *The Redemption of General Butt Naked* (2011), directed by Eric Strauss and Daniele Anastasion.
3 See P. Sands (2008) *Torture Team: Rumsfeld's Memo and the Betrayal of American Values*. New York: Palgrave Macmillan, 61–2.
4 Quoted in G. Didi-Huberman (2004) *Images malgré tout*. Paris: Éditions de Minuit, 34.
5 W. Benjamin (1988) *Illuminations*. New York: Schocken, 255.

(DE)ACTIVATING EMPATHY

PUBLICITY AND INDIFFERENCE:
MEDIA, SURVEILLANCE AND 'HUMANITARIAN INTERVENTION'

Thomas Keenan

'The price of eternal vigilance is indifference.'

– Marshall McLuhan

In his too-hasty indictment of the 1999 NATO air campaign over Kosovo, *Strategy of Deception*, Paul Virilio suggests that there was a determined relation between the 'humanitarian' dimension of this very first 'human rights conflict' and the 'truly panoptical vision' which NATO brought to bear on the battlefield (2000: 19–21).[1]

> After the eye of God pursuing Cain all the way into the tomb, we now have *the eye of Humanity* skimming over the oceans and continents in search of criminals. One gets an idea, then, of the ethical dimension of the Global Information Dominance programme, the attributes of which are indeed those of the divine, opening up the possibility of *ethical cleansings*, capable of usefully replacing the *ethnic cleansing* of undesirable or supernumerary populations. After oral informing, rumor, agents of influence and traditional spying, comes the age of optical informing: this 'real time' of a large-scale optical panoptic, capable of monitoring not just enemy, but friendly, movements thanks to the control of public opinion. (2000: 21–2)

This 'global tele-surveillance' (2000: 22) is for Virilio the signature of the 'globalist putsch' he denounces, 'a seizure of power by an a-national armed group (NATO), evading the political control of the democratic nations (the UN), evading the prudence of their diplomacy and their specific jurisdictions' (2000: 74).

Fig. 1 Border station near Globocica, Kosovo, April 1999; image from Bundeswehr CL 289 UAV (drone). Source: Bundeswehr.

Fig. 2 Bodies at Racak, Kosovo, January 16, 1999; news photograph from Koha Ditore (Pristina). Source: Koha Ditore.

The tropes are all-too-familiar, and not just to readers of Virilio. Democracy sacrificed to speed, accountability to total visibility. As if surveillance were just one thing. As if the images produced by the global panoptic were self-evident in their meaning or effect. And as if every project taken on by the Western military alliance, or what his [French] Foreign Minister Vedrine memorably nicknamed the hyper-power, was irremediably contaminated. But those are obvious commonplaces. What is interesting is the question of betrayal, denunciation, of this 'informing [délation]'. What difference does all the watching make? Especially where 'ethnic cleansing' is at stake – or to call it by its legal name, where genocide is underway? Virilio's dissident position, that what is truly to be feared and resisted is less the killing itself than the practices of global control it alibis or sets in motion, is at once unjustified and deeply flawed from a political standpoint.

But, interestingly, it also runs counter to the most cherished axioms of the international human rights and humanitarian movements. Since the end of World War II, indeed, the non-governmental movement has looked forward to

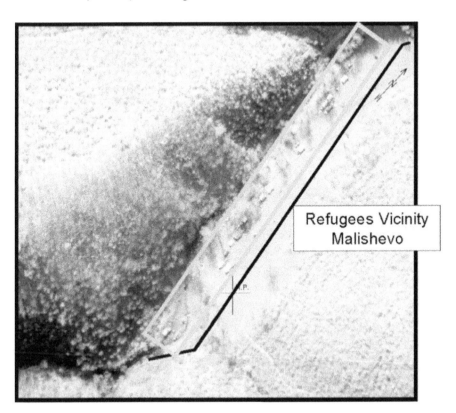

Fig. 3 Refugees, vicinity of Malisevo, Kosovo, April 1999; overhead imagery released at NATO briefing, April 10, 1999. *Source:* NATO.

17

the prospect of up-to-date information about crimes in progress, coupled with access to the public opinion that might enable them to be interrupted. With the creation of a rich and increasingly robust global network of human rights monitors, and the ability to relay acts of witness and evidence around the world in near real time, something like this transparent world is increasingly real. 'The media will carry the demand for action to the world's leaders; they in turn must decide carefully and positively what that action is to be', runs the axiom in its clearest formulation.[2] But what of the reaction, the action, and the public? Kosovo – where a limited military intervention probably prevented a genocide, protected a terribly endangered civilian population, and finally stopped a military and paramilitary apparatus that had terrorised primarily Muslim civilian populations in Southern Europe for most of the 1990s – was rather the exception than the rule. Global tele-surveillance and human rights monitors did not help much at Vukovar, Omarska or Srebrenica. Nor did these names confirm the omnipotence of NATO, or the unaccountable power of the transnational human rights movement. After a decade of genocide, famine and concentration camps, the very value of publicity – whether that affirmed by the movements or condemned by Virilio – seemed questionable.

Visiting Sarajevo at Christmas in 1993, less than a year into its suffering, the Archbishop of Paris Cardinal Jean-Marie Lustiger noted the strikingly public or visible character of the carnage there.[3] In an interview with Zlatko Dizdarevic of Sarajevo's *Oslobodjenje*, he compared the siege of the city to the horrors of World War II, but with a significant difference:

> Here, however, there are no secrets. There are journalists here, from here pictures are transmitted, there are satellite communications, all of this is known. In this city there are soldiers of the United Nations, well armed, and nonetheless it all continues to happen. This is unbelievable; this is overwhelming. One man yesterday told me that everyone here feels like they are animals in a zoo that others come to look at, to take pictures of, and to be amazed. And then, those up in the mountains also treat them like animals, killing them and 'culling' them.

Dizdarevic asked how it was possible that, 'all of this goes on without any end in sight, in spite of the fact that we are surrounded by hundreds of cameras [and] that everyone knows everything and sees everything?' Lustiger responded: 'There is no answer for that – I really do not have an answer. However, that means that it is always possible to get worse and worse.'

Lustiger's bold and uncompromising position, as rare as it was at the time, has now achieved the status of common sense. Among the too many would-be

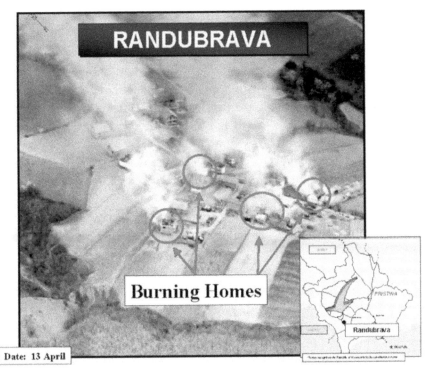

Fig. 4 Burning homes in Randubrava, Kosovo, April 13, 1999; overhead imagery released at NATO briefing, April 14, 1999. *Source:* NATO.

'lessons of Bosnia', this one stands out for its frequent citation: that a country was destroyed and a genocide happened, in the heart of Europe, on television, and what is known as the world or the West simply looked on and did nothing. 'While America Watched', as the title of a documentary on the genocide in Bosnia broadcast by ABC Television in 1994 already put it.[4]

The surveillance was as complete as the abandonment. Bosnians, said one to the American journalist David Rieff, 'felt as you would feel if you were mugged in full view of a policeman and he did nothing to rescue you.'[5] Or, as Rieff himself put it:

200,000 Bosnian Muslims died, in full view of the world's television cameras, and more than two million other people were forcibly displaced. A state formally recognized by the European Community and the United States [...] and the United Nations [...] was allowed to be destroyed. While it was being destroyed, UN military forces and officials looked on, offering 'humanitarian' assistance and protesting [...] that there was no will in the international community to do anything more. (1996: 23)

But what does 'in full view' mean, and what is the particular ethico-political force of this condemnation: not just genocide, but genocide in the open, transparent mass murder?

There is no denying the simultaneity of this watching and that destruction. They happened together – and what happened should not have happened. But what did the surveillance and the watching have to do with what happened? What links the thing we so loosely call 'the media' and its images with action or inaction? Or more precisely, when something happens 'in full view', why do we expect that action will be taken commensurate with what (we have seen) is happening? And what about that humanitarian assistance: what sort of 'action' is it?

This trajectory of this programme – from the camera to a response, but maybe nothing 'more' than a humanitarian one – appears everywhere today, in military and political and historical discussions of so-called postmodern wars or humanitarian crises, in legal or ethical commentaries on genocide and catastrophe, and in critical media-studies analyses of what has been called 'the CNN effect' or the-role-of-the-media in contemporary conflict. And what seems to concern us most, for better and for worse, are the media. It seems as if we cannot talk about what happened in Bosnia or Somalia or Rwanda without talking about the media.[6]

Consider, for (and unfortunately only for) example, the brilliant series of articles in the *New York Review of Books* in which Mark Danner chronicled the high and low points of the battles over Bosnia in the United States and Europe. He was in Sarajevo for much of it, but his articles insistently begin with watching television.[7] 'To the hundreds of millions who first beheld them on their television screens that August day in 1992, the faces staring out from behind barbed wire seemed painfully familiar', begins his 4 December 1997 report on the camps of Western Bosnia. The opening sentences of his 20 November article tell a similar story about Srebrenica:

Scarcely two years ago, during the sweltering days of July 1995, any citizen of our civilized land could have pressed a button on a remote control and idly gazed, for an instant or an hour, into the jaws of a contemporary Hell. Taking shape upon the little screen, in that concurrent universe dubbed 'real time', was a motley, seemingly endless caravan, bus after battered bus rolling to a stop and disgorging scores of exhausted, disheveled people [...] every last one a woman or a child. The men of Srebrenica had somehow disappeared. Videotaped images, though, persist: on the footage shot the day before, the men can be seen among the roiling mob, together with their women and children, pushing up against the fence of the United Nations compound, pleading for protection from the conquering Serbs. (1997: 55)

From 1992 to 1995, says Danner, we watched, and what we did and didn't do with what we saw was all the less forgivable, because we could see.[8] Many other versions of this protest could be enumerated, but the precise formulations of and differences among them are less interesting than their ubiquity. The recurrence of the gesture (we watched 'all that' but we did not act as we should have), across so many different accounts and styles and methodological predispositions, mirrors somehow the phenomenon it describes: the omnipresence of the gesture is the very ubiquity of the camera, the image or spectre of the camera that now seems to haunt our consciousness, and indeed, the in-full-view-of-the-camera seems now to have become the most privileged figure of our ethical consciousness, our conscience, our responsibility itself.

This was not always a rebuke. Television, publicity, surveillance of the affirmative sort, was supposed to help. This was the situation Michael Ignatieff described some years ago – before Bosnia and Rwanda, when the crises were those of starvation and Cold War proxies – in an essay on 'the ethics of television', now the first chapter of *The Warrior's Honor*.[9]

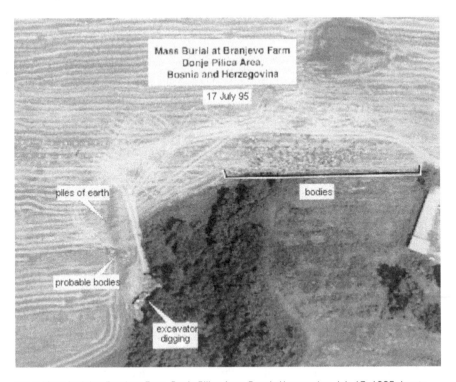

Fig. 5 Mass burial at Branjevo Farm, Donje Pilica Area, Bosnia-Herzegovina, July 17, 1995; image from United States U-2 aerial reconnaissance aircraft, released by US officials in Bosnia, March 22, 1996. *Source:* US Department of State.

Television is also the instrument of a new kind of politics. Since 1945, affluence and idealism have made possible the emergence of a host of non-governmental private charities and pressure groups – Amnesty International, [...] Medecins sans frontières, and others – that use television as a central part of their campaigns to mobilize conscience and money on behalf of endangered humans and their habitats around the world. It is a politics that takes the world rather than the nation as its political space and that takes the human species itself rather than specific citizenship, racial, religious, or ethnic groups as its object. [...] Whether it wishes or not, television has become the principal mediation between the suffering of strangers and the consciences of those in the world's few remaining zones of safety. [...] It has become not merely the means through which we see each other, but the means by which we shoulder each other's fate. (1997: 21, 33)

Fig. 6 General Ratko Mladic, Bosnian Serb Army, Potocari, Bosnia- Herzegovina, July 12, 1995; video still of RTS image on CNN, date unknown. *Source:* Radio Television Serbia via CNN.

Ignatieff allows us to orient this enquiry toward the special relationship between television and humanitarianism. International humanitarian action of the sans-frontières variety is unthinkable except in the age of more-or-less instant information. As Rony Brauman has underlined, the founding of the International Committee of the Red Cross in 1864 is linked non-coincidentally to the possibility of high-speed transmission by telegraph, and contemporary relief operations since Biafra and Ethiopia have been born and bathed in the light of the television camera and the speed of the satellite uplink.[10] Humanitarian action seems not simply to take advantage of the media, but indeed to depend on it, and on a fairly limited set of presuppositions about the link between knowledge and action, between public information or opinion and response. In some cases, like that of the international human rights movement, as Alex de Waal has argued, the conditions of action rest all too heavily on the concept of 'mobilizing shame'.[11]

In the humanitarian arena proper, the pioneering French activist turned politician Bernard Kouchner put the coordination between media and intervention in a simple epigram: 'sans médias, pas d'action humanitaire importante, et celle-ci, en retour, nourrit les gazettes [without the media, there is no important humanitarian action, and this, in turn, feeds the papers].' Kouchner calls this 'la loi du tapage', the law of noise.[12] And among military thinkers, practitioners, and diplomats, the sense that

television imagery or news dispatches 'drive' decisions about intervention has by now gained a name
of its own – 'the CNN effect' – and is the topic of
vigorous debates.[13] (1997: 3–4)

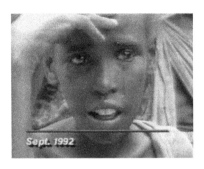

Sept. 1992

Fig. 7 Somalia, September 1992; video still
from CNN, date unknown. *Source:* CNN.

What does it mean? Thanks to what is loosely
termed 'public opinion' in the media age, which
displaces or warps of state institutions and power
through emergent alternative centres of power
like the media and non-governmental organisations, the so-called 'famine movement' (or what
Alex de Waal has nicknamed the 'Humanitarian
International') has emerged as a political actor, and of a new sort: apparently
unlimited by traditional notions of sovereignty, accountability, borders, interest
and the rest.[14]

We need to understand the 'humanitarian action' which triumphed in Bosnia
as something different from either of the two obvious options: it was neither
inaction (a passive acquiescence or a cover-up, a fig leaf that disguises the actual
doing-of-nothing), nor a heroic new non-state politics of the sort anticipated by
many of the founders of the movement. It was an action that – precisely because
it offered the possibility of a reference not to national interest or the defense of
the state but to what it called, alternatively, 'human beings', 'victims', 'misfortune'
or 'suffering', and did so by way of public opinion and the image, which is to
say by reference to the order of the ethical – opened the possibility of a political
discourse that, for better or more often for worse, did not have to justify itself
in political terms. In Bosnia, humanitarian action was action indeed, action that
threatened to totalise the field of all possible action: not simply to hide inaction
or offer alibis for not doing other things, but more radically to interrupt, to render impossible, to actively block or prevent those actions.

And this action had as its field or condition the image, sometimes precisely
the image and sometimes more generally what we nickname 'the media' or 'real
time'. Recall that for Walter Benjamin, in the 'Work of Art...' essay at least, the
invention of the motion picture introduced nothing less than a temporal explo-
sion, 'the dynamite of the tenth of a second', such that in what remained, the
'far-flung ruins and debris' of our daily lives or our familiar terrain, would open
up 'an immense and unexpected field of action.'[15] Film and today television do
not only collapse and annihilate, as is so often said, time and distance – they also
make unprecedented times and spaces available for action, real virtualities that
are marked by the affirmation of possibilities of engagement, 'action', as well as

by the negativity of this 'dynamite'. Field of action, yes, but what kind of action? The answer is also Benjaminian, though this time in a different way. The privileged example at the close of the 'Work of Art...' essay is war, what he labels the aesthetics of mechanised warfare, which he says is discerned more clearly or best 'captured by camera and sound recording' and not the naked eye (1969: 242, 251). Today cameras don't simply represent conflicts but take part in them, shape not only our understanding of them, but their very conduct. We need to attend to these sounds and images not just as accounts of war but as actions and weapons in that war, as operations in the public field, which today constitutes an immense field of opportunity for doing battle, as weapons in what we too easily call 'image contests' or 'publicity battles'.

'There was a cameraman there' – this is a fragment from a news report about a man shot by a sniper in Sarajevo:[16]

> Mr. Sabanovic got in the way at a particularly dangerous Sarajevo crossroads. That is why there was a cameraman there to film his near death. Because the spot is treacherous, the chances are good that a few hours of patience by a cameraman will be rewarded with compelling images of a life being extinguished or incapacitated. (Cohen 1995: 12)

What difference does it make that a cameraman is there, as he or she so often is? No matter where, it seems, a camera regularly happens to be there, when something happens to happen. So much so that it has become a cliché, a veritable commonplace, to say that today things don't happen *unless* a camera is there. Of course, it takes not just a camera, but an entire network of editing, transmitting, distributing and viewing technologies – and agents – that extend out from the camera, to make what Marshall McLuhan so famously and confusingly called a global village.[17] But it begins with the camera and its operator, with their already having been there.

What the journalist here wants us to understand is the complex structure of that 'there': was it a place where cameras waited patiently for things to happen (a particularly dangerous crossroads), or a place where things happened because cameras waited patiently (compelling images of lives extinguished)? The camera is there because of the danger, but its silent witness transforms the event and its 'there' – that is what matters here. Thanks to the camera, what it means for the event to occur, its taking-place, undergoes a mutation. The crossroads so precisely targeted in the sniper's gun-sight is also the blurred intersection of what our impoverished theoretical vocabulary allows us to call only event and representation, occurrence and image. This confusion cannot be written off as one more version of a timeless ontological conundrum (which comes first?), nor caricatured as a postmodern prejudice for the discursive over the real, nor simply eliminated with a declaration of the moral superiority of the things themselves. The confusion itself is all too real and – especially in the case of events like those at this crossroads – it constitutes something like an exemplary ethico-political difficulty and opportunity for us.

What is at stake, finally, in this confusion is a certain experience and definition of public space and time, of publicity and of a crisis in our sense of public information and exposure today. The corollary, of course, of the cameraman's being there is that, in some sense, we are too. The camera metaphorises the becoming-public of the event, because we who watch and listen are also caught in the intersection of the sniper's and the cameraman's viewfinders – not as potential victims exactly, but in some other sense as targets of those vectors (borrowing this sense of the word from McKenzie Wark in *Virtual Geography*).[18] What do we do in watching and listening? When I say 'we', I mean that hazy thing called the public, a rich concept sent to us by the Enlightenment and the French Revolution and in need of extensive rethinking. If the public means us, us in our exposure to others, then today 'we' cannot be something given in advance, not the sum total of all of us somewhere or sometime, not a community or a people but rather something that comes after the image, a possibility of response to an open address. The public, we could say in shorthand, is what is hailed or addressed by messages that might not reach their destination. Thinking about the images at hand, we could even say that what makes something public is precisely the possibility of being a target and of being missed.

So the television image constitutes a field of action – not just a representation of actions elsewhere but a field in or on which actions occur – a public field, we could say, but only if we're willing to part with some of the cherished predicates of that concept.

Somalia, December 1992. The first American soldiers of Operation Restore Hope land on an Indian Ocean beach at Mogadishu, met not by clan fighters or starving children but by hundreds of reporters, camera people, technicians, whom, as it turns out, the American military had informed in advance of the time and place of the operation. Kouchner's claim that without television, there is no humanitarian intervention, seems to come true in a multiple and almost perverse way here: not simply that images – there, of starving children – could shame governments into action, but that armies will undertake humanitarian rescue missions for the publicity value alone, and that publicity could also bring the mission to an end.

What happened there? We are not finished understanding the complex of clan politics and paramilitary violence, the liquidation of the post-colonial and post-

Cold-War state, famine and even starvation, and the succession of interventions, humanitarian and armed ones, and then nation-building which followed them.[19] But the images (from the starving children to the gun-belted fighters, the brightly-lit landing, the camcorder pictures of a helicopter pilot held hostage and a dead soldier dragged in the street) and the phrases (Mad Max vehicles, warlords, the photo-op invasion and the CNN effect, and the Mogadishu line) have already decisively shaped the interpretation and practice of humanitarian interventions in the decade since that fateful night in the lights.[20]

Fig. 8 Mogadishu airport, Somalia, December 9, 1992; live video still from NBC. *Source:* NBC.

Fig. 9 Mogadishu, Somalia, October 4, 1993; video still from CBS, October 4, 1993. *Source:* Reuters via CNN.

Fig. 10 Mogadishu airport, Somalia, December 9, 1992; live video still from CNN. *Source:* CNN.

The lesson of those lights was already clear, the morning after the event, to the grand old man of American foreign policy, George Kennan, who awoke that morning in December 1992 to watch the soldiers landing in real time, surrounded by reporters and interviewed on the beach, and offered a harsh assessment of the damage. He told his diary, and then the opinion page of the *New York Times*, that he had finally seen enough:

If American policy from here on out, particularly policy involving the use of our armed forces abroad, is to be controlled by popular emotional impulses, and particularly ones provoked by the commercial television industry, then there is no place – not only for myself, but for what have traditionally been regarded as the responsible deliberative organs of our government, in both executive and legislative branches.[21]

Kennan – the architect of the Cold War, the author of the doctrine of 'containment', Mr. X himself – watches his era end on his television, not with the fall of the Berlin Wall and the reunification of Europe, nor with the great borderless coalition and its triumph in the Gulf War, but with chaos on an African beach, disaster breaking out of new world order with such energy and confusion that it threatens to tear apart the institutions of government and publicity themselves. What is threatened in Mogadishu, not by the clans but by the cameras and the soldiers who are drawn to them, is nothing less than the basic structures of ethics and American democracy – responsibility and deliberation. The rational consideration of information, with a view to grounding what one does in what one knows, now seems overtaken and displaced by 'emotion', and responses are now somehow 'controlled' or, better, remote-controlled by television images. What disappears beneath the image or behind the screen is the place of politics itself. There is, Kennan confesses, not only no place for him but no place at all for a decision, for the organs that regulate the link between knowledge and action. Television – that virtual place – displaces the public place, substituting emotion for reason, immediacy for the delay proper to thought.

Fig. 11 Sarajevo, Bosnia-Herzegovina, January 1993; video still from CNN, January 26, 1993. Source: CNN.

In somewhat more complex, but no more theoretical, terms, Virilio has suggested that this phenomenon, the displacement of the traditional rational-critical experience of the public sphere by what is nicknamed 'emotion', characterises in general contemporary televisual publicity:

> The space of politics in ancient societies was the public space (square, forum, agora...). Today, the public image has taken over public space. Television has become the forum for all emotions and all options. We vote while watching TV. [...] We are heading toward a cathodic democracy, but without rules. [...] There is no politics possible at the scale of the speed of light. Politics is the time of reflection. Today, we no longer have time to reflect; the things that we see have already taken place. And we must react immediately... Is a real-time democracy possible? An authoritarian politics, yes. But what is proper to democracy is the sharing of power. When there is no longer time to share, what do we share? Emotions.[22]

This compelling immediacy of the media, the magnetic pull of the image and the microphone, has been testified to by the highest officials of our government and military.[23] Images, they certify, do make things happen and sometimes too quickly. We can and should dispute the contention that discussion or sharing disappear in the putative instantaneity of the live transmission (as if it does not have its own temporality, its own internal structure, its delays and frames and decisions) but there is no debating the claim that the image (and especially the image of catastrophe) has the power to circumvent or pressure political institutions, and not just in democracies.[24]

In Somalia events did seem dictated by this CNN effect, with the attendant displacement of deliberation by emotion and hence the short-circuiting of the public sphere, whether it was a matter of the starving children, the proud international forces, or the dead American soldier. But what then of Bosnia, where everything seemed to be visible as it happened, and yet, on the contrary, it is said, virtually nothing happened in response? As David Rieff has written, 'no slaughter was more scrupulously and ably covered' and 'it [did] no good' – 'we failed' (1996: 223, 222):

The hope of the Western press was that an informed citizenry back home would demand that their governments not allow the Bosnian Muslims to go on being massacred, raped, or forced from their homes. Instead, the sound bites and 'visual bites' culled from the fighting bred casuistry and indifference far more regularly than [they] succeeded in mobilizing people to act or even to be indignant. (1996: 216).

Fig. 12 Warrior armored vehicle, Cheshire Regiment/UNPROFOR, Amhici, Bosnia-Herzegovina, April 22, 1993; video still from CNN, April 23, 1993.

If the lesson of Somalia was that cameras made things happen, and sometimes too quickly, Bosnia seemed to tell the opposite story: a brutal combination of overexposure and indifference. Somalia was hyperactivity; Bosnia inactivity, just watching. This was the clichéd meaning for which Sarajevo became the metonym. We are back to where we started: let me cite a few examples, from war correspondents themselves, of the trajectory that travels from a certain expectation about the putative power of images to despair at their failure and even to anger, from Mogadishu to Sarajevo.

Only nine months into the siege, in a dispatch that won her the first of many prizes for coverage of Sarajevo, CNN's Christiane Amanpour reported on a creeping despair with the televisual:

Take any day in the life of this city. The sights are so familiar, perhaps they have lost their impact. Around noon another mortar falls. More people are killed and injured. They are rushed to the hospital. The emergency ward is full. Surgeons labor to save lives. The operating theatre is awash in blood. Early on in the war the staff were patient with photographers, hoping perhaps their pictures would shock the world into doing something. The world has done nothing and the doctors have lost hope and patience.[25]

Years later, Giles Rabine, reporting live for France 2 from Sarajevo on 13 July 1995, just after the fall of Srebrenica, commented simply that, after thirty-nine months of televised siege, 'the Sarajevans have had enough of being interviewed, being filmed, being photographed; they've had enough of us watching them die, live, without trying to do anything to save them. And who's to say they're wrong?'

They were not wrong. Roger Cohen of the *New York Times* took this as the premise for his searching front-page report on 'postmodern war' in the besieged city one Sunday in May 1995. Postmodern for many reasons, but mainly because it's a matter of images, of what the reporter finds to be a dangerously blurred boundary between event and representation, and of a certain paralysis, the apparent re- or dis-location of the field of knowledge and action to the screen of a monitor and the entry of those representations back into the field of the things and events they ought simply to represent. Here is his lead for an article headlined 'In Sarajevo, Victims of a "Postmodern" War', *New York Times*, 21 May, 1995:

Faruk Sabanovic, a pale and gentle-featured youth, is a thoroughly modern victim of war. He lies in the main hospital here with a video of the moment when he was shot and became a paraplegic. There he is, outside the central Holiday Inn, walking briskly across the street, his hair ruffled by the wind. The crack of a shot echoes in Sarajevo's valley. He falls. He lies on his side. He is curled in an almost fetal position. A United Nations soldier looks on, motionless.

A Sarajevan man arrives, screaming abuse at the soldier, who eventually moves his white United Nations armored personnel carrier. This slight movement is enough

Figs. 13, 14 & 15 Faruk Sabanovich, outside the Holiday Inn, Sarajevo, Bosnia-Herzgovina, March 3, 1995; video still from ABC, March 3, 1995. *Source:* RTV/WTN pool material via ABC.

to cover the civilian as he rushes out to retrieve Mr. Sabanovic, whose lithe body has turned limp. 'It's strange when I watch the video, I feel like it's somebody else', said Mr. Sabanovic, who is 20. 'But I remember it so well. After I was hit, I felt my legs in my chest. Then I saw my feet. I tried to move them. But I could not. This United Nations soldier was looking at me. He did nothing. He just looked. For me, it was so long.'

The scene is shocking, doubly so by virtue of the videotape. The civilian victim is not only crippled by a sniper but is also in possession of the images of his attempted murder. The reporter can thus not only interview the person but watch TV with him. And the image is somehow not just of Faruk Sabanovic or of what happened to him on the street in Sarajevo; it is for Cohen an allegory, an image of something else, more confusing, an image of the confusion and loss of orientation – in images – which have affected our sense of reality itself. Watching this tape, with its inert star next to him, Cohen seems paralysed by the sight of people watching: 'Faruk lies ... with a video'; 'a United Nations soldier looks on, motionless'; 'this United Nations soldier was looking at me. He did nothing. He just looked.'

Thanks to images like these, we are all like that UN soldier, just looking, or like the cameraman, waiting. That is their rich allegorical meaning, their hermeneutic supplement: they mean the inaction that they demand of their producer and their viewer. Cohen adds:

The images capture more than the maiming of Mr. Sabanovic; they capture the increasingly surreal and sordid nature of the three-year-old Bosnian war. A civilian is shot on a city street; a television cameraman, waiting at a dangerous crossroads to see somebody killed or mutilated, films the shooting; a soldier sent by the United Nations as a 'peacekeeper' to a city officially called a 'safe area' watches, unsure what to do and paralyzed by fear. The elements of this troubling collage are also elements of what some military analysts are now calling 'postmodern' or 'future' war.

In the tape, in the hospital, Cohen sees an image from Sarajevo and in it the whole new troubling thing metonymised. As the space and time of what happens shifts onto the screen, even 'there' in Sarajevo, all sorts of boundaries are collapsing with it. He enumerates the transformation or the decay that coincides with the emergence of the videotape: states are replaced by militias or other informal groupings; armies and peoples become indistinguishable; central authorities disappear; and 'live images of suffering, distributed worldwide, sap whatever will or ability there may be to prosecute a devastating military campaign'. Looking is not acting, in Sarajevo or in New York, and for Cohen the diffusion of images goes hand in hand with a more disturbing dispersion or evisceration of the conditions of action: lost are centrality, authority, borders and clear distinctions, principles, and all the rest.

The triumph of images figures this for Cohen: images sap the will in war, he says, and yet paradoxically it is a war of images, fought with images:

> Mr. Sabanovic got in the way at a particularly dangerous Sarajevo crossroads. That is why there was a cameraman there to film his near-death. Because the spot is treacherous, the chances are good that a few hours of patience by a cameraman will be rewarded with compelling images of a life being extinguished or incapacitated.

A 'compelling image' is, of course, a weapon, and the cameramen sometimes seemed like the best gunners the Bosnian government had, being deprived of almost all other military equipment. Certainly most of the journalists in Sarajevo understood this, and recognised that their work was not simply impartial. Didn't Somalia suggest, after all, that images could be compelling, that tele-guided public opinion could force action?

Cohen, in the late spring of 1995, has seen enough to withdraw that conclusion. There are no compelling images: 'Thus, just as the world has long watched the crushing of Sarajevo – so endless as to become increasingly unreal – the people of Sarajevo may now watch from their hospital beds the moment they were crippled, so abruptly that comprehension is difficult.'

The image sparks a crisis, not just in action but in comprehension, and the sentence that speaks of it also tells the story of a more profound disturbance. '...So abruptly that comprehension is difficult', he writes, but just what exactly happens so abruptly, the crippling or the watching? Surely Cohen means the suddenness of the rifle shot itself, caught on tape, but his dangling modifier betrays the ambiguity he is most alert to, the difficulty of discerning event and video repetition. In the face of this difficulty, Cohen proposes some reservations, or some objections, which although they are not formalised, and hesitant at best, do constitute something like a systematic critique of this 'postmodern' condition – it troubles him and with him, 'reality'. Sarajevo becomes surreal, unreal, endless; there is too much watching, too much mediation, even there in Sarajevo, so that even the subject of the image is himself alienated from it, split from himself. 'I feel like it's somebody else', says Sabanovic, now sharing the position of the immobilised one who just watches. The sniper and what Cohen calls 'the twisted video' together reduce everyone to a paraplegic – inert, paralysed by fear, just looking. And yet Cohen finds a moral for the story in the prone 20-year-old, 'a strength and a conviction that rise far above the banal violence of his video with its succinct accounting of a directionless war in which civilians die live on camera.' Without direction, pulling the very subject of the image apart from himself, the war of 'live death' comes to mean for Cohen at once an excess of imagery and a failure of the promise of those images – no action, no comprehension, only difficulty and a certain indetermination. Faruk Sabanovic, for his part, thanks the camera: the United Nations, he says, is 'just here to ease consciences. [...] And I know they brought me to the hospital in their ambulance only because the camera happened to be there. I have to say that I despise them.'

So in the end the two viewers of the tape disagree about its effects while agreeing that it has one, and these opinions recapitulate what I think represents the crisis of a certain idea of publicity. The symmetrical opposition of the interpretations – Mogadishu and Sarajevo – confirms that what is in question is the theoretical status and the actual function of the public image. Sabanovic believes in the CNN effect: 'they brought me to the hospital only because the camera happened to be there'. Cohen fears that the camera and the watching cripples our responses, that 'images sap the will'.

The strong version of his hypothesis has also been articulated by Jean Baudrillard, who thus forms a symmetrical pair with Virilio.[26] Baudrillard suggests that 'Bosnia exemplifies total weakness'; 'the West has to watch helplessly', in a 'military masquerade where the virtual soldier ... is paralyzed and immobilized' (1996: 87). And 'the Bosnians ... end up finding the whole situation unreal, senseless, and beyond their understanding. It is hell, but a somewhat hyperreal hell, made even more so by their being harassed by the media and humanitarian agencies ... thus they live amid a type of spectral war' (1996: 81).

Some American commentators have drawn radical conclusions from this proposition, and although it is in a certain sense highly disputable there is nevertheless something extremely important at stake here which this radicalisation can help clarify. In a collection of essays called *This Time We Knew*, edited by Thomas Cushman and Stjepan Mestrovic, an attempt is made to measure the significance of what seems an obvious failure: the last time around, we might have been able to say we didn't know what was happening, but throughout the second genocide in Europe in this half century, we have no such excuse. Because of television and the rest of the 'daily barrage of information and images', it is not possible for 'even the most disinterested viewer to ignore the grim reality of genocide'. Their 'Baudrillardian' hypothesis:

Lack of action proceeds ... from the fact that the mediated images of the world are mere representations that lend an air of unreality to the things they represent.

[...] Media watchers lose touch with reality ... stand passively by or engage in self-serving forms of ineffective action ... [their] voyeurism and individualism feed[ing] on televised images of evil. (1996: 79)

And that means that the crisis is not merely one of inaction. In fact, what is lost in Bosnia is nothing less than the Enlightenment, and with it the discovery of the public sphere as the site where knowledge and action are articulated. They feel obliged to ask, then, 'whether there is any relationship between the degree or extent of public information and practical or moral engagement by those who receive it' (1996: 7).

The important point is that there is a sharp discrepancy between what we know and what we do, and this discrepancy has been neglected in most previous analyses. Yet this gap between knowledge and action is full of meaning for apprehending history as well as the present. In addition, this contrast causes us to rethink the success of the so-called Enlightenment project: the passive Western observation of genocide and other war crimes in the former Yugoslavia amounts to a toleration of the worst form of barbarity and gives us pause to wonder whether, behind the rhetoric of European progress and community, there is not some strong strain of irrationality that, if laid bare, would call into question the degree of enlightenment the civilized West has managed to attain at the century's end. (1996: 8)

It is not clear just how far the two editors to that volume are willing to go in 'calling into question' the Enlightenment axioms that the 'gap between knowledge and action' in Bosnia provokes. The specter of 'irrationality' – always opposed to a normative reason – and the progressivist hint in the word 'attain' suggests that they remain committed to the project that has become questionable. But what happens if we seize on this insight – that the Enlightenment and its public sphere are in question – and try to move beyond the simple desire to recover it, to rescue it from its temporary loss. Suppose it were, precisely, the problem.

What failed in Bosnia? We often say that we failed, and we imply that *we* are just this well-known public of the 'so-called Enlightenment project'. But the more we rely on and retreat to the sense that the public sphere collapsed, the more we shore up just the notion whose apparent solidity may be implicated in the disaster. What if the belief in this public was part of the failure, if the faith in the obviousness, the evidence or self-evidence of the pictures and the automatic chain of reasoning they inspire, was not what failed but the very failure itself? What is at stake is the programme which expects that, as David Rieff put it, 'one more picture, or one more story, or one more correspondent's stand-up taped

Fig. 16 AP TV cameraman Miguel Gil Moreno de Mora (left, with camera), Kosovo, 1998; photograph.

KOSOVO REFUGEE CRISIS

Fig. 17 Christiane Amanpour, reporting from the Kosovo border, spring 1999, video still from CNN, date unknown.

in front of a shelled, smoldering building would bring people around, would force them to stop shrugging their shoulders, or like the United Nations, blaming the victims'[27] – one more picture would force something to happen – what if just that expectation about information and illumination was part of the problem?

To draw out the most radical conclusion from Cushman and Mestrovic: what if it is some part of the 'Enlightenment', and not its failure but rather the faith we put in the informative power of images, that didn't just fail to stop what happened but allowed it to go on? What if, because the cameramen and the images were there, and because they are supposed to make a difference simply by virtue of what they showed, the disaster continued?

Hypothesis: to the extent that we imagine or take for granted the articulation between knowledge and action, which seems to define the public sphere, it is bound to fail. But what can only be thought of as a failure in those terms is, in another sense, the success of a political strategy, and if we continue to think that images by virtue of their cognitive contents, or their proximity to reality, have the power to compel action, we miss just the opening of 'new fields of action' (Benjamin) that they allow.

So what if we think about this understanding of publicity not as a failure or as the re-emergence of irrationality, but as an alibi, a conceit or a consolation? These are words I borrow again from David Rieff, in *Slaughterhouse*, who suggests that it is this that has failed in Bosnia: a naive hope, a consolation and a conceit, the consolation of images and the dream of public information. Here's the collapsed public in a sentence: 'People ... console themselves with the thought that once they have the relevant information, they will act. It is an old conceit' (1996: 41). 'It was the conceit of journalists ...[:] if people back home could only be told and shown what was actually happening in Sarajevo ... then they would want their governments to do something' (1996: 216).

The conceit or fantasy of this kind of public sphere must, after Bosnia if nowhere else, contend with what we could call the rule of silence – no image speaks for itself, let alone speaking directly to our capacity for reason. Images always demand interpretation, even or especially emotional images – there is nothing immediate about them. This implies a second rule, that of unintended consequences or misfiring – the story of Bosnia is that images which might have signified genocide or aggression or calculated political slaughter seemed for so long to signify only tragedy or disaster or human suffering and hence were available for inscription or montage in a humanitarian rather than a political response. So what failed in Bosnia is an idea or an interpretation – and a practice – of publicity, of the public sphere as the arena of self-evidence and reason, an idea which now must be challenged, not to put an end to the public sphere but to begin reconstituting it.

As it happened, the images were open enough to demand only that we 'do something', and the problem concerns, in short, this something. The naive consolation is precisely that its content or meaning is self-evident, even analytically implied by the information itself, by 'what is actually happening'. And 'do something' they did, in fact, something which amounted to, as Rieff puts it in the sharpest phrases of his book, 'administering the Serb siege' and 'becom[ing] accomplices to genocide' (1996: 147, 189). The combination of the traditional tasks of peacekeeping – which require military observers to be stationed on or between the front lines, and hence in the zone of any possible offensive military operations like air strikes – and the new humanitarian tasks of escorting convoys across lines of confrontation meant that the 'humanitarian' operation was an active impediment to any other action. Not just the 'fig leaf' which Rieff too lightly calls it but an affirmative choice: 'the wish that there be no intervention' (1996: 189, 176). And this project was best accomplished by undertaking the other intervention: stationing peacekeepers close enough to Bosnian Serb forces that they would either be targets of Western air strikes or easy hostages for the Serbs, and escorting the convoys that always made it necessary not to, as the UN put it, 'compromise the humanitarian mandate' by antagonising the aggressor. 'This convergence of interest between the UN and the Chetniks was not an exceptional situation', as Rieff says, but the very structure of the situation (1996: 175).

And it happened thanks to the images, from which we expected something rather different. But images, information or knowledge will never guarantee any outcome, force or drive any action. They are, in that sense, just like weapons or words, a condition, but not a sufficient one. Still, the only thing more unwise than attributing the power of causation or of paralysis to images is to ignore them altogether. If they can condition some action – and indeed, in Sarajevo and elsewhere, that's exactly what happened – then it is only at the risk of this very indirection, the unexpected outcome, we might say: here, the humanitarian one. We cannot, at least not without repeating what seems to me to be the basic strategic error here, not expect the unexpected – we cannot count on the obviousness of the image, fall for the conceit that information leads ineluctably to actions adequate to the compulsion of the image, precisely because images are so important. There is no compulsion, only interpretation and re-inscription, and the image dictates nothing.

This fate of the image – left to wander and to drift from context to context, nothing but surface and frame – is what we can call, borrowing words from the reporter in Sarajevo, its 'banal violence', the banality of a 'succinct accounting' on video. The image has no guaranteed meaning, and remains only to testify, to demand, to induce a responsibility – even if, as Avital Ronell argues about the video-tape of Rodney King being attacked by the LA police, 'it is a responsibility that is neither alert, vigilant, particularly present, nor informed'.[28] The responsibility of the viewer is co-extensive with the lack of self-evidence of the image: it dictates nothing, compels nothing. It can always be used, though, which is to say that it can and must always be interpreted, and the terrible failure of Bosnia was that a certain understanding of the public sphere – 'the thought that once [people] have the relevant information, they will act' – allowed or even produced an interpretive complacency. 'Surely one more picture, or one more story, or one more … stand-up … would bring people around, would force them to stop shrugging their shoulders' – nothing is less sure, less certain, precisely because we think that it is.

The question of surveillance teaches us, finally, that there is no 'finally' where its images are concerned. Images never speak for themselves, never make anything in particular happen, even if they seem often to make something happen and are now indispensable in war. In Bosnia, they opened a gap, issued a call, and in response came the humanitarian option, displacing all others.[29] This means that the accounting, however succinct, does not stop – the image remains, without guarantees, always available for reinterpretation and reuse, of necessity the focus of an endless vigil and a struggle for re-inscription. The battle takes place in public, in fact the public sphere is constituted by the irreducibility of this battle, not the public as the last refuge of that dream or consolation of information properly acted upon, but another public, space and time, virtual and visual and nevertheless real enough, tenuous, uncertain, where everything is open to abuse and appropriation; shaky ground indeed.

Some years ago, Virilio warned in *Le Monde Diplomatique* that, far from merely offering new opportunities for exploration or relaxation, the media of which telegraph, telephone, radio and film were the merest announcements have by now radically accelerated and generalised the transmission of event and signification, and indeed absolutised it to the point of instantaneity, such that places no longer matter. He wanted us to believe that, when surveillance is ubiquitous and its output moves at the speed of light, new media now threaten to deprive us of places altogether, inducing not simply vertigo or disorientation but a more radical 'de-situation'. In an age of real-time communications, of 'instantaneous, globalized information', Virilio saw nothing less than the disappearance of the world itself in a 'tyranny of absolute speed'.[30]

In other words, the vertigo is absolute and unceasing, depriving us of ourselves. Far from creating a new world citizenry, a virtual community of humanity freed of allegiances to anything other than other humans as such, blown by the technologies of 'anywhere' out of the local particularities of place and identity, what disappears here is humanity, the relation to the other. When what happens there happens here too, in real-time, for Virilio what we lose is the fold of reflection, the gaps and delays that make decisions possible and debatable, that divide them into and across more than one instance.

'This goes beyond CNN. Actually, CNN is history', Virilio told a reporter. 'And it has nothing to do with the current surveillance of parking lots and street corners by security cameras. [...] We're witnessing today the deployment of a new, global tele-surveillance system whose impact will be far more profound than that of the traditional television.'[31]

But as surveillance goes global and speed crosses the barrier into instantaneity, do time and responsibility, and with then the possibility of democracy, disappear? Storage and montage happen in so-called 'real-time', of course excess time is built into the transmission, into the mediation that defines any technology of inscription. 'No longer time to share?' Not quite.

In addition to the vertigo of acceleration, there is also a more subtle vertigo of deceleration, of slow motion. What Benjamin called 'the dynamite of the tenth of a second' means that fast and slow cannot simply be opposed to one another. What is destabilised is the privilege of the present, the experience of the human subject and its self-present reflection (deliberation, reason, judgement), which would seem to regulate the transformations of speed. But only the most classical metaphysics of the subject and of presence can see in this the end of politics, the disappearance of the public sphere in the pure surface of the image. And only an excessive commitment to some ideology of the real imagines that time and decision evaporate in the light of the television screen. What speed teaches us is that this surface is itself folded, temporally or rhythmically complex and heterogeneous, that there is always an 'interior' lag which divides the subject from itself. It is this division which makes possible, in fact, the sharing that defines democratic conflict. We cannot simply say, 'warning! slow down!' – as if the distortions of speed could be undone and the self-identity of the present reinstated, and with them an anachronistic definition of the political, the public and the instance of decision. We can say, though, that the vertigo of deceleration – the slow motion of even the fastest and most 'compelling' image – tears us apart from our solid selves and opens the possibility of a decision, even of a properly political relation to others, in the question it poses. We are not quite out of time, but the image does not provide the answer for us either.

NOTES

The author and editors are grateful to PMLA for allowing this chapter to be re-printed.

1 P. Virilio (2000 [1999]) *Strategy of Deception*. New York: Verso. 'Hasty' because, as the example of Richard Falk shows, some left opponents of the war later became convinced of its necessity and justification. See R. Falk (2000) 'Kosovo Revisited', *The Nation*, 10 April.

2 M. Hudson and J. Stainer (1999) *War and the Media*. Phoenix Mill: Sutton, 300.

3 Cardinal Jean-Marie Lustiger, Archbishop of Paris, 'I am Ashamed as a Man', interview by Z. Dizdarevic, *Oslobodjenje* (European edition), 6 January 1994; http://www.bosnet.org/archive/bosnet.w3archive/9405/msg00021.html. See also Lustiger quoted in Z. Dizdarevic (1994) 'What Kind of Peace Is This?', *New York Times Magazine*, 10 April, 21: 'Here in Sarajevo, hundreds of TV crews parade before our very eyes; dozens of foreign journalists, reporters, and writers. Everything is known here, right down to minutest details, and yet, nothing…'

4 'While America Watched: The Bosnia Tragedy', Peter Jennings Reporting, ABC News, broadcast 30 March 1994.

5 D. Rieff (1996) *Slaughterhouse: Bosnia and the Failure of the West*. New York: Touchstone, 140.

6 Think of the feature films already available about the conflict in the former Yugoslavia: even skipping Marcel Ophuls' war reporter epic-doc *The Troubles We've Seen* (1994), from the British *Welcome to Sarajevo* (1997) to the Spanish *Territorio Commanche* (1997) to the Serbian *Pretty Village, Pretty Flame* (1996), the war apparently cannot be portrayed without putting a reporter and cameras at the centre of the action, which is to say, the war cannot be presented and its story told without putting its immediate presentation and the tellers of its story, then and there, at the heart of the story itself. See 'Media Art in the Balkans, a special issue of *Afterimage*, 28, 4, January/February 2001.

7 M. Danner (1997) 'The US and the Yugoslav Catastrophe', *New York Review of Books*, 20 November, 56–64; 'America and the Bosnia Genocide', *New York Review of Books*, 4 December, 55–65.

8 And consider, if you can bear it, the former President of the United States, Bill Clinton, whose extraordinary (in so many ways) confession, in Kigali in March of 1998, of his and our inaction in the face of the Rwandan genocide put him squarely – and immobile – in front of the television: 'Today the images of all that haunt us all: the dead choking the Kigara River, floating to Lake Victoria. [...] We did not act quickly enough after the killing began. [...] All over the world there were people like me, sitting in offices, day after day after day, who did not fully appreciate the depth and the speed with which you were being engulfed by this unimaginable terror' ('Remarks by the President to Genocide Survivors, Assistance Workers, and

U.S. and Rwandan Government Officials', 25 March1998, Kigali Airport, http://clinton4. nara.gov/Africa/19980325-16872.html, accessed April 13th, 2012). For further information, see S. Power (2001) 'Bystanders to Genocide, *The Atlantic Monthly*, September, 84–108.

9 M. Ignatieff (1997) *The Warrior's Honor: Ethnic War and the Modern Conscience*. New York: Henry Holt/Metropolitan Books.

10 See R. Brauman (1996) 'La pitié dangereuse', in R. Brauman and R. Backmann (eds) *Les médias et l'humanitaire: Ethique de l'information ou charité-spectacle*. Paris: CFPJ, 9–60.

11 See A. de Waal (1997) 'Becoming Shameless: The failure of human-rights organizations in Rwanda', *Times Literary Supplement*, 21 February, 3–4.

12 See B. Kouchner (1991) *Le malheur des autres*. Paris: Odile Jacob, 210.

13 The literature on the CNN effect is already significant, for example see J. Benthall (1993) *Disasters, Relief, and the Media*. London: I.B. Tauris; N. Gowing (1994) 'Real-Time Television Coverage of Armed Conflicts and Diplomatic Crises: Does it Pressure or Distort Foreign Policy Decisions?', Working Paper 94–1, Joan Shorenstein Barone Center on the Press, Politics, and Public Policy, Harvard University, Cambridge, MA; E. Girardet (ed.) (1995) *Somalia, Rwanda, and Beyond: The Role of the International Media in Wars and Humanitarian Crises*. Crosslines Special Report 1. Dublin: Crosslines; J. Gow, R. Paterson and A. Preston (eds) (1996) *Bosnia by Television*. London: British Film Institute; J. Neuman (1996) *Lights, Camera, War: Is Media Technology Driving International Politics?* New York: St. Martin's; L. Minear, C. Scott and T. G. Weiss (1996) *The News Media, Civil War, and Humanitarian Action*. Boulder: Lynne Reinner; R. I. Rotberg and T. G. Weiss (eds) (1996) *From Massacres to Genocide: The Media, Public Policy, and Humanitarian Crises*. Washington: Brookings Institution/Cambridge, MA: World Peace Foundation; M. Ignatieff (1997) *The Warrior's Honor: Ethnic War and the Modern Conscience*. New York: Henry Holt/Metropolitan Books; P. Seib (1997) *Headline Diplomacy: How News Coverage Affects Foreign Policy*. Westport: Praeger; S. Livingstone (1997) 'Clarifying the CNN Effect: An Examination of Media Effects According to Type of Military Intervention', Research Paper R-18, Joan Shorenstein Center on the Press, Politics, and Public Policy, Harvard University, Cambridge, MA; W. P. Strobel (1997) *Late-Breaking Foreign Policy: The News Media's Influence on Peace Operations*. Washington: U.S. Institute of Peace; and S. Moeller (1999) *Compassion Fatigue: How the Media Sell Disease, Famine, War and Death*. New York: Routledge.

14 See A. de Waal (1997) *Famine Crimes: Politics and the Disaster Relief Industry in Africa*. Oxford: James Curry/Bloomington: Indiana University Press, 65.

15 See W. Benjamin (1969) 'The Work of Art in the Age of Mechanical Reproduction', in *Illuminations*, trans. H. Zohn. New York: Schocken, 217–51.

16 See R. Cohen (1995) 'In Sarajevo, Victims of a 'Postmodern' War', *New York Times*, 21 May, 12; Cohen retells the story in *Hearts Grown Brutal: Sagas of Sarajevo*. New York: Random House, 1998, 377–9.

17 'As electrically contracted, the globe is no more than a village. Electric speed in bringing all social and political functions together has heightened human awareness of responsibility to an intense degree. It is this implosive factor that alters the position of the Negro, the teen-ager, and some other groups. They can no longer be *contained*, in the political sense of limited association. They are now *involved* in our lives, as we in theirs, thanks to the electric media' – M. McLuhan (1994 [1964]) *Understanding Media: The Extensions of Man*.

Cambridge: MIT Press, 5.

18 M. Wark (1994) *Virtual Geography: Living with Global Media Events*. Bloomington: Indiana University Press.

19 See, on the trade of images for food, M. Wark (1995) 'Fresh Maimed Babies', *Transition*, 5, 1, 36–47.

20 I have addressed some of these questions in T. Keenan (1994) 'Live from.../En direct de...', in E. Diller and R. Scofidio (eds) *Back to the Front: Tourisms of War/Visite aux armées: Tourismes de guerre*. Caen: F.R.A.C. Basse-Normandie, 130–63.

21 G. Kennan (1993) 'Somalia, Through a Glass Darkly', *New York Times*, 30 September, A25.

22 P. Virilio (1991) *L'écran du désert: Chroniques de guerre*. Paris: Galilée, 71–2.

23 See L. Minear, C. Scott and T. G. Weiss (1996) *The News Media, Civil War, and Humanitarian Action*. Boulder: Lynne Reinner, 46.

24 See S. Weber (1996) 'Television; set and screen', in *Mass Mediauras: Form Technics Media*. Stanford: Stanford University Press, 108–28.

25 Christiane Amanpour, Cable News Network, 26 January 1993. That was in January 1993, when she was just back from Somalia; in July of that year she again reported something similar: 'Those of us who've stayed in Sarajevo – which is the majority of the press corps – have been welcomed throughout most of this year. People have looked at us as their conduit to the West, and perhaps have looked at us as being able to jog, perhaps, some conscience in the West. The attitude towards us has been changing – certainly, in the last month. People have seen that really nothing has changed, that promises have been made and broken – promises from the Western allies have been made and broken. And people look to us and sort of vent their frustrations on us. [...] So the tide is turning somewhat, but that's a measure of people's despair, I suppose (CNN, *Larry King Live*, 30 July 1993).

26 See J. Baudrillard (1996a) 'No Pity for Sarajevo', trans. J. Patterson, in T. Cushman and S. G. Mestrovic (eds) *This Time We Knew: Western Responses to Genocide in Bosnia*. New York: New York University Press, 80–4; and (1996b) 'When the West Stands In for the Dead', trans. J. Patterson, in T. Cushman and S. G. Mestrovic (eds) *This Time We Knew: Western Responses to Genocide in Bosnia*. New York: New York University Press, 87–9.

27 D. Rieff (1996) *Slaughterhouse: Bosnia and the Failure of the West*. New York: Touchstone, 223.

28 See A. Ronell (1994) *Finitude's Score: Essays for the End of the Millennium*. Lincoln, NE: University of Nebraska Press.

29 See D. Campbell (2002) 'Atrocity, Memory, Photography: Imaging the Concentration Camps of Bosnia – The Case of ITN versus *Living Marxism*', *Journal of Human Rights*, 1, 1–33 and 2, 142–72.

30 P. Virilio (1995) 'Alerte dans le cyberspace', *Le Monde Diplomatique*, August; 'Red alert in cyberspace', trans. M. Imrie, *Radical Philosophy*, 74, November-December, 2–4.

31 See B. Giussani (1997) 'For a Philosopher, the Net Is a Whole New Perspective', *New York Times on the Web*, 9 December, http://www.nytimes.com/library/cyber/euro/120997euro.html.

SHOOTING WITH INTENT: FRAMING CONFLICT

Alisa Lebow

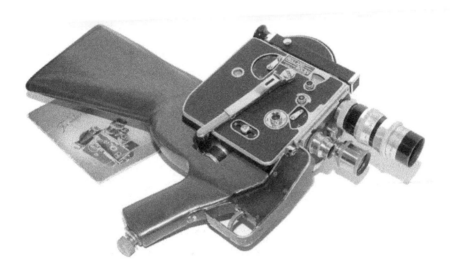

Fig. 1 Bolex with Pistol Grip.

It is a curious and not insignificant etymological coincidence that in some languages, the verb 'to shoot' is used to mean both the firing of a gun and the filming of an image. Ever since the invention of the moving image, there has been an intimate and mutually dependent relationship between the camera and the gun. One of the very first prototypes for the motion picture camera, Etienne-Jules Marey's 'Fusil Photographique', was fashioned out of and modelled upon the revolving rifle able to 'shoot' twelve photographs per second in rapid succession. Here, at the origins of cinema, we find an inspiration less innocent than implicated, where the sightlines of a camera mimic and will come to eventually support the sightlines of a weapon.

Fig. 2 Etienne-Jules Marey's 1882 invention, 'Fusil Photographique', an early experiment in recording motion on film.

Guns and cameras have an obvious affinity that precedes the invention of the cinema.[1] The framing and tracing of movement through the 'viewfinder' of a gun, along with the mechanisms supporting its agility and efficiency, are eventually mimed by the cinematic apparatus, further nourished by the vast investments in the development of weaponry that is guided by, and/or monitored through, the lens of a camera.[2] For several decades, weapons have been developed whose precision depends heavily on the 'eye' of the camera requiring only a technician, based in a far away post, to focus, aim and fire.[3] In his book *War and Cinema*, Paul Virilio writes extensively about the interpenetration between warfare and cinema – not exclusively about the gun, but about the entire apparatus of destruction. There is what he calls 'an osmosis between industrialized warfare and cinema' so ultimately enmeshed that he is moved to assert that, 'War is Cinema, Cinema is War' (1992: 58, 26).[4]

We learn from Virilio that wars are no longer fought without cameras – and have not been since World War II, when Hitler sent a cameraman out with every battalion (1992: 56).[5] By now there is a thorough integration of cinematic tools in warfare (and, at least in some countries, of the military's participation in the making and advising of war films). The gunsight and the camera eyepiece not only engage a similar operation of framing the target, with a shared privileging of the ocular faculty, but in fact the camera and the weapon are frequently conjoined, aiding and abetting the other's operations – as cameras are used to spot targets, perform reconnaissance, train marksmen, built into military aircraft and mounted onto rifles and missiles, to capture and record the moment of 'impact'.[6]

But if Virilio exhaustively recounts the relentless imbrication of armed conflict and cinema, he does so only in relation to fiction film. Despite the obvious fact that the images taken from aboard the unmanned planes, all-terrain vehicles, robots and anti-tank weapons are documentary in nature, Virilio and others writing about the relationship between cinema and war,[7] rarely if ever acknowledge the link between visual realist modalities of filmmaking and violent conflict.[8] Instead, their sights are set on the spectacle of the fiction film, especially the action and war genres, most particularly those made in Hollywood. This essay attempts to refocus attention back onto visual realist modalities – whether documentary or otherwise[9] – where in effect, it all began, and where it still continues to play an undeniable role in representing and mediating zones

Fig. 3 Rokuoh-Sha Type 89 WWII Vintage Machine Gun Camera, used mostly for target practice.

of violent conflict. It will trace its way through the question of the frame, initially in its literal sense, and ultimately in a more figurative fashion.

Initially, I want to situate the discussion by examining the two distinct positionalities that visual realist filmmaking can take within the context of violent conflict zones: the Gunsight POV – shooting from the perspective of the bullet; and the Barrel POV – shooting down the barrel of a gun, in the line of fire. As Harun Farocki's *Image of the World and Inscriptions of War* (1989–90) attests, the point of view from which visual material is shot does not and cannot exhaust its semiotic valences nor its hermeneutical potential.[10] It does, however, speak volumes about the relationship between aiming and framing, or said otherwise, the power of the frame, the power to frame and reframe. The purpose for which the images are collected and disseminated, the allegiances an image is meant to forge, the information and intelligence it is meant to gather, the power, or lack thereof, it may represent, and the way in which images are literally and figuratively framed, are all valid reasons to distinguish between these two divergent sightlines. It does, after all, matter from which side of the gun you're shooting, not to mention what is included in and what is left out of the frame. In this essay I will be discussing three specific projects, with attention to the pressing question of point of view and framing. The larger aim of this article is to explore the limits of the 'encounter', or better, the 'confrontation' between the two apparati – the camera and the gun – and the broader 'frame' in which these images are captured and disseminated.

The crucial distinction to be made here between the Gunsight POV and the Barrel POV is whether the camera is positioned as an extension of the gun or as a response to it, in effect 'shooting back'. In cinematic terms these two positionalities can literally represent the shot/reverse-shot structure, though the key difference would be that the 'shot' wields both literal and symbolic power while the 'reverse shot' in this case is arguably consigned to the symbolic.[11] In that both wield symbolic (and phallic) power we have to enquire as to the machinations and mobilisations of that power, and we must then consider what may occur in the one instance (the Gunsight POV) where symbolic power is concomitant with destructive force.

Scopophilia and voyeurism, the twin regimes of the repressive patriarchal cinematic gaze, clearly take on more than symbolic implications when allied with, and to a much lesser extent against, a lethal weapon. Not unlike the dagger at the end of the tripod leg in Michael Powell's *Peeping Tom* (1960), the camera is more than a threat in representational terms, becoming part of a much larger apparatus of death and destruction. Today's riot police squadrons routinely dispatch their minions, interchangeably wielding batons, tasers, guns and cameras, all in pursuit of the same repressive goal.

Although the visual images rendered from the Barrel POV remain in the symbolic realm, they are nonetheless caught in the sight lines of an 'adversary' for whom this is not the case, posing potentially very real and dire consequences in this lopsided 'Mexican stand-off'. Whether there is any such thing, really, as purely symbolic power, and whether indeed the effects of the Barrel POV-oriented camera do in fact also have 'real world' effects, remains to be explored.

GUNSIGHT POV – THRILL OF THE KILL

The most common modality from the Gunsight POV is official, governmental, military or paramilitary imagery. The Gunsight POV can, of course, also partake of several other visual realist modalities. When, during the second Gulf War, the US Defence Department gave journalists access to its maneuvers as long as they agreed to be 'embedded' within a military platoon, we see a clear example of journalism's collusion with the Gunsight POV. A spate of documentaries made from the soldiers' POV, some making extensive use of helmet cams (*Gunner Palace*, Petra Epperlein, Michael Tucker, US, 2004; *Restrepo*, Tim Hetherington and Sebastian Junger, US, 2010, and; the British TV documentary series *Our War*, a three-part series produced for BBC3 by Colin Barr, 2010–11) all attempt in a sense to put the audience in the shoes (or head?) of the invading military units as they make their way in unknown and dangerous territory, eagerly taking on the Gunsight POV, albeit one that also has guns aimed at it. The effect of much of this material can be insidious. In the case of both *Restrepo* and *Our War*, the spectator's perspective essentially mimic's the soldier's, and just as they at first find themselves disoriented and uncertain of their feelings (why are we here, what is this place), so does the viewer. As soon as the first soldier is killed, the identification between viewer and soldier, by virtue of POV, is strengthened. The viewer is brought into the war as a virtual participant, the soldier who gets shot in front of 'us' could just as easily have been 'us'. Thus as the soldiers gain a sense of purpose that suddenly gives meaning to the operation – revenge and retribution – even if that meaning masks the vague and unconvincing premise that may have brought them there, the viewer has been positioned to share their vengeful sentiment, identification having been seamlessly effected; this process, of course, conveniently sidesteps those nagging questions (why are we here, by what right), insinuating the viewer as part of the 'we' who are going to make 'them' pay.

Not all Gunsight POV is one-sided. There are countless YouTube postings of amateur video shot on camcorders or mobile phones by soldiers, militia fighters, jihadis and mercenaries in places like Iraq, that when seen back to back in compilations such as Mauro Andrizzi's *How We Fight, Part I* (Argentina, 2008), give a sense of the shot/reverse-shot that can occur strictly from the Gunsight POV. That is to say, both sides are shooting to kill.

I would like to briefly describe a clip from Mauro Andrizzi's *How We Fight, Part I* to give a sense of the investments of the Gunsight POV. The play of the title empties the promise of an ethical answer to the question of 'why we fight' (the title of the US War Department's World War II documentary propaganda series directed by the likes of Frank Capra and John Huston – a promise admittedly never fulfilled) into the more mechanistic and pragmatic problematic of 'how'. The project as a whole is a compilation video comprised of footage taken by participants in the Iraq conflict (Iraqi militia fighters, Iraqi military, US and UK military, mercenary fighters, civilian workers). The majority of the material was downloaded from YouTube by the Argentinian director, Andrizzi. In one brief extract we hear the voices of several young American soldiers, as their unsteady camera peers out of their vehicle's windshield, looking at a generic industrial landscape. The moment is charged with their agitated anticipation. The young man behind the camera asks the presumably more experienced soldier how long he should continue to film for, to which he receives the sage response: 'until you turn it off'. They wait impatiently for the missile to come, launched, we understand, from a nearby position, perhaps by members of their own battalion. They clearly know the target and the timing of the launch and it's only the filming of it over which they seem to lack mastery. Nonetheless, there is thorough identification between the missile strike and the filming of it, as the soldiers exclaim with whoops and hollers and phrases such as 'hell yeah, bitches,' 'that was so fucking beautiful', 'see you in fucking hell', when the projectile finally hits its mark. Ultimately, when the missile strikes, mastery over the visual image is also achieved, as we hear the novice videographer brag before cutting, that he 'got it all' on tape.

This clip differs dramatically in tone (but not in alliance between the camera's POV and the attack) from its countershot, as it were, one of the many Iraqi militia clips also included in the compilation, where we hear a fighter chanting Allah's name repeatedly, with strained voice, before and after we see a (usually successful) strike. Faith and discipline characterise the tone of the latter extracts, whereas the unruly excitement of a high-octane videogamer characterises the former. In both cases, however, we witness the unity of vision, a shared objective between the camera and the apparatus of destruction. There is a clear affinity here, a symbiosis of vision as a nexus of power. The gaze acquires its properly lethal aspect where to be shot by the camera is in essence, synonymous with being shot. The objective of the camera here is to capture the moment of impact – the 'money shot' if you will. It goes without saying that there are, of course, even more explicit and direct affilliative scopic relations between the camera and the gun, and the position in which the viewer is placed vis-a-vis this material is inevitably fraught, implicating the spectatorial gaze in the military might being brought simultaneously to bear. For instance, watching reconnaissance footage taken from an unmanned drone flying a mission over Iraq and broadcast on the corporate/commercial news conglomerates in the US, or footage from a 'smart missile' moments before it strikes its target, combines the thrill of being let in on a secret, the satisfaction of prosthetically allying one's gaze with high-tech precision aim, and the vertiginous dawning realisation that one is being made to identify with a lethally destructive force, which has a passive dimension of approbation: by witnessing, not to mention taking pleasure in the spectacle, we are tacitly interpellated into the frame as accessories, no longer ignorant of the destruction, but in a manner of speaking, aligned with it.

When used in the 'theatre' (perhaps we should call it the 'cinema') of combat, a camera cannot be conceived of as a passive recording device. It is transformed into an instrument of war. As Allen Feldman suggests in his article 'Violence and Vision: The Prosthetics and Aesthetics of Terror', optical surveillance such as this can and often is regarded by the opposing force – with good reason – as tantamount to aggression.[12] The identification of the camera with the gun in these settings is not merely an allusion to repressive power, it is a direct mechanism of that power. The footage recorded amounts to intelligence gathering, and can be used in any number of ways against human and other targets. To be caught in the sightlines of the enemy's camera, is to foreshadow being caught in the crosshairs of the enemy's gun.

When Feldman was conducting his fieldwork in Northern Ireland in the late 1970s and into the 1980s, he saw very little in the way of oppositional or activist media, though it is known to have developed there later. Still, from the beginning of the conflict, the camera was an integral weapon in the defensive arsenal of warfare and it was treated as such. Framing and focusing a camera lens on a human subject by any of the warring factions was tantamount to an act of hostility.

BARREL POV – SHOOTING BACK

Civilians shooting back with a camera, without the apparatus of warfare supporting and sustaining it, while perhaps still regarded by the state and its militaries as a provocation, cannot and would not be eager to claim, I believe, such a thorough-going imbrication with destructive force. It is also rarely allied with the governmental and official realist modes of filming (such as reconnaissance, or target identification), but is much more commonly affiliated with the journalistic, documentary, activist and civilian modes of filmmaking.[13]

I will focus my attention here on two 'Barrel POV' projects: the first is a documentary entitled *Burma VJ* (2008), and the second is an NGO-sponsored activist project associated with a well known human rights organisation based in Israel/Palestine, called, appropriately enough, Shooting Back.[14]

Burma VJ is credited as a film by Anders Østergaard, a filmmaker initially working on a project about a group of Burmese video journalists/activists who had been shooting news footage illegally and sneaking it out of the country, in defiance of their government's harsh censorship laws, when the so-called 'Saffron Revolution' broke out in 2007. In the end, the film chronicles the events of the Saffron Revolution made to look almost as though the amateur video journalists (the VJs of the title) were coordinating its developments. The film shows the monks of Burma leading popular demonstrations for days on end in a face-off with the currently ruling military junta, one of a succession of juntas that have mercilessly ruled the country without respite since 1962. *Burma VJ* features the raw footage shot by the video journalists/activists who braved life and limb to capture the month-long uprising on their small, easily hidden, camcorders. The mere possession of a camcorder in Burma at the time was a prosecutable offense-carrying a prison sentence of up to 25 years. A powerful film, it took the festival circuit by storm, winning top prizes at IDFA in 2008 and Sundance in 2009.

The footage is gripping, and the bravery of the citizen journalists turned video activists is beyond doubt. Their stated goal (as conveyed via voice-over of a VJ code-named Joshua – not credited as writer, however, in the film) is to show the world what was happening in Burma, then as now, a country closed to foreign press. As these images were successfully smuggled out of Burma during the course of the events, finding their way onto CNN, BBC and indeed via satellite back into Burma, the video activists can claim to have been successful in their aim.

The film has been praised by the Western press as being as suspenseful as an action film, made all the more powerful because it is 'real'.[15] What critics seem to be moved by is the sense that the events are unfolding before their eyes. This effect is partly created by the interspersed re-enactments stitching this raw material together, preserving a sense of immediacy – placing the spectator 'in the moment'.

This illusion of 'presence' is of course a conceit, because while the archival footage was shot live during the events' unfolding, the story that weaves it into a coherent narrative is constructed for the purposes of the film. The 'lead character' Joshua, played by an actual Burmese VJ who did indeed escape Burma, is seen in several scenes set both within and outside of Burma, engaged in conversation with his comrades, often coordinating their elicit activities or receiving breaking news about the whereabouts of one of their number. This was scripted and re-enacted for the benefit of the film, yet by seamlessly intercutting the re-enacted material with the archival, the film's sleight of hand renders it somewhat suspect, as if entertainment value and narrative flow take precedence over the historicity of the archival material. There are also re-enacted scenes that are shot so as to appear as if they were part of the secretly filmed footage of the VJs, for instance, a scene where the activists aren't sure anybody will turn up for a demonstration, and the footage appears to be shot illicitly from across the road, as protestors start coming, first one, then another, and soon many begin to stream in. This footage, though one might never suspect it, was staged, and its power to move the viewer rests precisely on the fact that we think it's an artefact produced under extremely dangerous conditions; a testament to the grit of the intrepid VJs.

This relentless staging and re-enacting in the service of the all important demands of narrative coherence, also serves to suppress the gaps, the lacunae, the ultimate inadequacy of the coverage, rather than considering such shortcomings to be a consequence of the general state of repression which would have allowed it to be imagined and understood as such by the viewer. The staged material does provide a dramatic platform on which to set the tense and engaging, if chaotic, original footage. But one wonders if it doesn't also reduce this unique event into a generic action/suspense spectacle, with all of the habitual responses to such genre films, at the ready.

Also in the service of a seamless narrative – the conventional film's ruthless master – a great deal of relevant information is elided, such as the fact that the monks in the film appear to be a unified force, though after nearly half a century of military dictatorship in which the monks are 'highly respected', and where religious sites turned tourist attractions like Manderlay are major sources of for-eign currency, it is impossible to imagine that there weren't conclaves of corrupt monks. This, alongside the fact that no real reason is given for this spontaneous uprising, though of course there were many factors that triggered it, including the neo-liberal move by the junta to eliminate fuel subsidies which caused the price of diesel and petrol to suddenly rise as much as 66 per cent in less than a week,[16] make one suspect that the director wanted to streamline the story so that it was freed of any geopolitical particularities and could appeal to a 'universal' audi-ence. Armed with the platitudes of 'freedom' and 'democracy', and the elements of a particular struggle with all of its local cultural specificities effectively erased, what is left is a good crackling drama, of the sort any movie goer is familiar: a tense, action-packed, adrenaline-fuelled stand-off with high stakes, augmented by bright, 'exotic' colours. By conceding to the generic demands of an action film, keeping the viewer on the edge of her seat, heart pumping, palms sweating, one senses that the effect and political potential of the Barrel POV here, where real not 'pretend' lives are at stake, is flattened into well-worn formulas, rendered generic, made utterly familiar, and thus ultimately blunted.[17]

One aspect of this conventionalisation is the highlighting of the sense of dan-ger. This is done by frequently foregrounding the act of filming itself. In this age of cynicism, there is something almost irresistible in the prospect of real-life hero-ism, which is to be had in abundance with our fearless videographers, putting themselves in the line of fire at every turn. Their heroism, in fact, is not at issue. They truly are worthy of great admiration and respect. Their footage may at times appear to be shot from the vantage point of a sniper, but even so, we cannot help but be aware that it is they who are potentially caught in the crosshairs of the sniper's gun. Throughout the film, the risk to the video 'shooter' is palpable.

A pivotal scene in *Burma VJ* features the shooting by the Burmese military of a lone foreign journalist, Japanese cameraman Kenji Nagai, at point-blank range. It is captured by several of the VJs from different angles (from a position above, from street level, head on, side view) – a testament to what appears to be their surreptitious ubiquity, at least at this particular moment. The footage is slowed down and played both forward and in reverse for the viewer. Here we are shown the consequences of being caught filming in Burma. Just as Feldman indicated with reference to Northern Ireland, in Burma too the camera is treated as a provocation, tantamount to a gun: a challenge to absolute authority and a claim to the right to frame and thus attenuate that power, despite the fact that this 'gun' would appear to be shooting blanks. The power of the media is in effect affirmed, in that it is deemed worthy of extreme measures of repression, perhaps even regarded as an enemy of the state. We learn earlier in the film that Joshua –

Fig. 4 Japanese cameraman Kenji Nagai shot by Burmese military at point blank range.

our narrator's codename – had been caught filming days before but only briefly detained. But by the time this Japanese journalist enters the fray, the situation had become even more critical.[18] The consequences of filming seem real enough, and the high stakes motivation would seem to be to mediate the moment for the world to witness.

Despite the airtime the original footage received on Western media outlets, even prior to its recontextualisation in this film, I believe it is necessary to question the efficacy of such exposure, or at least to question whether exposure, in and of itself, ensures a response. Is seeing and being seen, including garnering airtime on major media outlets in the West, an effective organising strategy in and of itself? Put another way, 'what difference does it make that the camera was there?', a question provocatively posed by Thomas Keenan in relation to the heavily mediated yet relatively ignored battlegrounds in Sarajevo. Keenan argues forcefully against any assumption that would automatically link the mediation of an event with a call to action. He reminds us of the distinct lack of interest in, and the extremely delayed response of European and North American governments to, what by all accounts was a policy of ruthless genocide taking place in plain sight. By Keenan's reckoning, the siege of Sarajevo was one of the most heavily mediated conflicts of the 1990s. And yet, the saturation of images of the atrocities, instead, seems to have had a palliative effect, reassuring viewers that someone was there to witness in their stead (2002: 113).[19] Of course the Burmese VJs have multiple tactics and strategies beyond simply wanting their footage aired on international news outlets (including boycotts, litigation and using their footage to lobby foreign governments and mobilise student groups), but they are not alone amongst activist media groups to have international television exposure as a key component of their campaign. The emphasis placed on such televisual outlets by this group and by B'Tselem, the group I will discuss shortly, suggests the need to interrogate just what the role of the media may be. After all, as it stands today, it is by no means a neutral platform.

Having footage broadcast (pre-edited or otherwise) – and thus 'framed' – by global corporate and/or national media conglomerates, Keenan reminds us, does not guarantee a response, nor is it certain to influence policy. It is not even certain to change opinions. All it can do is inform and that within a contextualisation of the network's own design. One cannot expect the corporate and/or national media of the world to act outside of its self-interest, as a neutral conduit of the information presented to them by activists. If anything, it serves as inexpensive content, shot in places where the Western media either does not have access (Burma, or more recently, Syria), or has not gotten the footage in time (for example, footage from the Egyptian events in Tahrir Square at the beginning of the revolution of 2011, or in Iran during the Green Revolution). Such footage, shot by amateurs, is often circumscribed with the caveat that the news media outlet cannot verify the material as it was not shot by one of their own camera people, thus not only indemnifying them from legal claims, but also instilling doubt in the viewer as to the veracity of the footage itself.[20] Furthermore, entire discourse analysis theses could be written on juxtapositions, both within newscasts, and with intervening advertisements when present.

Emphasis on getting the message out through every available channel, without consideration of the way that footage may be framed, can lead to matters going well beyond the makers' control. While this risk may be deemed worth taking, the arguments in favour of exposure, without attending to context and framing, seem amiss. Yet it is not only the corporate or national newsmedia whose framing devices can be suspect. I will argue that *Burma VJ*'s own framing device has motivations beyond the Burmese VJs control, an issue explored further in due course.

THE ACTIVIST PROJECT: SHOOTING BACK, B'TSELEM

The Israeli human rights organisation B'Tselem's Shooting Back project, whose name was changed in 2008 by court order to the anodyne Camera Distribution

Project (and as of the writing of this article, simply referred to on their web-site as 'the Camera Project'), also actively invites international press attention, with a high degree of success. Here, as with *Burma VJ*, we have amateur video-graphers facing off against aggressive, potentially lethal, forces. The project, however, does not produce documentaries *per se*, but rather activist clips usu-ally edited by B'Tselem staff, sometimes complete with an English or Hebrew commentator track, which can be sent out as press packages and propagated over the internet. They are also compiled on DVDs, usually based on themes or geographical areas.[21]

Another key difference between *Burma VJ* and the Shooting Back project would be that the latter constitutes an exercise or expression of a legal action, one that is meant to test the limits of an already existent legal framework in which the actors have the right to film and document the situation (a right that may be arbitrarily and prejudicially enforced, but one that nonetheless exists). The mate-rial gathered can and frequently does serve as visible evidence of the most literal sort – evidence of abuses and excesses to be used not only in the 'court of world opinion' but in an actual court of law. Relative to the circumstances surrounding the shooting of the Burmese material, there would seem to be a tacit permissive-ness associated with the B'Tselem project, as it is clearly known in the region and lends some measure of credibility, if not protection, to its videographers.[22]

To wit, in one of the video clips released in 2007, and in another shot in 2008, we hear a Palestinian cameraperson who is being attacked by settlers and/or confronted by soldiers, respond in Hebrew to the provocations with the claim, '*Ani mi B'Tselem*' ('I am from B'Tselem') which is particularly intriguing for the authority that statement hopes to invoke.[23] The two cameramen's responses are meant to convey an entitlement: 'I have the right to shoot, I'm with B'Tselem.' This claim is all but unimaginable, of course, in the Burmese context. In one of the more recent clips though, it is the B'Tselem affiliation of the camera person that provokes a soldier to arrest him, saying on camera, 'if you're with B'Tselem, I'm arresting you too'. This despite the fact that the camera person had a legal right to shoot.

Several of the Shooting Back project's shorts depict direct encounters with hostile forces. Some are shot surreptitiously, as when a man secretly films an ille-gal Israeli Defence Force (IDF) house demolition from his window.[24] Others film direct confrontations with soldiers and/or Israeli settlers who mean them harm. Some are shot in the absence of actual guns, as when a young Palestinian boy manages to avert Israeli settler violence by chasing them with his camera. The camera here operates with a similar deterrent effect as a gun. Yet what is mobil-ised is not might but *sight* – the potentially damaging effects of witnessing, being caught (on tape) in the act of violent activities, tacitly supported by the state, reveals something of the limits to the settlers' own internal justifications of their actions. Clearly they know they are doing something wrong, if not immoral (and all of these settlers are wearing the garb of religious Jews), as at least the settlers in this video seem to fear being seen by others. However, there are other videos on the B'Tselem website where settlers are seen throwing rocks in plain view of the camera with no restraint,[25] and in yet another video, a young Palestinian girl catches on camera masked settlers with clubs attacking a shepherd in his field. Despite the likelihood that these are different settlers in a different field, it is as if the settlers learned their lesson from an earlier video and simply went back to get their masks to hide their identities while they continue with their brand of terror.[26] In these cases, the camera may be a witness, but it is no deterrent.

One of the best known videos of the project, *Tel Rumeida* (2008),[27] is shot by a Palestinian woman in Hebron, who is being tormented by her Israeli settler neighbours. She videotapes their abuses, which include verbal provocations as well as physical assault with stones, as Israeli soldiers look on. When the fully armed soldiers do intervene, it is generally to tell her to stop shooting, as if she is the one provoking the violence and her camera is obviously seen as a threat. At one point she runs out of her barricaded house into the perilous streets (as several young settler children pelt rocks at her and her little brother, who she is attempting to protect), and the soldier addressing her is apparently less concerned for her safety than about her continuous videotaping. He repeatedly tells her to stop shooting and although she keeps the camera rolling throughout, we see an image that indicates she has pointed the lens downwards, in essentially the same position as the soldier's gun. There is a meeting of the 'guns', both pointed downward in a gesture of non-confrontation: a tense conciliatory stance that nonetheless implies the potential for a standoff – camera lens to gunbarrel – but manages to avert it. While the camera may not have the same lethal force as the soldier's machine gun, the power it does have, to record, to witness, to confront, to intimidate, is clear for all to see.

We can see that the camera in these shorts, shooting from the Barrel POV, has different and at times conflicting effects. It can act as a deterrent, a witness or, indeed, a provocation. When acting as a deterrent to violent confrontation and/or illegal and illegitimate exercises of power, one can see the justification for its use. Similarly with witnessing, as the material can be used as evidence in both legal courts and the 'court' of public opinion. However, when it acts as a provocation, inciting or exacerbating an already volatile situation, there is a questionable value to the footage, both in terms of its status as witness and in terms of the risk in which it places the camera person. Suddenly and without warning, the B'Tselem affiliation shifts from shield to target, making it a liability for the person shooting from the Barrel POV.

I'd like to now shift the discussion from the question of the literal sightlines (POV) of the camera to the positioning of the material more broadly – the figurative framing devices of the two projects, B'Tselem's Shooting Back videos and *Burma VJ*.

The stated intent on the B'Tselem website (and on the jacket covers of the widely distributed free DVDs) is to expose the everyday reality of occupation, the daily abuse and indignities, the relentless and demoralising struggles, 'to show', as they would have it, 'the seldom seen'. However, in this decades-long occupation is there really any aspect of this struggle that can be said to be seldom seen? Not unlike the siege of Sarajevo that Keenan writes about, this conflict is easily one of the most mediated of all conflicts in history, with what seems like every angle covered by every possible mode of representation. It is perhaps not the specific situations that we haven't seen, but the POV that is new. But this is not what is emphasised on the promotional materials. It is simply asserted that we are to see the seldom seen, as if in and of itself, this 'seeing' could catalyse change. Now, this is not to reduce the work that B'Tselem is trying to do more broadly. This project is just one facet of the campaigning work they do against the excesses of the occupation. B'Tselem is a human rights organisation that uses all of the tools at its disposal, including video, to attempt to affect the conditions under which Palestinians are living in the Israeli-occupied territories.[28] I will not address B'Tselem's mandate as a whole here. I am strictly addressing myself to the claims made on behalf of the Shooting Back/Camera Distribution Project, which figures quite prominently in the organisation's promotional material.

Taking into consideration Keenan's important intervention, we must acknowledge that over-mediation, regardless of the POV, can misfire badly, and rather than inspiring the intended political response, can easily be naturalised as a site of ongoing human suffering, inciting in the viewer only pity and at best leading to some form of modest humanitarian intervention. There are consequences to this strategy, hinted at in Slavoj Žižek's book *Violence*.[29] While ameliorating harsh conditions is welcome, it may nonetheless ultimately mask larger problems. Žižek urges us to consider whether liberal humanist representations and condemnations of violence, such as those promoted by the Shooting Back project, merely register 'subjective' violence (the most visible yet superficial of all violences), while remaining mute in the face of underlying causes, unable to intervene in systemic, or what he terms 'objective' violence (2008: 9–10). How can the images of this project help us analyse the systemic violence of the Israeli occupation or even more profoundly, the military-industrial complex that sustains it and Israel's economy? In what ways can such representations hope to disrupt the relations of domination inherent in that system?

Žižek, in line with several prominent leftist thinkers including Michael Hardt and Antonio Negri, Naomi Klein and Eyal Weizman,[30] finds the ameliorative effects of 'humanitarian'projects, of which activist media such as Shooting Back is a part, neither address the constitutive issues enveloping the violent oppression (in this case the Israeli Occupation), nor can they hope to lead to an end to the injustices that they depict. All they can achieve within the logic of the occupation, is to alter the superficial conditions of such abuse, of the 'subjective violence', and of course, while some relief is not to be rejected, unless the root causes are addressed, the misery will be no closer to an end. The change they may bring will be minimal and often, temporary, as we see in the Hebron video where a B'Tselem team films a break in the illegal blockade of a main street, only to find soldiers days later ignoring the law and continuing to bar Palestinians access to that same street. Change can be fleeting and even reversible. Israeli law, based on precedent like the British model, is arguably affected by any case that is won on behalf of human rights. However, the logic of these precedents is such that they apply only very limitedly and specifically so perhaps a type of roadblock will be removed or a shelter for the sun provided; perhaps soldiers will be disciplined for particular practices, or a type of torture outlawed, but change at that pace – case by case – means it will take a few lifetimes for the occupation to be dismantled.

Don't get me wrong, the act of shooting back with a camera is not without its uses. It may be used as a visual record for future war crimes trials, and as stated it can and has been used as evidence for courts of law. The videos are indeed, as mentioned earlier, used as legal evidence, and may actually have a limited effect. Such effects are welcome in the short run, but whether they can end the excesses of the occupation as a whole remains an open question. In addition, it is not unprecedented for such projects to be used by the repressive forces to make the occupation more efficient, possibly more legally viable, and ultimately more entrenched. There are countless ways in which the Israeli government and the IDF have 'improved' their legal standing vis-a-vis the occupation, studying material made available through projects like Shooting Back, or Yoav Shamir's *Machso-mim* (*Checkpoint*, Israel, 2003), and then making minor adjustments to their practices so as not to be held legally liable.[31] Remember, these video images are widely available, and not only to those who might wish to 'help'. One can imagine too, if we want to extend the metaphors of warfare here, that there is ample opportunity for people caught in the frame (say, neighbours or fellow protesters), to be hit by 'friendly fire' – harassed, arrested, killed – simply by having been caught in the 'line of shooting' of these activist's cameras, and thus potentially targeted by hostile forces who have access to this footage by virtue of its sheer availability – the eagerness to be seen and shown (on the internet, on television, on free DVDs) means that the footage is readily available for many possible applications.[32] It all depends on who is watching the material and for what purpose.

I say this not to undermine the good work being done, but to refrain from over-valorising the role of Barrel POV in the service of NGOs and humanitarian projects (whether activist or documentary) with the ultimate goal, if that is indeed their goal, of toppling repressive regimes or dismantling unjust administrative structures. I don't particularly want to join the ever-growing chorus of NGO-bashers who position themselves as more radical and more committed, while in the end justifying their right to do nothing in the face of massive injustice – precisely in fact, what Žižek proposes (2008: 180). I launch this critique as a kind of internal reckoning, an attempt to imagine how video activism might do more than flood the world with images that will likely never be watched, heroically and dramatically facing off camera to gun, getting caught up in the crossfire of individual micro-conflicts while, in effect and in actuality, the junta in Burma retrenches and the West Bank remains captive.

B'Tselem is a multi-million-dollar operation with a very slick and effective media team. They retain shared rights to the material shot in the territories and they edit it as they see fit.[33] Sometimes they package the shorts for national and/or international news, the package is even available complete with British-accented commentators. According to their publicity, they have a high degree of success placing their stories on news outlets such as BBC, CNN and Al Jazeera.

It is important to consider that B'Tselem as a whole is a project conceived and run by leftist Israelis, whose main aim as stated on their website is to 'educate the Israeli public and policymakers about human rights violations in the Occupied Territories, combat the phenomenon of denial prevalent among the Israeli public, and help create a human rights culture in Israel.'[34] B'Tselem shows a kinder, more compassionate face of Israel – the very existence of the organisation, and the fact that their website and videos are not censored, goes some way to prove the 'benevolence' of the Israeli state. Yet despite its successes (in court, in the media, in fundraising), it surely cannot be said to have aided in the dismantling of a single settlement, let alone the now 45-year occupation (only a few years shorter than Burmese military rule), nor as suggested earlier, is that even one of its stated goals. Yet the Shooting Back project is considered so successful and has gained so much attention worldwide, that a new organisation called Videre, led by the first director of the Shooting Back project, has been set up to export the 'video intervention model' to other conflict zones, initially in South Africa and shortly thereafter, elsewhere. The Videre website states: 'Realising the impact of the project, the head of Shooting Back joined forces with a reputable group of filmmakers, businessmen, lawyers and human rights activists to found Videre in 2008.'[35]

Which brings me to my final point, to do with the framing of the 'raw' material of these projects, transforming them into internationally disseminated productions. Both *Burma VJ* and Shooting Back take footage from 'the field', shot primarily by civilian activists in the line of fire, and contain and contextualise the material, framing it for an anticipated audience of concerned (or soon to be concerned) viewers. Anders Østergaard is now, due to the success of this film, a well known, award-winning Danish filmmaker. The likes of Dame Vivienne Westwood and Richard Gere lent their presence to *Burma VJ*'s European premieres. The film was sold to HBO, screened on BBC and other broadcast outlets around the world, had theatrical release in most major cities in the United States, and was nominated for an Academy Award in 2010. The UK-based Cooperative Bank even sponsored a campaign in conjunction with the UK release of the film to raise awareness about Burma. Surely this is good news.

Yet something is amiss. The model is too familiar. Of course the Burmese VJs could not risk exposing their identities to collaborate as named partners on the project, but they could surely have been listed as collaborators – even if only as DVB (Democratic Voice of Burma – an Oslo-based satellite broadcaster featured in the film) – and Østergaard could have been, say, the project coordinator, rather than the sole named director. Instead, their only credit is as camera people, anonymously and collectively credited as 'The Burmese VJs', a credit they share with the explicitly named Danish Director of Photography, Simon Plum. As it stands then, we've got the classic colonial model of the raw materials extracted at low cost, to the European video producer, yet at an extremely high human cost in terms of risk to the actual producers. It is then transformed, out of context, into a consumable good (that is, a well-worn generic story that Western viewers can comfortably consume), and that accrues cultural and presumably economic capital for the filmmaker, and hopefully some international attention paid to an urgent political crisis, perhaps concrete measures taken by governments and organisations in a position to make a difference, but essentially these come as biproducts of the film's great success. In the film world, it is ultimately Østergaard who gets the acclaim; he is, in effect, the hero who brings the story to the all-important West's attention.

B'Tselem's project is not, or not primarily, an export, nor is it primarily conceived for the film world as a documentary. Yet the dynamic is not entirely dissimilar from that which we've seen in *Burma VJ*, in that you have an Israeli-run organisation taking footage shot primarily by Palestinians under occupation, and although the stated intent is to improve the lives of those very Palestinians, you begin to see the benefits that accrue not to any individual Palestinian, let alone the whole population, but to the reputation of this organisation to the point of spawning predominantly Israeli-run off-shoot projects. What gets exported here is the know-how, the organisational acumen, the skills – all still firmly in the hands of Israeli occupiers, not Palestinians – not to mention the international image of the Israeli state as ultimately tolerant and benevolent in its willingness to allow public critique.

The aim of this intervention is to identify in the larger framing of these projects, the reproduction of systemic power relations and hierarchies of control that the micro-frame of the camera – shooting back – pretends or intends to deny. What we see in relation to the examples given here is that the potential does exist in these shoot-outs to undermine the power structures that be – using the weapon of mass communication – but it remains an empty threat as long as the operations of power are only exposed at the subjective level, neglecting or ignoring its systemic aspect, and worse, perpetuating structural relations of domination in their making.

The relationship between the camera and the gun is a provocative one, worth parsing in more detail that I am able to do justice to in this essay. Yet beyond the apparent framing and POV, which accounts for the thrills and the heroism associated with this sort of imagery, we must attend to the figurative framing to which this material is subjected if we are ever to understand the power relations as well as the subtending violences which these images may not only document but perhaps unwittingly reproduce. Shooting visual realist imagery in zones of conflict is never free of ideological implications, but it is a complicated operation to identify and distinguish between the intention and the effect, or if you will permit me to stretch the shooting metaphor one last time, the 'target' and the 'impact' of the material.

NOTES

1 The earliest known camera to mimic the design of a gun was Thomas Skaife's Pistolgraph of 1856/59. Legend has it that Skaife was arrested when he attempted – with his pistolgraph – to 'shoot' (a photo) of Queen Victoria near her castle in Windsor, despite the fact that the camera bore only passing resemblance to a pistol; see B. Jay (2009) 'Passing Shots: The pistol/rifle camera in photographic history, 1858–1938', www.billjayonphotography.com/Passing%20Shots.pdf.

2 Alphonso Lingis lists an extensive catalogue of contemporary camera-guided weaponry, such as the 'Predator drone', the 'Global Hawk', the 'Sand Dragon', the 'Fire Ant', and so on; A. Lingis (2006) 'Ethics in the globalized war', *Eurozine*, http://www.eurozine.com/

articles/2006-11-29-lingis-en.html; accessed 13 April 2012.

3 This distance is, in fact, one of the themes of Harun Farocki's film *War at a Distance* (2003), where the images from the first Gulf War, mostly taken from the perspective of the weapon upon which they are mounted, become indistinguishable from video game imagery and other technological imaging that have the effect of expunging any real-world consequences of war. Several of Farocki's films and installations thematise the relationship between the camera and weaponry (see *Images of the World and Inscriptions of War* (1989–90), *Eye/Machine I-II* (2001–2), *Serious Games I-IV* (2009–10)). They investigate the interpenetration between the technology of warfare with the technology of everyday life, without actually taking on the issue of the relationship between the camera and the gun as such. Indeed Farocki dismisses claims of any affinity between the camera and the gun as 'narcissistic' on the part of filmmakers. See his interview with Frieda Grafe, *SüddeutscheZeitung*, 1 August 1982, as excerpted on his website: http://www.farocki-film.de/

4 P. Virilio (1992 [1984]) *War and Cinema*. London: Verso.

5 There are countless books published featuring Gun Alignment and Sighting Photography (GASP), most of which, like *Gun Camera: World War II Photography from Allied Fighters and Bombers over Occupied Europe* by L. Douglas Keeney (Shrewsbury: Airlife, 1999), gleefully celebrate the POV of the shots, in the thick of the fray, as it were.

6 The interdependency is not entirely mutual, I hasten to note, as most cameras are obviously not outfitted with lethal weapons. However, the photographic and cinematic image can and does 'pose a threat' and can, or can at least be intended to, be used as a weapon.

7 Some studies on the topic include: Guy Westwell (2006) *War Cinema: Hollywood on the Front Line*. London: Wallflower Press; C. Boggs and T. Pallard (2006) *The Hollywood War Machine: US Militarism and Popular Culture*. London: Pluto Press; and C. Copps and G. Black (1987) *Hollywood Goes to War*. London: IB Taurus.

8 'Visual Realist' is a term I borrow from Allen Feldman, who uses it to dislodge the images from association with any single mode of non-fiction filmmaking, whether journalistic, documentary, official, activist or artistic. Along with Feldman, I want to emphasise that these modes are neither 'passive reflection nor naturalized mimesis' (2000: 59) – they all constitute a type of 'political vision'.

9 This 'otherwise' is meant to denote a range of visual realist modalities that the word documentary does not fully account for, such as government surveillance and reconnaissance footage, journalistic imagery, activist media, artist films, etc.

10 In this film, we are shown a still aerial photograph taken in 1944 during an Allied reconnaissance mission over the IG Farben factory. It wasn't noticed until thirty odd years later, when CIA agents were re-examining the material, that the photograph contained detailed information from the Auschwitz/Birkenau complex, just next to the factory of interest to the initial mission. Because the World War II analysts of the photograph were not looking for the labour/death camp complex, despite the fact that it was staring them in the face, they did not see it. Nora Alter argues that Farocki's film ultimately reveals that 'the historical purpose of photography has been not only to record and preserve, but to mislead, deceive, and even to destroy: that is, to aid, yet also to obfuscate vision'; N. Alter (1996) 'The Political Im/perceptible in the Essay Film: Farocki's *Images of the World and the Inscription of War*', *New German Critique*, 68, 165–92. This fascinating subject remains outside the ken of the pres-

ent essay, but is beautifully argued in Alter's essay.

11 In the case of direct combat, it is possible to imagine that a POV may be simultaneously that of the Gunsight and of the Barrel (shooting while being shot at), yet in those instances, for our purposes here, I will consider this still to be the Gunsight POV, since each camera here is fortified, as it were, with an actual lethal weapon.

12 A. Feldman (2000) 'Violence and Vision: The Prosthetics and Aesthetics of Terror', in V. Das and A. Kleinman (eds) *Violence and Subjectivity*. Berkeley: University of California Press, 46–78.

13 In order to suggest the direction the Barrel POV has taken in the various modes mentioned, here is a very partial sketch. The journalistic mode, clearly when not 'embedded', is often taken from the position of the victims or targets of aggression, though it is complicated by a range of factors including the pretense of objectivity, or what we can call here the 'unaligned gaze' – permitting the journalist to switch sides at will. The documentary mode includes examples such as *Death in Gaza* (James Miller, UK, 2003); *My Dear Olive Tree* (Osama Qashoo, Palestine/UK, 2004); *Burma VJ* (Anders Østergaard, Denmark, 2008). For the activist mode, associated with the oppositional Barrel POV a good example about which I will go into some detail later in this essay is the Shooting Back project of the Israeli-based human rights organisation, B'Tselem. Two more modes, civilian and 'artist' can also be identified from the Barrel POV; think of the footage emanating from the so-called 'Green Revolution' of 2009 in Iran – as seen on YouTube, twitter, Facebook, and other social networking sites. Two films have pieced these online images together: *The Green Wave* (Ali Samadi Ahadi, Iran/Germany, 2010) and *Fragments of a Revolution* (Anonymous, Iran/France, 2011). An example of the artist mode might be Annamarie Jacir's *Like Twenty Impossibles* (2003), a blend of documentary and fiction about trying to make a film in the Israeli-occupied West Bank.

14 Ironically, B'Tselem was forced to change the name from 'Shooting Back' to 'the Camera Distribution Project' when they lost a bid in court to a Washington DC-based organisation that claimed rights to the name.

15 See K. Thomas (2009) 'Burma VJ Vividly Details Monk Uprising', *LA Times*, 29 May; C. Bass (2009) *The Independent*, 28 May; D. Edwards (2009) Mirror.co.uk, 17 July.

16 Source: http://en.wikipedia.org/wiki/2007_Burmese_anti-government_protests; BBC News, 'Burma's Leaders double fuel prices' 15 August 2007, http://news.bbc.co.uk/1/hi/world/asia-pacific/6947251.stm; accessed 13 April 2012.

17 An example of a documentary that refuses the temptations of the generic lure of the action film, despite its riveting subject and the blatant potential to be exploited as such is the impressive *Bus 174* (Jose Padilha, 2002), which details the four-and-a-half-hour hijacking of a public bus by a desperate, glue-sniffing, homeless teenager in Rio de Janiero. Despite the film's use of sensationalist live television coverage, the film steps back and proposes to analyse the deeper social, economic and political causes that might have led to such an event. See A. Villarejo (2006) '*Bus 174* and the Living Present', *Cinema Journal*, 46, 1, 115–20.

18 At least three of the other VJs faced lengthy prison sentences as a result of their participation as videographers in the uprising. The sentencing of some of the VJs of the film is discussed in the interview held with Anders Østergaard and 'Joshua' for the online film magazine *Film 24*; see http://www.film24.com/NewsAndArticles/NewsAndArticles.aspx?NewsID=A0529;

accessed 29 August 2009.

19 Keenan made a similar argument in an online interview several years before his 2002 article; see T. Keenan (1997) 'Media Wars and the Humanitarian (non)Intervention', interview with G. Lovink, *Documenta X*; www.nettime.org/Lists-Archives/nettime-l-9708/msg00001. html; T. Keenan (2002) 'Publicity and Indifference (Sarajevo on Television)', *PMLA*, 117, 1, 104–16.

20 When CNN showed amateur footage from events in Tehran during the events of the Green Revolution, the anchor disclaimed thus: 'We need to stress, and we will continue to do so, that CNN cannot independently verify this stuff, but we feel it's important that people see this, see and hear what is coming in to us.' From the *New York Times* article of 17 June 2009, 'In Coverage of Iran Amateurs Take the Lead' by Brian Stelter. http://mediadecoder. blogs.nytimes.com/2009/06/17/in-coverage-of-iran-amateurs-take-the-lead/; accessed 13 April 2012.

21 For example, two DVDs released in 2007 are *Hebron Stories* and *B'Tselem Shorts: Documenting the Seldom Seen*.

22 Actually, the B'Tselem camera is often treated as a threat by the Israeli officials and the military, with soldiers at times assaulting the camera people as they shoot. See, for instance, the video entitled *28.2.10: Soldiers disturb and assault B'Tselem's video photographers in the West Bank despite army's declaration that filming is permitted*. This particular video begins with the declaration from the Israeli Army that there is no legal prohibition against filming in Judea and Samaria (otherwise known as the West Bank) including filming the Israeli Defense Force, as long as it does not aim to obtain sensitive or classified information or 'significantly disturb the forces' activities'.

23 See a compilation of videos of this phenomenon shot between 2008 and 2010 on a video called *Soldiers disturb and assault B'Tselem's video photographer* (2010): http://www. btselem.org/video/2010/02/soldiers-disturb-and-assault-btselem-s-video-photographerswest-bank-despite-armys-dec. Many of the videos from the DVDs and many more can be found on B'Tselem's website as well: http://www.btselem.org/video. When possible, I have listed the exact url for the individual video referenced. Accessed 13 April 2012.

24 'Ruin and Humiliation in Qalqilya, http://www.btselem.org/node/118940; accessed 13 April 2012.

25 'Saturday Violence – A-Tuba' (2007) http://www.btselem.org/video/2007/09/saturdayviolence-tuba; accessed 13 April 2012.

26 'Settlers Attack Shepherds in Southern Hebron Hills' (2008), http://www.btselem.org/ video/2008/06/settlers-attack-shepherds-southern-hebron-hills; accessed 13 April 2012.

27 http://www.btselem.org/video/2008/11/tel-rumeida-hebro; accessed 13 April 2012.

28 It may nonetheless be worth recognising that nowhere on B'Tselem's website or in their description of the organisation's aims do they mention working to end the occupation; rather they claim to be working to ensure human rights under the occupation. http://www.btselem. org/about_btselem; accessed 13 April 2012.

29 Žižek, S. (2008) *Violence*. London: Profile Books.

30 See M. Hardt and A. Negri (2001) *Empire*. Cambridge, MA: Harvard University Press; N. Klein (2008) *The Shock Doctrine*. London: Penguin; and E. Weizman (2009) 'Lawfare in Gaza: Legislative Attack', *Open Democracy*, 1 March. http://www.opendemocracy.net/ar-

ticle/legislative-attack.

31 For a further elaboration of the position that the Israeli government and the IDF work in extremely clever ways in order to legally indemnify themselves from accusations of criminality (illegal warfare, attacking civilians, crimes against humanity, etc), see Weizman 2009. For the source of the report that *Checkpoint* was used by the IDF for training purposes, see 'Is the film "Defamation" defamatory? … No, but it certainly is provocative,' by Patricia Aufderheide, Laura Katz Cutler, Lisa Moses Leff and Yoram Peri, *Washington Jewish Week*, 6 April 2011; http://washingtonjewishweek.com/main.asp?SectionID=31&SubSectionID=49&ArticleID=14723, and Mitchell Miller's 'Frontline Films' in *The New Humanist*, 119, 6, 2004; http://newhumanist.org.uk/807/frontline-films; both accessed 13 April 2012.

32 There is one well publicised case of alleged retaliation by the IDF after B'Tselem released a video shot by a teenage Palestinian girl, Salaam Amira, of an Israeli soldier shooting a blindfolded Palestinian youth in the foot with a rubber bullet at point blank range. The soldiers began to regularly shoot at Amira's house in Ni'ilin on the West Bank, and arrested her father. See news item, 'Israeli Army Targets Family over "Brutality Film"', by Jonathan Cook, *The National*, 1 September 2008; http://www.thenational.ae/apps/pbcs.dll/article?AID=/20080901/FOREIGN/87166974; accessed 31 August 2009; see also 'B'Tselem: Views to a Kill', Matt Reese, *The Telegraph* 16 January 2009.

33 Though according to one blogger, they attempt to cut the footage minimally, so as to avoid claims of manipulation; http://gordolobos.vox.com/explore/neighborhood/tags/israel/

34 http://www.btselem.org/english/About_BTselem/Index.asp.; accessed 13 April 2012.

35 http://www.videreonline.org/; accessed 13 April 2012.

IMMERSION (2009)
2 videos, colour, sound, 20 minutes (loop)

Harun Farocki

[Exposé – text written in 2008 in advance of the production of *Immersion*.]

We are familiar with worlds of artificial imagery from computer games. We would like to show how they are used constructively in ways that go beyond self-contained fictional universes. How they are used against the sobering backdrop of military reality, namely in the training of US troops before their deployment to combat zones and in the provision of adequate post-deployment care on their return.

The possibilities presented by virtual reality offer obvious advantages when it comes to preparing soldiers for the difficult tasks awaiting them in often unfamiliar, exotic surroundings.

A hybrid of actual and virtual reality known as *augmented reality* is employed in the Advanced Simulator for Combat Operations and Training at Camp Pendletonin, California. In shadowy light, soldiers comb through plywood structures in front of projected backgrounds. They act out stressful situations in the studio and practice communicating with the virtual inhabitants of the foreign country. The scenario can be modified at any time; it is controlled by a 'director' who can add imponderables and vicissitudes at will. Just as pilots of passenger aircraft use a flight simulator to practice flying at night or how to respond when they run into computer-programmed storm clouds, recruits practice what to do if they encounter injured persons when searching a house and how to form a convoy when driving through the desert in enemy territory. The aim is the same: optimising responses to difficult situations.

Precisely the opposite happens when soldiers sustain injuries in the reality of

Iraq and Afghanistan. They often only become aware of these much later, when what they have experienced leads them to react in ways they cannot control, with frequently fatal consequences, and the neural pathways formed in their brains cause them to return home as traumatised veterans. For those suffering from post-traumatic stress disorder, or PTSD, a simple car trip can become a nightmare because they have witnessed vehicles blown up by bombs exploding under roads. A family outing to a crowded shopping mall can be sheer torment because it brings back memories of how a buddy at their side was fatally shot in a Baghdad market.

Albert Rizzo of the Institute for Creative Technologies at the University of Southern California in Marina del Rey has developed a new form of behavioural therapy for the treatment of war veterans suffering from PTSD. Using their accounts of what they experienced, the reality they lived through is recreated virtually in the console game Full Spectrum Warrior. The scenarios devised in the lab in California are then compared to the frame of reference, i.e. they are sent to the Iraq Combat Stress Control Team and submitted to a 'reality check'.

The veterans are taken back to the time and place where they suffered the traumata now affecting them in ways beyond their control and relive the situation that triggered their disorder. In this form of exposure therapy, patients are literally *immersed* in the experiences they lived through during the war.

However, the traumatised soldiers do not have to face the situation alone: this time there is someone at their side – the therapist – who can intervene. For instance, the therapist can increase the level of threat and thus provide clients with the experience of coping successfully with a difficult situation. Alternatively therapists can use the Wizard of Oz, the game's control unit, to modify the virtual reality so as to mitigate the situation, suspend it, or break it off altogether. The aim is to reprogramme the neural connections that have such a devastating effect on patients and help them come to terms with their trauma by facing the original situation that triggered it rather than remaining in denial. With this form of exposure therapy, Rizzo has succeeded in finding an effective means of treating deep emotional scars that break open repeatedly and uncontrollably and help patients find closure by reliving their traumatic experiences cathartically.

Rizzo and his co-workers have devised several ingenious modifications to the video game that enhance the therapy's efficacy even further. The veteran wears a *head-mounted display*. The perspective of the images he sees on the data goggles change in accordance with the position of his head and body, and the sounds he hears over the headphones – children screaming, fragments of words in Arabic, shrapnel exploding, rescue helicopters approaching – are spatially modulated. The low-frequency rumble of engines and explosions sends shudders through the platform he is standing on. Olfactory cues can be fed in, as well: the fragrant aroma of Arabic spices, the acrid odour of sweat, biting smoke of burning oil-fields, the stench of singed hair. The ex-soldier holds a gun in hand, just as he used to on the battlefield. But this weapon is not loaded, it is merely the ballast of the soldier's reality, for Rizzo is convinced that revenge is not the way to come to terms with traumatic experiences.

During the sessions, patients are encouraged to put what they are experiencing and feeling into words. They are hooked up to various monitoring devices so the therapist can see the curves of the heartbeat, perspiration, brain activity, adrenalin output on his screen. The various peaks and troughs in the curves tell him to what degree patients are affected by what they are reliving at a particular moment. Simply by assuming this small degree of responsibility for the patient, the therapist takes part of the burden off the patient's shoulders.

This is not the first time wartime experiences have been reconstructed using virtual reality. The method has been used in the past with Vietnam veterans and to treat 25,000 survivors of Portugal's colonial wars in Mozambique, Angola and Guinea-Bissau from 1961 to 1974. It has also been applied to help the traumatised witnesses of bus bombings in Israel and those who lived through the horrific attacks and collapse of the World Trade Center on 9/11. Exposure therapy incorporating virtual reality is also used to help people overcome more commonplace problems such as acrophobia, arachnophobia, social phobias, fear of flying, abnormal fear of pain during medical treatments and learning disorders.

We would like to give viewers an insight into how therapists succeed in making the imprint left in traumatised individuals' brains by a real-life spatiotemporal experience recede and replacing it with an artificial reconstruction of reality. The aim is to fade out the painful memories and involuntary mental images that cause such torment by using state-of-the-art technology to achieve a virtual reality that is as vivid and convincing as possible.

This new therapy developed by Albert Rizzo, Virtual Reality Exposure Therapy for Combat-related PTSD, is the focus of our documentary film.

In the fall of 2008, Rizzo will train military psychotherapists in Fort Lewis, Washington in the techniques of Virtual Reality Exposure Therapy for Combat-related PTSD; the therapists will subsequently test the techniques on themselves.

The fact that theoretical instruction and practical application will be so closely linked and concentrated in a period of two days will allow us to elucidate the technical equipment, its use, and the approach employed in treatment without the need for explanatory comments or interviews as an aid to comprehension. The therapists learning the technique themselves will ask the questions required to understand the principles on which it is based and how it works. We will not need to add anything to the footage filmed on site; it will be self-explanatory because we are there each step of the way.

As we film the therapists and test subjects, we will use a scan converter (which is hooked up to VGA or DVI and interposed between the head-mounted display and a computer to simultaneously record the images the soldiers see on their display and the arousal curves (heartbeat, breathing rate, etc.) the therapists see on their screen.

If possible, we would like to go beyond the laboratory situation by being present at three or four therapy sessions, even if we will not go into any details of individual stories and will not show the faces of those undergoing therapy to protect their privacy. Maintaining their anonymity is made easier by the fact that their features are obscured by the head-mounted display anyway – they are already wearing the 'black bar' on their faces, so to speak.

To render the principle of inversion, we will also show how virtual and augmented reality are used in the training of soldiers – as exemplified in Immersive Infantry Trainer and Advanced Simulator Combat Operations and Training.

To illustrate that this kind of therapy is not limited to use within the military, we will extend our observations to include 'civilian applications' such as its use in the treatment of acrophobia, arachnophobia and social phobias.

We will be filming with a crew of three people (director, Harun Farocki; camera/cinematography: Ingo Kratisch; sound: Matthias Rajmann). We will be using a high-speed camera so that we will not require any additional light sources. Our approach to documentary filmmaking means we never intervene in the situation, we simply allow it to unfold as (it would) if we were not there.

Director, scriptwriter: Harun Farocki
Research: Matthias Rajmann

ANAESTHETISING THE IMAGE:
IMMERSION, HARUN FARCOCKI

Kodwo Eshun

Following a public screening of the first rough-cut version of his film *Immersion* in 2009 at the Goethe Institute in London, the German director Harun Farocki discussed his film project with the artist and critic Kodwo Eshun (co-founder of the Otolith Group).

Kodwo Eshun: *At the end of the film we see the first session in what these therapists call VRET – virtual reality exposure therapy.*

Harun Farocki: What you saw was a workshop, or training seminar. There's a group in America that has invented virtual reality exposure therapy. The man with the ponytail at the beginning, he's one of the leading figures. He's a therapist, he works for the centre for experimental science in San Diego with other therapists who have been working with traumatised patients for a long time. One of them was the woman who played the therapist here, who always says, 'You are doing a great job', in a slightly mechanical, perhaps hypnotic way. They are all free-lancers: the others, those in camouflage uniforms, are all in life-time – twenty-year-long – employment with the American army. It was all filmed in an army base, Fort Louis, in the State of Washington, very close to Seattle. The therapists want to sell their virtual Iraq device to the army, for use for the therapy of traumatised patients. The idea is to treat patients with so-called exposure therapy, which means they have to go back and re-create the experience that caused their trauma. In this case they've speeded the process up a little; in reality, of course, not all aspects of the treatment are covered right from the first session.

First, you find out what the trauma is about, and so on, and then the idea is (it's a well-known strategy, but now it's conducted with virtual images) that you can somehow re-create, more or less, the atmosphere in a more suggestive way. So they have built virtual Iraq, and I was told that they are also working on adding some mountains so that it can also be used it for Afghanistan! Of course, the mosques are the same, so some of the sounds can also be used; not only the explosions, but also the muezzin you heard at the beginning. There is also a virtual Vietnam, and a virtual World Trade Center. Perhaps one day we could re-tell the story of America using those images, but for the moment the scope of my project is limited. They [soldiers] see a virtual desert, or a virtual city, and learn how to patrol, how to avoid ambushes, and so on. So there's an interesting coincidence. At first you use these images to be de-sensitised. The army has also huge military facilities; one is even in Germany, for NATO, but run by the Americans. There, large scale role-plays are carried out: they hire extras. If they have Arabic-looking features, they get ten euros more per day. So they use real people, and also real locations, but they also use studios in which soldiers learn, as if they were in a huge video game, how to react. So these are two aspects of how you make use of images [VR and role-play] and of a course, wonderful examples as they open up many questions.

KE: *These therapists [in* Immersion*] need to find a market, they need to find a demand. So I think economically we can understand this, but I think what's interesting for us is what happens when a filmmaker begins to magnify some of these processes. One thing that strikes us immediately is the fact that what you were interested in filming here was role-play; that you didn't film an actual therapy session between therapist and soldier. You filmed a therapist playing a soldier, so that the kinds of image repetitions at play are doubled by the fact that roles are being performed before an audience, an audience that we don't see but that we hear. Obviously this feeds into your interest in role-play, an interest that extends back to* How to Live in the FRG *(1990), to works like* The Interview *(1997), and others. I know the decision is in part pragmatic – in the sense of being able to film the role-play – but I also sense there's an interest for you in exaggerated gestures and the kind of demonstrative capacity that role-play demands, where you have to find a kind of language of presentation that conveys and connotes to everybody. And I wonder if you could talk a bit about this question of role-play.*

HF: Yes, I think there are even more layers here. If you analyse it, it's not the soldier telling of something he has experienced, it's the therapist, who has treated many patients; or his colleagues, who have treated patients in other cases. So he creates this scenario, and this scenario is the imagining of a patient; the therapists are the listeners, and they have to imagine. So that's already the third or fourth layer on which they refer to this real war in Iraq. The astonishing thing – otherwise it wouldn't work at all – is that nevertheless you sense something about this war. It has something to do with the filmmaking process; there are so many processes before you have something on screen, you can't believe that there is still something visible, because after all these artificial attempts you made, how can something...

KE: *How can something immediate emerge from all this mediation? How can you be touched by something so obviously artificial?*

HF: Yes, exactly. In that sense, I think, it's a good, and also a very specific, imagination of the war, about which we don't know much. Perhaps fifty years ago there would have been a novel by a smart American; he'd have written a novel about the experience in Iraq, as with the Phillip Roth generation, the post-World War II generation of writers. Today, I think images have to capture some of this memory, and I think that the material here is an interesting comment on them. I imagine the association that came to everybody's minds when they first saw these images was the video game. We all probably are not great video-gamers, otherwise we wouldn't be here tonight – yet in some sense it is true. Although the process is a bit more complex. The VRET developers got the footage from the game industry. They then adapted it to their needs, but the main features derive from the video industry. What you have here are only two locations; one with some interiors in Baghdad, as well as some Baghdad streets and blocks that you can navigate through. Here you can see a statue of Saddam Hussein: that's Saddam standing here in front of this little village. So you have a game controller at this M16 rifle, so you can navigate through the streets when you are on patrol. In the car, of course, you can also speed up or steer wherever you want. So it's a kind of interactive game also. Of course, in this case you don't fire; it's not about firing, it's about healing now. But the feeling of a gun somehow is important. The first step was that they got the main features, the structure of the images, of the software, from the game industry, but the game industry got it from the army beforehand. So a lot of money, I think, hundreds of millions were spent to develop this material. For these two locations, they spent twenty to thirty million dollars. So they are nearly already on a film production level with these games. So you see that it's not much, so they have to get it back from them. For me it's so interesting that, perhaps that is the modern strategy, that today you no longer make a film about as they did when they hired John Ford in World War II to, say, make a battle in the Pacific. Then we had a film which really showed what our war is about, which made it attractive, or which explained it, let's say – propaganda. I think today propaganda doesn't have to be specific in this way, it's like advertising; you don't have to advertise for a special brand, I think advertising for cigarettes or Gucci or whatever, also helps Mercedes and others. It's not specific. In this sense, you introduce the war into the imaginary, and the location as well. I think that all these Vietnam films have helped to do it, that has become a *topos*, Vietnam. The exposure to this danger, the fact that you don't know who is firing on you, and that you are surprised, and all these things have become part of the common imaginary, it's a genre like the western. That is probably smarter to confirm what you are doing than by having a special message. So the real economy is an aesthetic economy.

KE: *Yes, Marizio Lazzarato talks about how advertising works by life-worlds. By creating a life-world that you feel before you experience it, but this feeling is already a kind of experience, and then there's a kind of mismatch between the feeling and the experience and you hunger after to make your feeling actual. But your specific point about topos, about topoi, that specific kind of image trope, that we saw circulating around, let's say the Vietnam era, I think, would you say that these kinds of images suggest or imply a new genre of images? A new kind of digital image? I sense that your interest in these images is not just for the images in themselves. There's a sense that these images signal some kind of shift in the production of images, so a part of your project is to use your camera to reveal to us a new shift, a new mutation, in what the image can now do.*

HF: Yes, I think that these kinds of images are nowadays the standard. This is probably due to all that is possible, that you can navigate within the image, this carnival effect, that you can turn your head and see whatever you want to within the limits of the programme, that you can walk through it, that it's interactive, and so forth. I think that displaces these kinds of images into a field of so-called scientific superiority. So if you look at advertising, in the 1950s every ad was still painted, or drawn, and then all these photographic images came, and it was unthinkable to not have a photographic image, because one thought that is the real thing, and that really proves that it exists. I would say that this function is nowadays at play within the digital image, and not the photographic image. One aspect is the technical standard – just as writing with the typewriter is bad, but with the computer it's modern – in the sense that to use such an image is to align yourself to the real technical world, this world which we are processing, and the aspect of symbolical 'mastering' is so strong in it. I don't know if it's possible to see it if you see a person talking about it – confronting a narration with an image – but my hope is that you see, or that it becomes somehow accessible, the idea that these images are not so far from an oil painting on canvas, which you can find here in some museums. When a war is made classic, by making art of it. It also says that this is not just an event, it is something which belongs to the continuity of all these sea battles which we have depicted in our museums. Today you no longer have painters for it but you need digital images for it.

KE: *So you're saying these images for you are operating as something like a contemporary history painting. A painting of contemporaneity now operates through this, and those who have the power of technical standardisation, they can control, or they have the capability to operate what we think of now, as History.*

HF: Yes, or even the reverse. The public believes that such an image is true, as a real snapshot from the location, because the entire infrastructure is included in the image. It's not just an image, with one person taking a picture, there's this huge infrastructure. It's a little bit like what you have in a war, that there's not just one soldier walking there. In World War II, behind every soldier were 270 people behind the front, and I think today it's 1,500 or so in the case of the Americans. So this infrastructure is somehow palpable.

KE: *Every pixel shows its industrial force. Every pixel celebrates its industrial might. Its something like the kind of carnival of attractions that Tom Gunning talked about, the way in which the image displays itself, and shows off to us, and reveals its power, and its industrial superiority, and that if you can attach yourself to that, that you too are on the winning side of History. Because of course History is written by those who have the means of reproduction. So of course you would have Virtual Reality Exposure Therapy for soldiers, rather than for Iraqi civilians. The soldiers who carry out the 'shock and awe' are the people who are repaired, in order that they can go out and do more shocking and more awesome damage.*

HF: And also this PTSD – post-traumatic stress disorder. The word isn't known in Iraq – it's something like colour TV, or digital cameras, or whatever. In World War II, which was also a traumatic event, it was not known, this word. It has to do with an already very elaborate culture, of course.

KE: *So you only showed, as you said, it's first stage, just some initial episodes from your shooting, but it's clear that the project as such is to study a way in which the* *image comes with the claim to both inflict harm and then to repair that harm. The dialectic of the contemporary image, and the way in which the image holds out a promise of curing the havoc that it creates. All of this is summed up in the notion of de-sensitisation, and in the notion of immersion. And I guess an initial instinct of any person, any kind of cultural worker, is to be entirely suspicious of this, is to think of it almost as a kind of advertising claim; the ministry can't possibly think this, the military can't possibly think that the image that creates harm is also the image that will cure that harm. They can't really think that. But when you talked to them, did you find that this kind of double nature was something that they were quite happy with, and quite familiar with?*

HF: We avoided every philosophical and meta-debate, and tried just to get permission to shoot something! I don't know what these guys think about it, it could make things more difficult with access, and so on. It's already difficult enough to get permission, it's a long process. But as Chris Marker says in *la sixième face du pentagone* [1968] – if the Pentagon is inaccessible from five sides, you must use the sixth.

You asked something earlier, perhaps we can go back to it, I have not yet addressed it at all. I always loved that role-play has this second layer; you don't make a documentary where people are really having a conflict, which is mostly not the case, and then a stage, and it's badly played, and so on. But here you have the consolation in which bad playing can be great. I think, and I hope that you agree, that many people for some minutes believe that it must be a real experience, what he's going through and conveying here. This wonderful abstraction that you have when the woman has a rifle, and she stands in a classroom, a quite sleazy classroom, and says, 'It was so terrible', and she has to raise her voice because the sound in her earphone is too high. In a kind of Brechtian way that reminded me of one of his early plays – *Man Equals Man* [1926] – when the soldiers go to India and you don't really see India – it's just an imagination. For me this is what's so strong – this kind of condensing which you get in a role-play, as you get in a film as well.

KE: *The idea of role-play opens out the wider question of, on the one hand repetition, and on the other re-enactment – the differences between those two modalities, and the kind of entanglement between them both. And re-enactment is something that has, as I said, been operative in your work from* How to Live in the FRG *onwards. But here, re-enactment has, we can call it almost a predatory, and directly commercial aspect. And so I was thinking about how to consider the changes in re-enactment since* How to Live in the FRG *in the early 1990s,* *and now the early part of the twenty-first century. And now, what happened in between, which is the art world becoming totally fascinated by re-enactment. I think it's a lot to do with temporality, a lot to do with the particular time-zone that a re-enactment adopts. On one hand, it's clearly looking back, it's clearly re-working something that's past, but it's also looking ahead to something that couldn't emerge then, and has to be projected now. So there's this kind of Janus face, this kind of double face to re-enactment. My interest is in how you capture that, and what that has to do with the way in which you frame the image as two images, so that you have a comparative eye, and a kind of editor's eye, and part of your practice is to invite an editor's gaze from the viewer, so that the viewer is placed in this role of comparing images, comparing these different modalities of re-enactment, which are simultaneously harking back to something and simultaneously gesturing forward to something. I guess it's a roundabout way of asking you about form, a roundabout way of asking you why you framed the work in the way you have, and some of your thoughts about that.*

HF: Yes, so first of all I think that here, the use of these two screens is really very simple. You see what he sees, or what she sees, and I had mounted display, in future cases you will see HMD [head-mounted display]. So that's quite simple. Then of course you can make dramatic use of it. The moment when he really speaks of Jones I switch it off, and when he says, 'Ok, I must continue', then the image comes back. So there are little ruses, but in general it's just about showing what they're looking at, and to see how and why it is used. In other cases, the use of it in my other works, which are not present here so perhaps we should not talk too much about them, there are also different approaches. Different approaches where one can use it as some form of montage between two present images, but in this case, I think of course in its affect it doesn't limit itself to it. But you create a very obvious off-space with these two images, because the audience is always in the 'off'. Also there's an interesting tension for me in that on one screen he's talking only to people we never see.

You asked about re-enactment. If we take this idea seriously we aren't talking about a remake; it's not that you have the image and then you do a re-enactment. Today's artists can't believe that a kind of realism, or naturalism, can be mimesis. And therefore something other has to be imitated or re-created. If you instigate a process of re-enacting, of having the original and the copy, as with a remake of a Hitchcock film or so, then you have lifted this mimesis to a different level, to a more intellectual sphere, and that is perhaps an interesting approach to this practice, but that could not justify it. You had asked, what has changed, in the last twenty years? First of all, in the West, when I made *How to Live in the FRG*, and

I showed it in Latin or Catholic countries, even in France, where family values are still strong, people didn't know what I was talking about, because they didn't have these forms of experience, which of course in America are quite prevalent.

KE: *These practices of simulation and rehearsal.*

HF: Of practice therapies, cheap or community college therapies and so forth. So that has changed, and became a common language. The middle-class professional must today be able to participate in a role-play. Today it's like having a driver's license. So that has changed, but the interesting aspect is that usually a role-play is not so much for the audience as for the participants, the audience or therapist to comment. In this case it was pure theatre, because they didn't have to experience anything; they just played it for the others, but still there was something real about how she as a therapist showed how she would behave. So it's very tricky because they only *referred* to a real role-play. And the weird thing is that later they even have a second act, where they were talking about, 'How did you experience what you just had when you were looking at these images?' when I said, 'No, continue, vomit into the bucket there', and so on. And he said, 'Well I felt...' So he gave the answers which the ideal patient would give, and that's also an invocation of course, a magical aspect, and this session was already called 'working with difficult patients', who are not difficult at all, but his resistance was only to say, 'Could we stop...?' The fact is that many drop out and don't continue. Many go in the first instance because it's more attractive to say, 'I'm going to a video game centre', than to say, 'I'm going to a shrink', because it's not good for your reputation. Although Hitchcock would be astonished. But somehow a shrink is too middle-class! That's what they say; but on the other hand many people drop out. There's a huge state-funded programme to monitor success, effectiveness, drop-out rates, and so forth – $900 million; it's not chicken feed, even though it wouldn't save a car company, but $900 million is invested into this research programme.

KE: *So that makes a difference between the second Gulf War and between the first Gulf War of 1991. That's a key difference between the generations of new industries of vision, new kinds of machine vision, broadly speaking. When between 2001 and 2003 in your trilogy* Eye/Machine *you looked at images you called 'operational images', the images that came out of the first Gulf War, and now, when you look at the images that emerge from this war, if you make a comparison across those years, I wonder, how would you characterise that difference? I guess one immediate way is that the operational images of the first Gulf War seem* *to promise to take the human out of the loop; they promised the automisation or weaponisation of the image, whereas here in these immersive images, the human is back in, you have this mixture of the talking cure, the image as cure.*

HF: I'm not a sociologist of military technology but it seems to me that this project was already started with the first Gulf War in the 1990s. To have these so-called smart weapons, a kind of automisation which did not really work out, because nobody was prepared to invest the means you really need for that. It's a bit more expensive than just trauma research, and ironically one could say that there was never ever a single smart weapon used. I don't know in court if I would ever succeed but I swear there was never such a weapon. It's only a project and this project was launched and many people believed in it in the 1990s because they wanted to sell it. That's also a good idea; first you create the idea that something already exists and then you ask for finances to make it, because logic tells you it should exist. This project was more or less called off, but this other idea, the problem is that Saddam in a sense, because he had the biggest army and the most weaponry in the entire region, there you can really have this war at a distance, you have some ships and you somehow hit the infrastructure of the country and so on... But where is the next enemy? It's so difficult to find one where you can. So for these other projects which are more police-like, where you can say, so you can kill him and not her and so on, then things become really difficult and this doesn't work as a traditional warfare and would need far more complicated intelligent weapons.

KE: *But you made a really interesting point. You're not a military sociologist or historian, you're a filmmaker, and sometimes it seems like all along you've been interested in war, but not just in war. All along you've been interested in thinking about the relationship between the image and violence, and sometimes it seems as though your whole career has a thread running through it and that thread is of finding ways to make the relationship between the image and violence visible, sensible. Visible and audible. It's something that's consistent, you've been, you could almost say, obsessed with this question, a question that is answerable in so many ways. How to make the connection between images and violence audible and visible. How to organise that so that we begin to see something which is often quite abstract. Something we're involved with but excluded from, something we see at the level of television but which informs us of nothing, and affects us all the time. Would you say that if we start to look back across the breadth of your work that it's one of the threads that's been forming your work in many different ways?*

HF: When you say so I must admit it's true; it's somehow a terrible idea. Why this preoccupation with images and violence? Of course, somehow this offers itself to be the subject of research. So in a Max Weberian term, 'ideal type', somehow these images are very close to an ideal type. I think they are asking reality to be as calculable as these systems are. Of course there can be some contingencies and so on, but you know already, the ambush must be behind the bridge, and this calculability is somehow, when you deal with images and you are astonished that also in the last war sometimes they didn't show the real thing but rather the simulation or 3D, less realistic, cheaper – they showed it with computer animation. This has become part of the news now. Then of course I became interested in what these images mean. So the main aspect is of course that images and science, or images and real meaning, or social meaning, were totally diverted towards distraction and entertainment. Certainly, when computers started to process images suddenly images had a technical meaning again, and came to a different level. So that's one aspect, which made it so interesting for me, because the status of the image was changing. The other aspect of course we have not yet talked about, we always talked about the fact that somehow it's a symbolic act; one feels guilty about the victims and everybody knows that these so-called veterans, after some years nobody cares about them, they can't find jobs and end up in a trailer park or whatever, if they're white, otherwise it's worse... So the symbolical generosity, *we care about you*, that is a social programme, and then you have given them this icon that you are caring about them, not forgetting what they've done by re-enacting this war.

KE: *So then what's interesting is the role that you as a filmmaker in this symbolic restitution of the soldiers and of those that were victims of the war; where are you in all these different ways of looking at the image and violence? The symbolic and restitutive way, as well as tracking the shifts in the image from the image as representation to one as calculating algorithm? My sense is that as a filmmaker, your interest precedes this shift from, say, signification to calculation, that you have an interest that goes back to the 1960s and perhaps before. It's not that I'm interested so much in origins, as the particular relation you open up which is thankfully a very un-English, deeply un-English relation. It's a distanced involvement, it's a kind of cool low affect, low emotional threshold, which allows one to observe things which are quite difficult to put into images, quite difficult to create a montage of, and my sense is that this low emotional affect is something like a signature that again is a thread. So if it's possible for you to talk about the kind of affective relation you want to create with these images...*

HF: I think you've said it already. Perhaps I'll try to elaborate that it's not only mimesis, but of course also affect; you can't create it by having an actor explaining something true. If you have doubts about this approach, then of course by opposing the banding of many stratas of such a signification then some of the rays are refracted in a way that they shed a different light. I've become very metaphorical now. I think that approach is that you see how they are creating a fact here, which is somehow not only a parody but also an epitome of the war.

KE: *You make a film around every 12 to 18 months, and you make installations as well. How do you keep going? Where do you draw the enthusiasm to continue your quest that is both personal and at the same time something that is much bigger than you, clearly a demand you continue to make on images, a demand you continue to fulfill. How do you keep going in the face of so many demands?*

HF: It becomes a custom, just like making music. Some live musicians always need to perform, and the only meaningful performance is to have found something and to show it to others. Therefore I have to continue, because this drug doesn't last forever.

KE: *I think part of it is that you've found a way to operate that is fast and cheap; you work with a minimal crew.*

HF: Yes, that's important, that it's a small niche. It's terrible if you make features and you have to apply and wait seven years before the film is produced. For my temperament that would be terrible, a little bit rather than oil on canvas you make drawings, and then you can work in a relatively autonomous way. That's of course an important approach.

KE: *For this film I believe the crew was just three people. Ingo Kratisch, the cinematographer you've worked with for many years, and your sound person, who is also your researcher, Mathias.*

HF: Yes, he's also my researcher. It's very important in this field of course. Research is so crucial because it's such a big problem to find out what's happening where and to fly over at the right time, and get permissions and so on. He's a very creative researcher and he can work nicely independently, so he shapes his research and has an idea of how to pull the string with companies – things I'd never know how to do.

KE: *That's critical, as your images are a kind of ongoing research. Your films and your installations are a kind of knowledge production, and that's where a lot of us value the work, the fact that it's an ongoing production of a certain kind of knowledge into what a certain kind of image is becoming, so that one can track the production and mutation of images through your films, which facilitate the reflexive analysis of images. Nobody takes out an advert in the newspaper saying, 'Greeting comrades, the image has now changed its status'. Images now become calculable. Nobody has ever announced it, so it happens without anybody knowing, but one day you find yourself obliged to talk in a language that recognises it.*

HF: It is the same as with Vilhem Flusser, who published his books of philosophy in the 1980s, theories that later proved to become true. Then of course the sensitivity existed to address these issues.

KE: *Well, that's an interesting point, because Flusser's media analysis of what images are becoming suggests partly that your work is in dialogue with certain theoretical formulations and investigations. Were there particular theoretical ideas you were reading at the time of the production of this work, or is this work not really based around theory? Because there's a sense that this work is in itself a theorisation, in a sense it doesn't need to refer to theory.*

HF: I didn't find theoretical texts in this field until now, so it's based on the research we did for this warfare research in general, with *Eye/Machine* and so forth. In the case of *Immersion*, the research was only the background of the subject, and to consider how one could figure out a meaning from their intentions?

[Audience member]: *The question is about resistance, but also about the real in relation to the image. How can we create a space of resistance?… because I have an aversion to this, despite the fact that I find it extremely interesting to see it, and have it accessible, I wonder for you, what is the question? Is this enough for you? Or how far do you want to go in relation to this?*

HF: I think it's a little bit like in economics. You are happy nowadays to understand how finances work but you don't dare to propose how one should run the world. One doesn't want to reform it; one doesn't have an idea what a different model could be. I understand that one looks for some agency, but I'm very far from agency in this case. I'm just looking at which things are happening and under which contradictions. In the case of the army military complex I'm not even sure; probably the military in general is in a bigger crisis than the banks at the moment. We are not based so much on them as we are on banks, so it's not so bad for us that they are in a crisis, so I'm not totally negative about it. I'm quite content to find out about things, and my agency is to comment on them; if it's possible to provoke the ideas that we have alluded to tonight, then I'm perfectly happy with that, that is agency for me.

REVISITING ROCHA'S 'AESTHETICS OF VIOLENCE'

Michael Chanan

1

At the end of the first part of *La hora de los hornos* (*The Hour of the Furnaces*, 1968) by the Argentine filmmakers Fernando Solanas and Octavio Getino, after a lengthy analysis of the history of neo-colonialism in Argentina, we arrive at a cemetery in the desolate countryside of the northwest province of Jujuy, bordering on Chile and Bolivia, where a funeral is taking place. Indigenous peasants in bedraggled clothing, heads bowed, men and women walking in silent desultory procession; the camera walks with them, weaving in and out, a solitary voice intones a prayer, they drink from old bottles. We watch and then, one more time, comes the calm and serious voice of the narrator:

> The Latin American peoples are condemned peoples. Neo-colonialism does not allow them to choose either their own life or death. Life and death are marked by everyday violence. This is our war: of hunger, curable diseases, of premature old age, today in Latin America four people die per minute, 5,500 per day, two million per year. This is our war, a genocide that in fifteen years cost twice as many lives as the First World War.

The moment evokes a scene from another film of the same year, by the Cuban director Tomás Gutiérrez Alea, *Memorias de subdesarrollo* (*Memories of Underdevelopment*) – indeed they were shown alongside each other at the Pesaro Film Festival in Italy that year. Over a montage of images of hunger in Latin America, Sergio, the protagonist is reading from a book by an Argentine journalist:

In Latin America four children die every minute due to illnesses caused by malnutri-
tion. In ten years twenty million children will have died, the same number of deaths
as were caused by the Second World War.

Somehow four people a minute has been transmuted into four children a minute,
and the First World War into the Second, but these texts are echoing figures first
given in 1962, in a document whose wide dissemination testifies to the powerful
influence on the Latin American left of the Cuban Revolution three years earlier.
Known as the Second Declaration of Havana, this was Cuba's response (doubt-
less written by Fidel Castro) to its Washington-orchestrated expulsion from the
OAS (Organization of American States). The Declaration also gives another sta-
tistic: 'a continuous torrent of money flows to the United States: some $4,000 a
minute, $5 million a day, $2 billion a year, $10 billion every five years. For each
thousand dollars which leave us, there remains one corpse. A thousand dollars
per corpse: that is the price of what is called imperialism! A thousand dollars per
death, four deaths every minute!'[1]

This equation, in which the brutal economic exploitation of the continent by
the all-powerful North (acting through the local oligarchy) is the cause of so much
deprivation south of the Rio Grande, is also the underpinning of a pithy manifesto by the Brazilian director Glauber Rocha, *The Aesthetics of Hunger*, known
alternatively as *The Aesthetics of Violence*, first delivered as a short speech at a
film festival in Genoa, Italy in 1965 and then widely reprinted.[2] Hunger in Latin
America, says Rocha, is not simply an alarming symptom; it is the essence of the
society. 'This hunger will not be assuaged by moderate government reforms, and
the cloak of technicolor cannot hide, but rather only aggravates, its tumours.' The
language of film has to be different; it has to be capable of revealing the causes
of this inequity.

The rejection of Hollywoodian spectacle was one of they key traits of *el nuevo
cine latinoamericano* (The New Latin American Cinema) – a term adopted in
1967 at a foundational meeting of filmmakers from across the continent in the
Chilean seaside town of Viña del Mar. It also characterises other manifestos of
the 1960s, especially, at the end of the decade, *Hacia un tercer cine* ('Towards
a Third Cinema'), which Solanas and Getino wrote after making *La hora de
los hornos*, and in Cuba, Julio García Espinosa's *Por un cine imperfecto* ('Towards an Imperfect Cinema').[3] The former held that militant cinema (wherever
it's found – some of their examples are from first-world countries) is indifferent
to the technical means of production and division of labour, because it needs to
be collective, small-scale and agile. The latter argued that any attempt to match
the 'perfection' of the commercial movie of the metropolis was mistaken, and

contradicted the implicit endeavour in a revolutionary cinema to arouse an audience, because the beautifully controlled surface of commercial cinema was a way of lulling the audience into passive consumption; and besides, filmmakers in a third-world country could hardly afford such profligate ambitions. Both pieces are substantial essays which could be read as explications of the aesthetic dialectic already implicit in Rocha's call to cinematic arms. Rocha's brief text is short on analysis but high on rhetoric, but it's this rhetoric, which interests me here.

2

In an interview with Julianne Burton, Rocha admitted to a personal predilection for imagery of violence: 'In my case, I have a particular preference for violent films because I like the epic genre.' But he also spoke of the problem of the audience's alienation: 'rather than use the alienating elements of imported commercial cinema to accomplish our goals ... [f]or us, the violent elements typical of Brazilian films are a means of provoking the public out of its alienation'.[4] Which implies, like every avant-gardist, a certain readiness to assault his audience's sensibilities.

Glauber Rocha was the shooting star of Brazilian cinema, the *enfant terrible* of the *cinema novo* of the 1960s, the pioneering Brazilian branch of *nuevo cine latinoamericano*. Born in Bahia in northeast Brazil, he entered cinema as a teenager through the film clubs, studied law for two years, made a couple of shorts, wrote prolifically, joined the group around Nelson Pereira dos Santos (whom he called the father of *cinema novo*), and directed his first feature in 1962. (He would die young in 1981.) Rocha not only opposes Hollywood but also the kind of Brazilian artist for whom misery becomes a form of exoticism 'that vulgarizes social problems'.[5] He proposes an equation between hunger and violence; violence, he claims, is normal behaviour for the starving; and an aesthetics of violence is revolutionary rather than primitive because it not only reflects the culture of hunger back to itself but undermines and destroys it.

The context for this combativity is important. This is the young trio of Brazilian *cinema novo* talking to Italian cinephiles at a small festival of Latin American cinema, the year after a military coup, just as political repression was beginning. The humanistic project represented by *cinema novo* was in crisis, but the mood was defiant, and Rocha did not hide his feeling that Europeans hadn't got the message: 'For the European observer, the process of artistic creation in the underdeveloped world is of interest only in so far as it satisfies his nostalgia for primitivism.' (Not only primitivism, of course, but exoticism, imaginary geographies, and other kinds of projection.) But *cinema novo*, he insisted, is an ongoing process, which opposes 'commercialism, exploitation, pornography and the tyranny of technique', by filming the truth and opposing 'the hypocrisy and repression of intellectual censorship'. However, it is also 'a project that has grown out of the politics of hunger and suffers, for that very reason, all the consequent weaknesses which are a product of its particular situation'. In a word, it was what was known throughout Latin America as *cine pobre* – the cinema of poverty.

Inevitably, films that Rocha himself describes as 'those ugly, sad films, those screaming, desperate films in which reason has not always prevailed', came to be seen as metaphors for what they pictured. As Robert Stam has put it: 'films which would not only treat hunger as a theme but also be "hungry" in their own impoverished means of production. In a displaced form of mimesis, the material poverty of style would signal real-world poverty.'[6] This kind of aesthetic is in Fredric Jameson's view allegorical, but it's also ambiguous. If technical perfection, says Jameson, connotes advanced capitalism, then 'imperfect cinema' signified not merely underdevelopment but a knowing kinship with the 'contemporaneous practices of First World oppositional filmmakers like Godard, with their use of handheld cameras, deliberately sloppy and foregrounded editing, and their ostentatious valorisation of amateurishness in place of Hollywood'.[7] Of course this is a calculated sloppiness, born of a different type of gaze and a different sense of rhythm, intended to disrupt the familiar patterns of what the new film theory of the day called the institutional mode of representation. But if this affinity is cogent, then we're not talking of an underdeveloped cinema in the sense frequently assumed by metropolitan observers, that of being 'backward' and even 'primitive'. Rocha is quite within his rights to protest: 'The violence of a starving man is not a sign of a primitive mentality. Is Fabiano primitive? Is Antão primitive? Is Corisco primitive?' He is speaking of the protagonists of Pereira dos Santos' *Vidas Secas* (*Barren Lives*, 1963), Ruy Guerra's *Os fuzis* (*The Guns*, 1964) and his own *Deus e o Diabo na Terra do Sol* (*Black God, White Devil*, 1964). With *Vidas Secas*, dos Santos carried the spirit of neorealism deeper into new territory with a stark adaptation of a novel by Graciliano Ramos about the appalling conditions of rural northeast Brazil, a zone of underdevelopment within underdevelopment. The same aesthetic and the same locale served Guerra for *Os fuzis*, a drama of hunger in the *sertão* and violent confrontation between soldiers and peasants. Rocha's film we shall come to shortly.

The intellectual context – the affinities and intertexts evoked by the manifesto – also calls for attention. In effect, Rocha raises the same classic questions posed by Walter Benjamin in his early essay, 'Critique of Violence':[8] can violence, as a principle, be a moral means to just ends? Is violence ever justified? Or is the use of violence incompatible with its ends? What about the right of self-defence? What of the situation of someone impelled by anger, for example, to an act of violence which is not a means to an end but a manifestation? Above all, perhaps, does violence follow a natural law, or is it a product of history? For Rocha there seems no contradiction in saying that the cruelty perpetrated by the system on its vulnerable underclasses is not natural but historical, but the counter-violence of the oppressed is its natural result – but as long as it remains only a manifestation, then it remains caught up in a hopelessly repeating circle of strife and brutality which is transcended only by the conscious turn to revolutionary violence.

When Rocha declares that revolutionary violence is distinguished by its moral justification, there is a profound correspondence with Che Guevara playing beneath the surface: it is 'not filled with hatred; nor is it linked to the old, colonising humanism ... because it is not the kind of love which derives from complacency or contemplation, but rather a love of action and transformation'. For this is sure to evoke Guevara at his most paradoxical, in a published letter to a Uruguayan journalist in 1965 which became known as 'Socialism and Man in Cuba': 'At the risk of seeming ridiculous, let me say that the true revolutionary is guided by a great feeling of love' – that is to say, a deep sense of humanity and love of justice; for according to Guevara, only this will save the revolutionary from 'dogmatic extremes, cold scholasticism, or isolation from the masses'.[9] Perhaps it is psychoanalysis we should turn to here for help, because it knows about the way that affects can turn into their opposites.

Above all there is Rocha's affinity (which is shared by Solanas and Getino) for Frantz Fanon, the Martinique-born psychiatrist whose culminating work, *The Wretched of the Earth*, born of his experience in Algeria, published in France with its famous introduction by Sartre in 1961, is in Robert Young's phrase, 'both a revolutionary manifesto of decolonization and the founding analysis of the effects of colonialism upon colonized peoples and their cultures'.[10] The kinship between them, which Rocha signals in his phraseology without mentioning Fanon's name, arises because the Brazilian filmmaker identifies the condition of his country as one of colonisation, not independence. The history of Latin America – this is a view that is widely shared – is that of exchanging one coloniser for the next, one type of colonisation for another, and 'What distinguishes yesterday's colonialism from today's is merely the more refined forms employed by the contemporary coloniser.' Thus it is Fanon from whom Rocha draws his rationale: 'The moment of violence is the moment when the coloniser becomes aware of the existence of the colonised. Only when he is confronted with violence can the coloniser understand, through horror, the strength of the culture he exploits. [...] The first policeman had to die before the French became aware of the Algerians.'

The film screen presents the symbolic expression of this confrontation with the violence inherent in what Fanon's teacher Aimé Cesaire called the 'colonial trauma', of which poetry may carry the trace, a wound which persists in the pseudo-independence of postcolonial governance which continues to the haunted by the spectre of colonialism.[11] In the new wave Latin American cinema of the 1960s and 1970s, violence is a presupposition, a systemic feature of the world, and at the very centre of the plot in paradigmatic films like *Yawar Mallku* (*Blood of the Condor*) by Jorge Sanjinés, and *El chacal de Nahueltoro* (*The Jackal of Nahueltoro*) by Miguel Littin. The violence represented in these two films – the first Bolivian, the second Chilean, both dating from 1969 – is of different kinds, but both provide a synoptic analysis of its ramifications through all levels of society. Both are based on fact. *Yawar Mallku*, which recounts the response of a Quechua community to the sterilisation of its women who attend a maternity clinic run by the American Peace Corps, not only treats of an explicit racist violence, but also the structural racism of Bolivian society. *El chacal de Nahueltoro*, a sociologically precise reconstruction of the murder of a woman and her children by an illiterate casual worker, not only discloses the workings of the forces of law and order through which the criminal is caught, convicted, imprisoned and finally executed, but also exposes the role of the social agencies – school, church, mass media – in producing the social discourse of criminality. In both cases we see how violence of one kind begets violence of another, how this may produce a chain of responses, a kind of negative feedback process, and this is a seemingly endemic and everyday condition. It should be added that these were not esoteric films. *El Chacal de Nahueltoro* was Chile's most successful film at the domestic box office to date, and clearly articulates the feelings that led to Salvador Allende's election the following year as President of the Popular Unity government. *Yawar Mallku* has the distinction of being one of the few films anytime anywhere with a direct political effect: it led to the expulsion of the Peace Corps from Bolivia.

3

Rocha's manifesto, in all its brevity, lumps together the various different kinds of violence that are dramatised in the films, and thereby placed in complex narrative and symbolic relationship to each other. Already in Rocha's first film, *Barravento* (*The Turning Wind*, 1962), there are several kinds of violence. The setting is a fishing village in Bahia, where the huge net the villagers use for the catch is owned by the local white boss who reaps all the profits. Firmino, whom the police have down as a troublemaker, returns to his native village to seek refuge, and begins to challenge the fatalistic beliefs of the villagers. Violence first breaks out physically in a clash over one of the women between Firmino and Arua, whom the whole village believes to be protected by Yemanya, the goddess of the sea; symbolic violence is perpetrated through the casting of spells; Firmino commits instrumental violence when he cuts the net; and when the wind turns, the violence of nature is unleashed both physically and symbolically by the storm that it brings.

Technically speaking, *Barravento* is still close to the practices of Italian neo-realism, shooting on location in black-and-white with non-professional actors led by a few select professionals, and with the sound dubbed and mixed in post-production. Rocha claimed the film not really to be his own because he took it over in the middle, but it already shows the mark of his baroque, and in his own word, 'tropicalist' sense of style; not least in the extensive use of music and dance over long takes, sometimes in long shot, sometimes with a swirling camera, which helps to give the film its pervading tone of heightened lyricism: long takes of the fishermen singing as they haul in the net, of macumba drumming on the sound-track, of candomblé and even capoeira. Indeed the first third of the film is more like an ethnographic musical than a political drama, and later on, when Firmino and Arua fight again, but in the form of capoeira, their struggle takes on a ritual and allegorical quality which lifts the film entirely out of a naturalistic vein (not in the spectacular manner of kung fu movies, but neither does Rocha here assault the viewer's sensibilities as in later films).

Five years later, in *Terra em Transe* (*Land in Anguish*, 1967), still using basi-cally the same technical means, a curious thing occurs. A baroque allegory about Brazilian politics, conceived in the wake of the traumatic 1964 coup d'état, this is the tale of Paulo, a poet, who in a neat account by Roy Armes, 'veers erratically between the mystic conservatism of his first patron, Díaz, and the empty popu-lism of the pseudorevolutionary leader Vieira'.[12] The film is pervaded throughout by a sense of violence – the threat of political violence is introduced explicitly in the very first scene – but it is never directly observed. It is seen only in the form of threat or aftermath. It can be heard, however, several times in the form of gunfire on the soundtrack, unconnected with the diegesis, and therefore fulfill-ing an ambiguous symbolic function. Like the Sternberg of *The Scarlet Empress* (1934) says Armes, Rocha scorns the primacy of narrative clarity and puts his faith in violent, expressive imagery, arranged in short sequences joined jaggedly and abruptly.

In between, in *Deus e o Diabo na Terra do Sol*, violence spills out of the screen in abundance. Manuel is a tenant farmer who kills the cheating and physi-cally abusive *terrateniente* in self-defence, and is forced with his wife Rosa to become a fugitive, where they enter the realm of legend. They first seek the holy man Sebastião, who preaches a mystical salvation, but Sebastião demands total submission, including physical trials and even the sacrificial killing of Manuel's child. Rosa, in her horror, stabs Sebastião, but the couple are spared by the arrival of Antonio das Mortes, killer of bandits and hireling of church and landlords, described by Armes as 'a man without a past who strides through the film with the invulnerability of a Clint Eastwood hero'. Das Mortes, who will become the eponymous protagonist of Rocha's next film, shoots down Sebastiâo's followers, allowing the couple to escape, only to encounter the bandit Corisco, who kills the poor to spare them from starving and metes out to the rich a justice that consists solely of rape, mutilation and slow death.

Rocha's special fascination is the violence expressed in and through popular religious practices. His masterpiece, *Antonio das Mortes* (*The Dragon of Evil Against the Warrior Saint*, 1969) is again set in northeast Brazil, with emblematic characters performing stylised actions, in a strange amalgamation of fact and legend, epic and lyric. For Rocha the mysticism of popular religion, a syncretistic fusion of Catholicism and the motifs of African religion transplanted with the slave trade, became the expression of a permanent spirit of rebellion against unceasing oppression, a rejection and refusal of the condition in which the common people had been condemned to live for centuries. It also provided him with a model for the syncretism of his own film language, where the exuberant torrent of images, the mix of mysticism and legend, cult and ritual, were married to surrealistic symbolism to achieve a visionary force.

4

Rocha wishes to de-naturalise violence. He shows a strong affinity with Brechtian ideas, which are also found in García Espinosa, about breaking the illusionism of traditional realist forms of representation. The filmic equivalent of the theatrical *Verfremdungseffekt* is understood to require a negation of conventional mise-en-scène, and Rocha's aesthetics of violence, as he practices it himself in different keys in successive films, always employs an anti-classical form of montage – including the paradigmatic alternation between long takes, sometimes static, sometimes mobile, and the sudden violent outburst of visual and musical energy. The interruption often produces narrative ambiguity and elision, in short, a form of aesthetic aggression against the good narrative.

It is integral to this style that when it comes to the direct representation of violence, the mise-en-scène is motivated by the refusal of spectacle. As Stam explains, speaking of *Terra em Transe*:

> Violence, above all, is consistently de-realized by the editing. Guns are omnipresent but they are never coordinated with their sounds. We see pistols and hear machine guns; we hear machine guns but see nothing. A policeman on a motorcycle

presumably shoots Paolo, but we see no wound. Violence is treated in a fragmented and anti-realistic way, in keeping with Rocha's expressed desire to reflect on violence rather than make a spectacle of it.[13]

Armes remarks that the opening of *Deus e o Diabo na Terra do Sol*, in which Manuel kills the *terrateniente*, 'would not be out of place in a 1940s realist drama', but the way it's shot and edited is quite different. Not only does Rocha avoid focusing the camera on the act of violence itself, but there is an elision after the killing in which a whole chunk of narrative is omitted that the Hollywood genre movie, telling the same story, would expand inordinately in order to create suspense. But here, instead of seeing the *terrateniente*'s henchmen going after Manuel, we cut directly to the end of the pursuit, and even then, the camera hangs back as the second bout of killing occurs. You could almost say that Rocha constructs his narrative out of precisely those bits and pieces of footage which, if this were a Hollywood movie, would have been left on the cutting room floor.

Another example occurs in *Terra em Transe*, when a humble peasant leader, Felicio, defies Vieira, and Paulo menaces him, a tussle we see from a distance, immediately cutting to the apartment where Paulo confesses to Sara, Vieira's dedicated secretary, how he 'beat a poor peasant because he threatened me' (although what we saw was the opposite – Paulo was the one doing the threatening); abruptly we cut again, to the wailing of the *campesinos* who have discovered Felicio's dead body – there is a moment of ambiguity until we hear them accusing Vieira of the murder. Again a whole tranche of narrative is omitted that would be meat to a Hollywood movie. This is not the same as poor plotting, and there is no plot lapse in the narrative gap, for this is a different mode of fiction altogether.

All this presents us with a conundrum, because Rocha's aesthetics of violence is clearly not the only or the usual aesthetics of violence. On the contrary, violent imagery – artificial, highly stylised and spectacular – is the daily bread of both Hollywood and television drama; television is also the site for the raw representation of violence in the news, and each of these strands of imagery has its own codes and its own aesthetic of violence. There are critical differences between fiction and documentary. Much of what fiction portrays, which the viewer knows to be illusory, is unavailable to documentary, which is taken to be veridical. This doesn't mean that the truth of documentary is the whole truth: an impossible idea, because the documentary camera is always seeing from a partial point of view, and certain things remain hidden, taboo or invisible. In consequence of these differences, each of these representational codes or sub-codes has its own ideological implications, arising essentially from what the code foregrounds and what it suppresses – not even comedy is innocent. Rocha's version is concerned with forms of social violence which are systemically suppressed in the cinematic codes he opposes – the silent everyday violence perpetrated by the system, the hunger and disease, the social violence of political deception, the popular spirit of rebellion that these forces engender, which needs to be brought back down from religious messianism into revolutionary focus.

Societies of hunger generate fear – but different fears in the hungry multitude and the few who eat well, whose politics are geared to controlling the masses and blocking their tendency to rebel – the army is their agent, but sometimes gets uppity, and acts on its own behalf. What happens when the masses acquire leaders who represent their authentic interests, and they enter into politics? The oligarchy's fear of losing control is subsumed by the military, who take on the role of defender of the nation, and the politicisation of the military brings the supreme act of violence which is constituted by taking over the State. There were sixteen military coups in Latin America in the twenty years from the end of World War Two to the moment Rocha wrote 'The Aesthetics of Hunger'. (Costa Rica and Venezuela, 1948; Peru, 1948 and 1962; Nicaragua and Haiti, 1950; Bolivia, 1951 and 1964; Cuba, 1952; Colombia, 1953; Paraguay, 1954; Argentina, 1955; Honduras, 1956, 1963; Guatemala, 1957, 1963). This too is part of the context of Rocha's manifesto, and the historical intertext of his films.

5

There is another difficulty. The discourse around the representation of violence is all too loose. It has a habit of conflating violence and aggression, strife and struggle, force, brutality and cruelty, as well as differences between individual and social violence. Nowhere have these differences been investigated as fully as in the literature of psychoanalysis, where treatment requires that violence be distinguished from aggression, and the physical from its psychological forms, verbal and symbolic. Foundational figures like Freud, Melanie Klein and D. W. Winnicott all had something to say about it, as Richard Mizen and Mark Morris (2007) remind us in a recent study of the subject, although they disagree whether the source of violence is reactive or instinctual (Freud himself characteristically changed his mind). The problem in turning to psychoanalysis is the shift in focus from the social to the individual: we will have to understand the relation between them. Mizen and Morris have little to say about the social, but they're clear on one thing: aggression, they attest, is a basic instinctual and affective component of the human being, at the deep level where the psyche and soma, mind and body, meet, which equips the subject to deal with threat and lack. Violence, however, despite the cliché 'mindless violence', is neither mindless nor innate, 'and no more a part of the human condition than, say, starvation, even if eradication seems insuperable...'[14]

Rocha's aesthetic of violence is not very interested in individual psychology. The perpetrators of violence in his films are representative and symbolic figures, icons of social forces or sectors. We should take heed, however, that the level of the individual is not spirited away. There is in the experience of violence an irreducible psychic experience. Physical violence is perpetrated and experienced bodily; and all violence is experienced subjectively. This includes the film viewer, for whom the sight of violence on the screen is always liable to produce a physical shudder. Neuroscientists have recently discovered what they call 'mirror neurons' in the brain which not only fire when a subject is poked with a needle, for example, but also when they watch someone else being poked. According to V. S. Ramachandran these neurons comprise a network that allows us to see things 'from the other person's point of view', they 'dissolve the barrier between self and others' and might be called 'empathy neurons'.[15] This is not empathy in its deep ethical sense, but as the term 'mirror' neuron implies, only on the surface, but we can predict that these neurons will be found to be firing overtime in the brain that is watching a movie.

Neuroscience has little to say about the causes of violent behaviour, which psychoanalysis perceives as the result of a failure of psychic integration, or a process of psychic disintegration, which becomes manifest in pathological forms (which remain outside the comfort zone of analytic treatment). However, what counts as pathological behaviour (and therefore subject to incarceration in a secure asylum) is a matter of social definition, medical and legal, and thus historical in character. Moreover, there are also forms of violent behaviour which cannot be morally regarded in this way because they are socially sanctioned and institutional – the foremost are war, where men are licensed to kill and maim the enemy; and policing, where the agents of law and order are licensed to use physical force. These of course are the legitimate forms of violence which in classic accounts are monopolised by the state, but there are also others. Benjamin mentions organised labour and the strike; and nowadays, in the neoliberal state, some of the means of law and order have been privatised. But here's the rub: within the appropriate institutional milieu, people are able to satisfy psychological desires which otherwise, unprotected by the sanction of their social function, might be judged psychopathic – the mercenary in Iraq; the prison guard at home; the manager in a company who engages in bullying and intimidation (or any institution: a university, for example); the politician drunk on power.

This masking also happens in the formation of crowds and mobs (as we know from Elias Canetti's study of *Crowds and Power*), where the multitude and the collective provide protection for individuals to express themselves in a manner they would otherwise suppress. You can see it in the 'tribalism' of football hooliganism. Or breakaway factions of militants in political demonstrations who lash out. It is seen in symbolic form in the street dancing of crowds of religious in Rocha's films, whose aggression borders on rebellion. In short, violence and agression must also be seen in the context of their social, institutional, economic and cultural milieu, where 'economic, political, ethical, moral and religious factors play their part, even where these are obscure or ambiguous'.[16] The only essential difference here from Rocha's view is that for him the 'economic, political, ethical, moral and religious factors' are not at all obscure: the same goes for Fanon, who turned to the historical and the material to identify the political source of the mental distress he saw in the clinic. They agree that violence, whatever its psychic mechanisms, is socially and historically produced. But still, is it possible to talk of a social psychopathology where these behaviours play out at a collective level? To which we must add, because we're speaking of countries like Brazil and Algeria, will it be the same social psychopathology as in Europe, where psychoanalysis originated? Can the psychiatric categories of the coloniser be applicable to the colonised?

Psychoanalysis itself has generally refused political questions, partly out of appropriate caution about notions of a collective psyche, and partly preferring to render its practices as apolitical and neutral, for fear of the charge of political complicity. But this is not the end of the story, as attested by writers like Fanon, Octave Mannoni and Albert Memmi, not to mention Sartre. According to Ranjana Khanna, in her study of psychoanalysis and colonialism, *Dark Continents*, Fanon discovered in Algeria the ill fit of European categories of psychic disorder to Algerian patients, including their imprecise symptoms when they presented themselves at the hospital.[17] Criticising colonial doctors for their racist politics and patronising address toward their patients, he suggested different explanations: perhaps the patient was faking for the sake of a warm hospital bed when it was cold; perhaps what they suffered was a form of illness unrecognised by the received psychiatric categories; perhaps they were suffering psychosomatic effects of colonial conditions, including cultural confusion and physical displacement. Khanna records how a certain Antoine Porot had formulated 'a contorted concept' of 'pseudomelancholy' to explain what he identified as a susceptibility to violence among Algerian Arabs, quite distinct from the introspection which supposedly characterised European melancholy; but perhaps, she says, the violent behaviour thus identified can be understood as a form of political protest rather than moral degeneracy. The doctors' failure to read the signs of political rebelliousness, protest, moral outrage at colonial oppression, amounted to disavowal, even denial.

Khanna takes Porot's notion of pseudomelancholy and turns it about to arrive at a concept of colonial melancholy. In Freud, melancholia is closely related to mourning, but unlike the work of mourning, it can never be brought even near to completion. Mourning assimilates the loss. Melancholia is an affective state caused by the inability to assimilate a loss, and the consequent nagging return of the thing lost into psychic life. The lost object may be a person, but also an idea – something as abstract as an ideal, a country, or a sense of liberty. Colonial (and postcolonial) melancholy arises from an unresolvable contradiction within the (post)colonial subject. If the melancholy of displacement, expatriation and exile expresses a crisis of identity which begins as a dislocation of the subject's civic affiliation and nationality (and gives rise to different senses of self), then colonial melancholy is a condition in which the concept of the nation is falsely embedded through the colonial relation, which has created a psuedo-nation-state where none existed before, often dividing cultures with arbitary borders, creating states which betray an alien system of social classification and categorisation. The result is a condition of psychic damage produced by the experience of a discrepant modernity, manifested in a haunting by the spectre of colonialism, an inability to assimilate the ideal of nation-statehood, the ghost of a dimly imagined community which can only remain utopian.

In the meantime there is poetry. As Césaire put it: 'All the dreams, all the desires, all the accumulated rancor, all the formless and repressed hopes of a century of colonialist domination, all that need[s] to come out and when it comes out and expresses itself and squirts bloodily carrying along without distinction the conscious and the unconscious, lived experience and prophecy, that is called poetry.'[18] But this seems to me an exact description of Rocha's aesthetics of violence.

6

The dialectic of the image of violence lies in its relation to fear, and this leads to one final difficulty, perhaps the most intractable – the differential position of the viewer in place and time. All viewers are born with the same neurocircuitry, but some are granted comfort and some are granted pain. Judith Butler observes that violence, produces not only fear and grief, abhorrence and anxiety, it also produces the fear of fear, especially in the media,[19] but this depends on where you are, and whether the violence you see in the media refers to your own or another society. While terrorism, above all since 2001, when it came home to the heart of empire, is treated by the mainstream media with moral outrage and public ceremonies of mourning – and the same media regularly whip up hysteria and practice psychological terrorism against dissenters of various kinds – still, it makes a difference whether hunger, homelessness, misery, destitution and deprivation are hidden away or in your face.

Rocha's position can be seen as an aesthetic wager on the capacity of the image to break out of its own frame, and we should ask how it stacks up against the ubiquity of violent imagery in general cultural circulation. It is frequently alleged that this plenitude brings its own risk, that of desensitisation – the idea that in a world hyper-saturated with such images, they have a diminishing effect, we become callous, there is a deadening of feeling. This is what Susan Sontag believed when she first wrote about photography in 1977, and revisiting the subject 25 years later, she observed that 'there is a mounting level of acceptable violence and sadism in mass culture: films, television, comics, computer games. Imagery that would have had an audience cringing and recoiling in disgust forty years ago is watched without so much as a blink by every teenager in the multiplex.'[20] Today she would add computer screens of various sizes. The vast majority of this imagery is artificial, unreal, cartoon-like, lacking emotional depth, essentially iconic, but psychologists have indeed found a certain amount of evidence for desensitisation, and the US military nowadays uses first-person shoot-'em-up computer games to condition soldiers to shoot reflexively at human targets.[21] Sontag, however, returning to the subject, now thought that it isn't quite as it seems, because not all violence is watched with equal detachment.

This is clearly true of the veridical images of documentary and news reportage, which are introduced with warnings that 'some viewers may find these scenes disturbing' – damn right! Some of it is seen with morbid fascination, some elicits a deep well of compassion and sincere waves of charitable donations to aid campaigns. Sometimes this leads to political demands for more aid and consumer pressure for more fair trade. Some people turn away, but people don't become inured to it, says Sontag, 'because of the quantity of images dumped on them' – they stop looking precisely because of the responses they call up. The states described, she says, as apathy or moral or emotional anaesthesia, are full of feelings: feelings of rage and frustration, undesirable emotions, which are therefore displaced by a kind of vague sympathy, which disguises the impotence of the privileged viewer.[22] Sontag was speaking from the perspective of Manhattan, but feelings of rage and frustration also populate the mental strife, which Fanon discovered as a practising psychiatrist in Algeria in the psychopathology of the colonial subject. And these of course are the feelings, which Rocha's aesthetics of violence wishes to liberate.

NOTES

1 See www.walterlippmann.com/fc-02-04-1962.pdf; accsessed 8 June 2010.

2 For example, in M. Chanan (ed.) (1983) *Twenty-five Years of the New Latin American Cinema*. London: British Film Institute/Channel Four, 13–14.

3 See M. Chanan (ed.) (1983) *Twenty-five Years of the New Latin American Cinema*. London: British Film Institute/Channel Four, 17–27; 28–33.

4 J. Burton (1987) *Cinema and Social Change in Latin America*. Austin: University of Texas Press, 108–9.

5 This and subsequent quotations from the Manifesto, in M. Chanan (ed.) (1983) *Twenty-five Years of the New Latin American Cinema*. London: British Film Institute/Channel Four.

6 R. Stam (2000) *Film Theory: An Introduction*. Oxford: Blackwell, 95.

7 F. Jameson (1992) *Signatures of the Visible*. London: Routledge, 218–19.

8 W. Benjamin (1979) *One Way Street and other writings*. London: New Left Books.

9 'Socialism and Man in Cuba' (1965). At www.marxists.org/archive/guevara/1965/03/man-socialism.htm; accsessed 14 April 2012

10 R. J. C. Young (1990) *White Mythologies: Writing History and the West*. London: Routledge, 158–9.

11 R. Khanna (2004) *Dark Continents: Psychoanalysis and Colonialism*, Durham, NC: Duke University Press, 126.

12 R. Armes (1987) *Third World Film Making and the West*. Berkeley: University of California Press, 262.

13 R. Stam (1976) 'Land in Anguish: Revolutionary lessons', *Jump Cut*, 10–11, 49–51.

14 R. Mizen and M. Morris (2007) *On Aggression & Violence: An Analytic Perspective*. New York: Palgrave Macmillan, xiii.

15 V. S. Ramachandran (2000) 'Mirror neurons and imitation learning as the driving force behind "the great leap forward"', *Human Evolution*, 69, May 29, 2000. http://www.edge.org/3rd_culture/ramachandran/ramachandran_p1.html; accsessed 14 April 2012.

16 R. Mizen and M. Morris (2007) *On Aggression & Violence: An Analytic Perspective*. New York: Palgrave Macmillan, 3.

17 R. Khanna (2004) *Dark Continents: Psychoanalysis and Colonialism*, Durham, NC: Duke University Press, 175–8.

18 Ibid., 126.

19 J. Butler (2004) *Precarious Life: The Powers of Mourning and Violence*. London: Verso.

20 S. Sontag (2003) *Regarding the Pain of Others*. London: Hamish Hamilton, 90.

21 See D. Trend (2007) *The Myth of Media Violence: A Critical Introduction*. Oxford: Blackwell, 22.

22 S. Sontag (2003) *Regarding the Pain of Others*. London: Hamish Hamilton, 91.

MEMORY OF VIOLENCE:
VISUALISING TRAUMA

'ÇA VA DE SOI':
THE VISUAL REPRESENTATION OF VIOLENCE IN THE HOLOCAUST DOCUMENTARY

Brian Winston

In memory of Miep Gies, Secretary and Resistance Worker 1909–2010

> *Si j'avais trouvé un film existant – un film secret parce que c'était stricte-ment interdit – tourné par un SS et montrant comment trois mille juifs, hommes, femmes, enfants, mouriaent ensemble, asphyxiés dans un cham-ber à gaz du crématoire II d'Auschwitz, si j'avais trouvé cela, non seulement je ne l'aurais montré cela, mais je l'aurais détruit. Je ne suis pas capable de dire pourquoi. Ca va de soi.*[1]

– Claude Lanzmann, *'Holocauste, la representation impossible'*
Le Monde, 3 March 1994[2]

We have exactly 1'59" of moving images of the mass execution of Jews in East-ern Europe during World War II. Taken by a German non-commissioned naval officer, Reinhard Wiener, out for a stroll with his 8mm Kodak movie camera in the port of Liepaja, Latvia's third city, sometime in July/August 1941, it shows members of an *Einsatzgruppe* – mobile killing squad – at work. There are civilian bystanders, local Latvian militiamen and German police in attendance as well as the SS as Jewish men are offloaded from an open truck and forced to run to an open pit where they are shot. There has been, of course, argument about the authenticity of this material but its provenance is fully documented.[3]

It is estimated that the *Einsatzgruppen* killed a man, woman or child every thirty seconds of every hour of every day for five hundred days between the

summer of 1941 and the autumn of 1942; but the Nazi order forbidding photography of the murders – which was in line with a general inhibition about
publicising the industry of death – was obeyed, almost to the letter. Wiener's film
antedates Himmler's prohibition against making any form of record of the killings and it was hidden from the Nazis (see Hirsch 2004: 94).[4] It is easy to see why
Himmler so ordered; the killings were not something of which the Nazis wished
to boast. On 3 October 1943, for example, Himmler addressed the SS general
staff in Posen and, even in such company, despite claiming that he would be 'for
once' – '*einmal*' – '*ganz offen*' 'totally open' about 'the Event', it was only so he
can say that 'we will never speak of this openly'. In Peter Haidu's account of this
speech, Himmler argues that

> He and they have been hardened by the experience of seeing 'a hundred corpses
> lie side by side, or five hundred, or a thousand. To have endured this ... and in
> spite of that to have remained decent' that is what has made them hard...' The
> extermination of the Jews, the goal to be effectuated, is to be 'a never-written and
> a never-to-be-written page of glory [*Ruhm*] in SS history'. (1992: 286)[5]

This Himmler describes as '*takt*', delicacy of feeling (1992: 285); a delicacy re-
enforced, of course, by his direct interdiction of photography, introduced within
weeks of the killing starting (but after Wiener's footage was safely hidden by his
mother back in Germany). Even the rare shame expressed by a very few bravely
uncooperative Germans at having to obey the SS's murderous orders did not often yield permanent records.

So the brief Liepaja footage, and a rather fuller collection of stills, are the
only records of shootings – actual images of extreme violence. Of the processes
of killing in the extermination camps – '*die Endlösung der Judenfrage*'/'the final
solution of the Jewish problem' – which replaced the somewhat inefficient procedures of the *Einsatzgruppen* with gas chambers and crematoria, there is no
photographic evidence, except for four surreptitious stills taken in Auschwitz
II (Auschwitz-Birkenau). For the extermination camps of Chelmno, Treblinka,
Sobibór, Majdanek and Belzec there are no photographs whatsoever; nor indeed
traces of much of anything. As Laurence Rees says of Treblinka: 'Put simply, there
is nothing there' (2005: 147).[6] No wonder Nazi guards taunted their prisoners
that, should they survive, they would never be believed and no wonder that bearing testimony has been such a powerful concern of the survivors: 'Not to live and
to tell' as Primo Levi put it, 'but to live to tell' (1961: 13).[7]

There is, then, a rather prosaic response to the vexed philosophical question
as to the ethical viability of using archival film to represent the central horror of

the Holocaust – the supposed *Bilderverbot*, ban on images, as it has come to be called. The issue is actually moot. Cinematographic representation is not possible simply because there is no cinematographic evidence of the processes of mass extermination and few stills either, except for the four mentioned above. And what there is otherwise is problematic whatever its source. According to Elizabeth Cowie, 'that the recorded "seen and heard" is not simply knowable or evidential, but requires interpretation that can become misinterpretation [and] presents a peculiarly acute dilemma for the documentary representation of the Holocaust'.[8] Cowie's point is true, of course, of all images, but those of the Holocaust pose a 'peculiarly acute dilemma' because, implicitly, they are required to meet the standards of criminal evidential truth. As the Common Law has it, their authenticity must be 'beyond reasonable doubt'. The iconicity of the photograph, however, is never sufficient in and of itself to meet this legal test.[9] The issue becomes so acute in the case of representing the Holocaust that perhaps the solution is to avoid the photographic entirely. This does not mean avoiding the documentary entirely because its compass now embraces animation. I want to suggest, in this essay, that at least one viable solution to the dilemmas of representing the Holocaust in documentary is, indeed, animation.

1. THE FIRST PROBLEM OF THE ARCHIVE: MISREPRESENTATION[10]

Realist factual Holocaust footage falls into three basic categories. There is a smattering – much increased by the assiduous work of film researchers in recent decades – of amateur material, taken by victims or 'perpetrators' (see Hirst 2003: 34).[11] This has been most tellingly recycled, for example, by Péter Forgács in a number of films to devastating effect (see Renov 2007; Fisher 2008).[12] Secondly, there is the deliberately misleading official Nazi film of the ghettos and operations around them designed either to fool the world (for example, *Theresienstadt: Ein Dokumentarfilm aus dem jüdische Siedlungsgebeit/ Theresienstadt: A Documentary Film from the Jewish Settlement Area*).[13] An alternative purpose of these commissions was to demonstrate the degeneration of the victims as in the footage of the Warsaw Ghetto, shot to a script discovered by Ilan Ziv.[14] Finally, there is the Allied footage of the liberation of the concentration camps.

This last is where the most disturbing pictures were made, for example, at Bergen-Belsen by the Army Film & Photographic Unit (AFPU) attached to the British 11th Armoured Division. Here are the living skeletons, the bulldozed bodies and the emotionless faces of the guards. Here is the indelible record of the consequences of otherwise unimaginable violence, the very *fons et origio* of our collective visual memory of the Holocaust.

To say that they are nevertheless 'misleading', as Hannah Arendt did in 1955 is not to deny their authenticity.[15] Despite the limitations of the photograph as evidence, these images are part of a dossier of overwhelming weight and it is a mark of serious, sinister delusion to deny their authenticity. They mislead, however, because they have been forced, in the absence of other photographs and films, to represent the whole of *die Endlösung*, which they cannot do. It is as synecdoche that they fail. Concentration camps were not extermination camps where people were dispatched within hours of arrival, not starved to death; and at the moment of filming the concentration camps were not what they had been earlier. The camp system had imploded as the Reich collapsed. This is not to dispute the obscenity of these hellholes through the long years of their existence but it is to remember the context. German city after German-held city had been reduced to rubble so it is little wonder that the camps had become charnel houses, repositories for the living dead.

Hence Claude Lanzmann's strategy in *Shoah* (1985) of avoiding the liberation footage in favour of the austerity of witness statements. This was as much determined by necessity as by any self-imposed *Bilderverbot*. *Shoah* is specifically about the extermination camps, of which there is no footage; Lanzmann's strategy is, first and foremost, a response to this absence of imagery. He avoids what had become the somewhat regular misuse of the specific horrors of one location at a specific point in time to provide images, as 'little more than illustrative wallpaper' (Haggith 2005: 33)[16] for other different locations at different times.

2. THE SECOND PROBLEM OF THE ARCHIVE: PROTUBERANCE

The laudatory response to *Shoah* for eschewing archival footage of any kind was in part, I believe, exactly because there was, in Britain and North America at least, a sense that by the 1980s audiences had become anaesthetised to the images, especially the liberation horrors. The images had become 'a protuberance' (Lebow 2008: xvii);[17] 'Used sparingly at the time [i.e. 1945–48] to prove the existence of the camps, these images have become so widely used in film and television progammes that they are now familiar icons' (Haggith 2005: 33).[18] Now bereft of close identification, without place and date for example, the images were being transformed from evidence into 'wallpaper'. Such familiarity seemed to have leeched the force of these shots, and primarily they now produce distanciation, if not alienation, in the audience.

By the 1980s when Lanzmann was working, there was some justification for filmmakers to feel that using the liberation footage would be counter-productive. To take – as it might be – an average case, Alan Rosenthal, working at this time on the Holocaust episode of the PBS series *Heritage: Civilization and the Jews*, felt that this footage had become 'chaser' material, literally a turn-off; and I, as his script-writer, certainly agreed with this. Although there was no audience research directly on the matter, that this was so had became very much a given within the industry.

Had it been remembered (which it wasn't) some classic early mass communications research offered support for this belief. This had apparently shown, in laboratory conditions, that horrific imagery in educational films – in this case designed to inculcate dental hygiene practices – did not work if the consequences of malpractice were overstated, i.e. suggesting very serious disease and even death as a consequence of hygiene failure (see Winston 1973: 33).[19] Audiences dismissed these messages.

For Rosenthal, moreover, the camps were the most familiar part of the story we had to tell and cliché was unavoidable. Defamiliarisation – *ostranenie*, to use the fashionable film studies jargon of the day – was required. He suggested that we deal very briefly, say in a minute, with the extermination camps over black using a montage of voices delivering very brief witness statements. I thought this was a brilliant way of avoiding the worst emotionalism of the 'Jews v. Nazis' norms but it was too 'de-familiar' for US public television and in the event Rosenthal himself backed off.

The sequence in the finished film takes the impressionistic, overly-sentimentalised approach first seen in Jean Cayrol's commentary, as polished by Chris Maker and spoken by an actor, in Alain Resnais' *Nuit et Brouilliard* (*Night and Fog*, 1955). Witness interviews apart, with this film Resnais, in line with normal *Groupe de Trente* documentary practices of the time in France, established Holocaust documentary's repertoire.

Here is perpetrator archival footage of deportations and ghettos, and the horrific Allied liberation material (the template for its misleading subsequent use as illustration of all varieties of camp). Also to be found for the first time is evocative colour cinematography of the remains of the concentration camps – at that date simply abandoned and not yet the site of tourist attention. The objection here is not to the aesthetic as such; rather it is an extreme example of what Joris Ivens called 'exotic dirt', images which prettify deprivation or horror (1969: 87).[20] Ivens has to be understood as saying, not that the aesthetics can be considered independently of a film as a whole – mere decoration; rather, it is that the aesthetics accurately reveal the errors of analysis conditioning the totality of the film. If prettifying images of the slums (the occasion prompting his remark) was an 'error', how much greater is the 'error' of producing prettified images of the Holocaust? *Nuit et brouillard*, the pictorialism of its colour footage amplified by the poetic voice-over, was accused of aestheticising an obscenity at the time. Of course, criticism of the poeticism of the commentary falls silent 'in the face of authorial good intentions' (King 1981: 7).[21] Actually, in this instance, it falls silent in the face of authorial experience – Cayrol survived Mauthausen.[22]

It has been claimed that 'Alain Resnais' film structured the commemoration of the Holocaust from the mid-1960s onward' (Knapp 2006c: 165).[23] To an extent, this is irrefutable and the film's effectiveness justifies Resnais' aesthetic choices.[24] So close to the event, this was perhaps the only way to cauterise the horror sufficiently for it to be remembered. This rationalisation, though, has since long timed out, its positive effectiveness swamped by the negative reaction *Nuit et brouilliard*'s successors are now deemed to produce in audiences. In fact, *Nuit et brouilliard* points the way to problems which were to be exacerbated in the subsequent deployment of its repertoire.

That certainly was our thinking when we approached the *Endlösing* sequence in our *Heritage* film. We eschewed the horrific but otherwise followed this poeticising pattern of *Nuit et brouillard*. A survivor provided – and indeed spoke – the words. In his autobiography Rosenthal describes this sequence as 'one of the most devastating scenes in the film' (2000: 246);[25] but for me it represents the one moment when we betrayed our desire not to make a standard 'Jews and Nazis' film. Elsewhere we insisted on the political dimensions of the Holocaust, the variety of its victims other than Jews, the activities of 'the righteous' and the efforts of the Jewish resistance. But with the camps we fell, in my view, too much into line with the by then standard procedures of what had become post-*Nuit et brouillard*, dare one say it, Holocaust industry documentaries.

Yet I want to suggest that this sense of familiarity, bolstered by the constant injunction not to forget, depended as much on the enduring indelible dreadfulness of the violence depicted in the images rather than on their ubiquity. In fact, they were not 'so widely used'; they just seemed to be. The sense of the Holocaust's omnipresence was as much sustained by the ever growing library of written and other materials as by the documentary, anyway a somewhat marginal form.)

As pointed out above, Toby Haggith notes that the movie material had been used sparingly in the late 1940s. After a flurry of newsreel and compilations, presented as incontrovertible evidence of the horrors uncovered by the liberation of the concentration camps, the production of documentaries slowed dramatically. In the UK, Sidney Bernstein's attempt to make a full-scale archival film of the material – under the supervision of his then business partner Alfred Hitchcock – was thwarted exactly because the images were deemed to be too abhorrent.

Between that initial wave in the late 1940s and *Nuit et brouillard* in the mid-1950s the material was not being much circulated. Even in 1955 the French censors hesitated over the horrors in Resnais' film (as well as, of course, objecting to the glimpses in the archive footage which he had included of French police overseeing deportations). The film, nevertheless, was shown at Cannes and achieved instant canonical status, aided by the scandal of an official West German attempt to prevent the screening (see Resnais 1994).[26]

Certainly, for nearly two decades after 1955, no other documentary specifically dealing with the Holocaust was repeatedly screened enough to gain canonical status. There is more fictional representation, which had begun with *Ostatni Etap/ The Last Stage* (Poland, 1946), a forgotten feature actually shot in Auschwitz and based on the director's – Wanda Jakubowska – experience as an inmate of the camp. This, too, continued fitfully. More than a decade passed before Hollywood addressed the topic: *The Diary of Ann Frank* (USA, 1959, dir. George Stephens).[27] Nevertheless, the non-fictional figures even less than the fictional in the Holocaust filmography.[28] Leaving aside general World War II compilation films, there are only a few other titles on the Holocaust specifically.[29]

Five years after *Nuit et brouillard*, Jean Rouch, in *Chonique d'un été* (*Chronicle of a Summer*, 1960) provided the last component of the Holocaust film, the testimony of the witness. The mise-en-scène of this element – Marceline Loridan's memory of being deported through the Gare de l'est in Paris – was filmed in the Gare de l'est itself, with her voicing-over shots of her walking to the station. The constructed nature of this sequence is at odds with the rest of this self-proclaimed 'experiment in film truth', the prototype *cinéma vérité* documentary. The film is actually about 'the strange tribe that lives in Paris' (Morin 1985: 13),[30] not the Holocaust; and the deportation sequence is, with its voice-over technique, its most retrogressive element. In the final on-camera exchange between Rouch and his co-director Edgar Morin, they question the sequence's authenticity – was Marceline acting, they ask?

The question of acting, though, is, in my view, of less ethical consequence than the danger of causing victims psychological damage by making them recall these traumas. Of course, the need to bear witness is a compelling reason for their willingness to subject themselves to any form of acting. Indeed, it can be therapeutic, but the possibility of uninformed consent on the part of the subject and insensitive proceedings on the part of the filmmaker are nevertheless a potential danger. Such qualms, though, did not prevent others from taking the technique and running with it. Rouch's discovery of 'a cinematic discourse of history without archival image to anchor it' (Hirsch 2004: 67),[31] however, has proved too seductive to resist. (As for filming perpetrators, the therapeutic value of having them re-live their actions re-traumatising them is not at issue. Exposure is.)

Donald Brittain, a major Canadian filmmaker, would have known of *Chro-*

nique d'un été when he took Bernard Laufer, an Auschwitz survivor, back to Germany for the NFBC's *Memorandum/Pour memoire* five years after *Chronique d'un été*. *Memorandum* expands from testimony from survivors to witness statements by their relatives as well as by surviving Nazis and other members of the German public. Although not so readily available as to be a canonised text, the film won the Silver Lion at Venice that year as best documentary. The same year, Mikhail Romm made *Obyknovennyy fashizm* (*Ordinary Fascism*), the opening sequence of which uses horrific images *à la Nuit et brouillard*, to set the scene for an account of pre-war Nazism in terms the regime's use of propaganda, both via high culture modes and through popular platforms to represent its militarism. It won the East German documentary prize at Leipzig in 1965.

Overall, this level of usage does not suggest that Holocaust images were, in fact, being widely used in cinema documentaries during these years. The only canonical film noted in Haggith and Newman's *Holocaust and the Moving Image* filmography between the mid-1950s and the mid-1970s is Marcel Ophüls' *Le Chagrin et la pitié* (1969) – a film not about the Holocaust, but rather about French responses to occupation and fascism. Although commissioned by French Television (ORTF), it was deemed politically too sensitive to be screened on TV. Controversy over its release as a feature provoked a crucial debate in the vexed process of France's 'coming to terms with the past': or *Vergangenheitsbewälti-gung* as the Germans call it.

The potential *Bilderverbot* over horrific *Endlösing* material, already apparent by the late 1940s, would have also been sustained by the conservative norms of taste and decency which governed television whence the documentary had largely migrated by the 1960s; although Danish television (DR) screened an hour, directed by Henning Knusden, on Simon Wiesenthal, the Nazi hunter, in 1967 (*Mordere iblandt os/Murderers Among Us*). It can be noted, contrary-wise, that *The Rise and Fall of the Third Reich* (Jack Kaufmann's televising of William Shirer's book and a pioneering mini-series) did not receive a network screening in the US the following year but was, instead, sold in syndication. Again, not an overwhelming number of titles.

Eventually, though, evolving standards and television's appetite for history programmes on the two World Wars – TV's first documentary hit, it should not be forgotten, was Henry Salamon's archive-based *Victory at Sea* for NBC (1952/53) – was slowly to change this. The first Holocaust documentary after *Nuit et brouillard* noted in Haggith and Newman's list is Michal Darlow's 'Genocide', the twentieth episode of *World at War* (1974); the next is Peter Morley's *Kitty – Return to Auschwitz* (1979) where the documentarist goes a step further than Brittain had done and takes Kitty Hart, a survivor, back to the camp.

Of more significance, perhaps, in creating the sense that Holocaust movies were becoming a 'protuberance' are the fictional representations. The Hollywood TV miniseries *Holocaust* (1978) was a mega-hit in the US, and in Germany 'its reception nearly caused mass hysteria' (Kaes 1992: 208).[32] One in every two German adults watched it – over twenty million people. WDR got 30,000 calls and thousands of letters – these were invited with an on-screen telephone number. Discussion shows followed the transmission of each episode and ran for hours. The German language acquired 'holocaust' as a neologism. Even more than *La Chagrin et la pitié* had been in France, *Holocaust*'s transmission was a crucial event in the vexed process of *Vergangenheitsbewältigung* for the Germans. In Britain, however, the series was dismissed. Dennis Potter famously began his *Sunday Times* review: 'Excuse me if I splash you with my vomit... ' He then went on to complain, with bitter cynicism, that, among many other deficiencies, the extras were all too fat (see Lawson 1994).[33]

Be all that as it may: by the 1980s it was widely felt that the archive's usefulness was approaching exhaustion. The Holocaust, and especially *die Endlösing*, had boxed the documentary filmmaker into a corner. The very violence depicted in the photographic record of one of history's most violent episodes was inhibiting its representation on the screen. Representations had an aesthetising effect, which was inhibiting Holocaust image circulation. It was this rather than any philosophical *Bilderverbot* which accounts for the comparative paucity of titles in the archive. A documentary filmmaker might want to 'wound' the audience into 'a new, more vivid awareness of what had taken place' (which was, for example, Lanzmann's intention according to Stuart Liebman (2007: 61)).[34] Nevermind whether or not images do, in any meaningful way, wound; for a filmmaker with such ambitions, audience distaste and dismissal was an very much immediate problem.

3. *NACH AUSCHWITZ...*

This is not to say that the issues implied by the *Bilderverbot* debate were not of equal importance. Lanzmann certainly held passionate views on this, as demonstrated by the quote that opens this chapter. That he feels unable to say why he would destroy such images of course does not echo Himmler's concept of '*takt*'. Rather it could be that he refers to a moral ban on using 'perpetrator' footage, especially that designed to demonstrate the degeneracy of the victims. In the same way, a prohibition inhibits the citation of the results of murderous 'scientific' medical experiments conducted in the concentration camps (see more below). To use such data as evidence makes one complicit, contaminated.

There is also the possibility that there are dangers in consuming footage of mass killings. I do not mean that screen violence begets actual violence in the straightforward manner experimental psychology has been trying, and failing, for the better part of a century to prove that it does. That exercise is tantamount to blaming the rustling of the leaves for causing the wind because imitative violence is a mark, rather than a cause of socio- or psychopathic behaviour. Rather, it is the possibility that not only was the event itself traumatic, it was so traumatic that even images of it can cause trauma vicariously, and not just to a socio- or psychopath.

Although this is, in mental health terms, an unproven hypothesis, certainly some research does suggest that, post-disaster, rescuers, carers and family of victims can vicariously suffer from post-traumatic stress disorder (PTSD) (see McCann and Perlman 1990: 142);[35] even journalists reporting such catastrophes can (see Winston 1996).[36] Of course, none of these are viewers and the evidence for seriously 'wounding' effects of speech remains elusive.

On the other hand, filmmakers who have reported their own stress when working on Holocaust films will have no difficult in appreciating this possibility. In my own case, I mark down the writing of the Holocaust script for Rosenthal the saddest and most disturbing task of my life. And, as pointed out above, it is a truism of early mass communications sociology that horrific messages are counter productive for the audience. On remembering her first sight of stills from Bergen-Belsen and Dachau, aged 12, Susan Sontag recalled: 'When I looked at those photographs, something broke. Some limit had been reached ... something went dead; something is still crying' (1990: 20).[37] It is, then, an implicit duty of care – that no harm be done to the viewer – which is what goes without saying.

But there is, of course, more to it than that. A person seeking to represent the Holocaust – filmmaker, novelist, journalist, artist of any kind – even if they are completely careless of the potentially harmful impact of their work, cannot, supposedly, hope to explain, much less capture, the experience of the Holocaust, however much vicarious trauma they might, or might not, inflict. 'There really is no word or means to capture the totality of the event' in Elie Wiesel's opinion (1985).[38] For some, it is beyond not only words and the realistic image, it is beyond imagination. '*Nach Auschwitz ein Gedicht zu schreiben ist babarisch*': 'To write poetry after Auschwitz is barbarous', as Theodor Adorno famously put it in an aphorism, possibly coined as a response to the very greatest of Holocaust poems, Paul Celan's *Todesfuge/Death Fugue* of 1947. The remark, though, has been commonly applied to more than poetry. Any attempt at representation – especially in popular mass media – is, if not barbaric, then certainly suspect because inadequate.[39]

The impossibility of representing the Holocaust is now something a received opinion, a strand in the 'tendency to privilege that cataclysmic event' (Lebow 2008: xvii); a compelling, if black, justification for the rhetoric of Jewish exceptionalism. Yet if other horrors and outrages, catastrophes and massacres, other genocides and cleansings continue to pile up (as Walter Benjamin imagined them doing at the feet of the Angel of History) – and they do, then the very claim of exceptionalism must be discarded.

And, I would suggest, with that goes the assertion that *die Endlösung* cannot be explained or effectively represented. For example, the particularly heinous behaviour of the doctors conducting murderous experiments in the camps can be explained in terms of public health. The victims were, literally, vermin in their eyes, a public health hazard which the Nazi medics had convinced themselves was in line with their general untoward medical responsibilities. Killing the mentally deficient, the disabled, homosexuals, communists, Jehovah's Witnesses, the Roma, the Ruthenes and the Jews, and so on, brought an added benefit in the name of increasing scientific knowledge (see Lifton 1986).[40] On the general point, Saul Friedlander, a major pillar in Holocaust Studies asserts, briskly: 'The extermination of the Jews of Europe is as accessible to both representation and interpretation as any other historical event' (1992b: 2).[41] But, as with any other event, there are boundaries, limits – as he also points out. Nevertheless the existence of the myriad of texts and artifacts across the whole gamut of expressive modes – from *Todesfuge* to *Shoah* – attest to the correctness of Friedlander's assertion. *Todesfuge* alone rescues poetry from the Holocaust.[42]

In sum, while there are issues involved in representing the Holocaust, it can be done and there is no overriding basis for a moral *Bilderverbot*. Lanzmann's strategy, for example, answers the problem of the contamination of the archive by ignoring it; and the result is the almost unanimous positive reception of his film. 'There is near unanimity that *Shoah* is a masterpiece' (Bathrick 2008: 10).[43]

Rarely has any film received the unqualified praise widely accorded *Shoah* ('brilliant' is a starting point for most comments), let alone a film about the Holocaust with the many pitfalls and tempting misdirections surrounding that subject. (Lang 2008: 76)

4. IS MORALITY A QUESTION OF HELICOPTER SHOTS?

The response to *Shoah* repaid Lanzmann for his years of effort, which had included being physically attacked by the family of a Nazi war criminal, which put him in hospital for eight days (see Liebman 2007: 63). The received opinion of *Shoah* nevertheless can be challenged. Lanzmann arguably has not actually solved the 'peculiarly acute dilemma' of the Holocaust documentary – not remotely.

His ethics as a filmmaker remain questionable. He is, it should not be forgotten, a journalist and his effectiveness as such speaks to certain ruthlessness: 'His is a direct, investigative, even combative strategy ... His style is aggressive, he takes no prisoners, lets no one off the hook' (Lebow 2008: 29). This is, in my view, just fine when he entraps, with or without a hidden camera, unrepentant Nazis or exposes the systemic anti-Semitism of contemporary Poles with *faux naïf* questioning. That speaks to the time-honoured journalistic imperative of 'afflicting the comfortable and comforting the afflicted'. For me, this is not the unethical behaviour of a documentarist but rather the admirable, legitimate inventiveness of the investigative journalist uncovering something I, and society, needs to know.

This is most emphatically not true of two of his interviews with survivors. In one, at Chelmno, where the killing began in mobile gas chambers on 7 December 1941, a day that should, indeed, as President Roosevelt said in another connection, 'live in infamy', Lanzmann allows a dozen or so elderly Poles to confront, indeed surround, Simon Sribnik, cheerfully detailing for Lanzmann how the Jews were killed. Sribnik is one of only two survivors of the camp and the Poles discuss him, whom they remember as a 13-year-old in leg-irons kept alive to sing for the entertainment of the SS, in the third person; as if he were a lost pet dog returned at last. They profess themselves to be delighted to see him. He stands uneasy and mute amongst them. Why does Lanzmann do this? Certainly not to gain information from Sribnik who says nothing. And it cannot be that he thought Sribnik's presence would encourage the Poles to, in effect, confess their complicity. No, this is a set-up worthy of a crass and reckless Reality Television producer seeking cheap sensation.

What he does with Abraham Bomba is even worse. Bomba, who was detailed to cut women's hair at Auschwitz as they waited to be gassed, is taken to a barber's shop in Tel Aviv where he pretends to cut a man's hair while Lanzmann grills him in excruciating detail as to how he performed this task. After nearly 15 minutes of this meaningless snipping accompanied by increasingly horrendous memories, Bomba, with a furtive glance at the camera, falls silent, broken. Lanzmann's response is to badger him. 'You have to', he tells Bomba, cajoling him eventually into continuing. My reaction is Potter's reaction to the mini-series *Holocaust*. Lanzmann's 'You have to...' is a blatant and outrageous lie. It is the last thing the man has to do. Rather, the imperative to have Bomba re-live the horror is Lanzmann's. He needs it for his film; whether Bomba, palpably distressed, needs to be (or run the risk of being) re-traumised is, to be charitable, an open question.

The justification for documenting trauma for an audience is to preserve memory and gain the experience of history; but this can only be done if the bearing of witness is therapeutic for the traumatised. It is hard to see how this was the case with either Sribnik or Bomba. These scenes are, in my opinion, as egregious examples of morally reprehensible behaviour as Flaherty's endangering of the Aran Islanders physically in the climactic storm sequence of *Man of Aran* (1934). That Lanzmann can then equate Bomba's distress, which he has engineered, with his own situation as a filmmaker is a final (dis)grace note: 'There was a fantastic tension for him and for me' (Lanzmann 1990b: 156).[45] To claim his distress is equivalent to a survivor's borders, for me, on the obscene.

Lanzmann's ethical lapses are, unfortunately, of an all too familiar kind but one does not have to buy into Holocaust exceptionalism to find them particularly offensive and irresponsible in this context. Not that he is without scruples. He recognises the possibility that there are things he should not be doing but – I confess I find this bizarre – these have to do with what he calls 'artistic' transgressions; an aerial shot, for example. To use an aerial shot in *Shoah* would be, apparently, to cross a moral boundary line. He thus, he reports, voiced strong objection to his cameraman's suggestion that they should get a helicopter shot of Chelmno to help the audience follow the geographic details of the interviews. 'This', says Lanzmann firmly, 'would have been a crime. A moral and an artistic crime' (1990b: 153).

This strident desire to distance himself from any charge of pictorialist indulgence is of a piece with Grierson's 'man against the sky' v. 'man in the bowels of the earth' rhetoric (see Grierson 1979: 64).[46] For Lanzmann, as for Grierson, the pictorial has to be avoided because it undercuts seriousness of purpose: cf 'exotic dirt'. The irony is that Lanzmann, like Grierson, fails to avoid this 'error'. The Griersonian archive is replete with exoticised images of slum, factory and mine; and *Shoah*, despite being prosaically shot, is nevertheless not so journalistic as to avoid the seductions of image-making. The film's 566 minutes[47] are sustained by many misty and mystic forestscapes, rutted tracks and, above all, trains – especially the evocative contemporary Polish steam trains, the romance of steam becoming repulsive in this context. Lanzmann is enough of a filmmaker to write *finis* to his film with this image.[48] Lanzmann's poetic shots, overall, are less effective in *Shoah* than those in, say, *Nuit et brouillard*; but that is only because Resnais is so much the greater filmmaker. Lanzmann was not really as hostile to the aesthetic as has been claimed and so Simone de Beauvoir was not wrong to talk of *Shoah*'s 'beauty and horror' in her review for *Le Monde* in 1985 (in Liebman 2007: 4). Raye Farr finds the landscapes 'starkly beautiful' (2005: 161).[49] Nor is Liebman out of order (although clearly over the top) to see *Shoah*'s opening sequence in which Simon Sribnik, is filmed being romantically punted down the Narwa river singing a Polish folk song as 'haunting': 'The simple images are imbued with an astonishing, almost mythic density as Sribnik, a modern incarnation of Orpheus crossing the River Styx, appears to call the dead back to life' (2007: 80). So much for anti-aesthetism.

In sum, then, Lanzmann, even as he demonstrates that the Holocaust can be represented, shows how flawed such representation is. As I have said, he only saves himself from the contaminations of the archive by ignoring it; but the viability of his personal *Bilderverbot* is compromised by his unethical proceedings. *Ostranenie* eludes him. As Alisa Lebow suggests: 'after nine-and-half obsessive hours, one realises that no amount of questioning will ever satisfy our unquenchable thirst for answers' (2008: 29).

My point, though, is not merely to criticise *Shoah*. Yes, Lanzmann's ethical faults are his alone. His manipulations and interventionism, though, are sanctioned by mainstream practice and the rest of these failings are not Lanzmann's, not *Shoah*'s alone, either. *Shoah*, in effect, sums up the strategies available for the realist Holocaust documentary and, one way or another, finds them wanting. These failings, plus the inevitable fetishising of surface which is the realistic image's doom, come with the territory. So, is this the end of the matter? Is the Holocaust, after all, beyond the documentary's reach?

5. 'BY INDIRECTION SEEK DIRECTIONS OUT'

I think not. *Shoah* does not mark an end point for the Holocaust documentary – not even for the use of realist images. There is, after all, more to be done than simply 'wounding' the audience into remembering. Of course, implied in the remembering is a subsumed objective: we remember to prevent recurrence. Prevention, however, requires the analysis of cause, which goes beyond remembering only to grieve. This objective is not necessarily best served by wounding memory, standing alone as despotised tragedy. A rhetoric which suggests the scope and horror of the *Shoah* cannot be comprehended as human disaster can obstruct analysis of it as an historical phenomenon. Given the freight that the realist image of the Holocaust has acquired, approaching the material with a more direct preventative analytic agenda requires avoiding the established tropes – the protuberant repertoire which begins with *Nuit et brouillard*. Doing so leads the filmmaker to other modes of representation, one that bring a necessary degree of *ostraninie*.

Like far too many others, Joram ten Brink, a scion of European Jewry, has his own family Holocaust saga, which was more fully discovered by him in the 1980s when examining his grandmother's papers. That generation of his family were protected, like the Franks in Amsterdam, by being hidden by a neighbour in her attic. As his name indicates, ten Brink's ancestors were a well-established northern Dutch family. In fact, they had lived there for more than three centuries. Yet it was not simply that he wished to commemorate the righteousness of the family's neighbours. His motivation was more immediately pressing. In the late 1980s Le Pen's anti-immigrant rhetoric in France was buying him considerable political support; ten Brink, appalled by this, was moved to recall his family's story as an indication of where such glib easy intolerance of the 'other' led.

In the film he made for Dutch television in 1989, *Jacoba*, he reconstructed his grandmother's story. In order to achieve a degree of *ostraninie*, he cast the descendants of his family's rescuer – the eponymous Jacoba – as his family. Jacoba's grandchildren, Christians, played ten Brink's grandmother, grandfather, father and great uncle, Jews. In other regards, too, he was at pains to reveal the past in the present as a way of drawing attention to intolerance as a contemporary clear and present danger. For example, he was deliberately not meticulous in the period detail of his reconstructions.[50] I would argue, because of these defamiliarisations, *Jacoba*'s hegemonic intention is achieved.

Other approaches to achieve *ostraninie* are also possible. The archives themselves are not static, limited to overused images. In fact, they have been growing through the accretion of witness statements and the recovery of material such as home movies, not least (but not only) via access to sources and people long contained behind the Iron Curtain. In the hands of Péter Forgács, say, this work of recovery is no mere matter of uncovering further illicit images of the Holocaust, which can then be used as a way of 'wounding' us into paying attention. In his films, which deal with 1939–45, images of the Holocaust are rare, overt images of violence rarer yet. They come to us, as with, for example, footage of a Jewish work camp taken by an inmate, in circumstances that defy explanation (*Az örvény/Free Fall*, 1996) (see Fisher 2008: 244).

What really matters, though, is the very domestic familiarity of the activities being filmed, which produces an effect of unbearable poignancy and doom – without a trace of explicit horror and without the danger of exposing or re-traumatising survivors. Paradoxically, Forgács films de-familiarise through the display of the familiar. Any need for a *Bilderverbot* is avoided – the subjects are, almost all, past our care; clearances, we are assured, have been obtained from the living, those who hold the original material. He exploits, not his subjects, but us, creating what he calls 'the tension of double knowledge. [...] To do this I needed to mobilise the viewer's existing historical knowledge but put it to a different end'; Forgács 'wounds' us into understanding by getting us 'to see the overall banalities of life during wartime' (Macdonald 2005: 314, 317).[51]

Repeatedly, the effect is devastating. Footage of a Dutch Jewish family, the Peereboms, packing, as if for a holiday, becomes an image of impending disaster. We know, and Forgács re-enforces that knowledge by detailing the items they are being allowed to take, and what their destination, Auschwitz, portends (*A Malestrom/The Maelstrom*, 1997). All images become images of doom, no matter their actual subject content. The context – the catastrophe inflicted on European middle-class life in the mid-twentieth century – dominates their meaning. The War and the Holocaust suffuse every frame. One longs to shout at the figures on the screen, as children by tradition are encouraged to shout at actors being threatened by a theatrical villain at an old-fashioned English Christmas pantomime: 'look behind you, look behind you!'

Ostranenie is not a consequence of happenstance, Forgács being merely a skilled – if not just consistently lucky – film researcher. He burrows, as he put it,

> beneath the surface of the home movies and amateur films I have access to, not because I want to patronize these films or see them merely as examples of some idea but because they reveal a level of history that is unrecorded in other kind of cinema. (In MacDonald 2005: 299)

Although a scrupulous historian as regards provenance and identifications, Forgács's practice is not otherwise bound by the protocols of the archivist. He is, in a way, no respecter of the integrity of original material. He reworks the archive, primarily through use of titles and tinting, with music, by manipulation of film running speeds and introduction of stop frames and occasional voice-over reciting legal ordinances and the like. The result is that 'these rescued images are imbued with uncanny historical resonances through a stunning display of Forgács's editorial élan' (Renov 2007: 21), augmented over twenty years and thirty films by composer Tibor Szemzo's music.

Forgács thereby prevents the footage being received as unmediated 'evidence' because of these interventions. He prevents them from misleading us, as, say, Frederic Wiseman's observationalism misleads through a spurious implied transparency. After all, beyond the accident of its survival, the material, however quotidian the events it depicts, is inevitably partial, untypical, as limited in view in its way as is the liberation footage. The home-movie archive represents the catastrophe inflicted on European life in the mid-twentieth century seen through the eyes of the economically privileged middle class who could afford the expensive hobby of home-moviemaking. We are, assuredly, not watching a species of surveillance camera. The amateur cameraman Max Peerebom might have shot a wild sea in peacetime but he did not intend it to be a presaging metaphor of the war that we know was soon to engulf the world on the screen. Forgács does that.

With Forgács and ten Brink, we are still in the realm of the realist image, still trapped on the surface, despite the deep resonances they create. There is, though, another totally non-realistic technique to consider.

Silence is an animated film and is therefore as different from *Shoah*, say, as any film on the Holocaust could be. For one thing it lasts only eleven minutes – and it is an animation. As Orly Yadin who co-produced and co-directed it with Sylvie Bringas, has pointed out: 'It contains no archival images of the Holocaust no shots of the locations where these events took place, and yet it is a documentary and a true story' (2005: 168).[52] Animation obviously can serve to achieve *ostranenie* and overcome the over-familiar, the protuberant.[53] It can also illustrate, concretise a *mentalité*.[54] The question arises, though, 'is it a documentary?' to use the title of her article.

This question counter-balances Lanzmann's claim that *Shoah* is not a documentary because 'scenes in it are staged and rehearsed' (1990b: 295). Lanzmann raises a sterile definitional issue that would seem to be grounded in the usual journalistic ignorance of documentary aesthetics and history (see Farr 2005: 162). Seemingly seduced by Direct Cinema's *dogme*, Lanzmann appears to be taking a view of documentary which denies legitimacy to anything but the observational in its Direct Cinema mode. Remembering *Nanook of the North* (1922), we need not be detained by this. And Yadin's doubts about the documentary status of *Silence* need not detain us either. *Shoah* and *Silence* are both documentaries.

Documentary film has always embraced the possibility of reconstructing images to match testimony. In *Nanook of the North*, Flaherty not only conspired with Allakarialuk to capture on film typical Inuit activities. The more dramatic incidents actually illustrate testimony – the walrus-hunt he learned about from an Inuit called Omarolluk; the impossible sledding across the pack-ice, the seal-hunt and the race to the deserted igloo happened to an Inuit called Comock (or Koomak) whom Flaherty met in 1912. These Inuit and others provided Flaherty with the prior witness essential to preserving the documentary value of reconstructed material.

On the basis of this precedent, can animation be a legitimate technique to illustrate the reconstruction of prior witness? Certainly it has been an albeit rare but not unknown strategy from Windsor McKay's fact-based animation, *The Sinking of the Lusitania* in 1916 on. So why should a soundtrack of the memoire of Tana Ross, who survived the war in Therienstadt, hidden from the Germans by her grandmother, not provide the testimony to vouchsafe *Silence*'s documentary value? I would claim this is a legitimate documentary soundtrack and illustrating it by animation a legitimate documentary strategy.

Illustrating the memoire posed a particularly vexed problem not unlike that facing Art Spiegelman when grappling with representing his father's experience as a survivor. Spiegelman, reflecting a 1980s sense of exhaustion with the *Nuit et brouillard* approach, felt he needed to avoid 'some kind of odd plea for sympathy or "Remember the Six Million"' (quoted in Huyssen 2001: 34).[55] In his hands, *ostranenie* took the form of a comic book with predator Nazi cats exterminating Jewish mice (*Maus*, 1986). 'I resist', said Spiegelman, 'becoming the Elie Wiesel of the comic book' (in Huyssen 2001: 28). This is not just an issue of *Bilderverbot*. Yadin and Bringas had early decided to avoid the horrific drawn image, just as Spiegleman did; or others, notably Lanzmann, did in eschewing the horrendous photographic one (see Lingford and Webb 2005: 173).[56] Nor was the problem lack of archive.[57] The real difficulty was that Ross was not simply recalling what had happened. She was concerned to share a question, one that had haunted her emotionally for fifty years. Could her family in unoccupied Sweden have rescued her as others with Swedish relatives had been rescued? It was this suppressed idea in her mind which demanded representation:

> I was not interested in filming yet another interview with a survivor talking about events she experienced at a much younger age. So, I kept on saying no to the idea of making a film. Tana, however, was persistent. She was determined to end her silence, but didn't want to face an audience herself. (Yadin 2005: 168)

(Which – given, say, the Bomba interview in *Shoah* – is entirely understandable on her part, just as one can understand her contrary pressing imperative to bear witness.)

Yadin counts among the advantages of the animation the fact that it involves no journalistic subterfuge of transparency, no voyeurism and, positively, of course it allows the visualisation of what she calls the 'unreachable'. Moreover, because of its history as a technique for children's film, an animation on so serious a subject as the Holocaust automatically de-familiarises its subject matter. *Silence* seizes this possibility. Yadin and Bringas worked with two animators. One, Ruth Lingford used a stark black and white woodcut style for the camp half of the film; the other, Tim Webb, drew a colourful children's cartoon for the Swedish half. Tana Ross, born in 1940 in Berlin and liberated as a five-year old, is among the youngest of Holocaust survivors. Her insight is of the very young child. The infant's perspective is a different order to that of other survivors', even other somewhat older young witnesses', testimony. Animation brilliantly allows the filmmakers to visualise her infantile memory of the nightmare.

Silence has moments of blinding illumination. That the Nazis justified their bestiality by treating the existence of their victims as a species of health hazard is summed up in seconds as scurrying black figures morph into insects being swept up by an enormous broom.[58] A child's traumatised horror of all adults is captured when a uniformed Swedish railway man morphs into a menacing armed SS man and back again. *Silence*, indeed, makes the Holocaust new and it does so at no moral or ethical cost. It also allows us to understand a child's sense of betrayal by her own people. Yadin writes, as a provocation: 'Animation can be the most honest form of documentary filmmaking.' I do not believe this is just a provocation. *Silence* demonstrates its truth. That is why I think it is amongst the most telling Holocaust films.

There is one simple answer to the problem of illustrating *die Endlösing*. Not that it cannot be done, but that, as Forgács, ten Brink, Yadin and Bringas demonstrate, it must be done by obeying Hamlet's injunction 'by indirection seek directions out'. *Ca va de soi.*

NOTES

I wish to thank Alisa Lebow her help in preparing this chapter.

1   'And if I found a film existed – a secret film because it was strictly forbidden – shot by a member of the SS and showing how 3,000 Jews, men, women and children died together, suffocated in a gas chamber in crematorium II in Auschwitz, if I found that not only would I not have shown it but I would have destroyed it. I can't say why. It goes without saying.'

2   Quoted in T. Haggith and J. Newman (eds) (2005) *Holocaust and the Moving Image: Representations in Film and Television Since 1933*. London: Wallflower Press, 15.

3   The possibility that the material was reconstructed by DEFA in East Germany post-war has been suggested (see S. Bardgett (2005) 'Film and the Making of the Imperial War Museum's Holocaust Exhibition', in T. Haggith and J. Newman (eds) *Holocaust and the Moving Image: Representations in Film and Television Since 1933*. London: Wallflower Press, 25 n.1) but Raye Fare (USHMM) believes it to be authentic with a full history of how it was shot, processed and preserved attested to by Wiener in an interview (via personal communication). Wiener deposited a copy with Yad Vashem, while the film remains copyrighted to Mrs Henny Weiner, presumably a relative of the cameraman. Stuart Liebman suggests that Claude Lanzmann, for *Shoah*, interviewed the cameraman, but did not finally include him, but this was a different Wiener; see S. Liebman (2007) 'An Introduction to Claude Lanzmann's *Shoah*', in booklet issued with *Shoah* DVD, Masters of Cinema Series. Incidentally, USHMM gives 1'42" as the running time. See also R. Farr (2005) 'Some Reflections on Claude Lanzmann's Approach to the Examination of the Holocaust', in T. Haggith and J. Newman (eds) *Holocaust and the Moving Image: Representations in Film and Television Since 1933*. London: Wallflower Press, 161– 7.

4   J. Hirsch (2004) *Afterimage: Film, Trauma, and the Holocaust*. Philadelphia: Temple University Press.

5   P. Haidu (1992) 'The Dialectics of Unspeakability' in S. Friedlander (ed.) (1992) *Probing the Limits of Representation: Nazism and the 'Final Solution'*. Cambridge, MA: Harvard University Press, 277–99.

6   L. Rees (2005) '*The Nazis: A Warning from History*' in T. Haggith and J. Newman (eds) *Holocaust and the Moving Image: Representations in Film and Television Since 1933*. London: Wallflower Press, 146–53.

7   P. Levi (1961) *Survival in Auschwitz*, trans. Stuart Woolf. New York: Macmillan.

8   E. Cowie (2005) 'Seeing and Hearing for Ourselves: The Spectacle of Reality in the Holocaust Documentary', in T. Haggith and J. Newman (eds) *Holocaust and the Moving Image: Representations in Film and Television Since 1933*. London: Wallflower Press, 189.

9   See the Rodney King case for a most vivid demonstration of this point; see B. Winston (2008) *Claiming the Real II: The Documentary Grierson and After*. London: British Film Institute/Palgrave Macmillan, 142–3.

10 Michael Chanan warns (via personal communication) that this word and its synonyms (e.g. 'distortion') need to be used with care so as not to give the erroneous impression that undistorted images are possible.

11 M. Hirst (2003) *Jurisdiction and the Ambit of the Criminal Law*. Oxford: Oxford University Press, 34.

12 See M. Renov (2007) 'Away from Copying: The Art of Documentary Practice' in G. Pearce and C. McLaughlin (eds) *Truth or Dare/Art and Documentary*. Fishponds: Intellect, 13–24; and J. Fisher (2008) 'Peter Forgács's Free Fall into the Holocaust', in D. Bathrick, B. Prager and M. Richardson (eds) (2008) *Visualizing the Holocaust: Documents, Aesthetics, Memory*. Rochester, NY: Camden House, 239–60.

13 Better known by its later title: *Der Führer Schenkt den Juden Eine Stadt/The Fuhrer Presents a Town to the Jews*.

14 In the course of his research for his film *Tango of Slaves* (1994).

15 See H. Arendt (1955) *Elemente und Ursprünge totaler Herrschaft*. Frankfurt: Eoropäische Verlangsanstalt, 219.

16 T. Haggith (2005) 'Filming the Liberation of Bergen-Belsen', in T. Haggith and J. Newman (eds) *Holocaust and the Moving Image: Representations in Film and Television Since 1933*. London: Wallflower Press, 33–49.

17 A. Lebow (2008) *First Person Jewish*. Minneapolis: University of Minnesota Press.

18 In his analysis of the Bergen-Belsen footage, Toby Haggith notes that some British cameramen (all holding the rank of sergeant) described the camp inmates as 'zombies' or 'ragdolls' on the written dope-sheets they prepared. ('Dope-sheets' term the camera operators' written notes to identify undeveloped material for processing and editing) (2005: 43–4). While Haggith makes quite clear the extent of the enormous impact the experience had on these men and their overall sympathy for the inmates and hostility to the Nazi guards, I want to add one small personal comment to balance the impression perhaps created by his reference to the dope-sheets. One of these men became a well-known BBC reporter/cameraman in the late 1950s, Slim Hewitt. He was an important pioneer in 16mm sync-sound filming with whom I had the privilege of working on *24 Hours* in the following decade. Slim once told

me that, while filming in Bergen-Belsen, he had fallen deeply in love with a survivor – obviously for him she was neither a zombie nor a ragdoll. The relationship did not survive those days in the camp except, vividly, in his memory. Slim died in 1987.

19 B. Winston (1973) *Dangling Conversations: The Image of the Media*. London: David-Poynter.

20 See J. Ivens (1969) *The Camera and I*. New York: International Publishers, 87.

21 N. King (1981) 'Recent "Political" Documentary: Notes on *Union Maids* and *Harlan County, USA*', *Screen*, 22, 2, 7; originally said of *Harlan County, USA* (1976) where the filmmaker, Barbara Kopple, was also attacked, shot at on camera, by strike-breaking thugs while making her documentary.

22 Yet, to his eternal credit, he had written a script which so universalised the *Shoah* that some voices objected to the film's lack of specific reference to anti-Semitism; for example, see J. Petersen (2006) 'A Little Known Classic: *Night and Fog* in Britain', in E. van der Knapp (ed.) *Uncovering the Holocaust: The International Reception of Night and Fog*. London: Wallflower Press, 106–28. 111.

23 E. van der Knapp (2006) 'Tracing (Holocaust) Memory and Re-reading Memory Matters', in E. van der Knapp (ed.) *Uncovering the Holocaust: The International Reception of Night and Fog*. London: Wallflower Press, 165–72.

24 In Germany, for example when the film was finally widely seen on television in 1978, its impact 'eclipsed all other films on the same subject with its enormous power'. Its *court-métrage* length, at just over 30", also aided its educational use; see E. van der Knapp (2006) 'Enlightening Procedures: *Nacht und Nebel* in Germany', in E. van der Knapp (ed.) *Uncovering the Holocaust: The International Reception of Night and Fog*. London: Wallflower Press, 46–85.

25 A. Rosenthal (2000) *Jerusalem Take One: Memoirs of a Jewish Filmmaker*. Carbondale, IL: Southern Illinois University Press.

26 A. Resnais (1994) excerpts of audio interview for *Les Étoiles du cinéma* included on the Criterion Collection DVD release *Nuit et brouillard* (2003).

27 Stevens had made one of the earliest 'evidential' liberation compilation documentaries, *Nazi Concentration Camps* (USA, 1945).

28 See, for example, the extensive filmography in T. Haggith and J. Newman (eds) *Holocaust and the Moving Image: Representations in Film and Television Since 1933*. London: Wallflower Press, 288–95; or in D. Bathrick, B. Prager and M. Richardson (eds) (2008) *Visualizing the Holocaust: Documents, Aesthetics, Memory*. Rochester, NY: Camden House.

29 For example: *Den Blodiga Tiden/The Bloody Time* (1960, Sweden, dir. Erwin Leiser) but this, typically, eschews the most traumatic images of *Nuit et brouillard* in the short section it devotes to the Holocaust; as do even those with prurient tag-lines such as the curious *After Mein Kampf* of 1961 which deals with Nazi indoctrination of the German people.

30 E. Morin (1985) 'Chronicle of a Summer', *Studies in Visual Communication*, 2, 1, 1–37.

31 J. Hirsch (2004) *Afterimage: Film, Trauma, and the Holocaust*. Philadelphia: Temple University of Press.

32 A. Kaes (1992) 'Holocaust and the End of History', in S. Friedlander (ed.) *Probing the Limits of Representation: Nazism and the 'Final Solution'*. Cambridge, MA: Harvard University Press, 206–22.

33 Edgar Reitz, whose TV series *Heimat* (1984), a species of response to *Holocaust*, attacks the

American series, somewhat more sinisterly than does Potter, by claiming *Holocaust's* aesthetics were the 'real terror' of the twentieth century; see E. Santer (1992) 'History beyond the Pleasure Principle', in S. Friedlander (ed.) *Probing the Limits of Representation: Nazism and the 'Final Solution'*. Cambridge, MA: Harvard University Press, 143–54. This sort of remark chimes with the right-wing rhetoric that was fuelling the *Historikerstreit* – a conflict among West German intellectuals, provoked by an attempt to equate Stalin's Gulag with the Holocaust – in the 1980s. Reitz's remark chimes with Lanzmann's concept of the aesthetic 'crime'.

34 S. Liebman (2007) 'An Introduction to Claude Lanzmann's *Shoah*', booklet issued with *Shoah* DVD, Masters of Cinema Series.

35 L. McCann and L. A. Pearlman (1990) 'Vicarious Traumatization: A Framework for Understanding the Psychological Effects of Working with Victims', *Journal of Traumatic Stress*, 3, 1, 131–49.

36 B. Wnston (1996) 'No wimps in Wanatchee', *British Journalism Review*, 6, 32–5.

37 Sontag, S. (1990) *On Photography*. New York: Anchor Books.

38 E. Wiesel (1985) 'A survivor remembers other survivors of the Shoah', *New York Times*, 3 November, quoted in R. Farr (2005) 'Some Reflections on Claude Lanzmann's Approach to the Examination of the Holocaust', in T. Haggith and J. Newman (eds) *Holocaust and the Moving Image: Representations in Film and Television Since 1933*. London: Wallflower Press, 161– 7.

39 Subsequently, Adorno backtracked on this opinion; see T. Adorno (2003) *Can One Live After Auschwitz?* Stanford: Stanford University Press, xvi. Anyway, it is clear from the outset that he never intended it to be understood as a more general statement of difficulty. That, however, is what the remark has commonly come to mean. See also DeKoven Ezrahi, S. (1992) 'The Grave in the Air', in S. Friedlander (ed.) *Probing the Limits of Representation: Nazism and the 'Final Solution'*. Cambridge, MA: Harvard University Press, 259–76.

40 R. J. Lifton (1986) *The Nazi Doctors: Medical Killing and the Psychology of Genocide*. New York: Basic Books.

41 S. Friedlander (1992) 'Introduction', in S. Friedlander (ed.) *Probing the Limits of Representation: Nazism and the 'Final Solution'*. Cambridge, MA: Harvard University Press.

42 Celan had translated Cayrol's commentary for the German-language version of *Nuit et brouillard*; see Kligerman, E. (2008) 'Celan's Cinematic: Anxiety of the Gaze in *Night and Fog* and "Engführung"', in D. Bathrick, B. Prager and M. Richardson (eds) *Visualizing the Holocaust: Documents, Aesthetics, Memory*. Rochester, NY: Camden House, 185–210.

43 D. Bathrick (2008) 'Introduction: Seeing Against the Grain', in D. Bathrick, B. Prager and M. Richardson (eds) (2008) *Visualizing the Holocaust: Documents, Aesthetics, Memory*. Rochester, NY: Camden House, 1–20.

44 B. Lang (2008) 'Review: *Claude Lanzmann's Shoah: Key Essays* (Stuart Liebman ed.)' *Cineaste*, 33, 4, 76.

45 C. Lanzmann (1990) 'Seminar with Claude Lamzmann, April 11' in booklet issued with *Shoah* DVD, Masters of Cinema Series (2007).

46 J. Grierson (1979) *On Documentary*. Ed. F. Hardy. London: Faber and Faber.

47 The UK running time. In the US it was released with 1 hour and 3 minutes excised.

48 And, of course, the film is now branded by the image of the train driver, leaning out of his engine.

49 R. Farr (2005) 'Some Reflections on Claude Lanzmann's Approach to the Examination of the Holocaust' in T. Haggith and J. Newman (eds) *Holocaust and the Moving Image: Representations in Film and Television Since 1933*. London: Wallflower Press, 161–7.

50 This can create a measure of ethical difficulty. In the *Heritage* episode, a lengthy (for mainstream television) description of the successive waves of anti-Jewish legislation passed by the Nazis is illustrated with contemporary 1980s footage. Thus, for instance, the degree forbidding Jews to use trains is illustrated by shots of a modern train. The danger is that this improperly imputes guilt to today's Germans; the advantage is that it makes the clear and present dangers of intolerance more real for the audience. It is not just a matter of history.

51 S. MacDonald (2005) *A Critical Cinema 4: Interviews with Independent Film Makers*. Berkeley: University of Californai Press.

52 O. Yadin (2005) 'But is it a Documentary?', in T. Haggith and J. Newman (eds) *Holocaust and the Moving Image: Representations in Film and Television Since 1933*. London: Wallflower Press, 168–72.

53 I have in mind Aardman Animation's use of actuality interviews with disabled people as a soundtrack for *Creature Discomforts*, a 2007 series of television advertisements made for the Leonard Cheshire Disability charity. Chair-bound lobsters, birds, hedgehogs, a deaf cat and a visually impaired lizard forced us to see afresh what we might usually ignore (see Winston 2008: 281).

54 *Animated Minds* (Andy Glynne, UK, 2003), a series of four animations, for example, uses a variety of non-realistic, somewhat avant-garde techniques to illustrate testimony from mentally ill patients describing their condition. (The use of actuality audio recording as a soundtrack was pioneered by animators John and Faith Hubbley who won an Academy Award in 1959 for their film *Moonbird*. They had secretly recorded their young children's bedtime fantasising which they then visualised in the animation.)

55 A. Huyssen (2001) 'Of Mice and Mimesis', in B. Zeliser (ed.) *Visual Culture and the Holocaust*. London: The Althone Press, 28–42.

56 R. Lingford and T. Webb (2005) '*Silence*': The Role of the Animators', in T. Haggith and J. Newman (eds) *Holocaust and the Moving Image: Representations in Film and Television Since 1933*. London: Wallflower Press, 173–4.

57 Although the most obvious source, *Der Führer Schenkt den Juden Eine Stadt/The Fuhrer Presents a Town to the Jews*, is the most egregious, propagandistic example of the official Nazi film.

58 A criticism of Spiegelman is that his cat and mouse metaphor echoes the Nazi equating of the Jews with vermin, e.g. in Frtiz Hippler's notorious (and very poorly and boringly made) documentary, *Der erwige Jude/The Eternal Jew* (1940). This reading, though, simply fails to see 'how Spiegelman's mimetic adoption of Nazi imagery actually succeeds in reversing its implications' (Huyssen 2001: 34). The Nazis had forgotten the status of the treatment of mice as a measure of tolerance. 'I promise you' says a father admonishing his cruel son in a bestselling children's book of 1783, 'the smallest creature can feel as acutely as you. I never knew a man that was cruel to animals and compassionate towards his fellow creatures' (in J. Lamb (2009) *The Evolution of Sympathy in the Long Eighteenth Century*. London: Pickering & Chatto, 70–1.

SCREEN MEMORY IN *WALTZ WITH BASHIR*

Garrett Stewart

A cartoon anti-war movie? In Avi Folman's *Waltz with Bashir* (2008), given an Israeli combat plot cast into flashback within an animated story of post-traumatic stress disorder and memory loss, what kind of hurdles to political conviction or even good taste does this animation erect? Or what ironies release? Following on from all the contemporary war films about American incursions in Kuwait, Iraq and Afghanistan (with the digital blitz of their high-tech quasi-documentary treatment),[1] what is *Waltz with Bashir* after in returning us not just to a former Middle East bloodshed, but to the literal drawing board?

Despite assumptions in the press, there is no rotoscoping (digital tracing) involved. The technique is 'cut-out animation', with the videotaped movements of real actors used as rough models for the 'animatics' of a 'videoboard' whose subdivided jigsaw shapes are only then fed into a computer programme that calibrates the sectored rhythms of human movement. Though the level of kinetic detail has been limited (as Folman explains on the DVD commentary) by his electronic production budget, such constraints are in fact cashed out stylistically, with the film's troubled bodies, heavy with dream and guilt, wading through a lurid quagmire of deflected memory. The nightmarish atmosphere is offset by such hyper-cinematic gestures as warp-speed transitions between Dutch and Israeli locales or battleground overviews higher than any crane shot, steadier than any helicopter pan. In line with the developing ironies of psychic artifice in the film, these effects are not just associated with surrogate visual memories; they are surrogate cinema.

Twenty-five years after serving as a teenager in the Israeli army during the early 1980s occupation of Beirut, a middle-aged director sets out to discover why he has so completely blocked the memory of a notorious massacre of Arab civilians carried out by Israeli allies, the Christian Phalangists, in reprisal against the assassination of the newly elected Lebanese President Bashir Gemayel. Only later in the film does a friend suggest that the director, Folman, must have distanced his role in this whole operation from the start, since policing the Palestinian camps, let alone facilitating a mass extermination, would have been intolerable for a child of Auschwitz survivors to reflect upon. Rather than see himself as a Nazi, he took refuge in illusion.

But his private mirages are hard to sort out from the toxic phantasmagoria of combat, which, according to Folman, assaults the mind like 'a bad acid trip'. Right from the start, the film's palette is eerily acidic. The animators have found just the right sulfuric glow for the delirium and mayhem. With a gangrene orange saturating one bombed-out urban space after another like a stain rather than a hue, bodies flow past in their fragile animation as if struggling to keep life in their limbs. And in contrast to the shell-shocked canvas of metropolitan Beirut, we get the occasional beachside or sylvan respite exploded by violence. In one of the most mordantly gorgeous episodes, we look on at a sun-speckled forest ambush in which, with a web of shadows turning Israeli uniforms into a balletic animated camouflage, a pre-teen Arab boy comes out of hiding to fire a rocket grenade straight through our line of sight into an approaching tank.

In a film about scrambled memories painfully drawn out of hiding, Folman's narrative is especially difficult to remember in the exact order of its realist flashbacks and its delusional cover stories. As a psychic topography, it amounts less to an autobiographical through-line than to the layering of a collective unconscious. The surreal opening nightmare of ravening dogs unleashed on an Israeli street sets the pattern for subsequent flashbacks sprung from the separate monologues of former soldiers. The friend who tells the director of this recurrent dream explains how he was too green a recruit to be trusted with killing enemy combatants, so he was assigned instead to the shooting of dozens of dogs to prevent their warning yelps. Plunging us unprepared into the gruesome nightmare that haunts him years later, the film thus begins in anticipation of its own dead end: a howling revenge for the slain that will later, when fantasy has been scoured away, emerge as an accusatory human chorus of mourners.

In the next interview, we see in flashback another friend's escape from seasickness into the absurdist vision of a giant naked woman on whose breast, maternal and erotic at once, he floats off while the rest of the crew is bombed. Based on second-hand reports like this, the climactic revelation for the Folman character is that a languid swimming episode in the pre-dawn, flare-lit sea, his one recurrent flashback, is a defensive fiction as anaesthetising and desolate as it looks.

This is the spectral leitmotif that erupts at three separate points, less often than one might remember, and not with the echoing of a charm but as its own gradual exorcism. Neither of the two friends rising naked with him from his remembered Mediterranean interlude zombie-like but still armed, recalls the event at all. Locating him outside the circuit of killing in this alternate picture of male camaraderie, Folman's numbed skinny-dipping fantasy is of course as much a libidinal sublimation of carnal violence as is that other soldier's hallucination of sea-borne feminine salvage: each a regressive fantasy at once oceanic, laving and amniotic – as well as an amphibious flight from the nightmare of all those boots on the ground. In this somnambulism of disengagement, Folman goes night-bathing with his buds while others conduct the bloodbath – only for him to remain, afterwards, quite at sea about the facts this fiction has kept submerged. Denaturalised further by the unnerving electronic score (Max Richter's accompanying music is entitled 'The Haunted Ocean'), such are the condensations and displacements of the traumatic unconscious in the protective mind's eye.

These figurative means for keeping himself in the dark, his guilt at bay, stand in contrast to alternate visual mediations familiar in part from other recent war films and their ubiquitous digital replays of Middle East violence. Certainly every chance *Waltz with Bashir* gets, it throws the chromatic and somatic estrangement of its own animation effects into relief against the recessed treatment of other media, regularly dropped back into black-and-white format so as to forefront the alternate intensity of the prevailing narrative mode. Like zones of grisaille monochrome cordoned off in oil painting, these include everything from an aerial surveillance monitor tracking a self-guided missile in the bombing of an Arab neighborhood, through black-and-white photos repeatedly pinned-up in the background of separate interview sessions, to an abrupt detour into the exaggerated historical fidelity of pre-colour treatment to animate a World War II anecdote about furloughs from the Russian front. Then, during Folman's own bleak leave in Haifa, there are alternating broadcast images of a political harangue and a rock video on a storefront's bank of TV monitors, all the screens blaring in their own anachronistic version of jittery black-and-white focus. These appear just before he passes a video arcade and sees, in full colour this time, a *Desert Patrol* war game, exactly the garish digital simulation of combat pyrotechnics that the cautionary animation of his own film rejects.

The building impact of these embedded photomechanical and electronic mediations helps orient an extended filmic conceit about psychological blockage. When Folman consults a trauma specialist, she mentions another soldier who, being 'an amateur photographer' before the Lebanon War, staved off the 'horror' of its carnage by the 'dissociative' maneuvre of seeing everything – through an 'imaginary camera' – as a parade of merely 'great scenes'. At just this point in her monologue, we get a series of separate animated rectangles decelerated to a graphic novel's equivalent of cinematic freeze-frames. Reverting to the single drawings that underlie the narrative's whole technique, these combat shots turn the postures of a continuous battlefield tension and ravage into instantaneous poses. 'Then one day the camera broke', says the psychologist in voice-over. Suddenly a dozen or so still shots rush by in a vertical file with sprocket noise accompanying the 35mm roll, as if serial record were clutching at filmic motion in the moment of its dysfunction.

Indeed the psychiatrist's own terms have slipped, across a simile, from photography to movie-going, for her patient 'had used a mechanism to remain outside events, like watching a film' of the war rather than participating in it. Completing this photomechanical emblem, the last two frames of the broken roll don't just flutter past but settle into place to reveal moving images in their own right, one animated miniature screen on top of the other. Once the prophylactic 'mechanism' has broken down, the perils of real time seem to be breaking through. Even the smallest increments of the track register an involuntary index of history in passing: the tattered banner at the Beirut Hippodrome flapping overhead to the left of each jammed, stacked frame. No matter how much the mind tries to lock down such disturbing pictures, their incrimination will return from the repressed, in this case precipitating a long panning shot across a circus of horror strewn with the bodies of slaughtered 'Arabian' horses – until we close on the convex blur of a fly-swarmed eye, where an anonymous soldier sees his own reflection in death's brute anamorphosis.

This pitiable instance of shot/reverse-shot in the same organic lens points straight – along a similar ocular axis – to the exchanged points of view at the film's close. On the way there, and to complete the motif of the dead eye, we hear of a hellish urban hinterland known as the 'slaughterhouse', where everything is 'like an LSD trip', including the spectacle this time of human rather than equine Arab bodies viciously desecrated, their organs and limbs exchanged in macabre triumph. No sooner is this memory dispatched on the soundtrack by another interviewed soldier that we see, sped past as if in revulsion by the camera itself, the gouged-out retinal globe and optic nerves of a swollen eyeball in a formaldehyde jar.

Following this monstrous flashback, the final interview with a renowned TV journalist, who was formerly there on the scene in Lebanon, summons the image of his cameraman crawling along on the ground in front of him to keep beneath the line of fire. With 'women, children and old people' crowding the high-rise balconies, the seasoned reporter was stunned to see them watch the gun battle raging around him in real time 'as if it were a film'. But when the kind of video footage his crew was actually there to record is shown to us in the end, it seizes attention with the disjunctive force not of a film but of unmediated recall. Here is on-site video retrieved from the vaults – but no longer the tomb – of memory and made present, as if in its original sighting, to Folman himself at last. Burst through the labours of animated reconstruction is the true archive of terror – and the final trope of recognition. You had to have been there. The trouble is that Folman was – and must now take up the video image by proxy as his own admitted view.

To earn its culminating disclosure, *Waltz with Bashir* must of course dismantle the screen memory of those naked swimmers safely adjourned from the murders and all but drowning out their guilt under cover of darkness. In each repetition of this shielding fantasy so far, the three men return to the morning streets still buttoning up their fatigues, with the Folman character leading them straight toward the camera. At that point, however, alone in the frame this third time, he turns a corner past posters of Bashir and finds his line of motion slowed by a procession of grieving women in pantomime, their wails symptomatically dialed out by the electronic score. Though in reverse directions, paths visibly intersect. He is already in the thick of things. But this isn't 'factual' either, any more than was his enervated idyll in the sea, from whose false dawn he must awake. Both the lulling retreat, bracketed off from political reality, and his return to the fray in the aftermath of violence is linked cover stories. The actual reality lies between, rests in fact on a more candid marking – and impossible bridging – of the admitted *distance* between: a distance more rigorously acknowledged at last, even while being visually traversed in the closing camera movement. What memory has involuntarily spliced together of this sundered experience until then – the defensive sea dream and the terror that still infiltrates it – is their final disjunction, where Folman must recognise himself not immersed in suffering but confronted by it from his own official if rapidly vanishing distance.

Folman knows now that he was always present at the atrocities, but only on the outskirts, standing guard with fellow Israeli soldiers at the perimeter of the camps, *looking the other way* during the orgy of executions. With the beach fantasy shattered, its closing interpenetration of on-duty hero and the inexorable tread of Arab grief is replayed finally at the truer remove of his disengaged complicity: that of an emotionally detached onlooker forced finally to see – and, by suddenly direct sound, to hear. On the brink of recovered memory, he is separated now across the gulf of a rapidly telescoped long shot. Animation again generates a hyper-cinematic effect, a preternatural tracking shot burrowing through the train of bereft women with more precision than any Steadicam, closing by its own force the distance between their virtual funeral march and Folman's sentinel duty in the distance. The intervening and despoiled no-man's land, previously elided in the dream's commingling of Folman and the suffering women, here yawns between them to mark the breached gap – across time as well as space – between a censored private vision and the returned look of mass grief.

Closing upon the formerly glazed eyes of denial, the pinioning camera bores in on a prolonged close-up of Folman in his emerging awareness – until the abrupt reverse-shot seems to echo and complete, in an analogous vector, the early assault of the Arab rocket in our direct line of sight. By this point, however, it is any remaining screen of fantasy that is exploded on contact with the approaching spectacle of pain. Overtly yanking him back to the aftermath of slaughter as it actually transpired, we see as if through his eyes a montage of 1982 documentary images of bereavement, then death itself. There is nothing knee-jerk in the resulting spasm of ocular recoil. The shock is knowingly twofold – and first of all in its visual letdown. Until now we've never seen screen images like *Waltz with Bashir*'s, whereas we've seen all too much Middle East affliction on TV. Throwing us back on the too familiar, the sudden visual privation is as barren as it appears.

But in no way facile or anodyne. There is no formal capitulation to routine *verité*, as some reviewers have objected, in this plummet through a hyperbolic, computer-assisted imaginary to the analogue real; nothing pat about the 180-degree turn from show-stopping graphics to a straightforward graphic violence. After all the animated soul-searching close-ups, there must, at any aesthetic cost, be real faces looking back. And a fact faced – no longer masked or countenanced. After all the artful pains taken to picture the veils of repression, the actual pain: real mourners and – following that sound video – real corpses as if beginning to disintegrate in an even grainier file of soundless and nearly still frames, none of them 'great' shots at all, let alone photographic buffers against the event. After the screams of grief, its cause: absolute final silence. After so much animation, and our gradual acclimation to its spooky allure, its opposite in rank death.

We don't know for sure who took these documentary images, if or when they were ever broadcast, whether or not they correspond to what Folman was positioned to see on the scene. All we know is that, in the mental recognition they emblemise by the initial eye-line match of this distended reverse-shot, the agonies they index are now meant to be, as they once weren't, felt. By their insistence – over against an animated image to whose mode of visualisation we never return – the Folman figure has been taken finally, and the film with him, beyond the cartoon world of his deferred witness and the earlier phantasms of his self deceit. In a jolt to our vision as well, a decisive shock of recognition, past atrocity is rerun as full-frame recall.

Screen memory gets erased form within by video trace. But the pivotal wrench of transition has been dialectical rather than reductive, let alone cathartic. Documentation dislodging fantasy turns fantasy itself into a document of disavowal, the superseding archival footage into a ghostly apparition – as much a haunting by history as its straightforward record. Though cut loose from actuality over the course of the film, an unconscious screening-out of one's guilt is no less true than the archived bloodshed it papers over with the desperately etched imagery of denial. The retreat to virtuality (and its techniques of animation) is therefore as much a record of the ordeal, in its psychic response, as is the video transcript of flailing misery. Together they are the truth of trauma, spelled out as such only in collision – and searing aural overlap – in these final moments, whose dialectical clash pictures each in the other's terms.

Prerecorded human sounds, mostly articulate voices, have anchored the film's recovered memories throughout, though usually suspended in the episodes of hallucination. In the last sequence, the keening grief of the approaching women is on the track (for the first time in this third iteration of their image) well before we enter the assailed vision of the hero, switching there from painted frames to the recorded source of the wails in live-action despair. After all those webcam and satellite transmits in other Middle East war films, those hand-held or unmanned captures that keep death at arm's or armament's length, after all that contemporary 'period style', here both ears and eyes are opened to a moral abyss that still cannot be mastered, neither faced down nor fully faced up to, but which remains all the more blistering for the images previous arisen to repress it. Less an unflinching acknowledgement than a residual haunted-ness, the act of mourning that now swallows up the film is its own. The narrative reversion from drawing to automatic record has come with a cinematic suture from which no healing is to be had.

NOTE

The author and editors are grateful to *Film Quarterly* for allowing the chapter to be re-printed.

1   See my essay 'Digital Fatigue: Imaging War in Recent American Cinema,' *Film Quarterly*, 63, 4, 45–55.

ANIMATING TRAUMA :
WALTZ WITH BASHIR, DAVID POLONSKY

Joram ten Brink

David Polonsky, art director of the animated documentary film *Waltz with Bashir* (2008), lives and works as an illustrator and art director in Tel Aviv, Israel.

Joram ten Brink: *The film is about war, trauma, memory and trying to recover images of war.* Waltz with Bashir *is extraordinary in the way it takes documentary and pushes it into areas beyond representation of war; how do we understand war and violence through animation?*

David Polonsky: I think my main concern was not to get carried away with the aesthetics of war. Because it's really easy to make 'pretty pictures' that are very effective and very dramatic within a film on any war. One of my main concerns was to try to avoid pathos. And try not to show beautiful explosions and interesting splashes of blood. It sort of directed me to a more modest and restrained style of drawing, because we didn't want to glorify war in any way. And because it's so easy to do it in animation and in painting ... like when you see paintings of historic battles ... they're beautiful! So that was one concern. On the other hand we had to be communicative, to carry emotion, in a good way and also in a dramatic way. It needed to be dark, and a little scary of course, so that's the simple reason why there are so many blacks in the film; it's darker that way.

JtB: *The main character in the film says that the landscape was beautiful and pastoral – southern Lebanon with its olive groves, fields, orchards, and so on. But there's very little of the beauty of the landscape and the city in the film. On the* *soundtrack everybody talks about Beirut being a beautiful city, with its big villas, beautiful streets, the beach…*

DP: I did not want to illustrate the text because it was beautiful, but because it was also devastated and scary. And the point of view of the film is of the soldiers themselves. Many of the landscapes – as I couldn't go to Lebanon myself and I've never been there – were basically drawn from what I know to be very similar to Lebanon, that's the northern part of Israel where I grew up. So I drew the old Haifa/Tel-Aviv road, with armoured vehicles along it. And the light, the dust, the floor, everything is the same. But it's disrupted by war.

JtB: *And the idea of using animation to investigate trauma and memories of war?*

DP: That was Avi's idea [Avi Folman, the film's director]. Throughout the whole film there were many decisions taken; one example would be the use of photographs within the drawings. I use bits and pieces of photographs in the background, but there is not one frame of the film that is absolutely clear; everything is reinvented and shifted around, and so that's the way it addresses the nature of memory and its subjectivity. The result is that the viewer is perplexed – is it true or false? Is it made up or 'real'? So that addresses this aspect of memory. And then there's the nature of dream and it results in different pace to events, that is supposed to carry you into an almost hypnotic realm.

JtB: *The dream is the first thing we see in the film…*

DP: Yes. It's not just the visuals, it's the pace itself, and of course, later, the music. It's repetitive; it has an episodic structure. Each time we get too close … at the moment we get too involved and things get too sad, or too scary, or too hilarious, we switch the story; we start a new story, new cycle, it's kind of poetic device. I'm saying this in hindsight; it wasn't planned. Until eventually, it's abruptly cut. There is no redemption.

JtB: *The film contains different stories and experiences of war – that of the soldier who was stuck on the beach, Avi's story, the Dutch…*

DP: …and the guy who stormed the beach after having the dream … losing his virginity (this is the macho guy who danced) … So the film is made up of a great number of episodes. Actually, the preliminary script had two more episodes, it was even more diverse, and the final film had to be a little bid toned down.

JtB: *It had to be toned down because in the end we do get into a very traditional ending, as the second half of the film becomes about Sabra and Shatila...*

DP: I wouldn't go as far as saying that the film is about Sabra and Shatila, because there's nothing new about what we say about Sabra and Shatila. There's no journalistic value whatsoever in the film. It's a personal story, it's as much about Sabra and Shatila as it is about repressed memory.

JtB: *But the repressed memory of Sabra and Shatila is the most important one in the film, or that is how it is perceived?*

DP: Yes. So for the reconstruction of the memories I used references, mainly from the Internet, some old newsreels, and again remembering Haifa, my home town.

JtB: *The memory is built on the tension between the soundtrack made of a pure old-fashioned documentary interview and your drawings that could not be further from documentary. The image of Bashir Gemayel himself is the only real image cut inside the drawings...*

DP: [laughs] It's actually a picture that I drew ... well, it looks like him but there isn't a picture of him exactly like mine...

JtB: *But it's the nearest reference to a real photographic image...*

DP: There are of course also the guys themselves, those who are telling the stories, the interviewees. In a way there's nothing really new in a documentary animation. In fact, I think, the first surviving animated sequence, that still exists today, is about war, it's about a warship that was sunk.[1] The drawing of the warship was about the spectacle. A lot of short animated films are what you would call documentary. So the idea is not new. It's new in feature format, I don't know of another feature-length animated documentary. In some aspects it's even more truthful than a traditional documentary, because when you photograph or shoot in video you have the pretense of truth. You declare that what you are showing is the truth whereas you may be manipulating it in countless ways, through editing, music, whatever. In reconstruction especially, when you stage a reconstruction within a documentary, you, as a viewer have to suspend your disbelief watching the actor before you. Whereas, when you draw it you eliminate the middleman. Once again it doesn't even pretend to be real, it's just telling the story, like any other documentary. Before we started working on our film, we looked at *Touch-*

ing the Void [Kevin McDonald, 2003], and we were influenced a lot by the nature of its construction, because in that film you know that these are not the people who are being interviewed, but there are many cinematic devices, which cause you to forget this. And that's okay.

JtB: *One of the strongest images in the film is the image of washing the blood in the back of the troop-carrier after the delivery of the wounded soldiers. It is a long shot with only a little blood drawn. In certain places it looks like a graphic novel ... As an experienced illustrator who works in diverse styles, how did you arrive at your decision about the particular style of the film?*

DP: It's kind of circumstantial that the look is 'graphic novel-ish'; I wasn't thinking of graphic novels, although it later became a graphic novel in a way. I wasn't thinking about it when we were working on the style. We had a lot of technical restraints ... it couldn't be too stylised, too 'caricature-ised', because we were trying to create this feeling of 'participation' and the moment you stylise a character too much you cannot make your own presence very evident, so it had to be fairly realistic, with real proportions. At the same time it had to be very expressive, very strong, involving the viewer. Or, it had to be just very intriguing visually. So that's the reason for the black outlines and the dramatic colours etc. Together it works out that it looks like a mainstream American graphic novel, but that wasn't what we were aiming for in the beginning.

JtB: *Was there a struggle in the design between How do I represent violence and how do I represent memory? Where is the truth? As the film is digging deeper and deeper into the psyche of our man?*

DP: I think first of all just the choice to tell the story in animation is what makes the biggest difference. The rest, the political considerations, are very important but they are secondary. The main thing is that you realise that we are dealing with memory and inner journeys and the fact that it's done through drawings. You realise that the voice is 'real' and that the image is fabricated. So you see that the images are the manifestation of something subliminal, something that you don't obviously see in the world but that came out of somebody else's mind. In a way it's a method of turning yourself into a third person. It is like when you need to make a mathematical calculation – you write down the numbers to multiply. You know how to do it in your head and you ask yourself – why do I need to make a mark on the page? Because you take this knowledge and you look at it from the outside. In the same way, drawing lets you look at what's in your mind.

JtB: *You chose to give the overall film realistic dimensions – in its proportions; the skyline of an Arab village, of an orchard, of the military vehicles, even the figures are human-size...*

DP: This is the manipulation we were trying to create. That if you were making something that is too inventive, you wouldn't carry the audience. You have to pretend to be neutral.

JtB: *And the one extraordinary scene on the love-boat where he jumps...*

DP: But we say it's a dream so it's okay.

JtB: *The whole film is in a fact a dream, also the dogs are a dream ... But the dogs are treated in a very realistic manner; through using the camera's positions – the dogs run toward you, they knock the chairs on the street ... it's hyper-realist almost...*

DP: In a way, yes. But it's a delicate balance between two different directions. One is to express yourself to the maximum and the other is to remain truthful. And the very simple way to describe this in drawing is to create naturalistic drawings.

JtB: *You were never inclined to draw something non-naturalistic in style; to delve further into the world of trauma and the memory of war ... adopting a naturalistic style may also tone down the nature of war and its representation...*

DP: I'm not sure; if you think, for example, of Francisco de Goya and the drawings of the Napoleonic wars in Spain, which were gruesome and vivid. I don't think there is anything more powerful, a more powerful depiction of war. And if you think of Picasso's 'Guernica', which is much more expressive and free in terms of style, it's also an extremely strong painting, an amazing one. But if I choose which gets me in the gut, it's Goya's, it's not 'Guernica', the beautiful 'Guernica'. It's so beautiful. It's not really scary. And when you look at tormented corpses hanging from the trees it's ... And yes, these are all different artistic/aesthetic decisions, but if you look at the same time what [Goya] has done to depict war ... you see many things; the composition, the nature of the lines, everything. And it's realistic. I think it's by nature, it's who I am; it's the way I work. I work consciously, thinking a lot about the works from Germany in the late 1920s, by Otto Dix and those guys, namely, the New Objectivity. Again there's this kind of expressionism but with restraint, with this pretense of objectivity, that's why it's called New Objectivity. I will show you in my film what I think about the officers, you know the caricature ... I'm going to show you it as it is, I'm going to exaggerate but pretend that it's journalistic.

JtB: *And that will fit into the bigger picture of the film as being a documentary?*

DP: Yes. This is Avi's way, it's not exactly mine ... but I go along with it, because I find it very exciting – this kind of extreme expression. It's not trying to show complexity. He knows what he wants to say and he's out to say it. It's not about nuance. And my job as a designer is to add nuance and not to go along with the grandeur of the statement.

JtB: *It was a new adventure for you, the first film you've ever done?*

DP: Yes, it was fun. I had some experience of animation for television, so I had some understanding of the process, and then again, I'm not doing it alone, there's a process that places me in a very convenient position to start drawing. And that is Avi, and Yoni Goodman, the director of animation, and myself. We'd met and discussed each scene, and then Yoni would proceed to make a storyboard. They were very rough drawings initially; you realise that you have a long shot of the street, with an 'American' shot of two figures from the knees up. And then I had a lot of freedom to create the atmosphere, the specific look, in which the street, the lighting, the characters themselves ... whatever, but I do have an image. And that's different to my usual illustration work where I choose, where I'm also the director, and that what takes up most of the time and thinking. But with the film where the story is being told in many other ways, I was more free to go into the details and tell the story by showing the posters on the wall, or choosing a colour, and so on. But I'm a little bit 'pre-directing' and helping things that are already in the script or storyboard. The primary choice, to use animation, was Avi's, and that was the most important artistic decision in this film. Everything else is an interpretation of this idea.

JtB: *And the idea came to Avi because he was trying to deal with war and memory in a different way, or he didn't believe that a documentary film made of a set of interviews with his friends would be satisfactory?*

DP: Actually we had that film – interviews with fiends. It exists. First of all it was filmed, and we had a straightforward talking heads documentary with all the interviewees. I know that Avi was looking for a way to tell his story about the war for a while but he just didn't see any reasonable way, because to make another documentary ... we've had enough of those, especially here in Israel. But the possibilities he gets from animation, to move freely, to reconstruct cities and so forth are immense. We have worked together on another project that was also a documentary, and it had little bits of animation, and I think there he realised that he can try it on a larger scale. Everything on the screen is your decision; it's absolutely the opposite of usual documentary. If you have an interview, and the interviewee takes a long pause, or he deviates from the subject, you have to throw it out. In a 'regular' documentary it's very difficult to do because you see the jump cut. In animation it's acceptable.

JtB: *Was there any time that you were worried that this kind of animation, or any kind of animation, would actually damage the degree of believability in the story about the Lebanon War?*

DP: No, we didn't think so. And actually it's not the most important thing for us to make people think that it was 'real'. It's very important, but it's not the most important issue. It's not a journalistic film, it's not about the truth; it's about the process of discovery of memories of war, which is something else. Of course the live sequence at the end is there to make sure that everybody realised it's true. That it's not made up.

JtB: *And you got a lot of flack for it...*

DP: For the last part of the film? Yes, we did.

JtB: *I don't have a problem with it one way or another. The filmed images are not more dramatic than the drawings. The drawings of the dead children in the rubble and those of the killing of the old man are as powerful as the 'real' footage.*

DP: I don't know; there were a lot of arguments against this and some for it. I think it works, again, not for moral reasons but for aesthetic reasons. Because the film has an episodic structure, the moment you break the device, you make it clear that this will not continue. The film is based on cycles of beginnings, followed by 'something' becoming very dramatic, very stressful, and then ending with the 'start of a new story'. And this is the most violent way you can break the story in the middle. By using the live footage in that way, you leave the audience waiting for the end, and in many screenings we noticed that people sit throughout the credits. It's not because they're interested in reading my girlfriend's name, it's because they're waiting for the end. I think, in fact everybody realised that it's the end, but emotionally we're on this wave and it's broken in the middle, so it's kind of 'what next?' feeling. This is the kind of feedback we got from audiences.

JtB: *In a sense the first scene is the film's strongest.*

DP: Yes, some say that.

JtB: *Alongside the last section with the filmed footage – these are kind of strong bookends to the film. The first scene in the film really gives you the shivers. It draws you into the film with the men looking down through the window, through 'the window of the mind'...*

DP: I didn't think of that...

JtB: *...and you see the dogs that are running on their own; there's very little detail, as an image ... as an image of violence. It is an image of memory of violence...*

DP: Which again has many precedents in art. You have the expression 'Dogs of War'.

JtB: *That type of 'full-blown' violence, in long shots, in close up, full of energy, they are moving ... fast ... the dogs are almost more threatening than the tanks in the film.*

DP: Because they have eyes! The tanks don't have eyes. And it was my choice to use the stretch of the street in Tel Aviv, because it's the heart of bourgeois Tel Aviv. It's the 'safest' place in the country because Tel Aviv feels itself to be protected from the madness and violence around. This street is at the heart of the seemingly protected bubble. So I chose to bring the dogs into the heart of this 'safe' place.

JtB: *And the dogs bring back the horrors of the past, of war ... the nightmare of the trauma...*

DP: The best part is that it's true, in a way. It's really a dream that a friend of ours dreamt. In fact it was even more gruesome, but it didn't connect very well to the rest of the film.

JtB: *The explanation for the image appears much later in the film...*

DP: Yes, so you don't know what you're seeing at first…

JtB: *But the images are not repeated…*

DP: No, but you do see them again in his memory, when he actually shoots the dogs, and you have the explanation.

JtB: *But the violence is restrained then…*

DP: Yes, it's only one dog, and in his dreams there are 26 of them. The dream was even more gruesome, too gruesome for our film…

NOTE

1   *The Sinking of the Lusitania*, Winsor McCay, USA, 1918.

SPACES OF VIOLENCE:
HISTORY, HORROR AND THE CINEMA OF KIYOSHI KUROSAWA

Adam Lowenstein

In 2005, the Japanese director Kiyoshi Kurosawa attended a special screening of his breakthrough horror film *Kairo* (*Pulse*, 2001) at the Japan Society in New York. The film was on the eve of a belated, limited theatrical release in the United States just ahead of its American remake. In his comments before and after the screening, Kurosawa located himself squarely within the resurgence of Japanese horror films beginning in the 1990s called 'J-horror', mentioning two of the phenomenon's most successful examples, Hideo Nakata's *Ringu* (*Ring*, 1998) and Takashi Shimizu's *Ju-on* (*The Grudge*, 2003), as reference points. However, Kurosawa did not promise the audience that *Kairo* would deliver more of the same in terms of J-horror expectations. Instead, he asked viewers to keep an open mind about what he called 'the elasticity of the horror genre', which he believed could accommodate even films like *Kairo*.[1]

In this chapter, I will argue that Kurosawa's remarkable exploration of the horror genre's 'elasticity' can be framed through his articulations of violence as a matter of cinematic space structured by traumatic history. In contrast to much J-horror, Kurosawa prefers vast, empty spaces rather than the tight, claustrophobic spaces typified by *Ringu*'s haunted well or *Ju-on*'s cursed house. I have written elsewhere about J-horror's doubled investments in the overlapping traumatic histories of World War II and the collapse of the Japanese bubble economy in the 1990s, but Kurosawa's use of space opens up these histories to new forms of spectator address.[2] Kurosawa's films encourage viewers to place themselves, both spatially and temporally, within traumatic histories they may not wish to see themselves as complicit with or responsible for.

Kurosawa (b. 1955) is an extraordinary and extraordinarily versatile director whose output over the last 25 years consists of much more than horror films, but even the breadth of his horror genre work alone is impossible to encompass in this essay.[3] His three most well-known horror films, *Cure* (1997), *Kaira* and *Sakebi* (*Retribution*, 2007), form something like a loose thematic trilogy organised by relations between space and violence; these relations, as I will explain, provide maps of communal responsibility for historical trauma. I will concentrate on *Sakebi*, the latest and perhaps most ambitious entry in the trilogy, to illustrate how Kurosawa weaves together cinematic space and traumatic history.

Sakebi, which was written as well as directed by Kurosawa, is set in contemporary Tokyo. Yoshioka (Koji Yakusho), a tough police detective, investigates a mysterious series of murders in which victims are drowned in puddles of sea water. His work on the case draws him to an infamous sanitarium closed just after World War II, and to the ghost of a woman in a red dress (Riona Hazuki) who was tortured to death by being drowned in sea water at the sanitarium during the war. The ghost of this woman in red is behind the murders Yoshioka investigates – she has possessed certain ferry commuters who once passed by the ruins of the sanitarium on their way to work. These commuters then re-inflict the manner of her death on others. As Yoshioka delves deeper into the murders, he begins to feel that he is not just an investigator but also a prime suspect. After all, he took that ferry past the sanitarium himself, and he becomes less and less certain of what he remembers and forgets about the mysterious appearances and disappearances of his girlfriend Harue (Manami Konishi). Eventually, Yoshioka makes the shattering realisation that it was he who killed Harue in his apartment six months ago. So he is haunted not only by the woman in red, but by Harue's ghost as well. The film's enigmatic final shot shows Harue's ghost crying a silent scream, wearing the clothes she was murdered in – a dress imprinted with red flowers that evoke the dress of the woman in red. Harue seems to cry out to Yoshioka, but the space that surrounds her is not the empty city streets Yoshioka walks through. Instead, she occupies the barren wasteland of an abandoned construction site by the sea where two of the murders took place and where the woman in red's ghost has wandered throughout the film.

As striking as Harue's gesture is in the final shot of *Sakebi*, the blurred outlines of the landscape behind her may be even more important for charting how this film intertwines space and history. The three most important spaces of the film are Yoshioka's apartment, the abandoned construction site, and the dilapidated sanitarium. These spaces orient spectators toward the initially rather puzzling temporal coordinates presented by the film. *Sakebi*'s three key spaces correspond to various moments in time: the sanitarium is the repressed past of World War II;

Fig. 1 Harue's silent scream in the final shot of *Sakebi* (Kiyoshi Kurosawa, 2007).

Yoshioka's apartment is the repressed present of Harue's murder; and the construction site is a crossroads between past, present and future. The identity of the construction site as a temporal crossroads is conveyed in a number of ways. It is land reclaimed from the sea that was planned, in pre-recessionary times, to be a condominium development. But now all construction is frozen, and the land is subject to earthquake tremors that cause puddles of sea water to emerge all over the site – puddles that become deadly when those possessed by the woman in red drown their victims in them. In other words, land reclaimed from the sea during an economic boom is now slipping back into the sea during an economic bust. In this sense, one temporality captured by the construction site is that of Japan since the recessionary 1990s, a time so traumatic for the nation's concept of itself as an ever-expanding economic power that historians such as Harry Harootunian and Tomiko Yoda have called it 'the long-deferred end of the postwar' in Japan.[4]

But other temporalities course through the construction site as well: the woman in red's appearances at the site evoke the past of World War II, with its traumatic legacies of military aggression, atomic victimhood and national defeat;[5] the current murders that occur at the site characterise the recessionary present; and the dream of what the site was going to be before the recession, the condominiums that never materialised, gesture toward a deferred future. The fact that these multiple temporalities are condensed within the single space of the construction site means that the site also functions as a setting for horrific conflicts over remembering and forgetting, history faced and history erased. The woman in red haunts the site so that others may remember her forgotten agony that dates back to World War II; Yoshioka returns to the site again and again to investigate the grisly murders while testing his own tortured memory about whether he may have committed them; Harue's ghost seems trapped inside the site at the film's end – she appears doomed to remain in a painful limbo between past, present and future.

The construction site dominates *Sakebi* – it is where the film begins and ends, and it infects the other key spaces of Yoshioka's apartment and the sanitarium. It is significant that this contamination between spaces is facilitated by water, as water is the primary sign of history in the film. Water as conquered force characterises those dreams of the future staked on the condominium development, while water as conquering force characterises the present economic realities when the recession paralyses that development. In addition, the waterways traversed by the ferry allow the past trauma of the World War II-era sanitarium to meet the present trauma of the murders. Water also carries connotations of pre-modernised historical time, since Tokyo's pre-1868 past includes a long era when water was much more central to the city's character than it is during the period from 1868 to today.[6] As the architectural historian Jinnai Hidenobu puts it, 'it is all but forgotten today that Tokyo's low city was once a city equal to Venice in its charms'. Today, Jinnai explains, 'Tokyo's unused canals have become no more than white elephants. They have come to belong to the 'wrong' side of the city, removed from human view and treated as shabby 'parts of shame' left behind in the wake of modernization.'[7] Or, as Kurosawa described it to me, 'Tokyo was originally just part of the sea, a swamp. Since it is impossible to go back to that time, I decided [in *Sakebi*] to draw a line to the past that began with World War II. Tokyo burned during World War II, and I wanted to show the city before and after the war, but it was so hard to do. The war was a key term for the film. I was trying to make a sort of map in the film from World War II to the present, but there are so many factors that change a city over time that it was hard to accomplish.'[8]

Kurosawa's comment sheds light on how *Sakebi* suggests links between Tokyo's pre-modernised past as a water-centered city and the traumatic modernity of Tokyo's destruction during World War II. But where Jinnai sees in Tokyo's pre-modernised past a romantic rival to Venice, Kurosawa sees a city always on the apocalyptic verge of slipping back into the sea, an apocalypse nearly accomplished by other means during the catastrophic bombing of World War II. Another iteration in this series of Tokyo apocalypses is the Great Kantō Earthquake of 1923, an event Kurosawa evokes (perhaps alongside the Kobe Earthquake of 1995)[9] in *Sakebi* by staging multiple earthquake tremors that unite all three of the film's major spaces: Yoshioka's apartment, the sanitarium and the construction site. In fact, it is the earthquake tremors that lead to the flooding of the construction site, that in turn facilitate the murders at the site, which are motivated by the death of the woman in red during World War II. This non-chronological yet simultaneously historical logic of recurring trauma is given shape in *Sakebi* through a corresponding spatial logic, one where the film's three major spaces provide viewers with a guide to Kurosawa's 'map in the film from World War II to the present'. But since Kurosawa's map uses encroaching water and demolishing earthquakes to reference multiple historical coordinates, *Sakebi* encourages viewers to imagine traumatic history beyond conventional cause/effect linearity, and space beyond boundaries dividing discrete locations. By making the film's spaces into sites where history and horror converge, Kurosawa asks spectators to refigure their own relations to traumatic aspects of Japan's past, present and future.

To gain a more specific sense of how Kurosawa accomplishes this form of spectator address through strategic deployments of space as signs of traumatic history, I would like to examine a particular moment from *Sakebi*. A sequence from roughly midway through the film begins with Yoshioka at the construction site, sitting alone. He has just experienced (imagined?) a terrifying encounter with the woman in red at the site – she spoke to him and insisted that it was Yoshioka who killed her all those years ago by drowning her in a puddle of sea water. He vehemently denies her accusation, for it makes no sense in terms of time. Yoshioka could not possibly have been at the sanitarium during World War II to commit the murder. But the accusation makes chilling sense in terms of space, and Kurosawa even inserts a few violent 'fantasy' images (Yoshioka's imagination/memory? The woman in red's memory/suggestion?) depicting Yoshioka assaulting the woman in red at the sanitarium to underline this point. If the construction site is a crossroads between multiple temporalities, then the possibility arises of Yoshioka occupying a space where his direct but denied participation in Harue's murder in the present can bleed into his indirect, even unconscious participation in the woman in red's murder in the past.

Throughout the sequence, Kurosawa emphasises this possibility of temporal contagion through spatial dynamics. The medium-shot of Yoshioka cradling his head, tortured over violent memories of the past and present he cannot fully own or disown, gives way to an extreme long shot with Yoshioka dwarfed in the far right corner of the frame. Yoshioka is no longer the centre of the viewer's perceptual attention – he is secondary to the vast space that surrounds him. From background to foreground, that space is the modern urban vista of contemporary Tokyo; then the gray expanse of the sea (including a ship that catches Yoshioka's eye, foreshadowing his later revelations about the commuter ferry and the sanitarium); then the brown mud of the construction site with its puddles of water

Fig. 2 Yoshioka dwarfed by the vast space that surrounds him.

indicating the sea's infiltration of the land. Just as Yoshioka struggles to remember, so too does the open space function as an invitation for viewers to place themselves somewhere in this landscape that is also a time-scape, whether it be the present of the urban skyline, the past of the sea, or the contested past/present/future of the construction site. Kurosawa's address of the spectator through space can be detected through the relegation of Yoshioka to such a tiny and imbalanced area of the frame – the suggestion is that the spectator must balance the space, mark the time.

This invitation to the viewer extends to the second half of the sequence, which transpires in Yoshioka's apartment and involves a striking long take of a conversation between Yoshioka and Harue while they embrace each other tenderly. Yoshioka, like the audience, does not yet know that Harue is a ghost, but Kurosawa's use of space as an entry into traumatic time encourages spectators to intuit this shocking fact. Kurosawa's use of the long take, together with Yoshioka's slow, measured delivery of the questions 'What have I done a long time ago?' and 'What have I done lately?' to Harue leaves viewers plenty of time to contemplate what these lines might mean for the film's organisation of space as history. Is the violent threat of the construction site really so far away from this apparently cozy domestic scene? The similarities in colour between the brown wooden floor of Yoshioka's apartment and the brown mud of the construction site, between the red flowers of Harue's dress and the woman in red's dress, coupled with the persistent sound of a faucet dripping inside the apartment to remind us of the potentially deadly puddles of sea water outside, make the two spaces more contiguous than discrete. The same goes for what at first seem like stark contrasts between the woman in red, with her frightening demand that Yoshioka remember his involvement in the past of her death, and Harue's ghost, who comforts Yoshioka and encourages him to forget the past as an illusion irrelevant to their relationship. Yoshioka's fetal-like collapse into Harue's arms confirms how seductively regressive the lure of forgetting is, but Harue's unnerving stare, accompanied as it is by a streak of red fabric that dominates the right side of the frame and a subtle reflected light on her face that suggest the ghostly presence of the woman in red, counteracts the possibility of forgetting. At the level of space, the woman in red and Harue's ghost are doubles, not opposites. When Harue stares into the camera, she may be looking toward the woman in red offscreen, but since Kurosawa provides no reverse-shot to confirm this, her stare remains directed squarely at the spectator. And in that stare, we can barely miss Yoshioka's questions rebounding back to us: 'What have *you* done a long time ago?'; 'What have *you* done lately?'

Kurosawa's address of the spectator as complicit in violence, along the axes of space and time, can be elucidated further through Michel Foucault's concept of a 'heterotopia'. For Foucault, a heterotopia is a physical space that functions as a sort of cultural counter-site in which 'all the other real sites that are found within the culture, are simultaneously represented, contested and inverted'. Examples of heterotopias include the cemetery and the cinema, two spaces that are 'capable of juxtaposing in a single real space, several sites that are in themselves incompatible'. The cemetery simultaneously encompasses a sacred and immortal space, as

Fig. 3 The unnerving stare of Harue, directed toward the spectator's relation to history.

well as a dark space associated with bodily illness and decay. The cinema is constructed on another apparent spatial impossibility: the projection of an illusory three-dimensional space in the cinematic image onto the two-dimensional space of the movie screen. Foucault distinguishes between a heterotopia of illusion, where a space is created that 'exposes every real space, all the sites inside of which human life is partitioned, as still more illusory', and a heterotopia of compensation, where the space created is 'as perfect, as meticulous, as well arranged as ours is messy, ill constructed, and jumbled'.[10]

Kurosawa's heterotopic spaces of Yoshioka's apartment, the sanitarium and the construction site are heterotopias of illusion. They each expose the illusion that the violence committed there is a unique event removed from any other space (similarities in the method of the murders and their watery surroundings collapse space) or any other time (ghostly connections unite World War II and contemporary recessionary Japan, as well as pre-modern and modern Japan). In fact, Foucault insists that 'heterotopias are most often linked to slices of time – which is to say that they open onto what might be termed, for the sake of symmetry, heterochronies. The heterotopia begins to function at its full capacity when men arrive at a sort of absolute break with their traditional time.' Once again, the cemetery provides an example of heterotopia as heterochrony: a space associated with both 'the loss of life' and life's 'quasi-eternity', where signs of memorialised permanence take shape through 'dissolution and disappearance'.[11] Focuault's formulation of heterotopia as heterochrony in terms of an 'absolute break with traditional time' moves suggestively toward the disjunctive temporalities of historical trauma – events whose shattering impact exceed 'pastness' and infect the present. Following Foucault's formulation illuminates how Kurosawa's mapping of World War II onto the present works as a violent compression of space and time, as well as the stakes of that violence for spectatorship.

In *Sakebi*, the sanitarium functions as the spatial centre for the traumatic history of World War II. Yoshioka learns of the sanitarium's significance from an officer who identifies the building on an old, pre-World War II map. The officer tells Yoshioka about a rumour he heard that the inmates of the sanitarium were subjected to corporal punishment: their heads were dunked in washbowls full of sea water until they suffocated. Even though the sanitarium closed shortly after the war concluded, the officer notes that some of the inmates continued living there. When Yoshioka finally visits the ruined, rotting hulk of the sanitarium, he treads across partially flooded floors (again, water conjoins this space with others in the film) and discovers several markers of past habitation that function as traces of the woman in red. These include a half-empty washbowl, a weathered photograph of a woman with an infant in her arms, and a pile of human bones

Fig. 4 The ghostly human stain that evokes 'atomic shadows'.

linked to a stain on a nearby wall that resembles the outlines of a human body. This stain bears a remarkable likeness to the 'atomic shadows' created when victims of the atomic blasts at Hiroshima and Nagasaki were incinerated at such high temperatures that their bodies left nothing behind but scorched blots on the buildings or pavement next to them.[12]

This spectre of Japan's victimisation during World War II is coupled with evidence of Japan's role as wartime victimiser – the torture of the sanitarium inmates evokes some of the most painful revelations about Japanese wartime atrocities, including medical experiments performed on prisoners of war. Yoshioka sees the woman in red for the last time at the sanitarium, but her statement that she now forgives him proves misleading. She does not absolve him from the traumatic history of World War II she is embedded within as both human victim and ghostly victimiser, but dispels the blindness that has prevented Yoshioka from seeing his own complicity with that history. When Yoshioka returns home from the sanitarium, he faces Harue's corpse for the first time and admits his guilt in her murder. When he combines Harue's remains with those of the woman in red he recovers from the sanitarium, he acknowledges symbolically these mixed remains as one body – the violence of the past merges with the violence of the present, and Yoshioka finally recognises his responsibility for both.

Kurosawa's decision to present Yoshioka as a murderer who deflects and then finally owns his responsibility for violence that traverses history already demands a lot from spectators who may be uncomfortable sharing an intimate connection with such a 'compromised' protagonist. But Kurosawa presses even harder on audience complicity by having Yoshioka's fellow commuters on the ferry that passes the sanitarium in the early 1990s (the era of the recession's beginning) come from such a broad cross-section of Japanese social life. Like Yoshioka, these commuters become possessed by the woman in red and commit murders that repeat her own drowning in sea water. In the process, they enact the philosopher George Santayana's famous dictum that 'those who cannot remember the past are condemned to repeat it' as well as the structures of repetition common to traumatic experience – failure to absorb the trauma when it occurs results in its haunting recurrence in forms such as nightmares.

The commuters include Sakuma (Ikuji Nakamura), a doctor who murders his rebellious teenaged son whose last act is to ask his father for a large sum of money that he owes; Miyuki Yabe (Kaoru Okunuki), a female accountant who kills her company's boss after he promises to leave his wife and legitimise his ongoing affair with Yabe; and Ichikawa (Ryo Tanaka), the boyfriend of another young woman in a red dress, Reiko Shibata (Sakiko Akiyoshi), whose parents must endure Ichikawa's extortion of money from them after he murders her. The consistent theme of troubled economic transactions across all three of these murders foregrounds the recessionary context, while the relative randomness of the connections between the murderers highlights the complicity of all of Japan in their actions. As in so many other instances in *Retribution*, Kurosawa channels this invitation for audience self-recognition through space's relation to time. The temporalities of World War Two and the recessionary 1990s commingle not only via the ferry that crosses water literally and time allegorically when it passes the sanitarium, but also through an actual and metaphorical mirror that is held up to the audience.

This mirror appears first during *Sakebi*'s opening scene: the murder of Reiko Shibata at the construction site. In the first of the film's long takes, the spectator witnesses Shibata's drowning in a puddle of sea water, but our view of the murderer's face is obscured by bright light reflecting off metal debris at the construction site. This visual motif of shimmering light reflected from a mirroring surface recurs throughout the film, always to announce a ghostly presence. It often appears in conjunction with a long take, as is the case here with Shibata's murder and in the previously mentioned scene between Yoshioka and Harue's ghost. The combination of mirrored light and the time provided by the long take for the audience to locate this light in space results in viewer awareness of the mirror on at least two levels. At the level of plot, the mirrored light signals the ghost's presence and introduces uncertainty about what the viewer is seeing – for example, hiding the identity of the killer during Shibata's murder. At the level of spectator address, the mirrored light encourages viewers to involve themselves in the film's

Fig. 5 A murder in which the killer's identity is hidden by reflected light.

violence. The mirrored light may conceal the face of Shibata's murderer, but since we do not see the source of this light, doesn't the mirror direct that light back to us? Don't we recognise ourselves on the other side of the mirror?

Kurosawa drives these questions home for the spectator by supplementing the mirrored light and long takes with actual mirrors. Yoshioka and Harue's first interaction in his apartment is mediated by a full-length mirror, as is his encounter with the woman in red when she appears inside the same apartment; Sakuma's interrogation at the police station (another long take) occurs in a room with two large mirrors, one of which reflects the ghostly bright light; Yabe studies her face in the mirror both before and after the murder she commits, with the woman in red appearing alongside her reflection in the second instance; Yoshioka's visit to the sanitarium includes seeing his face reflected back to him in a broken mirror, providing a literalised image of his split subjectivity; and Yoshioka's police partner touches his own reflection in a bowl of sea water prior to the arrival of the woman in red, who appears first as a reflection in the water and then as a flying ghost that drags the partner along with her when she 'dives' into the bowl of water from above. The proliferation of these mirrors, coupled with the visual motif of the woman in red appearing within the mirrors alongside the reflections of characters studying themselves, conveys an insistent theme realised in space: to look at yourself is to see the violence of the past and to recognise your place in it. Kurosawa's strategic deployment of mirrors in cinematic space transforms this theme from one addressed solely to the characters inside the film to one directed equally toward the spectators outside it.

A startling switch point between the mirror as character address and spectator address occurs near the end of the film, when Yoshioka must face the fact
that he murdered Harue. As Yoshioka desperately clings to the hope that he can
somehow hold on to Harue even after realising he killed her – he promises her
that 'I know how to forget, it's easy' – Kurosawa inserts two shots in which we
see Yoshioka embracing what he thinks to be Harue, but what is revealed to the
viewer as empty space. In performing this revelation, Kurosawa transports the
spectator to the other side of the mirror, the side where Yoshioka's fantasies of
Harue's presence disintegrate alongside his impossible desire to forget about the
traumatic past. Although the mirror in this instance is metaphorical (structured
by shot/reverse-shot editing that alternates between Harue's appearance and disappearance in Yoshioka's arms) rather than an actual component of the mise-en-
scène, its evocation of the mirrors littered throughout the film is unmistakable.
Indeed, this final encounter between Yoshioka and Harue in his apartment recalls
their original meeting in this space, when they look at each other for the first time
– through their reflections in a mirror.

When Kurosawa deploys the mirror to collapse the distance between Yoshioka
and the spectator, he supports Foucault's understanding of the mirror as a heterotopic space. For Foucault, the mirror functions as a heterotopia because 'it exerts
a sort of counteraction on the position that I occupy'.[13] Foucault describes this
'counteraction' as a self-recognition quite different from the idealised self-image
of the psychoanalyst Jacques Lacan's mirror stage, at least as Lacan tended to
be mobilised in film theory of the 1970s. Laura Mulvey, for example, likens the

Fig. 6 Yoshioka's face in a broken mirror, crystallizing his split subjectivity.

Lacanian mirror stage to the experience of cinematic spectatorship in this way: 'The sense of forgetting the world as the ego has subsequently come to perceive it (I forgot who I am and where I was) is nostalgically reminiscent of that presubjective moment [during the mirror stage] of image recognition.'[14] Compare Foucault on this point:

> From the standpoint of the mirror I discover my absence from the place where I am since I see myself over there. Starting from this gaze that is, as it were, directed toward me, from the ground of this virtual space that is on the other side of the glass, I come back toward myself; I begin again to direct my eyes toward myself and to reconstitute myself there where I am.[15]

Foucault's emphasis on the mirror as a device for seeing oneself clearly, unsparingly, 'there where I am', captures Kurosawa's insistence on heterotopic space as an inoculation against forgetting whether for character or spectator. We are a long way from Mulvey's nostalgic cinematic mirror where the world is forgotten.

And yet *Sakebi*, for all its commitment toward never forgetting the traumatic past, does seem to gesture toward forgiving by the film's conclusion. Both the woman in red and Harue forgive Yoshioka for his sins in the past and the present. Still, Harue's silent scream in the film's final shot inevitably recalls the ear-splitting shrieks of the woman in red throughout the film. These shrieks, the sound of anguish that refuses to be contained by any conventional registers of time and space, reach out toward the spectator in ways perhaps more visceral than any im-

Fig. 7 Yoshioka embraces only empty space, not Harue herself.

age. Again, Kurosawa encourages the audience to fill in the woman in red's voice for the silence of Harue. And what would that voice *say* if its pain could be rendered in words? *Sakebi*'s final image is Harue, a body with no voice. But the film's final sounds belong to the woman in red, now a voice with no body. Three times, her voice-over intones, 'I'm dead. Please, I wish everybody would die, too.' On the final repetition, she completes only the first of the two sentences. So perhaps Harue's silent scream might be translated as the missing words of the woman in red: 'Please, I wish everybody would die, too.' Death, in this sense, seems to encompass not so much forgiveness or forgetting as a desire for communal self-recognition – that everyone will know death through their shared responsibility to past, present, and future others.

What I have described in this chapter as Kurosawa's masterful manipulation of what he calls the 'elasticity' of the horror genre to forge connections between haunted space, traumatic history and complicit spectatorship began by noting his simultaneous proximity to and distance from the phenomenon of J-horror. So I will conclude by returning to where I began, with a brief speculation on what makes *Sakebi* more 'elastic' in its use of horror than comparable J-horror efforts like *Ringu* and *Ju-on*. Ghosts, curses and the theme of revenge are essential to all three films, but *Sakebi* departs from the other two by mapping space not in terms of traps that kill victims unlucky enough to step into them, but as a series of sites that offer victims and spectators alike opportunities for recognising links between horrors of the past and horrors of the present. The victims of *Ringu* and *Ju-on* die at the hands of angry ghosts seeking revenge for yesterday's sins. The key victims in *Sakebi* do not die themselves, but kill others as the ghostly woman in red was once killed. They must live with guilt and search for meaning, rather than suffer and die unknowing. The horror of *Sakebi* is not the cat-and-mouse game of traps laying in wait, but the fear of loss attached to the fact that the spaces offering modes of understanding between present and past, responsibility and history, are always on the verge of disappearance. Perhaps this difference is what Kurosawa gestures toward when he states that his horror films are not particularly frightening.[16] And maybe they are not, at least not in the manner of the jolting, adrenalised terror generated by *Ringu* and *Ju-on*. But whatever Kurosawa's films may 'lack' in the instant they make up for in sustained haunting – the kind of haunting that invites spectators to find themselves on the spatial maps he presents as guides to the violence of traumatic history.

NOTES

1   Kiyoshi Kurosawa, personal appearance at the Japan Society, New York, 3 August 2005.

2   See A. Lowenstein (2009) 'Ghosts in a Super Flat Global Village: Globalization, Surrealism, and Contemporary Japanese Horror Films', *Post Script*, 28, 2, 59–71.

3   For further background on Kurosawa's work, particularly in relation to horror, see C. Kinoshita (2009) 'The Mummy Complex: Kurosawa Kiyoshi's *Loft* and J-horror', in J. Choi and M. Wada-Marciano (eds) *Horror to the Extreme: Changing Boundaries in Asian Cinema*. Hong Kong: Hong Kong University Press, 103–22; J. McRoy (2008) *Nightmare Japan: Contemporary Japanese Horror Cinema*. Amsterdam: Rodopi, 135–70; J. White (2007) *The Films of Kiyoshi Kurosawa: Master of Fear*. Berkeley, CA: Stone Bridge Press; and T. Mes and J. Sharp (2005) *The Midnight Eye Guide to New Japanese Film*. Berkeley, CA: Stone Bridge Press, 92–110.

4   See H. Harootunian and T. Yoda (2006) 'Introduction', in H. Harootunian and T. Yoda (eds) *Japan After Japan: Social and Cultural Life from the Recessionary 1990s to the Present*. Durham, NC: Duke University Press, 1–25.

5   For additional context on postwar Japan through the lens of historical trauma, see A. Lowenstein (2005) *Shocking Representation: Historical Trauma, National Cinema, and the Modern Horror Film*. New York: Columbia University Press, 83–109; Y. Igarashi (2000) *Bodies of Memory: Narratives of War in Postwar Japanese Culture, 1945–1970*. Princeton, NJ: Princeton University Press; and L. Yoneyama (1999) *Hiroshima Traces: Time, Space, and the Dialectics of Memory*. Berkeley: University of California Press.

6   It is important to note that 1868 is the date of the Meiji Restoration in Japan, a major political shift that is often understood as the dividing line between pre-industrial and industrial Japan. However, historians such as Conrad Totman note that although 'one can, certainly, date the rise of Japan's industrial society from the Meiji Restoration ... industrialization did not really get underway and start to have a broad social impact until the 1890s or even later'. See C. Totman (2000) *A History of Japan*. Oxford: Blackwell, 141.

7   J. Hidenobu (1995 [1985]) *Tokyo: A Spatial Anthropology*, trans. K. Nishimura. Berkeley: University of California Press, 66; see also S. Yoshimi (2010) 'Tokyo: Between Global Flux and Neo-nationalism', in C. Berry, S. Kim and L. Spigel (eds) *Electronic Elsewheres: Media, Technology, and the Experience of Social Space*. Minneapolis: University of Minnesota Press, 245–59.

8   Kiyoshi Kurosawa, interview with the author, Tokyo, 25 June 2008. I am grateful to Yuka Sakano for translation, to Chika Kinoshita and Koichi Maeda for coordination of this interview, and to Kiyoshi Kurosawa for so generously sharing his time with me.

9   In the wake of Japan's catastrophic Tohoku Earthquake of 2011, *Sakebi* seems destined to inhabit an especially uncanny cinematic afterlife – its haunting iconography of quakes and floods will appear to anticipate the future as well as reflect the past.

10 M. Foucault (1986) 'Of Other Spaces', trans. J. Miskowiec, *Diacritics*, 16, 1, 22–7. Foucault's concept of a heterotopia has been remarkably influential on critical theories of space. See, for example, E. W. Soja (1996) *Thirdspace: Journeys to Los Angeles and Other Real-and-Imagined Places*. Oxford: Blackwell, esp. 145–63.

11 M. Foucault (1986) 'Of Other Spaces', trans. J. Miskowiec, *Diacritics*, 16, 1, 26.

12 This moment in *Sakebi* echoes the atomic-laden imagery of ashes and shadows that characterises *Kairo*. For a fascinating, related discussion of how Japanese visual culture is haunted by the atomic bomb, see A. M. Lippit (2005) *Atomic Light (Shadow Optics)*. Minneapolis: University of Minnesota Press, esp. 143–57 (on *Cure*).

13 M. Foucault (1986) 'Of Other Spaces', trans. J. Miskowiec, *Diacritics*, 16, 1, 24.

14 L. Mulvey (1986) 'Visual Pleasure and Narrative Cinema', in P. Rosen (ed.) *Narrative, Apparatus, Ideology: A Film Theory Reader*. New York: Columbia University Press, 202. See also J. Copjec (1994) *Read My Desire: Lacan Against the Historicists*. Cambridge, MA: MIT Press, esp. 15–38.

15 M. Foucault (1986) 'Of Other Spaces', trans. J. Miskowiec, *Diacritics*, 16, 1, 24.

16 Kiyoshi Kurosawa, personal appearance at the Japan Society, New York, 3 August 2005.

ON HISTORICAL VIOLENCE AND AESTHETIC FORM:
JEAN-LUC GODARD'S *ALLEMAGNE 90 NEUF ZÉRO*

Daniel Morgan

In the late 1960s and early 1970s, political cinema – both Western and non-Western – was largely defined by its connection to ongoing political struggles. It is an imperative found in European efforts, following May '68, to combine political commitment within films with a model of collective, collaborative production. It is also found in the declaration of a 'Third Cinema' by Fernando Solanas and Octavio Getino, in which all aspects of cinema – production, distribution, reception – were bound up with revolutionary activity.[1] This is the idea of political cinema most commonly held up as exemplary. Something began to change, however, in the late 1970s and early 1980s, perhaps due to the rise of right-wing figures, ranging from Reagan and Thatcher to Pinochet and Videla, and the apparent failure of revolutionary energy across international borders. In the midst of this reaction from the right, the self-evidence of what counted as political cinema was lost, and it began to splinter into a wide variety of forms.

I am going to focus on one of these new forms, defined largely by a marked turn to the history of cinema. This shift has seemed to critics as a kind of withdrawal from politics, a refusal to engage with the world, even a retreat to an 'auteurist' or apolitical view of cinema. By contrast, I think that it amounts instead to a different way of engaging with politics, one that attempt to come to terms with a legacy of revolutionary violence, historical upheavals and radical transformations. Put simply, investigations into the history of cinema became a central way of understanding history, a tool by which history could be analysed. Chris Marker's *Le fond de l'air est rouge* (*A Grin without a Cat*, 1977) may be the first major instance of this form. Marker looks back on the previous decade to see how and why the left had failed in its political ambitions, but his focus is equally on cinema. Not only does he incorporate documentary footage, he draws on the history of cinema – political, art house and Hollywood – to think about the events that had happened (or failed to happen). *Le fond de l'air est rouge* is not just the history of cinema, or even history represented or alluded to by cinema, but history done *through* (the history of) cinema. It's this form of political cinema that allows us to grasp the porous boundaries and complex relations that have existed (or been thought to exist) between film and history.

In this vein, I am going to discuss one of the key filmmakers who straddles the divide in political cinema: Jean-Luc Godard. Along with Marker, and perhaps even more so, Godard is exemplary of the shift that took place in debates over political cinema. In the late 1960s, the 'Groupe Dziga Vertov', founded with Jean-Pierre Gorin, had been central to the dominant strand of political cinema (indeed, it's precisely because of the importance of these films that Godard's work since then has incurred charges ranging from nostalgia to naïveté to indifference, frequently characterised as amounting to a wholesale withdrawal from political concerns).[2] Part of the shift that takes place involves Godard's rediscovery of the history of cinema, albeit on different terms than interested him in the 1950s and early 1960s. A familiar version goes as follows. In 1978, he stepped in for Henri Langlois – who had recently died – to give a series of lectures (or 'voyages', as Godard called them) on the history of cinema, and his own place within that history, at the University of Montreal.[3] This visit gave him the idea to develop a more substantial work on this topic, which became *Histoire(s) du cinéma* (1988–1998), his eight-part video series on the history of cinema, the history of the twentieth century, and the way those histories have shaped one another. Across its episodes, Godard tells a vast and idiosyncratic story about the interaction of cinema and history, on which cinema had an obligation to record historical world and show it to an audience, but at key moments – most notably, World War II and the Holocaust – betrayed this mission, thereby undermining its historical and political relevance.

Along with this, Godard also developed an account of cinema and history that explicitly drew on the question of politics and violence that preoccupied him in the late 1960s. We see this in the way his films across the 1970s continually revisit and revise his own work: *Letter to Jane* (1972), *Ici et ailleurs* (1974), *Comment ça va?* (1975), *Numéro deux* (1975) and even *Sauve qui peut (la vie)* (1979). More systematically, in *Soigne ta droite* (1987), Godard provides a detailed reworking of the famous discussion on the train from *La chinoise* (1967), where a student militant (Anne Wiazemsky) and an older activist (Francis Jeanson) debated the value of revolutionary terrorism. In *Soigne ta droite*, made twenty years later, the discussion takes place between two older militants, and the tone is now emphatically retrospective, about the problems of justifying violence by appeals to historical laws.

This particular way of engaging history provides a different genealogy to Godard's late career, revising the picture of a filmmaker engaged in a kind of cinematic solipsism. He uses cinema as a medium with a privileged, even unique, ability to understand and analyse the world, and the historical and political situation of his time. It may be less driven by an attempt to directly change the world, but his conception of cinema is still oriented by questions of politics. Not surprisingly, much of this turns on matters of historical violence: violence of the left and the right, but also in the mundane aspects of everyday life (this is, for example, the guiding logic of *Numéro deux*). In his films and videos since the late 1980s, Godard's project is to develop aesthetic resources through which he can confront and grapple with the legacy of a century marked by violence.

My particular interest here is *Allemagne 90 neuf zéro* (*Germany Year 90 Nine Zero*, 1991), where Godard makes a case for cinema as capable of providing an understanding of history in a way that other media and modes of analysis cannot. It's a large claim, and he stakes it out with some care.

Allemagne 90 neuf zéro is, significantly, made and set at a historically complex time, when major upheavals and transformations were taking place across Europe: the end of the Cold War, the collapse of the Soviet Union, the (re)unification of Germany, and the build-up of troops in the Persian Gulf.[4] It is a moment when it looked as though an era was coming to an end, when the dominant disputes and contestations that had occupied the bulk of the century were losing their sense of importance. This uncertainty is found in a play on words within the title of the film itself, since 'Neuf' means both 'nine' and 'new'. So is it 'Germany 90 *Nine* Zero' or 'Germany 90 *New* Zero'? A year suffused with a century of history, or one of clean beginnings? Or both simultaneously? The film works through the history and aesthetics of cinema to model a new form of historical knowledge appropriate to this uncertain world, one that takes shape in response to a set of discourses available in the public sphere.

The film is ostensibly about the journey of a secret agent – Lemmy Caution from *Alphaville* (1964), again played by Eddie Constantine – across Berlin in the aftermath of the fall of the Berlin Wall. Godard uses the figure of the abandoned agent, forgotten by history, to pose the difficulty of coming to terms with the changing conditions in the present. Caution's sense of shock and dislocation requires him both to understand the events that have taken place around him *and* to create a historical narrative into which they fit, including two World Wars, the Soviet Revolution, the Holocaust, a divided Germany, the corruption of the East and the materialism of the West. This task is repeatedly interrupted by the appearance of a variety of literary figures, from Freud's Dora to Goethe's Lotte Kestner to Cervantes' Don Quixote; Caution even takes a side-trip to Weimar.

Another thread runs through the film, in the form of a series of scenes in which a man named Count Zelten (Hanns Zischler) and an unnamed woman (Nathalie Kadem) read Hegel together (in both French and German) and discuss German history and politics. To an extent, *Allemagne 90 neuf zéro* is structured by these recitations of and reflections on Hegel's writings on the philosophy of history, which Godard seems to employ as a way to think about the viability of large-scale historical explanations. Early on in the film, for example, he quotes from the famous preface to the *Philosophy of Right*. The lines are spoken simultaneously in German and French, the different languages overlapping: 'When philosophy paints its grey in grey, then has a form of life grown old? By philosophy's grey in grey it cannot be rejuvenated but only understood.'[5]

A natural thing to think here is that Godard is taking Hegel as a model, and so the implication would be that film (and art more generally) needs to rise to the level of philosophy if it is to successfully provide an understanding of the world to an audience. On Hegel's account, this is part of a gradual process away from art's sensuous aesthetic qualities and towards a degree of abstraction and self-reflection (a thesis that's been labeled 'the end of art').[6] Many discussions of Godard's late work assume this line of thought. Fredric Jameson, for example, argues that *Passion* (1982) attempts to give art a 'trans-aesthetic vocation – in which the work of art wants to be much more than a mere work of art, but rather to replace philosophy itself (an august Hegelian and anti-Hegelian vocation)'.[7] To a certain extent, Jameson is right: Godard is part of an intellectual and artistic tradition in which the medium of the artwork is at least part of the content of that work. But he makes a mistake in assuming, albeit implicitly, that when Godard takes cinema itself as the subject of films it is tantamount to asking cinema to *become* philosophy, and thereby to renounce its aesthetic ambitions. Where Jameson goes wrong, in other words, is in assuming that Godard's cinema, insofar as it operates primarily in a reflexive mode, has to take a non-aesthetic form.

My sense is that the significance of Godard's late work in general, and *Allemagne 90 neuf zéro* in particular, has to do with the way its broader intellectual ambitions, vast and varied as they may be, emerge not by an evacuation of an aesthetic capacity – thereby modeling itself on philosophical discourse – but by staying with and working out the aesthetic potential of cinema. Historical understanding emerges only through aesthetic form.

Godard pushes beyond a Hegelian framework in another way: he will propose that film, precisely because its mode of presentation differs from philosophy, is the medium best equipped to serve a project of social and historical understanding. In making this case, Godard revises the very terms of the Hegelian project. When Hegel says that philosophy can understand a world only when the life of that world has 'grown old' and 'cannot be rejuvenated', this implies that philosophy gains its diagnostic value only at the end of an historical epoch, when there is no longer meaningful development or change. It can then provide a coherent explanation of the logic behind that history, taking a perspective from which the lived intricacies of history can be made sense of. Film, by contrast, is engaged in a history of the complex and changing present. If the twentieth century is coming to an end – and Godard's films and videos of these years are suffused with an awareness of this – it is only cinema, the central art form of the century that is positioned to enable an understanding of the nature of this historical transformation. *Allemagne 90 neuf zéro* sets out to provide an account of how this works.

The film's argument is at once a criticism and a positive declaration of intent. To get this out, I'm going to focus on an early scene, where Godard suggests that there is something philosophy wants to do but which it fails to accomplish, and that film, precisely because of its affinity with a sensuous aesthetic dimension, is able to do.

The scene begins when Lemmy Caution is discovered living above a hair salon in East Berlin and unaware of the changes taking place in the world around him; he has been abandoned in and by history. Zelten tells Caution that the Cold War has ended, and that history has moved on. The sudden intrusion of the reality of post-Wall Germany places him in an uncertain position: he is asked to make sense of a new historical fact, to change the way he makes sense of the world. Caution tries to assimilate the fall of the Wall to an older worldview: 'All the same, you have to admit that it's the triumph of Marx. ... When an idea penetrates into the masses, it becomes a material force.' Earlier, Zelten dropped a bouquet of flowers on a sign labeled 'Karl Marx Strasse', said, 'Happy non-birthday', and then kicked it. Here, he expresses mild skepticism towards Caution's pronouncement. The collapse of the Soviet Union's control over Eastern Europe, he suggests, constitutes a conclusion to the narrative of the twentieth century. With the end of an era, conditions have changed, and so a different way of understanding the narrative arc of history is required; the explanatory power of Marxism ended along with 'actually-existing socialism'.

We then get a stunning, brief sequence. Gradually accepting the fact that the Cold War is over, Caution wonders about the years that have passed him by. 'What am I to do?' he asks, and we are given an intertitle: 'O pain, have I dreamed my life? [*Ô douleur, ai-je rêvé ma vie?*].' Zelten leaves, telling him to fend for himself, while Caution, after chasing Zelten to the door, asks a woman in the salon to bring his lunch. Then, in a peculiar if characteristic move, Godard strays from the narrative line. Instead of following Caution as he tries to decide on a course of action, the film cuts to a shot of an elderly woman having her hair done. Over this shot, Godard plays a German pop song, almost a show tune, whose lyrics run: 'When a person falls in love / His heart soars like a dove. / It doesn't really matter why, / But the sun sparkles in the sky.' The song fades into the background as we hear Zelten begin to recite Hegel in German:

> For philosophy to make its stamp on a culture, there must have first occurred a break in the real world [*so muss ein Bruch geschehensein in der wirklichen Welt*]. Philosophy then reconciles the corruption created by thought. This reconciliation takes place in an ideal world, the world of the spirit into which everyone flees when the earthly world no longer satisfies him.

In the first sentence, right on '*Bruch*', Godard cuts to a clip of people waltzing, dressed in formal and military attire of the Nazi era;the camera is just above head-height, moving with and cutting between the dancing couples. But the clip is not simply inserted in its original form.[8] Godard films the image off a video screen in way that allows us to see the texture of the video image: the flicker of the monitor, the pixels of the screen. Through the same means, he also varies the playback speed, a technique that generates a kind of 'stuttering' effect; Godard slows down, stops and speeds up the clip, drawing us into the movement of the camera as well as of the couples. After the quotation from Hegel comes to an end, Godard cuts to a shot of a study, framed from outside the door; Zelten enters and repeats a line from his previous quotation from Hegel, this time in French: 'Philosophy then reconciles the corruption begun by thought' [*la philosophie alors concilie la corruption commencée par la pensée*].

This is a dense passage, one of the key moments in all of Godard's late work. The fulcrum of the sequence is the sudden shift from the smooth flow of the film to the stuttered playback of the video footage. It raises, in particular, two large topics that bear on Godard's account of the role film can play in historical understanding. The first concerns the evidentiary status of the clip that's inserted into the film. We might think that its position inside another film turns it into something like an object, a document of sorts, that rather than showing a fictional world it functions instead as testimony to a historical moment (it becomes available as history when it ceases to be fiction). But this would radically underestimate the complexity of Godard's understanding of cinema and history. One of his deep beliefs is that how we understand the historical world is shaped by the images we see on screens, and these images are fictional more than – or at least as much as – they are documentary. In this way, the opening montage of *Notre musique* (2004) shows our image of war to be formed by the legacy of both fiction and documentary, from Vietnam-era newsreels to westerns. Fictions may be documents, but not just of actions and settings: they show us our fantasies and desires, tell us new things about ourselves – we are involved in complex relations to them as images, worlds, even dreams. The clip Godard incorporates is thus already involved in a complex relation to history; the use to which he puts it simply brings this out.

The second topic concerns the manipulation of the video image. Godard is often taken to subscribe to a rather strict divide between film and video, largely because of his fondness in the late 1970s and early 1980s for using the metaphor of Cain and Abel to describe the relation between them (most famously in *Sauve qui peut (la vie)*). An enigmatic remark at best, it's generally been taken to mean that film and video are opposed by virtue of a difference in their material base, with cinema figured as the good brother (even though, in the structure of the analogy, 'cinema' actually matches up with 'Cain'). In reality, however, Godard has a more open relation to new technologies: 'I'd say there was no very big difference between video and cinema and you could use one like the other. There are things you can do better with one so with the other you do something else … above all you can alter the image easily with video.'[9] Godard implies here that cinema and video are not different media but different tools for the production of images, allowing for different formal possibilities and effects. Although the videographic manipulation of footage in fact emerged as a technique in *France/tour/detour/deux/enfants* (1977), continuing in his video projects of the 1980s,[10] the video clip in *Allemagne 90 neuf zéro* marks the first appearance of this technique in a film. The technological shift from film to video serves as the occasion for a corresponding formal and aesthetic rupture, while also being connected to – this is the alignment the sequence works with – a historical transformation and upheaval.[11]

The shift in media, and the attendant features it brings with it, coalesces around the Hegelian term that Godard inserts at this moment. The idea of a 'break' functions as the sequence's central analytic term, both literal (the breaking of the world of the film) and figurative, and three different ways to understand it quickly suggest themselves. One involves Hegel's own account of history, indicated by the voice-over; the other two involve aesthetic considerations. The first of the aesthetic readings has to do with the way the rhythm of the video clip produces a 'break' in temporal continuity. The film's opening voice-over had wondered if it was possible to tell the story of time 'in itself', and later on Godard returns to the topic:

There is a difference between narration [*la narration*] and music. A piece entitled 'Five Minute Waltz' will last five minutes. That's it, and nothing else matters in its relation to time. But a telling [*un récit*] of an action that lasts five minutes could be stretched into a period a thousand times longer if those five minutes were filled with an exceptional awareness. And it can seem short although to its imaginary duration it may be long.

Based on the distinction articulated here, we might treat the inserted clip on the model of narration. If, ordinarily, a shot has a continuous temporality – the model of the 'five-minute waltz' – the stuttering of the speed of the clip means that the duration of the shot is no longer identical to the diegetic time it presents. Time itself becomes a variable that can be expanded or contracted within the film. And yet the terms of music are present as well, highlighting a set of associated formal attributes at the heart of cinema. There is rhythm, not only in the movement of the dancers but in the variation of the playback as well, and a suggestion of formal regularity that gives order and structure to the expressive effect of the clip.

These models are not mutually exclusive. Godard positions film between them, able to manipulate time but without the unfettered freedom of narration. By making the image dance to its own tune – in conjunction with but different from the movement of the dancers – Godard pulls our attention to the sheer fact of that movement. The effect is to make the world of the clip embody the principles of a dance, and the kind of experience such movements offer. It's not just that we see dancers moving in a certain time, following set patterns and rhythms; time itself comes to take on the semblance of a dance, with hesitations and accelerations followed by a smooth glide at normal speed. The duet between dancers and 'stuttered' clip makes us physically follow and respond to the image.

The second aesthetic understanding of the idea of a 'break' has to do with the way the introduction of video creates a 'break' in the world of the film. Godard makes the shift explicit by filming the clip directly off a video monitor, so that we physically sense the difference in tone and texture between the clip and the surrounding images in *Allemagne 90 neuf zéro*. His emphasis on texture – the lines, the flattening of space produced by the monitor – draws our attention to the surface of the image. Rather than seeing 'into' that world, we are invited to focus on its appearance. We become concerned with how the image looks, with the different texture of the video format, and, most importantly, with the rhythm of the 'stuttering' effect. The shift between film and video thus emphasises an experiential dimension in our viewing of films. We are arrested at the moment where the shift occurs, struck by the sensuous dimensions of the image before us.

But the sequence doesn't stay at this level. Godard ties the emphasis on aesthetics, and a kind of experience, to larger historical and political concerns. In part, this happens because of the content of the image: the dance we see is a Nazi-era ball, men with swastikas on their uniforms. History, and the violence it contains, is the unavoidable content of the sequence. But there's something else going on as well, emerging from the way Godard insists on describing the shift from film to video in terms of the Hegelian account of a historical 'break'. For Hegel, the idea of a break is intimately connected to our ability to understand the progress of history, since only after a radical shift in history – an often-violent undoing of the previous order – are we able to understand the significance of what came before.

I think there is a specific reason Hegel is important to Godard, although it is not explicitly present in the film. In the months during its production, Francis Fukuyama's essay 'The End of History?' (1989) had provoked a set of discussions in Europe about the historical narrative into which the decline of the Soviet Union ought to be placed. Fukuyama drew explicitly on Hegel to make his case, proposing that history had in fact come to an end when Hegel said it did, when Napoleon's defeat of the Prussian army in Jena in 1806 allowed for the institutionalisation of the principles of liberal democracy across Europe. Fukuyama claimed that history there reached its *telos*, the next two centuries simply the process by which liberal democracy became universal.[12]

Thinking that Fukuyama is on Godard's mind helps explain the terms on which *Allemagne 90 neuf zéro* takes up these same topics, and allows us to see how the correlation of aesthetic and historical breaks forms an implicit critique that uses Hegel's own terminology to undermine his explanatory power. The critical project takes shape in the opening juxtaposition of the passage from Hegel's *Philosophy of History* and the lyrics of the German pop song, a juxtaposition, which turns on the terms of the pop song. From the perspective of someone in love, the mawkish sentiment goes, the world itself is brought into accord with his or her desires: 'It doesn't really matter why / But the sun sparkles in the sky.' At first blush, nothing could be further from Hegel, but the affinity is to be found in the way Hegel describes philosophy as offering a location from which apparently contradictory historical intricacies are reconciled through a grasp of the whole logic of history. Philosophy is taken to reside in a space above or outside the world in order to produce an order and harmony the world itself lacks. The problem, then, is not just that philosophy might arrive too late to help us understand the changes in our world. Godard suggests that philosophy, insofar as it tries to make sense of 'breaks' by fitting them into a larger explanatory historical narrative, betrays something of the phenomena it attempts to analyse.[13]

This point is emphasised through Godard's use of the inserted video clip. It's not just any 'break' that's at issue – a moment when a contradiction in the social order emerges – but one that poses the strongest challenge to the explanatory narrative: the rise to power of the Nazi Party. A Hegelian mode of treating the Nazi rupture in world history would be to move towards a higher reconciliation, towards a wider perspective of history and its developments, treating the 'break' as a moment in the historical dialectic, eventually leading to a better social formation.[14] Indeed, Fukuyama himself made such a claim, arguing that the traumatic events of the twentieth century – the two World Wars, the Holocaust, Stalinism, and so forth – mattered within the historical narrative as the means by which alternative systems to liberal democracy were successively discredited.

Godard invokes the Nazi era not simply as a reflexive gesture against this position – well, what about the Nazis? – but to bring historical concerns of the present into the film. In a sense, the main historical anxiety present in *Allemagne 90 neuf zéro* does not have to do with the demise of East Germany or the disintegration of the Soviet Union. It has to do, instead, with the prospect that, for the first time since World War II, Germany was moving towards a unified federal state – and doing so, at times, without awareness of the historical legacy of national (and nationalist) ambition and its genocidal consequences. A number of commentators, activists and intellectuals at the time worried that Germans would think that, by virtue of having been divided into two states for over forty years, a moral debt incurred because of the Holocaust had somehow paid off. Frank Stern, for example, quotes a 1990 pamphlet on the subject of German moral and historical responsibility whose author writes, 'By means of hard work, a feeling of responsibility and good will ... the Germans have created the pre-requisites for the restoration of what Hitler destroyed: national unity.' As Stern notes, at work here is a kind of moral calculation:

Nazi horrors and the Germans as victims after 1945 are weighed one against the other, suffering juxtaposed to suffering, an equation of victimization. In this view, the mass murder committed against the Jews of Europe has been repaid and 'recompensated' – what remains now as a task is the historical reassembling of a shattered Germany.[15]

It is in the position Stern argues against that we can discern a Hegelian logic. The argument would go something like this: the rise of the nation-state produced genocide; this led to the division of Germany, the suffering of which balanced out the earlier crimes; as a result, unification was now possible, albeit on new grounds. A resolved dialectic.

At stake in the debate over historical narrative is the question of whether the history of German militarism and violence can be left to the past. Godard's emphasis on this particular history places him firmly on the side of those who worried about the historical significance of the move towards unification – seeing it, rather, as a move towards reunification. The danger, on this view, is in arriving at a perspective from which it all fits into and is justified by a large-scale historical pattern. Godard correlates the violence he does to the image with violence done in history so as to refuse a presentation of that history in a way that effaces its violence. The sequence, in short, amounts to a refusal to let a claim to a logic of history do away with the violence and suffering it contains.

The movement from film to video within *Allemagne 90 neuf zéro* has another ambition as well, one that concerns a methodological project. This is the positive argument of the sequence. Through the emphasis on the idea of a 'break' as something aesthetic, technological and historical, Godard suggests an alternative to the Hegelian postulate of an ideal reconciliation, an alternative to the very historical framework that Hegel deploys. He does so through the texture of the image itself. What the manipulation of the image does – the ambiguous temporality, stuttering playback speed, and shift in media – is to give us an example of what it is to stay or tarry with the experience of a break, and thereby to understand something essential about it as a historical phenomenon. Godard, that is, uses the qualities of an *aesthetic* break as a way to model an experience of remaining with *historical* breaks without immediately abstracting to a larger pattern. If a Hegelian philosophy attempts to place events within a larger historical narrative, Godard suggests that film, precisely through an affinity with aesthetics, is able to give us a better account of how and why the break itself matters. To tarry with the break is not to forgo understanding, to ignore the task of looking for historical patterns and causes of violence. It is, however, to suggest that the move toward abstraction is incomplete without recognition of the phenomenology of violence, and that film – including its use of video – is able to provide us with the necessary form of experience.

The terms of the connection between the aesthetic break in form and the historical break in the world shown in the clip finds additional support in the figure of the dance itself. Not simply a category of ornament, dance can be seen as standing in for a vision of social order. There is a clear expression of this idea in a letter of Schiller's:

> I know of no better image for the ideal of a beautiful society than a well executed
> English dance, composed of many complicated figures and turns ... Everything fits
> so skillfully, yet so spontaneously, that everyone seems to be following his own

lead, without everyone getting in anyone's way. Such a dance is the perfect symbol
of one's own individually asserted freedom as well as of one's respect for the freedom of the other.[16]

But this is clearly not what's going on in *Allemagne 90 neuf zéro*. Godard's manipulation of the dance undermines the political ideal through aesthetic means.
Rather than harmony and play, a kind of formalised beauty, we have stuttered
play-back; rather than a distanced perspective, overseeing the patterns formed by
the dancers as a collective, we are immersed in the visual breakdown of their individual movements. What was, in the diegetic world of the clip, a rhythmic and
graceful movement that evoked a well-ordered, successful society – even if one
on the verge of collapse – is made into something distinctly messier: the patterns
are broken down, disrupted by internal forces. And so, we might think, it should
be. The dance takes place under the aegis of a violent and repressive state; we
can take Godard to be arguing that the means for representing this social organisation should therefore be different than for those social orders which express
Schiller's aesthetic and political ideal. In a sense, Godard undermines an already
undermined vision of politics.

The terms of this reading recur throughout *Allemagne 90 neuf zéro*. Indeed,
we only need to look a little further to find the argument reiterated. As Zelten
continues to read from Hegel, this time in both French and German, Godard cuts
to a series of clips staged against the content of the quotation. The brief sequence
runs as follows:

> Philosophy begins by the destruction of the real world. [*Cut to a clip of artillery firing
> at night: only the gun flashes are visible, though we hear sounds of distant guns. Then
> a clip of deportations.*] Philosophy makes its appearance when [*cut to a clip from
> Lang's* Metropolis, *where Maria is surprised by a noise in the catacombs and whirls
> around*] public life is no longer satisfying and ceases to interest people and when
> citizens [*cut to a clip from Fassbinder's* Lili Marlene, *where she and a Nazi official
> mount a large staircase to meet Hitler; a Nazi flag is prominent in the background*]
> no longer take part in the running of the state.

The choice of images here is again non-trivial (though not entirely surprising).
Each clip presents a moment that refers, explicitly or implicitly, to a historical mo-
ment where the historical present was treated as breaking sharply from its past:
World War I, 1920s industrial poverty and quasi-socialist utopias, and World
War II.[17] Godard again contrasts philosophy's desire to resolve contradictions or
'breaks' – to place them into a coherent narrative, as Hegel does by employing the

device of the 'cunning of reason' – with the way film can stay with and emphasise the experience of that rupture through aesthetic means. In *Allemagne 90 neuf zéro*, cinema – both film and video – is presented as a way to think about these changes that are taking place, a medium that contains a unique and invaluable set of tools for the purpose of historical analysis.

In his films and videos since *Allemagne 90 neuf zéro*, Godard has continued his efforts to adapt cinema's aesthetic resources as an analytic tool for new instances of historical violence. Much of this, at least in the 1990s, concerned the break-up of Yugoslavia and the wars that erupted there; in works like *Hélas pour moi* (1993), *Je vous salue, Sarajevo* (1994), *For Ever Mozart* (1996), and even *Notre musique*, Godard brings cinema to bear on the increasing complexity of nation-states, personal identity and problems of war and memory. *Histoire(s) du cinéma*, his main preoccupation in these years, takes this project further, proposing that film is implicated in the historical events it analyses and shows. In one of its strangest and most controversial claims, Godard argues that the cinema was obligated to intervene in World War II but failed to do so, and its inability to prevent the Holocaust from happening – quixotic as that hope may seem – marked its failure as a medium attuned to the world.

The reasons behind these claims are beyond the scope of this essay. But Godard is insistent in his work since the 1980s that it's precisely because cinema has an obligation to show the world to an audience, to render that world intelligible for them, that its failures constitute an indictment of its very possibility for mattering in the first place. It's the power of film's aesthetic resources to model and produce historical knowledge that makes its failures so devastating, its reinvention so important.

NOTES

1   See F. Solanas and O. Getino (1997) 'Towards a Third Cinema: Notes and Experiences for the Development of a Cinema of Liberation in the Third World', in M. Martin (ed.) *New Latin American Cinema, Volume One*. Detroit: Wayne State University Press, 33–58; see also Michael Chanan's contribution to this volume.

2   This critical evaluation is buttressed by an apparent correlation with biographical facts. In the wake of the failure of his collaboration with Gorin and a devastating motorcycle accident, Godard founded a new studio, Sonimage, in 1972, with Anne-Marie Miéville. He did so, however, not in Paris but in Grenoble, moving to the Swiss town of Rolle shortly thereafter. Away from the urban centres of Europe, Godard seemed to position himself as a cinematic and political outsider.

3   Published in 1980 as *Introduction à une veritable histoire du cinéma*. Paris: Albatros.

4 A build-up which included German troops in a combat situation for the first time since 1945.

5 G. W. F. Hegel (1967 [1952]) *Philosophy of Right*, trans. T. M. Knox. London: Oxford University Press, 13.

6 For Hegel, this does not mean that art will no longer be produced, or that it will not fill an important social need. But it does not, and will not, matter in the same way. The result of this historical narrative is that philosophy – over and against art and religion – emerges as the most appropriate mode of self-knowledge in the modern, bourgeois world. To the extent that art survives and remains vital, it does so by turning into philosophy, into a kind of abstract meta-discourse about its own conditions of being (see G. W. F. Hegel, (1975) *Aesthetics: Lectures on Fine Art*, 2 vols, trans. T. M. Knox. Oxford: Oxford University Press, vol. 1, 11).

7 F. Jameson (1992) 'High-Tech Collectives in Late Godard', in *The Geopolitical Aesthetic*. Bloomington: Indiana University Press, 164. Jameson is here following an account of modern art most forcefully articulated by Arthur Danto: that over the course of the twentieth century, art loses its interest in aesthetics and becomes attuned purely to philosophy. Danto argues, 'Art ends with the advent of its own philosophy … all there is at the end *is* theory, art having finally become vaporized in a dazzle of pure thought about itself' – A. Danto (1986) *The Philosophical Disenfranchisement of Art*. New York: Columbia University Press, 111.

8 It is clearly a fictional reenactment, but I have not been able to identify the source.

9 J.-L. Godard and Y. Ishaghapour (2005) *Cinema: The Archaeology of Film and the Memory of a Century*, trans. J. Howe. Oxford: Berg, 32.

10 See M. Witt (2001) 'Going Through the Motions: Unconscious Optics and Corporal Resistance in Miéville and Godard's *France/tour/detour/deux/enfants*', in A. Hughes and J. Williams (eds) *Gender and French Cinema*. New York: Berg, 171–94.

11 Godard had used material from other films before. Many of his films from the 1960s show characters watching movies in a theatre, and *Letter to Jane* relentlessly examines a photograph of Jane Fonda taken in North Vietnam. What is different about *Allemagne 90 neuf zéro* is both the manipulation of the image off the video monitor and the way Godard dispenses with diegetic motivation for its insertion.

12 Douglas Morrey has also suggested that *Allemagne 90 neuf zéro* responds to Fukayama; see D. Morrey (2005) *Jean-Luc Godard*. Manchester: Manchester University Press, 196.

13 It's a claim that resembles Theodor Adorno's argument that Hegel attempts a false reconciliation of contradictory phenomena, rather than staying with the negative moment of the dialectic; see T. W. Adorno (1993) *Hegel: Three Studies*, trans. S. W. Nicholson. Cambridge, MA: MIT Press.

14 See, for example, Hegel's discussion of the way poverty and institutional authority interact to produce a 'break' in civil society – namely, crime – eventually leading to its dissolution and the subsequent reconciliation in the higher sphere of ethical life and the state; Hegel 1967, 231–56).

15 F. Stern (1991) 'The "Jewish Question" in the "German Question", 1945–1990: Reflections in Light of November 9th, 1989', *New German Critique*, 52, 4, 159; see also A. Huyssen (1991) 'After the Wall: The Failure of German Intellectuals', *New German Critique*, 52, 4, 109–43. The opposing position was that, while German nationalism certainly had a morally vicious history, historical parallels could be overstated. The militaristic nationalism of Bis-

mark and Hitler were not part of the definition of the German nation, but rather a misappropriation of that idea (see, for example, K.-H. Bohrer (1991) 'Why We are Not a Nation – And Why We Should Become One', *New German Critique*, vol. 52, no. 4, 72–83).

16 Quoted in P. de Man (1984) 'Aesthetic Formalization: Kleist's *Über das Marionettentheater*', in *The Rhetoric of Romanticism*. New York: Columbia University Press, 263.

17 That is, the period of and leading up to the Third Reich. The images are from that period, about that period, or, with the clip from *Metropolis*, anticipate that period. In the latter case, we are firmly on the terrain of Siegfried Kracauer's *From Caligari to Hitler: A Psychological History of the German Film* (Princeton, NJ: Princeton University Press, 2004; first published in 1947).

BATTLE FOR HISTORY:
APPROPRIATING THE PAST
IN THE PRESENT

SUBVERTING DOMINANT HISTORICAL NARRATIVES:
AVENGE BUT ONE OF MY TWO EYES, AVI MOGRABI

Joram ten Brink

Avi Mograbi, a documentary film director, lives and works in Tel Aviv, Israel. *Avenge But One of My Two Eyes (Nekom Achat Meshtai Einai)* was produced in 2005 as a French/Israeli co-production.

Joram ten Brink: *One of things that strike me is your work at the checkpoints full of images of the violence, humiliation, frustration and pain in these places. You developed that style over the years, with you as the provocateur, as the man with the film camera.*

Avi Mograbi: It wasn't my intention to provoke or intervene in the situation. There are lots of situations in the film where I don't intervene. Actually, I prefer to remain an observer, and let the viewer see the reality in, let's say, in a 'direct cinema' mode. Of course it's very strange to talk about my work and mention 'direct cinema', but I prefer to just look at things and let the viewer appreciate it, or understand what's happening. But what happens in the occupied territories is that, first of all, sometimes the situations immediately put you in a position of intervention. I am travelling often in the company of activists who have come to do work. They are not just observers. Often you want to be a silent observer but one of the parties that is being observed, the soldiers, are reluctant to become subjects of observation. And of course what you see in the film is only a small selection of situations but there were so many situations where you would go to a checkpoint and stand even from afar, and then one of the soldiers would come up and say: 'if you don't put away the camera we'll close the checkpoint and then it's not us who are not letting the Palestinians go across, it's you!' You 'become' the person with the key to the checkpoint with his camera! Of course because you come there with a political intention, you say to yourself: of course it's a distorted way to describe the situation, but the people are waiting to cross through the checkpoint. The soldiers don't mind, they often say to the Palestinians, pointing at me: 'He is blocking your way.' And sometimes even the Palestinians say: 'Go, don't film now, you are creating a disruption.' And of course in *Avenge...* there is one scene where they actually try to block me from filming. It's so strange, because there was nothing to film. We'd just arrived there, me and the B'Tselem guys, and this was a checkpoint where nothing was happening, you know, really there was nothing to film. And if it wasn't for them [the soldiers], there wasn't a scene. But they were making a scene. And of course the scene of trying to block the 'eye' is a very strong one, and very important. Of course, there was supposedly no physical violence, but it was a very violent situation. It's hard to see in the film, because the camera has a very limited lens width, but four soldiers were actually touching my body with their jackets, and this is why, when I move the camera, I move from one place to another. Because they were in front, they were blocking me with their bodies. So, of course, when you are in such a situation, whatever you do, you react. Either you say – okay, I'll put down, I'll turn off the camera; or you say, as I did – you have no right to do that. But whatever you do is a reaction. I don't think I provoked anything. I think I was provoked. But the fact is, you are right, that in the occupied territories a lot of times, the presence of the camera is a provocation. Not because you do anything, or not because anything happens or that you create something that happens, but the fact that you pull out a camera means that you have 'intentions'. And those 'intentions', as the soldiers see them, unless they know that you are on their side, are seen as a provocation, and they try to block filming. In the last scene of the film where I do 'explode' violently and aggressively, not with physical violence, but definitely with foul language, you can say – here was a situation that I created, but never intentionally. I never planned to do that. Lately, my activism has been shifted from demonstrating and working with activist groups to doing something useful. Like today I drove a woman from the town of Tulkarem to Tel HaShomer hospital and back. She needed treatment for her eye. She has a permit to cross but for her to get from the checkpoint of Tulkarem to Tel HaShomer hospital would take a whole day if she had to do it alone. But, back to the last scene in *Avenge...* I was with Physicians for Human Rights at a certain checkpoint where they had an ongoing problem with children returning from school at two different times, namely, at twelve noon and at one-thirty. The younger kids who arrive to the checkpoint at twelve always have to wait until one-thirty for the gates to open. This has been going on every day for months. And you know, the ridiculous thing, of course, is that the soldier told me: 'I don't need to tell you the reason.' If he said 'there is a security problem ... there's a suicide bomber on the loose, we have to close the gates', okay. But he just said: 'I don't have to tell you.' And this sentence put me on fire. What do you mean you don't have to tell me? And of course it's the hottest day of the year and I lost my temper, which happens from time to time. And the most irritating thing of all was that, come one-thirty, the soldiers opened the gate wide open, people from both sides – adults with bags, cars – everybody crossed at once; no body checked, as if there were no checkpoint there.

JtB: *You also see it in this scene – there's a kind of little ritual, a kind of 'dance' between the activists and the soldiers; the activists, always with a camera and you're not the only camera in many of the shots, and there are also B'Tselem's camera people walking around. We witness those moments of violence, of humiliation, so much integrated with the image of cinema and with the need to document everything.*

AM: The activists have learned that the Israeli juridical system, the police, the press and the public, don't believe the word of the activists, of the leftist activists, because they are biased. But the public cannot resist an image, and this is why it has become very common that activists travel with cameras in order to create proof for the authorities or for the press or the public. My son was once arrested near the village of Bil'in. He was not arrested during one of the big demonstrations there, but there was a period when they [my son and his friends] were doing mid-week activities to try to interfere with the building of the fence near the village. One of the things they did was that they created a big cylinder made out of barrels that were welded into a big pipe, and they made holes for the head and the legs. Six or seven activists were seated inside this pipe, only heads and legs protruding and they were all chained, etc. They placed it on the road where the tractors were working. And my son was arrested afterwards, and was brought to Jerusalem, to the Russian Compound Police Station, and then later brought in front of a judge. His friends who were not arrested came back and told me that there is a video showing everything that happened there. I took the video and ran up to Jerusalem and arrived on time for the hearing in front of the judge. The police accused my son of interfering with the building work etc, but also they accused him of attacking a policeman. I showed the video to the judge, and after he saw it, he said – I see only violence on the part of the police, the activists didn't 'do' any violence. Because they [the protestors] were locked inside [the barrels], the police started beating them with clubs. And the judge said – excuse me, they can go home, because there is only police violence here, there is no activist violence. And so forth. B'Tselem eventually gave dozens of cameras to locals [Palestinians] and this is how you got to see lately the incident where a soldier shot the leg of one of the people arrested in the village of Nil'in. A twelve-year-old girl filmed it on video. So the camera has become, I wouldn't say a weapon but ... I mean of course, when you are confronted with the soldiers this is not your weapon, this doesn't win the confrontation, but it's a weapon for later times to clarify what has really happened. The army do the same – whenever there are demonstrations in the occupied territories, they always use at least one soldier whose job is to shoot a video.

JtB: *But the presence of your camera at those checkpoints actually changes the dynamics of the events in the checkpoints.*

AM: Yes, it does. There are two possibilities. It depends on who the soldiers are. On one hand it makes them softer, because they are aware of the presence of the camera and maybe they are not so happy about what they are doing or even a little bit ashamed of what they are doing, maybe there is a bit of fear...

JtB: *So the camera stirs their conscience...*

AM: Yes, or maybe the camera makes them think that perhaps their mother will see them and so sometimes they become softer, like in the situation in *Avenge...* when a person was made by the soldiers to stand on the stone. We were three cameramen there. Normally, this 'event' lasts for hours but because of our presence an hour after we arrived nobody was there any more. They let everybody go. Because they suddenly realised that ... maybe the camera didn't raise their conscience but it raised their awareness of the situation.

JtB: *That shot made me think of Abu Ghraib photographs. It's the image of humiliation. But [your soldiers] didn't see it as an image until you came with a camera. Then it became an image of humiliation for them.*

AM: Yes. And in other situations, like you see in the film, where the soldiers decide that the camera is an interruption, they may either attack the camera, or block the checkpoint until you go. So the presence of the camera or the presence of human rights activists affects the situation. Nowadays people are so aware of the power of the image that you cannot place a camera anywhere without people knowing it. I mean, in the back of their mind, even if they don't feel that they need to modify their behaviour, they are aware of the presence of the camera. And I think this is very interesting – the camera is very powerful. But also the soldiers themselves use the camera not only for documentary, for an 'official' documentary activity, but also for fun. You mentioned Abu Ghraib? People here have been taking photos of themselves with corpses of fighters they have killed from the other side and have been spreading them in internal net[work]s.

JtB: *You've seen it?*

AM: Yes.

JtB: *So they're taking trophies?*

AM: Yes. Sometimes holding the dead person standing up, sometimes... I should have a picture of them – they look sometimes like hunters, with their leg on the body of the dead person. Abu Ghraib...

JtB: *Is not an American invention...*

AM: No. Of course, it's different when, in Abu Ghraib the camera came only after a series of humiliations in the prison. The soldiers were trying to brag about their abilities to be 'strong fighters'.

JtB: *Back to your film, what struck me also were the ambulance scenes – the use of long shots and the attention to detail. Those scenes are played out almost in real time. As part of the image of violence and humiliation they contain a huge number of small details – the hand gestures, the soldiers' orders: 'Come! Go! Come! Go!' the repetitive nature of the event. It looks almost like a ritual that happens every day.*

AM: Yes, I believe in an image that tells you a story and not in a person that tells you the story from his memory, including his interpretation of what has happened before. Although you may say that the 'information' may be the same, but when you see it, when you just see the image, although the basic 'information' is no different, the impact of the real image is so much stronger.

JtB: *But it's the attention to the little details, which 'delivers' the horror.*

AM: I think this technique also brings out the irony and points to how crazy everything is. It was very important for me to zoom in, as you said, to the guy at the top of the observation point, because when you stand down there you don't understand how it works. The people are showing the soldiers on the top of the observation point, from a distance, their ID, or their travel permits. Tell me, how can a soldier sitting twelve meters high up tell anything? He is sitting there with his binoculars and it is so absurd. Because what are these documents? If you look at them from twelve meters away with binoculars, how can you at all know tell if they're authentic or not? It could be lousy photocopy, and how can you read the names with binoculars ... I think that the absurdity is part of the horror, but also it is an idea within itself.

JtB: *If there were no cameras around the checkpoints, would the world of the checkpoints be different?*

AM: Of course the world of the checkpoints would be different, I'm not sure I know how, but it's like anything ... if there were no reporters, not only cameras, and nobody to tell you what's happening perhaps the situation would be different. Not necessarily for the good. Like some two or three years ago a woman in the Hawara checkpoint witnessed a person trying to cross with a violin. He was asked to play in order to cross. She caught it with her cell-phone camera. This image speaks not about the humiliation only but about the historical context – the image of the violin player in Jewish history is very loaded – the orchestras in death camps and in concentration camps etc. So again, the information is not so significant or important but more important and significant is the context, which corresponds to your own historical reference.

JtB: *We are always aware of the way you are making the film. Do you think this kind of self-reflective way of working, one that many filmmakers reject, is important in this context? As most of your films deal with conflict, violence, humiliation...*

AM: Yes, and they also deal with filmmaking, with storytelling, with point of view. It's very important for me that my presence as moderator, interpreter and participant is clear in the films. It's very important for me to make sure that it's very clear to the viewer that this is a film made from a particular point of view. A lot of films conceal the presence of the filmmaker. This is why in my film *Happy Birthday, Mr. Mograbi* [1999] I ask the cameraman to shake the camera, because if the camera is shaking it must be true!

JtB: *I just wondered if it adds to the power of the scenes at the checkpoint, the fact that you are actually in the film throughout. By the time we get to the checkpoint we know you so well, we've heard your voice and we identify with you. We know who the man is – at the end of the film at the checkpoint – the man who 'blows his top off', because we've spent an hour and a half in his company, in his living room, or studio. He's not a stranger to us.*

AM: I understand what you are saying, but I don't think this was intentional. For me it's very important to bring in the reflexivity because this is what really happens to me when I make a film. When I make a film and I come up with this idea. The film, Z32 [2009],[1] for example started as one thing, and I thought it would just be a very simple film of just a person testifying, or giving a testimony of what he has done, but of course as you go along, and you start making the film, questions arise and you find yourself with certain dilemmas, moral and cinematic dilemmas, and you have to deal with them. I think that those dilemmas, as the filmmaker, are part of the issue. It's not just a production dilemma. It's not a problem just of a filmmaker who needs to resolve or to deliver the product. The issues that I raise in my films are the issues that perhaps become a bridge to the consciousness of the viewer. And maybe take the subjects of my films to more abstract spaces or areas, and allow a more general discussion, and not just a specific one. This is why when I travel for example with Z32, and people talk about Israel and Palestine, I say: this is not a film about Israel and Palestine. This is a film about soldiers. And your soldiers are the same. If you think they are different then you have a big problem. This is 'how you make soldiers', and this is why soldiers do these things. That's how they become what they become.

NOTE

1   See the interview with Avi Mograbi on his film Z32 in this volume.

RE-ENACTMENT, THE HISTORY OF VIOLENCE AND DOCUMENTARY FILM

Joram ten Brink

The philosopher R. G. Collingwood, in his seminal work *The Idea of History* (1946), discusses the notion of re-enactment in the modern philosophy of history.[1] As early as 1928 he had already introduced his idea of re-enactment as a valid concept and method in the work of an historian. The historian's work is incomplete if reliant solely on documents and artefacts from the past:

> How, or on what conditions, can the historian know the past? [...] The first point to notice is that the past is never a given fact which he can apprehend empirically by perception. *Ex hypothesi*, the historian is not an eyewitness of the facts he desires to know. Nor does the historian fancy that he is; he knows quite well that the only possible knowledge of the past is mediate or inferential or indirect, never empirical. (1946: 282)

Collingwood's philosophical enquiry was motivated by what he considered to be practical problems. He strongly believed that the study of history leads historians to ask questions that have practical application as a basis for laying the foundations for the future (1939: 88).[2] Margot Browning attributes the inception of Collingwood's ideas to his wartime experience working in the Admiralty Intelligence in London between 1914 and 1918, and later as part of the team preparing the post-war peace conference (1993: 21–2).[3] A survivor of the war, Collingwood witnessed the trauma of a generation of young men killed on the battlefields. His entrenched resentment of the British establishment's failure in times of crisis is manifest in his autobiographical writings.[4] 'I completed my answer to the question that had haunted me ever since the War', he writes, reflecting back on his work in the 1920s.[5] 'How could we construct a science of human affairs, so to call it, from which men could learn to deal with human situations as skilfully as natural science had taught them to deal with situations in the world of Nature' (1939: 115). Collingwood questions the usefulness of a simple acceptance of testimony, concluding that this is not satisfactory in order to arrive at full knowledge of an historical event. Collingwood proposes that the historian re-enact the past in his own mind. In his study, the historian must go beyond the examination of relics; he must endeavour to discover the thoughts and motivations of historical actors at the time of the event's unfolding. That is, to think it again for himself: to re-enact the experience (1946: 282).[6]

Thus 'historical knowledge becomes more like a condition of human understanding than an explanation of the past' (Johnson 1998: 80).[7] Collingwood refers to the old school of 'scissors-and-paste' history in which the past is inert and knowledge of it corresponds to a compilation of past authorities (see, for example, 1939: 99). The understanding of historical events must be from within the present, as the past is not dead. Collingwood developed this idea already in 1920 as his first principle of the philosophy of history: 'At the time I expressed this by saying that history is concerned not with "events" but with "processes"; that "processes" are things which do not begin and end but turn into one another' (1939: 97–8). Past and present don't occupy separate worlds but partly 'overlay' each other as evidence from the past is always available to us in the present: 'The historian cannot answer questions about the past unless he has evidence about it. If there was a past event which had left no trace of any kind in the present world, it would be a past event for which was no evidence and ... no historian ... could know anything about it' (1939: 96). A modern-day historian, Raphael Samuel, has put it in similar terms: 'We are in fact constantly reinterpreting the past in the light of the present, and indeed, like conservationists and restorationists in other spheres, reinventing it. The angle of vision is inescapably contemporary, however remote the object in view' (1994: 430).[8] The historian, according to Collingwood, uses imagination, based on evidence, to reconstruct and understand the past but 'the past can be reconstructed only on its own terms. Historical claims are truth claims and, as such are subject to challenge by appeal to evidence. Imagination in history, therefore, is substantially different from imagination in art' (Johnson 1998: 84). Leon Pompa seeks to clarify Collingwood's method by adding his observation that it is valid if we also accept the fact that the historian operates within 'a context of known historical facts which cultures acquire in the course of their historical development and which, as members of these cultures, historians must accept as true in advance of their more specialised research which they carry out as historians' (1995: 181).[9]

Re-enactment is a process of critical thinking. For the historian's experience is of course different from the events in the past; 'it is not a passive surrender to the spell of another's mind; it is a labour of active and therefore critical thinking. The historian not only re-enacts past thoughts, he re-enacts it in the context of his own knowledge and therefore, in re-enacting it, criticises it, forms his own judgement of its value' (Collingwood 1946: 215). According to William H. Dray Collingwood's notion of re-enactment is based on a thought process, which involves continuous testing (1995: 55–6).[10] Collingwood himself brings the example of writing a history of a battlefield or a war. The historian must 'see the ground of the battlefield as the opposing commanders saw it, and draw from the topography the conclusions that they drew' (quoted in Dray 1995: 56n).

As re-enactment is a process of critical thinking, does the desire to re-create experiences, as authentic as they might be, shut the door to questions of representation and interpretation? Forms of representation and interpretation of traumatic or violent events in history are crucial to the notion of re-enactment. Does the present day re-enactment bear no responsibility to the past? Past and present don't occupy separate worlds but do overlap each other, according to Collingwood's idea of re-enactment.

Alongside the development of the idea of re-enactment in the field of philosophy of history, re-enactment became a much wider, popular, method of studying history by using theatre, live historical public re-enactment events, museum work, 'live museum exhibits', film and television, to name but few of modern-day forms of re-enactment. Most of the various forms of re-enactment work concern battles, wars, colonial history, invasions, local conflicts and disputes. Because of the nature of battlefield re-enactments (the most popular form of re-enactment today) they are performed on a massive scale with often the participation of thousands of 'actors' and as such attract considerable interest from the paying public or from enthusiasts and 'heritage followers'. What all the above forms of re-enactment add to Collingwood's notion of the method is 'a body-based discourse in which the past is reanimated through physical and psychological experience' (Agnew 2004: 330).[11] The degree of 'body-based discourse' varies – some of the public re-enactments don't capture the feelings of war (for example, the participants aren't 'scared') but they rather ritualise a commemoration of the past in the present; others like museum-created re-enactments, for example colonial Williamsburg in Virginia (see below) attempt to do just that. Vanesaa Agnew continues by arguing that 're-enactments ought to make visible the way in which events were imbued with meanings and investigate whose interests were served by those meanings … Its broad appeal, its implicit charge to democratise historical knowledge and its capacity to find new and inventive modes of history representation suggest that it also has a contribution to make to academic historiography' (2004: 335).

Pre-cinema battlefield re-enactment spectacle shows took place in London and Paris as early as during the Crimean War, 1853–56 (see Keller 2001: 65–70).[12] The Crimean War was the first modern war which was frequently relayed back home by war correspondents. William Howard Russell, considered to be the first modern war correspondent (Roger Fenton, the first war photographer also reported back from the Crimean War), sent regular dispatches to the *Times* in London reporting in detail the battlefield movements and the general conditions on the front line as they were unfolding. Crimean War battle re-enactment shows became immensely popular and were performed with the help of large cast of army personnel and others in front of thousands of spectators in Surrey Zoological Gardens, in Astley Amphitheatre in Lambeth and in Cremorne Gardens in Chelsea. Tickets were cheap and in what can only be described as Victorian 'pre-cinema spectacles' the live re-enactments re-staged the newspaper reports from Crimea in front of large-scale painted canvas backdrops (of the city of Sebastopol, for example) to illustrate the landscape and the physical environment of the far away country. Alongside the enormous backdrops and the live re-enactments by hundreds of 'troops', giant model fortifications were built on the show ground and dramatic illumination and pyrotechnic effects were used to give as accurate as possible account of the events in Crimea. Although the shows' entrepreneurs used some soldiers as 'extras', these re-enactment events were not part of a propaganda machine; rather, a commercial 'news' spectacle, striving to bring to the people of London 'life as it is' in the Crimea. To increase the sense of reality and in order to represent accurately the reports from the frontline injured soldiers who came back from Crimea played themselves on stage (2001: 66). Remarkably, the shows were altered and updated regularly, requiring a quick turn around of the production of new painted canvas backdrops and newly-built models in order to stay 'in sync' with the war reports from Crimea. The shows' organisers prided themselves in bringing to London the latest, most accurate historically 'images and sounds' from the battlefield. Similar, and even larger and more ambitious re-enactment spectacle shows of war scenes, were taking place simultaneously in Paris.

Live re-enactments became an even more popular industry during the 1880s with the travelling re-enactment show of Buffalo Bill's Wild West. The shows were promoted as 'factual history' (see Whissel 2002: 227).[13] These re-enactments defined American 'history' through a mixture of an elaborate production of a spectacle and the collaboration of a 'participant observer' crowd 'primarily through violent conflict between (morally superior) agents of civilization and (morally inferior) obstacles to civilization' (2002: 230). Cinema was not far behind it to cash on the growing appetite for re-enactment. During the 1899 Spanish-American War, the Buffalo Bill's Wild West re-enactment shows started to include scenes from the war which in turn were filmed by Edison:

> In these superior films can be seen the dead and wounded and the dismantled canon lying in the field of battle ... you think you can hear the huge cannon belch forth their death dealing missiles, and can really imagine yourself on the field witnessing the actual battle. (From Edison Catalogue, cited in Whissel 2002: 233)

Another early record of filmed re-enactment of battlefield is the work of the Chicago based inventor/filmmaker Edward H. Amet who pioneered around 1895 the production of film cameras and projectors. It is reported that he was refused permission in 1898 to go to Cuba and film the Spanish-American War. Instead, he set out to produce films about the war around his Chicago workshop. Using local residents and following the newspaper reports from the war front, Amet produced a series of short war re-enactment films including the famous battle of San Juan Hill. (He also filmed re-enactments of naval battles using miniature replicas of American and Spanish ships). During the Boer War in South Africa, Amet hired fifty local men and built a battlefield scene comprising campsites. He dug trenches and issued uniforms and guns to the participants the filmed re-enactments. In 1900, during the Boxer uprising in China, Amet continued with the production of battle re-enactments films (based on contemporary newspaper reports), only this time the local authorities stopped his production from being screened on the ground that it was 'too real' as it included scenes of 'beheadings' and other bloody war images (see Kekatos 2002: 410–14).[14]

Are historical events re-enacted through modern public entertainment methods become just another form of Collingwood's 'scissors-and-paste' history? Re-enactment is a process of critical thinking, as defined by Collingwood. Many of the major re-enactment events of battlefield clashes and other acts of violence are performed (and marketed) as enjoyable and fun-filled entertainment events.[15] Yet one of the dangers of modern-day re-enactments, as observed by a regular participant of large-scale American Civil War re-enactment events, is that although an enormous amount of historical knowledge is presented in these events, they tend to perpetuate ideologies rather than question them and examine issues like racism or the ethics of war (see Turner 1990: 134–5).[16] Does participation in a public re-enactment imply collusion with an historic event? Does it imply a desire to celebrate or commemorate an event or can it produce a critical view of history? A well documented controversy is the re-enactment of slave auctions in Williamsburg, New York in the late 1990s:

This edgy new representation of Colonial life casts costumed actors as slave leaders and slave owners while paying tourists find themselves in the roles of slaves. The re-enactments are so realistic that some audience members have attacked the white actors in the slave patrol, who have had to fight to keep their decorative muskets. [...] One visitor even attempted to lead his own revolt against the slave handlers. 'There are only three of them and a hundred of us!' he yelled. The actors had to step out of character to restrain him. At an attraction that historically has appealed almost exclusively to whites, the skits have stoked particularly strong emotions among African Americans, some of whom welcome frank discussion of a topic often given short shrift, even as they and others are discomfited by repeated images of subjugation. Several black actors have refused to portray slaves because they find it demeaning and emotionally wrenching. (*The Washington Post*, 7 July 1999: A1)

Williamsburg's decision to stage slave auctions can be seen as an effort to subvert the largely racist nostalgia for colonial America. Remarkably, a museum that normally appeals to white senior citizens and school kids chose to re-enact the brutality of US history in a form that usually is commemorative and seeks to glorify the past.

Can re-enactment as a method for the production of a documentary film, rather than simply filmed records of re-enactment events, offer a better solution? In fiction film, for example, films can create illusions but not easily criticise or destroy them. In asking viewers to repress critical reserve, indeed to become part of the illusion, David Herlihy argues that 'films make history seem too easy and our knowledge of the past appear too certain' (1998: 1188).[17] Herlihy continues by asking: 'Can [a film] through the same sights and sound, install both belief in the narrative and critical disbelief in its total accuracy?' (ibid.).[18]

Re-enactment in documentary film can take two forms: first, filmed re-enactment, similar to historical fiction films, in which the cinematic language of the common formats of documentary films – filmed lectures, expository and observational forms – offer mainly linear story rather than complex analysis; second, re-enactment as a method in documentary filmmaking, closer to Collingwood's ideal as well as to re-enactment as an artistic method.[19] For the historian Robert Rosenstone a film should be regarded as a form of history in its own right as the screen evokes a sense of involvement with the past. According to Rosenstone, filmmakers ask questions of the past that are more like the questions traditional historians have wanted to answer: how did we (the state, this people) get where we are and what does it mean to be here? (1995: 4–8).[20] Re-enactments as a method in making documentary film can be seen as opposition to the public re-enactment events, as they are interested in the performative re creation of histori-cal events as relevant to present day. These re-enactments question the present through performing the past and are not merely interested in the 'authenticity' of the historical facts.

Probably one of the earliest and more curious examples of using re-enactments as a method of documenting history is *The Storming of the Winter Palace* in 1920 in Petrograd in the Soviet Union. The re-enactment went beyond the re-creation of the authentic event – here re-enactment (this time executed by the state) was used to offer the public an interpretation of the history of the Revolution. The mass spectacle took place on the third anniversary of the storming of the palace in 1917 and was directed by the theatre director Nikolai Evreinov.[21] The storm-ing of the winter palace in 1917 was in a fact a 'non event' in the history of the Revolution, compared with other much more crucial moments that year. Unlike the real events in 1917 when a modest number of men and women took part in the actual storming of the palace, the 1920 re-enactment involved 10,000 par-ticipants and over 100,000 spectators; 'the mass performance would distil and improve the historical event' (von Geldern 1993: 203). As a revolutionary artistic project, three years after the Revolution, the re-enactment of the storming of the winter palace had a clear political and artistic brief: 'The re-enactment of the Revolution in the precise place of the original events brought the past into the present directly' (Buck-Morss 2000: 14).[22] Re-enactment was used here to 'create' the collective memory of the audience. The event was simultaneously produced as a theatre performance and as a film. It was designed as a grand theatrical and film performance, with elaborate lighting set-ups and minute-by-minute choreo-graphy of movements and actions by different groups of 'actors' (mostly soldiers and workers). The idea was to create a series of cinematic shots in the palace win-dows' frames to be viewed by the participating crowd in the street (2000: 147). As there were no film material in existence of the original event, the filmed ver-sion of the re-enactment quickly became the 'authentic' 'historical' documentary archive image of the storming of the winter palace, neatly conforming to the con-temporary revolutionary ethos (today, only four minutes of the film survived in the archives).[23] As one of the iconic images of the 1917 Revolution, Sergei Eisen-stein based the scenes in his film *October* – a film produced in 1927 to celebrate the tenth anniversary of the Bolshevik Revolution – on the filmed re-enactment scenes from Evreinov's 1920 spectacle in Petrograd as act of appropriation. The scenes in *October* – a feature film – themselves became the main source of in-formation and one of the definitive 'documentary' images of the 1917 events for generations to come in the Soviet Union and outside the country.[24]

In the past fifty years, one of the most important documentary filmmakers who has been using re-enactment as his main method of documentary filmmaking is the British director Peter Watkins, who used re-enactment in two of his major films on war, violence and conflict: *Culloden* (BBC, 1964) and the *La Commune* (La Sept/Arte, 1999).

The National Trust of Scotland describes the battle of Culloden in the Scottish Highlands in 1746 inside the Visitor Centre built on the grounds of the battlefield as follows:

> Towards one o'clock, the Jacobite artillery opened fire on government soldiers. The government responded with their own cannon, and the Battle of Culloden began. Bombarded by cannon shot and mortar bombs, the Jacobite clans held back, waiting for the order to attack. At last they moved forwards, through hail, smoke, murderous gunfire and grapeshot. Around eighty paces from their enemy they started to fire their muskets and charged. Some fought ferociously. Others never reached their goal. The government troops had finally worked out bayonet tactics to challenge the dreaded Highland charge and broadsword. The Jacobites lost momentum, wavered, and then fled. Hardly an hour had passed between the first shots and the final flight of the Prince's army. Although a short battle by European standards, it was an exceptionally bloody one. (Text from the National Trust for Scotland Culloden's home page – www.nts.org.uk/Culloden/PPF/TheBattle)

In the tradition of 'scissor-and-paste' public entertainment battle re-enactment event, a filmed version of the battle is screened in Culloden Visitors Centre and is on view on YouTube.[25] 'We are trying to portray the brutality of war through realistic and powerful film. It will be screened across the four walls of the theatre and we're putting the visitor right into the middle of the battle', says Craig Collinson, the film's director. He continues: 'Attempting to dramatically reconstruct the Battle of Culloden for film – giving an impression of scale, accuracy and, above all, sense of visceral bloodiness, was always going to be a challenge.'[26] Visitors to the Centre are recommended to watch two films on the battle of Culloden: *Battlefield Britain: The Battle Of Culloden 1746* – part of a BBC series by Peter Snow and his son Dan Snow (2004) and BBC Scotland's *Around Scotland: The Jacobites* (2008) (this three-part series is aimed at pupils aged 9–14). Separately, a computer graphics animation re-enactment of the Battle of Culloden can also be accessed on the Internet.[27]

Huw Wheldon, head of documentary and music programmes at the BBC who commissioned Watkins to make his documentary film *Culloden* wrote in the *Radio Times* (10 December 1964) to announce the first screening of the film on TV on 15 December 1964:

The battle and its aftermath will be re-created in tonight's programme which constitute something new in documentary filmmaking. [...] Bringing the techniques of news reel cameras, for example, to bear on carefully reconstructed events has been done before but only within very definite limits. Again, there is here virtually no 'dramatic dialogue' of the kind used in main historical narratives and what Peter Watkins has done, using modern documentary methods indeed, is to make what happened a long time ago happen with the urgency, the sense of vivid occasion, we associate with brilliant coverage of contemporary events. Even to attempt such a thing is to try something very difficult. To succeed (and this is my claim) is to achieve a definite moment of originality.

On the following morning after the TV transmission of the film the *Times* reviewer added: 'heroic legend stripped of Glamour. [...] it is easier to love an historical legend than an historical fact ... compulsory viewing of historical reconstruction'. The *Sun* described the film as 'One of the bravest documentaries'; and the *Guardian* wrote: 'an unforgettable experiment ... that was new and adventurous in technique'.

On the surface, with its meticulous attention to detail and with the help of a large number of participants, the film resembles a traditional battle re-enactment public event but in reality the film uses re-enactment as a method and strategy to inaugurate a complex and critical analysis of the Battle of Culloden. The 'traditional' re-enactment of the battle forms only part of the film and it is used to build a much larger historical picture about the causes and the consequences of the battle. The film, relying partly on the work of the historian John Prebble (who published *Culloden* in 1962) was announced as a BBC documentary film and as such uses a variety of modes of documentary film production.[28] Employing a mixture of voice-over narration, on- and off-camera commentary, interviews and sync-sound scenes, the film seeks to explore, through the construction of detailed forensic-like re-enactment scenes one of the most bloody events in British history. The main players in the drama and the modes of historical analysis are presented in the film in frank, often brutal modes of descriptions, using modern-day language. The result is a detailed outline of the political, economic and military background to and the aftermath of the events in 1746. The film adopts Prebble's approach as far as it tells the story of the ordinary men and women (and children) who took part in the battle and offers rich biographical details concerning a large number of soldiers and rebels. Many characters in the film are identified by name and are used to build, throughout the film, a dramatic framework to the re-enactment. Like Prebble's book, this is not the history of kings and generals but of the 'small' people of history. Using re-enactment in documentary film offers a suitable strategy to tell the story of people at war. To achieve it the film breaks down the barriers between subject and camera using techniques of reflexivity, extensive use of hand-held camera in extreme close proximity to the faces of the people in the killing field and asks the soldiers to stare at the camera and address the viewer directly.[29] By including lengthy direct-to-camera commentary by a large number of participants of the re- enactment, the film goes beyond the attempt to reproduce an authentic image of the battle as it delivers a contemporary critical view of the events. The film is shot from behind both battle lines, thus alternating the story and the perspectives of the battle. It includes post-battle interviews and reflections with soldiers, civilians and family members on the effects of the battle on families, the community and the political developments. Throughout the interviews the re-enactors are challenged about their actions and ideas. As a result, viewers identify with various characters and the changes in their actions and the wider consequences of the battle. Watkins also cites his motivation to produce *Culloden* at the time of the Vietnam War, where the US army was engaged in 'pacifying' the Vietnam highlands, as one of his reasons to embark on an historical re-enactment of the events that led to the 'pacification' of the Scottish Highlanders by the British army (see http://pwatkins.mnsi.net/culloden.htm). Ina Rae Hark observes that in its visual style and depiction of atrocities, *Culloden* 'eerily prefigure those images which reporting from Vietnam would saturate the screen in the years immediately following *Culloden*'s release' (1985: 294).[30] The Vietnam War was the first 'TV war' and in one sense it was 'preceded' by TV images of a war in the seventeenth century – a century with no photographic record.

Culloden is not a film about the battle in 1746 – it presents the re-enactment of the battle as a platform for an in-depth historical analysis of events prior but mainly post the battle itself. The film is about the destruction of the Highlanders in Scotland. By putting the battle in a wider context, re-enactment is used as a tool, a method to critically understand historical events. Re-enactment as a method is particularly useful within documentary dealing with events of violence and war as it offers a complex reading of history. In this film re-enactment really comes into its own as a vehicle for exploring how the present understands the past. The use of traditional observational or evidence-based documentary methods (for example, through the use of interviews, photographs, maps, archive material) offers an incomplete and limited view of history. In *Culloden* 'a body-based discourse in which the past is reanimated through physical and psychological experience' (as described above), coupled with the critical discourse gained by the method of re-enactment, can offer a rich and detailed account of history of violence.

The historian Natalie Zemon Davies commented on Watkins' *La Commune*:

> [It is] an example of a re-enactment film that can present the qualities and experi-
> ence of the past as efficaciously as prose, even if the truth status of re-enactment
> film is different from written recital. The historical richness of cinematic suggestion
> lies in its connection with evidence, its balance, and its willingness to suggest
> where the story comes from. (Quoted in Toplin 2002: 24)[31]

La Commune, Watkins' most ambitious documentary re-enactment film project
to date (the film is over five hours long) tells the story of the uprising and the
bloody demise of the communards of Paris in 1871. As in *Culloden* the film tells
the story from both sides of the barricades, offering a comprehensive view of the
events. Watkins took re-enactment as a method of production of a documentary film even further by organising mass meetings to attract participants to his
film. In these meetings in Paris he briefed the potential participants in detail and
worked with each individual on his/her historical character. The participants in
the re-enactment were asked to research and collect detailed evidence about their
character in preparation of the action of re-enactment in front of the camera
(these pre-production activities are not presented in the film). In fact, the participants imagined their life and built their own history based on evidence (a practice
very much congruent with Collingwood's understanding of re-enactment). As in
Culloden, the history of violence and bloodshed in 1871 (when more than 30,000
Parisians were killed by government troops at the end of the uprising of the commune) is told through actions re-enacted by more than two hundred members
of the 'cast'; the past is retold from 'below', by the people, not by generals and
politicians.

The film goes further than *Culloden* in so far as it presents to the viewer the
process of the filmed re-enactment of the conflict 1871. Watkins takes the viewer
step by step through the different stages of setting up the events in front of the
camera, the working of the filming process itself and the role of the journalists
who are fronting the film. In addition to the use of intertitles to deliver the historical information throughout the film, Watkins introduces as part of the re-enactment a modern-day journalistic reporting element to bring history to the present
day, namely the repeated use of modern contemporary news reporting by journalists and TV crews. These fulfil an important function in collecting evidence for
history as part of the historically-filmed documentary re-enactment. The anachronistic use of modern tools of collecting and delivering history gives Watkins
the chance to comment on the media's role in times of violent upheavals in 1871
or today.[32] In addition, every once in a while, the characters in the re-enactment
would step out of character and reflect on the significance of the violent events
on the streets of 1871 Paris, delivering detailed historical and modern analysis.

As Parisians, living in the same streets where the 1871 events took place, they ultimately express their opinions about life in Paris 1999. This deconstruction of the re-enactment process allows the viewer the critical space to consider how the past may always be already implicated in the present (à la Collingwood). Thus, the viewer is constantly asked to make connections between past and present, between the traumatic historical events and contemporary conditions in France.

> History is an argument about the past, as well as the record of it, and its terms are forever changing, sometimes under the influence of developments in adjacent fields of thought, sometimes – as with the sea-change in attitudes followed the First World War – as a result of politics. (Samuel 1994: 430)

Using re-enactment as a method in the production of documentary film can significantly advance our understanding of history and in particular enhance our insight into acts of violence and war. More urgently, Watkins' work – *Culloden* produced in the years of the Vietnam War and *La Commune* during social upheavals in Paris – mirror and demonstrate Collingwood's pragmatism and desire to use history to understand the present. In a moving contribution to the journal *Philosophy* early in World War II, April 1940, Collingwood calls upon on his fellow philosophers of history to respond the challenges of the time when he writes:

> No facts, in my opinion, are of greater practical importance at the present time than Fascism and Nazism. Our own country is fighting Nazi Germany. [...] The most urgent theme I can think of is the necessity of taking Fascism and Nazism seriously; to stop flattering ourselves with the belief that they are baseless follies indulged by unaccountable foreigners, or the alternative belief that they are good examples, which we should be wise to follow. What our soldiers and sailors and airmen have to fight, our philosophers have to understand. (1940: 176n)[33]

NOTES

1   R. G. Collinwood (1946) *The Idea of History*. Oxford: Oxford University Press.
2   Nietzsche already introduced the idea that 'We need history, certainly, but we need it for reasons different from those of which spoilt idler in the garden of knowledge needs it. [...] We need it, that is to say, for the sake of life and action, not as to turn comfortably away from life and action' – F. Nietzche (1997 [1873–76]) *Untimely Meditations*. Cambridge: Cambridge University Press, 59.
3   M. Browning (1993) 'Collingwood in context: theory, practice and academic ethos', *Interna-*

tional Studies in Philosophy, 25, 3, 17–33.

4 See also Collingwood's own account of the effect of World War I on his work in *An Autobiography*, Oxford: Clarendon Press, 1939.

5 Ibid., 89.

6 Collingwood applied his ideas of re-enactment also to his writings on the philosophy of art. As an avid music lover, Collingwood often referred to the experience of appreciating and understanding music as an act of imagination and reconstruction: 'What we get out of the concert is something other than the noises made by the performers. [...] what we get out of it is something which we have to reconstruct in our own minds and by our own efforts; something which remains forever inaccessible to a person who cannot or will not make efforts of the right kind, however completely he hears the sounds that fill the room in which he is sitting' – R. G. Collinwood (1938) *The Principles of Art*. Oxford: Clarendon Press, 141.

7 P. Johnson (1998) *R. G. Collingwood*. London: Thoemmes Press.

8 R. Samuel (1994) *Theatres of Memory, Vol.1: Past and Present in Contemporary Culture*. London: Verso.

9 L. Pompa (1995) 'Collingwood's theory of historical knowledge', in D. C. Boucher and J. T. Modood (eds) *Philosophy, History and Civilization: Interdisciplinary Perspectives on R. G. Collingwood*. Cardiff: University of Wales Press, 168–81.

10 W. H. Dray (1995) *History as Re-enactment*. Oxford: Oxford University Press.

11 V. Agnew (2004) 'Introduction: what is reenactment?', *Criticism*, 46, 3, 327–40.

12 U. Keller (2001) *The Ultimate Spectacle: A Visual History of the Crimean War*. Amsterdam: Gordon and Breach.

13 Whissel, K. (2002) 'Placing the spectator on the scene of history: the battle re-enactment the turn of the century, from Buffalo Bill's Wild West to the early cinema', *Historical Journal of Film, Radio and Television*, 22, 3, 225–43.

14 K. J. Kekatos (2002) 'Edward H. Amet and the Spanish-American war film', *Film History*, 14, 3/4, 405–17.

15 Although the journalist Andrew Gilligan, the defence correspondent of the *Sunday Telegraph*, reported on a big controversy following a military re-enactment by a rather 'extreme' wing of the re-enactment fraternity in the UK. The group, based in the Midlands, offered the public re-enactment of the St Brice's Day massacre in 1002. It involved 'bloody crucifixion', scenes of 'torture and murder of the innocent' and 'ritual rape and sacrifice of girls'; all produced anger and averse reactions from the public (*Sunday Telegraph*, 19 October 1997).

16 See R. Turner (1990) 'Bloodless battles – the civil war reenacted', *The Drama Review*, 34, 4, 123–36. Re-enactments of battle scenes from the American Civil War are by far to day the most popular of historical public live re-enactment events. Starting at the end of the nineteenth century they have mushroomed into a large-scale 'industry ' including production of 'authentic' artefacts and various paraphernalia.

17 D. Herlihy (1998) 'Am I a camera?', *The American Historical Review*, 93, 5, 1186–92.

18 For a detailed discussion on re-enactment in fiction films, see also N. Z. Davis (2000) *Slaves on Screen*. Toronto: Vintage Canada.

19 For example Robert Longo's photographs on the American Civil War (2002), Jeremy Deller's *The Battle of Orgreave* (2002) or Heike Gallmeier's *War and Peace Show* (2004); see also Alice Correia's contribution to this volume on Deller's *The Battle of Orgreave*.

20 R. Rosenstone (1995) *Visions of the Past: The Challenge of Film to our Idea of History*. Cambridge, MA: Harvard University Press.

21 For a detailed description of the event see J. von Geldern (1993) *Bolshevik Festivals, 1917– 1920*. Berkeley: University of California Press, 200–7.

22 S. Buck-Morss (2000) *Dreamworld and Catastrophe: The Passing of Mass Utopia in East and West*. Cambridge, MA: MIT Press.

23 http://www.soviethistory.org/index.php?page-subject&SubjectID-1917newculture&Year-1917&show-video; accessed 3 September 2010.

24 See also R. Rosenstone (2001) 'October as history', *Rethinking History*, 5, 2, 255–74, for a discussion of *October* as an historical document.

25 http://www.youtube.com/watch?v=HR_ltIlAeYA; accessed 13 September 2010.

26 http://news.bbc.co.uk/1/hi/scotland/highlands_and_islands/6913173.stm; accessed 13 September 2010.

27 http://www.youtube.com/watch?v=n9sv-rqj53g&nr=1; accessed 13 September 2010.

28 See Watkins on the making of the film in an interview in A. Rosenthal (1988) *New Challenges to Documentary*. Berkeley: University of California Press, 594; see also J. Prebble (1961) *Culloden*. London: Secker & Warburg.

29 The film's cameraman, one of the BBC's best – Dick Bush – was initially very apprehensive about taking on the job. He did not trust Watkins' method with an un-blimped 16mm hand-held camera, but after an hour of shooting he was won over by the 'brilliant concept' behind the film (quoted in J. Gomez (1979) *Peter Watkins*. New York: Twayne Publishers, 34.

30 I. R. Hark (1985) 'On eye-witnessing history: the compromised spectator in Watkins, Peter, "Culloden"', *South Atlantic Quarterly*, 84, 3, 294–301.

31 R. B. Toplin (1998) 'The filmmaker as historian', *The American historical review*, 93, 5, 1210–27.

32 The anachronistic use of modern TV reporting also follows current thoughts among some historians on the usefulness of counterfactual history; see N. Ferguson (ed.) (1997) *Virtual History: Alternatives and Counterfactuals*. Basingstoke: Macmillan.

33 R. G. Collinwood (1940) 'Fascism and Nazism', *Philosophy*, 15, 58, 168–76.

INTERPRETING JEREMY DELLER'S
THE BATTLE OF ORGREAVE

Alice Correia

Jeremy Deller's *The Battle of Orgreave* (2001) has primarily been discussed in direct relation to the violent clashes between picketing miners and police during the 1984–85 Miners' Strike in the UK. As a performed re-enactment of violence which took place on 18 June 1984, the work has been positioned within a narrative of the Miners' Strike that allows retrospective consideration of the political

Fig. 1 Jeremy Deller, scene from *The Battle of Orgreave*, 2001. Commissioned and produced by Artangel. Photo credit, Martin Jenkinson.

and social ramifications of the industrial action.[1] Whilst these interpretations are undoubtedly important, it is my contention that *The Battle of Orgreave* needs to be considered from a variety of perspectives, and that identifying a broader range of subjects at work in Deller's performance event leads to a richer and deeper understanding of this multifaceted work of art.

The Battle of Orgreave is best understood as a dialogical artwork, containing multiple strands created though conversations between the artist, veterans of the Miners' Strike, re-enactment specialists, the audiences of the work and its art-historical context. While the 1984–85 Strike is undoubtedly the fulcrum of the work, Deller has allowed space for different themes to exist. Initially contextualising this re-enactment through a discussion of the Miners' Strike and its presentation in the media, I will go on to suggest that *The Battle of Orgreave* could be interpreted as an exploration of historical memory and a consideration of how the past is understood and transmitted in the present day. Deller's fascination with 'living history', a term he uses to denote the stories of people living in the here and now who were involved in, or are representative of, events deemed culturally and historically significant,[2] can be viewed within a recent museological tendency of promoting the narratives of those on the margins of historical memory. Presenting the past in the present, Deller's performance event encompasses the politics of re-enactment as historical methodology, whilst the realism of the re-enactment calls into question whether viewing such a performance can have historical authenticity. Thinking critically about the past, Deller sought to tell the truth of the violence at Orgreave, and in doing so undermined apparently authoritative versions of history.

The narrative of the 1984–85 Miners' Strike encompasses the steady decline of coal mining as a major employer within Britain's heavy industries. Since the end of World War II, the contraction of the coal industry has been steady, and between 1960 and 1970 43 per cent of Britain's collieries closed. The 1984 dispute can be directly linked to the National Union of Mineworkers' (NUM) strikes of 1972 and 1974, the latter leading to the fall of Edward Heath's Conservative government.[3] By the time the Conservatives returned to power with Margaret Thatcher as leader in 1979, they had already drafted a policy proposal for the denationalisation of primary and secondary industries which many on the Left feared would have the additional outcome of quashing the power of the trade unions.[4] When, in 1984, the government and the National Coal Board announced plans for colliery closures, industrial action swiftly followed. The miners believed they could win; the government, ultimately, proved they could not. Although ostensibly about pit closures, the strike became the site of an ideological contest between left- and right-wing politics, a contest between the older, working-class socialism embodied by the NUM president Arthur Scargill and the new entrepreneurialism promoted by Margaret Thatcher.

Prior to the confrontation on 18 June 1984, it had become clear to both strikers and government that Orgreave would be of significant strategic importance in the trajectory of the dispute. Picketing the coking plant in Orgreave, South Yorkshire, which provided fuel for the Scunthorpe steelworks, Arthur Scargill had hoped to break the government's will over pit closures. Throughout the early 1980s, Margaret Thatcher had aligned herself with the police force, being a vocal exponent of law and order. Having learnt the lessons of the 1981 urban uprisings, during the 1984–85 dispute police armed with riot equipment were deployed across mining districts. The eventual confrontation at Orgreave was the first time riot police had been used to contain an industrial strike in the UK. However, distancing government involvement in the causes of the strike, Thatcher claimed: 'Mob violence can only be defeated if the police have the complete moral and practical support of the government.'[5]

In his book, published following the performance event, Deller explained:

On 18 June 1984, I was watching the evening news and saw footage of a mass picket at the Orgreave coking plant in South Yorkshire in which thousands of were chased up a field by mounted police. The image of this pursuit stuck in my mind and for years I wanted to find out what exactly happened on that day with a view to re-enacting or commemorating it in some way. It would not be an exaggeration to say that the strike, like a civil war, had a traumatically divisive effect at all levels of life in the UK. Families were torn apart because of divided loyalties, the union movement was split on its willingness to support the National Union of Mineworkers, the print media especially contributed to the polarization of the arguments to the point where there appeared to be little space for the middle ground. So in all but name it became an ideological and industrial battle between two sections of British society.[6]

In an extensive study, the Broadcasting Research Unit (BRU) found that between the months of June and August 1984 televised BBC coverage of violence on the picket lines was rising in comparison to ITV, where the reporting of violence was falling (see Cumberbatch et al. 1986: 50). The bias towards covering the violent aspects of the strike by the BBC was to prove significant in its treatment of the confrontation between pickets and police on 18 June at Orgreave. In a detailed analysis of the BBC 9pm news and the ITV 10pm news of 18 June, the BRU found a marked contrast in the language of the reporting and the visual images broadcast. While the BBC juxtaposed images of pickets assaulting policemen with words such as 'battle', 'violence' and 'battlefield', ITV chose to broadcast a policeman truncheon-ing a picket, with the newscaster using words such as 'fight'. However, both channels presented footage of the mounted police cantering into the pickets as occurring after an escalation of picket violence.[7] Eyewitness accounts of that day at Orgreave testify to the mounted charge as occurring *before* any major escalation of violence, suggesting that police intervention was the cause rather than the consequence of picket violence.

Seeking to rectify this false impression, Deller made the mounted police charge a key feature in his performance, and as such *The Battle of Orgreave* can be understood as building upon the work of leftist documentary photographers. During the course of the dispute images of the mounted police charge became synonymous with the Miners' Strike, but they were not exclusive to Orgreave. Photographs by John Sturrock of mounted police charging towards a miners' picket line at Brodsworth capture the pace and ferocity of the event from a miner's perspective. Alongside images of the strike by Chris Killip, Sturrock's photographs bear witness to the violent struggle taking place in 1984 and characterise the social documentary photography of the early to mid-1980s.[8] These documentary images of the 1984 strike, alongside the televised news footage, are echoed in Deller's re-enactment.

On 18 June 2001, seventeen years after the original confrontation, Deller returned to Orgreave with a cast and crew to re-stage one of the most violent clashes of the strike. He had first conceived of re-enacting the conflict at Orgreave seven years earlier, and in 2000, having received financial backing from public-art commissioners Artangel, undertook eighteen months of research into the Miners' Strike, looking at newspaper archives and television footage and, most importantly, meeting former miners and policemen and listening to their testimonies and eye-witness accounts. By choosing to re-enact the confrontation Deller distinguished Orgreave as not only particularly representative of the Miners' Strike but also as individually worthy of commemoration. Describing in his statement a desire to tell the truth, of wanting to find out what really happened, he alluded to the biased news reporting of the British broadcast media and by mentioning families and the print media and making reference to the status of heavy industry and the conflict between political ideologies, Deller emphasised the breadth of the social and political issues in play during the strike, as well as its ongoing ramifications in contemporary society.

Approximately one thousand people took part in *The Battle of Orgreave* in 2001, of whom about two hundred were ex-miners, together with a handful of ex-policemen (exact number unknown) who had been involved in the original conflict, and local Orgreave residents. For the reconstruction Deller enlisted the help of Howard Giles, director of Event-Plan, a re-enactment specialist company, who had previously been the director of English Heritage's Special Events Unit. With Giles' contacts, Deller recruited the other eight hundred participants from historical re-enactment societies,[9] all of whom were more used to re-staging historical events from outside their own living memory or personal experience. Rehearsals took place on 17 June, when participants performed mini-re-enactments, practiced period swear-words and told their stories of the strike to each other.[10]

On the day of the re-enactment, Orgreave village came to a standstill; a marquee was set up containing archival material and images, ensuring that onlookers were aware that *The Battle of Orgreave* was a commemorative reconstruction. A commentary explaining what was happening and pop hits from 1984 was played over loudspeakers. Fashions of that year were revisited and participants were dressed in costumes appropriate to the time and place of the battle. Miners wore reprinted 'Coal not Dole' stickers, whilst police uniforms remained static in their familiarity. Although the weather was overcast in 2001, it had been a hot day in 1984 and Deller insisted on attention to detail: so miners played football and ate ice-lollies on the battlefield. Because the re-enactment was staged to be as 'real' as possible, the site specificity of Orgreave was central. Taking place in and around Orgreave itself, the production reactivated the everyday space of the village and

Fig. 2 Jeremy Deller, scene from *The Battle of Orgreave*, 2001. Commissioned and produced by Artangel. Photo credit, Martin Jenkinson.

the surrounding fields as a site of conflict, reoccupying it with scenes from living memory. Whilst
it was not possible to adhere to the time-scale of
the 1984 battle, care was taken to ensure that the
re-enactment occurred in the correct sequence,
and Howard Giles identified two phases of the
battle which dictated the organisation of the re-
enactment.[11] The first comprised lines of miners
and police in a stand-off in a nearby field and
consisted of miners throwing foam-rocks, chanting and occasionally pushing the front line of
police. In response, the police banged their trun-

Fig. 3 Jeremy Deller, scene from *The Battle of Orgreave*, 2001. Commissioned and produced by Artangel. Photo credit, Martin Jenkinson.

cheons on their shields and hit out at pushing miners. An actor playing Scargill
inspected the police troops. This was followed by a recreation of the notorious
mounted attack which scattered the miners, who were then pursued by police officers on foot. The charge led to mock-fighting between miners and police, both
sides suffering pretend injuries; fake blood was distributed to achieve authenticity. During the original battle, panicked miners had retreated from the field by
scrambling across a railway line, but for safety this event was omitted from the
re-enactment.

The second phase was the battle in Orgreave village; again miners threw foam-
rocks, whilst mounted police charged through the streets and eventually pushed
the miners towards the outskirts of the village, where the re-enactment came to
an end. Events that had originally occurred over approximately eight hours had
been condensed and scaled down, but Deller recalled later that the re-enactment
had at times veered towards real violence and contained an edginess not usually
found in staged historical-battle re-enactments.[12] By insisting upon the presence
and participation of 'veterans' of the 1984 conflict on the front lines of the re-
staged picket, Deller gained for his project a legitimacy and a level of authenticity
that eludes other re-enactments and that made the work more compelling.

For many of the miners taking part in the performance, *The Battle of Orgreave*
offered an opportunity to reassert their truth of what happened on that day in
1984. In challenging governmental 'truth' of the violence at Orgreave and its presentation on both the BBC and ITV news, and by providing a forum in which the
destructive stereotype of the miner could be reconsidered, *The Battle of Orgreave*
can be understood – following Bakhtin – as a means by which miners could 'express their criticism, their deep distrust of official truth' (1984: 269). Functioning
as personal catharsis and commemoration, Orgreave was also a comment on the
legacy of social and political change in the subsequent years, and the performance

Fig. 4 Jeremy Deller, scene from *The Battle of Orgreave*, 2001. Commissioned and produced by Artangel. Photo credit, Martin Jenkinson.

touched on concerns that continue into the present. The closure of the mining industry 'was not just a case of local economic decline but rather one of cultural crisis'.[13] In the wake of pit closures, many mining villages had to cope with the long-lasting effects of male unemployment, the dereliction of industrial buildings, a rise in petty crime, substance abuse and the collapse of community cohesion in areas whose raison d'être had been mining. By providing a platform to address the causes of these social problems, Deller can be considered as participating in the regeneration and rehabilitation of marginalised mining communities. Tom Morton's proposition that *The Battle of Orgreave* was not simply 'about' the Miners' Strike but was, rather, 'a part of its history, an epilogue to an experience', seems particularly useful.[14]

Similarly, using Deller's conception of the term 'living history' discussed earlier, the participation of real miners and real policemen in the artwork places it within the purview of an individual picket's or policeman's experience, and as such, the work becomes part of their narrative of the strike. Deller was conscious that this should happen and his book *The English Civil War Part II: Personal Accounts of the 1984–85 Miners' Strike* – whilst ostensibly a document of the artwork, containing photographs of the re-enactment and information about the day – is in fact, as its subtitle makes clear, a collection of personal accounts of the strike. Containing essays by a picket, a picket's wife, a policeman and an ambulance driver amongst others, as well as reproducing newspaper reports and protest-song lyrics and containing a CD of oral testimonies, the book becomes a record of those normally excluded from official historical documents.

During his research for *The Battle of Orgreave* Deller became an oral historian, interviewing witnesses of and participants in the event in order to record the experiences and opinions of those 'people who might otherwise have been "hidden from history"' (Perks and Thomson 1998: ix). The documentary film recording of *The Battle of Orgreave*, directed by Mike Figgis,[15] is interspersed with archival television footage and interviews carried out by Deller; he also undertook the interviews for the audio CD. Deller's foregrounding of oral history and the written testimony of the miners and their supporters enabled the 'empowerment of individuals or social groups', who were demonised for their actions in the mainstream press and by the government.[16] In his attraction to those on the margins of mainstream history, it is possible to see Deller as the artist-ethnographer aligning himself with the miners and their families, in order to tap into their subalterneity and produce an artwork with potentially transformative properties. However, whilst Deller's book contains transcripts from a cross-section of people involved in the strike, David Gilbert notes that 'other voices from the strike remain silent – those miners that returned to work in Yorkshire are shadowy figures to be demonised or pitied'.[17] Deller's book and the CD subscribe to the predominant collective narrative of the strike given by pickets and their wives; miners who continued to work and anti-strike policemen are excluded. The casting of the striking miners as 'right' and the police as 'wrong' in Orgreave avoids some of the complexity of how to position non-striking miners. In this context, Anna Green has raised a note of caution when considering individual oral testimonies and histories that collaborate too closely with an already existent (although under-recognised) narrative.[18] She suggests that, while collective memory fulfils a need to remember and to cement identity within particular groups, the dominance of collective over individual memory has the potential to stifle differentiation and dissent. Green argues that 'the need for an "affective community" ensures that individuals remember primarily those memories which are "in harmony" with those of others'.[19] In his desire to rectify wrongs done towards the miners, Deller prioritised those narratives that already had credence within the pro-strike mining community, with several of his narrators having already been recorded in print and oral history archives.[20] However, it is clear from his statement quoted earlier that this was always intended to be the case. In telling the truth of what happened at Orgreave and challenging the biased media narratives, the artwork and its accompanying publication would naturally lean towards the pickets' position.

Enlisting the expertise of Howard Giles was critical for the fruition of Deller's artwork and directed interpretations of *The Battle of Orgreave* towards issues of history and re-enactment. As part of his research, Deller undertook an investigation into re-enactment societies and the role of historical re-enactment within British heritage industries. Embedded within Orgreave is a probing examination of the validity of re-enactment as historical experience and of the types of people who involve themselves with re-enacting historical battles as a creative pastime. Giles, in his role at English Heritage, had actively supported the use of re-enactment within the heritage sector as an educational tool in the form of 'Living History', which brought the past to life. In 1989, 49 per cent of English Heritage special events were military re-enactments.[21]

Literature on 'Living History' argues that re-enactment offers up alternative ways of accessing the past.[22] 'Living History' activates the senses of both participants and spectators, enabling a physical experience in a way that other forms of historical investigation do not. As a strategy for interpreting and negotiating the past, it is suggested, 'Living History' also allows for communication between the past and the present and facilitates greater understanding. *The Battle of Orgreave* as a 'Living History' performance brought the past into the present and encouraged a reconsideration of the events of 1984. Historical re-enactment developed in the 1960s, stimulated by the centennial celebrations of the American Civil War, and re-enacting military battles remains at the forefront of this kind of activity. In Britain, The Sealed Knot and the English Civil War Society were the earliest and remain the largest re-enactment groups, with both societies specialising in battles from the English Civil War. With members of both of these groups participating, *The Battle of Orgreave* might be equally 'about' the hobbyists who take part in historical battle reconstructions. In an extended interview, Deller explained:

Living history is a good term to use. That's the phrase re-enactment groups use all the time to refer to what they do. But often their performances have no social or political context – you just see this battle and the details of war, cannons, horses, etc. It's not about why those men are fighting each other, especially when they are from the same country. What I wanted was for re-enactors to be in a situation where they would be fighting with and against men that were part of an unfinished messy history. I wanted some of them to see that history didn't end in 1945. That was initially almost as much of an interest as the event itself. A lot of the members of historical re-enactment societies were terrified of the miners. During the '80s they had obviously believed what they had read in the press and had the idea that the men that they would be working with on the re-enactment were going to be outright hooligans or revolutionaries. They thought it would turn into one huge real battle.[23]

In his criticisms of un-contextualised re-enactments Deller appears to echo David Lowenthal, who argues that watching or participating in an exciting reconstruction is not the same as having historical knowledge or understanding; Lowenthal suggests that 'factoids', or details, replace the intricacies of historical contextualisation and interpretation.[24] Re-enactment societies appear to unconsciously uphold this position, presenting themselves as fervently a-political.[25] A bipartisan position has been the touchstone of historical re-enactment, with specialists arguing that in their adherence to battle records and attention to costume detail, performances (and therefore performers) do not allow space for personal subjectivity or historical revisionism.[26] Deller attempted to position the re-enactors beyond factoids, by bringing them face to face with the people they were pretending to be. In doing so, he demonstrated that the past and the present are intertwined and that, in order to fully understand the intricacies of the past, re-enactment performances must go beyond simulacra to include critical engagement.

But whilst it is possible to see details such as the 'Coal not Dole' stickers or the presence of vintage coal trucks as 'structurally superfluous' to the narrative of the strike given during Deller's re-enactment, according to Roland Barthes' essay *The Reality Effect* these details can be seen as important descriptive notations which frame the action whilst not in themselves influencing the progression of the narrative.[27] Barthes argues that cumulatively, these details establish the reality of the scene so that, as Stephen Bann explains, it is the detail which 'guarantees the authenticity of the historical message'.[28] From this perspective, verisimilitude is the frame which facilitates critical historical interpretation. Countering the anti-heritage discourse, Raphael Samuel maintains that 'Living History' can offer productive entryways into the past. For him historical re-enactment is 'live interpretation', where the past becomes plural and where hegemonic histories ascribed from above become fractured.[29] In this way, *The Battle of Orgreave* gave new and experiential insight.

Nonetheless, Deller's film *History in Action* (2000–05) seems to support Lowenthal's identification of living history as failing as a rigorous tool of historical research. In 1996, Howard Giles oversaw English Heritage's first multi-period event, 'History in Action', at which re-enactment groups that specialised in different historical periods gathered at a single site. Since then, English Heritage has expanded its involvement with historical re-enactors and 'History in Action' has been held annually, 'becoming the largest and most spectacular event of its kind in the world'.[30] Deller's *History in Action* is a record of this type of multi-era re-enactment event, depicting a procession of American World War I soldiers, followed by French nineteenth-century soldiers and their wives and children, marching through two rows of Roman legionaries. There is a strange intermingling of historical times and the work appears to be a record of Deller's fascination with not only the people taking part but also their ability to conflate time, despite their commitment to historical accuracy. The work raises questions regarding what exactly these people are re-enacting and whether there can ever be anything truthful in the coming together of discrete historical periods in this way. While Deller's stance towards these people is ambiguous, his film, in its existence as an artwork rather than a documentary, does imply a position, as proposed by Kevin Walsh, that re-enactment events 'are nothing but mere titillation, meaningless amateur dramatics promoting the post-modern simulacrum, a hazy image of a manipulated and trivialized past'.[31] While *History in Action* may stand alongside Folk Archive as a record of individual creativity and expression, it is distinct from *The Battle of Orgreave* in that it lacks historical specificity and could therefore be regarded as a general comment on the non-contextualised activities of re-enactment societies.

In light of this discussion of Britain's heritage culture, if we return to Deller's initial intention – to show the Miners' Strike as a pivotal moment in British history, a second civil war in which socialism and the nationalised industries were defeated by Thatcherite free-market capitalism – then politicised interpretations of *The Battle of Orgreave* as a nostalgic dialogue between past and present become increasingly complex. Robert Hewison and others have argued that the proliferation of heritage sites is a by-product of cultural nostalgia, but that this nostalgia is itself 'felt most strongly at a time of discontent, anxiety or disappointment' and that 'the times for which we feel nostalgia more keenly were themselves periods of disturbance'.[32] Re-enacted in 2001, *The Battle of Orgreave* could be viewed as evidence of personal nostalgia for community solidarity on the part of the ex-miners and, more specifically, as a symptom of a left-wing disenchantment with New Labour's government.

Alongside the historical, cultural and political interpretations of *The Battle of Orgreave* its art-historical contexts need also to be identified. As a time-based artwork, it exists within a discourse of performance in which reality and mimesis are united. Performance has been positioned as an alternative, anti-establishment art form which can challenge the limitations of more traditional object-based art and institutional sites for viewing art.[33] Consequently, Deller's idea of staging a re-enactment of the 1984 conflict can be conceived as performance art dealing with socio-political concerns which challenge the biased histories of the dominant power. The performed artwork can be understood, in Katherine Stiles' terms, 'as intrinsically activist and socially subversive of state policies, earning a privileged position on the margins of culture, where it serves in the liminal capacity as a tester of cultural values'.[34]

The performed re-enactment as subversive act of liberation from the prevailing order can also be regarded as a form of Bakhtin's carnival, marking 'the suspension of all hierarchical rank, privileges, norms and prohibitions. Carnival was the true feast of time, the feast of becoming, change and renewal. It was hostile to all that was immortalised and completed.'[35] *The Battle of Orgreave* might be seen therefore as a Bakhtinian suspension of the norms and prohibitions set in place to prevent civilian disorder and violence and giving its participants licence to enter into a fight or battle scenario outside the norms of everyday life. As in Bakhtin's carnival: 'The boundaries between play and life are intentionally erased' so that 'life itself is on stage'.[36] The artwork's status as re-enactment extends Bakhtin's proposition of carnival as a true depiction of life. The re-enactment as time machine transported the veterans and witnesses of the original conflict back to a time of remembered experience. The fine line between performed and real violent action in *The Battle of Orgreave* is complicated by the re-enactment's ability to telescope time, so that participants were both remembering real violence from the past and re-living it. When Alex Farquharson could record that 'rumour had it that a small number of the real miners were applying too much gusto to their roles at rehearsals the previous day', it is clear that a blurring between the real and the performed bodies taking part in the re-enactment occurred.[37]

Deller's artwork provided a space in which a conflict over agency and ownership of personal identity could take place. For Adrian Heathfield, 'the performing body is often presented as a site of contestation between opposing dynamics; as a passive recipient of inscription by social institutions, cultural discourses, ideologies and orders of power, and as an active agent through which identity and social relation may be tested, re-articulated and remade'.[38] The inclusion of real miners in the performance challenged the stereotype inscribed upon them in 1984 and enabled the participants to control their own presentation. It is significant that a proportion of the participating miners chose to play policemen during the re-enactment, complicating the notion that identities are stable and that representation can be authoritative.

Bakhtin posits that when the lines between play and reality are erased the audience is also complicit in the performance. Directing *The Battle of Orgreave* in front of spectators, Deller ensured that the re-enactment had an existence beyond its active participants; in this performance, as in carnival, 'everyone participates because its very idea embraces all the people'.[39] The 'liveness' of the event challenged a cultural system in which experience is frequently mediated. Just as 'Living History' has been seen to enable a physical historical experience, so live art performances heighten sensory knowledges and utilise the audience's emotional responses. As part of a public art performance, the audience, as much as the re-

Fig. 5 Jeremy Deller, scene from *The Battle of Orgreave*, 2001. Commissioned and produced by Artangel. Photo credit, Martin Jenkinson.

enactors or the artist, were complicit in the political positioning of *The Battle of Orgreave* and Deller transformed his spectators from passive observers into active participants and witnesses. Tim Etchells has suggested that performance art has the power to transform disengaged onlookers into active contributors through their witnessing of events, whereby 'to witness an event is to be present at it in an ethical way. To witness is to feel the weight of things and one's own place in them.'[40] As Alex Farquharson observed, 'For many – participants and spectators alike – this *Battle of Orgreave* was more flashback than re-enactment', and audience members joined in the chanting and jeering as policemen ran by.[41] The inclusion of Orgreave's inhabitants within readings of Deller's artwork is not only a recognition of the role spectators play in completing the performance, but also recalls their presence and participation at the 1984 conflict. *The Battle of Orgreave* can then be interpreted as a public work of art, including not only the participants but also its observers.

Reactivating memories of the Miner's Strike through its re-enactment, *The Battle of Orgreave* presented what happened at Orgreave in June 1984 as a conduit to wider concerns. Not only did Deller's artwork take into consideration the personal memories of the artist and the original participants, it also highlights how collective and group memories are shaped. Challenging the truth of what was broadcast on television in 1984, Orgreave raised questions over the reliability of images, over who has control over the presentation of historic events and over how the past is remembered. Using the tools of the heritage industry, *The Battle of Orgreave* opposed a heritage system in which the past is remembered through sanitised memories. Orgreave was not the past seen from a safe distance, but rather history presented as unfinished business. Identified as an artist-ethnographer and oral historian, Jeremy Deller can be located within the current debates surrounding the ethics of collaborative and socially engaged art. In *The Battle of Orgreave* he initiated a multifaceted performance with a lightness of touch which has meant that, despite his having clear aims for the artwork, there remains enough dialogic space around it for it to exist beyond those parameters.

NOTES

The author and editors are grateful to *Visual Culture in Britain* journal for allowing this chapter to be re-printed.

1   See, for example, A. Farquharson (2001) 'Jeremy Deller: *The Battle of Orgreave*', *Frieze*, vol. 61, September, 108; J. Jones (2001) 'Missiles fly, truncheons swing, police chase miners as cars burn. It's all very exciting. But why is it art?', *Guardian*, Arts Section, 19 June, www.guardian.co.uk/arts/story/0,,509066,00.html' accessed 8 November 2005.

2   See J. Deller (2002) 'A Thousand Words', *Art Forum International*, November, 17–71.

3   See E. J. Evans (2004) *Thatcher and Thatcherism*. London: Routledge, 2nd edition, 39.

4   See 'Appomattox or civil war?',*The Economist*, 27 May 1978, 21, a leaked version of Nicholas Ridley's policy report for denationalising British industry. Also, T. Lane (1983) 'The Tories and the Trade Unions: Rhetoric and Reality', in S. Hall and M. Jacques (eds) *The Politics of Thatcherism*. London: Lawrence and Wishart/Marxism Today, 169–87); although written prior to the 1984 strike, this is a useful outline of Conservative attitudes towards the trade unions and notes how Tory economic policy was a key component of the ideological battle taking place in the early 1980s.

5   M. Thatcher (1993) *The Downing Street Years*. London: HarperCollins, p. 348.

6   J. Deller (2002) 'Foreword', in *The English Civil War Part II: Personal Accounts of the 1984–85 Miners' Strike*, ed. G. van Noord. London: Artangel, 7.

7   For transcripts of the BBC 9pm news and the ITV 10pm news from 18 June 1984, see G. Cumberbatch R. McGregor, B. Brown and D. Morrison (1986) *Television and the Miners' Strike*. London: Broadcasting Research Unit, 72–3.

8   See G. Badger and J. Benton-Harris (1989) *Through the Looking Glass: Photographic Art in Britain 1945–1989*. London: Barbican Art Gallery, 64.

9   Including The Sealed Knot (English Civil War specialists), The Napoleonic Society, The American Civil War Society, The Victorian Military Society, and The World War Two Living History Association.

10 See D. Butler (2001) 'The Battle of Orgreave', *AN Magazine*, September, 24–5, for an account of *The Battle of Orgreave* by a re-enactor; Butler played a member of the Welsh Con-

stabulary.

11 H. Giles (2002) 'The Battle of Orgreave from a Tactical Point of View', in J. Deller (ed.) *The English Civil War Part II: Personal Accounts of the 1984–85 Miners' Strike*. London: Artangel, 24–31.

12 Jeremy Deller in conversation with the author, 26 January 2005.

13 K. Bennett, H. Benyon and R. Hudson (2000) *Coalfields Regeneration: Dealing with the Consequences of Industrial Decline*. Bristol: Policy Press, 4.

14 T. Morton (2003) 'Mining for Gold', *Frieze*, vol. 72, 73.

15 Mike Figgis (dir.) *Jeremy Deller: The Battle of Orgreave*, Artangel Media and Channel Four, first broadcast on Channel Four, Sunday 20 October 2002. Despite Deller's involvement in the film he had no editorial control over it, and is adamant that it should be regarded as a document of the artwork, and not as interchangeable with the artwork; Jeremy Deller in conversation with the author, 26 January 2005.

16 R. Perks and A. Thomson (1998) 'Introduction', in R. Perks and A. Thomson(eds) *The Oral History Reader*. London: Routledge, ix.

17 D. Gilbert (2005) '"The English Civil War Part II: Personal Accounts of the 1984–85 Miners' Strike" by Jeremy Deller', *Oral History*, 33, 1, 105.

18 A. Green (2004) 'Individual Remembering and "Collective Memory": Theoretical Presuppositions and Contemporary Debates', *Oral History*, 32, 2, 35–45.

19 Ibid., 38.

20 D. Gilbert (2005) '"The English Civil War Part II: Personal Accounts of the 1984–85 Miners' Strike" by Jeremy Deller', *Oral History*, 33, 1, 105.

21 See K. Walsh (1992) *The Representation of the Past: Museums and Heritage in the Post-Modern World*, London: Routledge, 102.

22 See B. Goodacre and G. Baldwin (2002) *Living the Past: Reconstruction, Recreation, Reenactment and Education at Museums and Historical Sites*, London: Middlesex University Press, 13.

23 Jeremy Deller, transcribed in John Slyce, 'Jeremy Deller: Fables of the Reconstruction', *Flash Art International*, 36, 228, 76.

24 See D. Lowenthal (1998) *The Heritage Crusade and the Spoils of History*. Cambridge: Cambridge University, 168.

25 Here the similarity ends as the present Sealed Knot society is 'not politically motivated and has no political ambitions whatsoever'; see 'History of the Sealed Knot', http://www.sealedknot.org/index.asp?Page=about.htm; accessed 20 March 2006.

26 See V. Agnew (2004) 'What is Reenactment?', *Criticism*, 46, 3, 332.

27 R. Barthes (1982) 'The Reality Effect,' in T. Todorov (ed.) *French Literary Theory Today*, trans. R. Carter. Cambridge: Cambridge University Press, 11–17.

28 S. Bann (1995) *Romanticism and the Rise of History*. New York: Twayne Publishers, 43.

29 R. Samuel (1994) *Theatres of Memory, Volume 1: Past and Present in Contemporary Culture*. London: Verso, 280.

30 See 'A Brief History of Re-enactment', *Event Plan*, 2006, http://www.eventplan.co.uk/history_of_ re-enactment.htm; accessed 20 March 2006.

31 K. Walsh (1992) *The Representation of the Past: Museums and Heritage in the Post-Modern World*, London: Routledge, 102–3.

32 R. Hewison (1987) *The Heritage Industry: Britain in a Climate of Decline*. London: Methuen 45.

33 See L. MacRitchie (1998) 'Introduction: The Sincerity of Events', in N. Childs and J. Walwin (eds) *A Split Second of Paradise: Live Art, Installation and Performance*. London: Rivers Oram Press, 21–30.

34 K. Stiles (2003) 'Performance', in R. S. Nelson and R. Shiff (eds) *Critical Terms for Art History*. Chicago: University of Chicago Press, 2nd edn., 94.

35 M. Bakhtin (1984 [1965]) *Rabelais and His World*, trans. H. Iswolsky. Bloomington: Indiana University Press, 10.

36 Ibid., 258.

37 A. Farquharson (2001) 'Jeremy Deller: *The Battle of Orgreave*', *Frieze*, vol. 61, September, 108.

38 A. Heathfield (2004) 'Alive', in A. Heathfield (ed.) *Live: Art and Performance*. London: Tate Publishing, 12.

39 M. Bakhtin (1984 [1965]) *Rabelais and His World*, trans. H. Iswolsky. Bloomington: Indiana University Press, 7.

40 T. Etchells (1998) 'Introduction 2: Valuable Spaces – New Performance in the 1990s', in N. Childs and J. Walwin (eds) *A Split Second of Paradise*, 33.

41 A. Farquharson (2001) 'Jeremy Deller: *The Battle of Orgreave*', *Frieze*, vol. 61, September, 108.

REMEDIATING GENOCIDAL IMAGES INTO ARTWORKS:
THE CASE OF THE TUOL SLENG MUG SHOTS

Stéphanie Benzaquen

'You, guy! What's your name? What did you do during the Sihanouk regime? The Lon Nol regime?' They'd already asked us these questions when we got off the truck. Why were they asking us again? Every prisoner was interrogated again and then it was my turn. Afterwards, I felt someone undoing my blindfolds. At first my eyes were out of focus but then my vision cleared. In front of me was a chair with a camera set across from it. 'Go sit on that chair', the guard said, pointing at me. The others handcuffed to me went with me but they sat on the floor as I was photographed. The guard took a picture of the front of my face, and then the side. Another guard measured my head and then they made an ID card. After me, they photographed the other people attached to me. Then they put our blindfolds back on.[1]

The Vietnamese army reached Phnom Penh on 7 January 1979 after a two-week blitzkrieg in Cambodia. Their arrival in the capital city marked the end of Democratic Kampuchea, the regime established by the Khmer Rouge in April 1975. In less than four years, Pol Pot and his comrades had starved, worked to death and massacred hundreds of thousands of their fellow countrymen. While exploring the desolated streets of Phnom Penh on that day in January 1979, two Vietnamese photojournalists came across a barricaded high school. It was S-21 (the other name of Tuol Sleng), the prison where the *santebal* (Khmer Rouge state security police) had jailed, tortured and executed about 14,000 Cambodians. Inside the buildings, the two men discovered several bodies, recently killed, and torture instruments. The walls were covered with blood.[2] There were also tens of thousands of pages of summaries, entrance forms, torture reports, signed execution orders, daily execution logs and confessions that the S-21 commander Kaing Guek Eav –

better known as 'Duch' – and his staff had left when fleeing the city.[3]

Black-and-white mug shots of terrified men, women and children were attached to the confession files. The photography unit of Tuol Sleng took pictures of each inmate who was brought in. The first-hand account – quoted above – of the Cambodian artist Vann Nath, one of the few people who survived S-21, depicts the procedure that Nhem En, the Khmer Rouge in charge of the photography unit, and his colleagues followed.[4] The fact that many of the prisoners were actually high-ranking Khmer Rouge cadres arrested during purges explains why the prison personnel had to thoroughly record its criminal (Duch would have said 'investigative') activities. Industriousness was key to hunting interior enemies – a thriving business in the paranoid leading circles of Democratic Kampuchea. As proven by the archival fragments and remnants of physical structures scattered throughout the country,[5] Tuol Sleng was not the only Khmer Rouge interrogation/torture/execution centre, yet it is by far the most infamous – a sinister reputation it owes in part to these portraits.

S-21 was turned into the Tuol Sleng Museum for Genocidal Crimes in 1980 under the guidance of Mai Lam, a Vietnamese officer himself, and an expert in museology. The mug shots were put on permanent display in case Cambodians would recognise relatives, thereby helping identify the victims. It was only in the late 1990s that Western audiences became familiar with the pictures. In 1993, as the Kingdom of Cambodia had just been established following UN-monitored elections, two American photographers, Douglas Niven and Christopher Riley, found around six thousand original negatives in an old cabinet of Tuol Sleng. They set up the Archive Project Group with the aim of preserving and cataloguing them.[6] Twenty-two of these negatives were presented in an exhibition entitled 'Facing Death: Portraits from Cambodia's Killing Fields', first shown in the Museum of Modern Art in New York in 1997.[7] They were displayed in Gallery Three, next to rooms dedicated to the museum's permanent photographic collection and a retrospective of American photography between 1890 and 1965. They had no labels and were loosely contextualised by a few paragraphs summarising, altogether, the history of Tuol Sleng, the discovery of the negatives by Niven and Riley, the production of the prints, and the funding of the Archive Project Group.[8] Such lack of information with regard to the history of the Khmer Rouge regime or the involvement of the United States in Cambodia subjected, according to the anthropologist Lindsay French, the photographs to two main kinds of readings. One was formal and aesthetic; the other was a 'kind of heroic, allegorical' reading. Turned into observers of suffering, visitors who wanted to escape such voyeuristic position had no choice but look at the pictures as conveying 'something more abstract or general', our condition of being human.[9] Since then,

Fig. 1 View of Tuol Sleng, Phnom Penh, Cambodia. Photograph by W. Noud. 17 (Creative Commons)

the mug shots have been globally circulated in various media and settings, from book covers to tourists' blogs, and even to a Thai horror movie (*Ghost Game*, Sarawut Wichiensarn, 2006), to such an extent that the anthropologist Rachel Hughes, conducting interviews with Western tourists at the Tuol Sleng Museum in 2000, stressed 'the significant number of tourists who professed a familiarity with the S-21 prisoner photographs'.[10] Once scrutinised in utmost secrecy, since Duch handed over the confession files only to a restricted number of Khmer Rouge leaders (mainly Pol Pot and Nuon Chea), the black-and-white portraits can now be seen worldwide. It is this administrative record of extermination, the very symbol of Khmer Rouge's absolute power, which has become the icon of the Cambodian Genocide.

Over the past ten years several artists, Cambodians and non-Cambodians alike, have created pieces incorporating the Tuol Sleng mug shots. Appropriating such a specific kind of photograph into artworks raises a number of issues. Are they not, first and foremost, evidence of the crimes perpetrated at S-21? It bears recalling that some of the pictures had been shown during Duch's trial at the Extraordinary Chambers in the Courts of Cambodia in 2009. The particular context offered by art settings for looking at such images makes it compelling to ask to which extent aestheticisation affects the evidential status of these images. It is a recurring issue in discussions on artistic representation of mass atrocity. In her analysis of beauty and the sublime in Holocaust-related artworks, Janet Wolff underscores the risk that 'visual pleasure negates horror by aestheticizing violence and atrocity, by proposing redemption in the face of outrage or by providing consolation in the encounter with beauty'.[11] Her concern resounds all the more strongly when related to what Riley and Niven declared in an 1997 interview in the *Village Voice* regarding their selection of pictures for the exhibition 'Facing Death: Portraits from Cambodia's Killing Fields': 'Even though they were of horrible subject matter, with horrible stories, we saw the possibility of making beautiful photographs.'[12]

However, one cannot but acknowledge that the evidential status of the mug shots has already been seriously undermined as their reception in widening geographic and cultural circles charged them with new meanings. Captions on blogs or comments in television news stories make this clear: S-21 photographs have been turned into emotional portraiture, icons of atrocity and injustice that make us feel and even project ourselves into such suffering. This transformation, obscuring the reality of Tuol Sleng (for example, the actual identity of the victims, or procedures of control) has far-reaching historiographic consequences. It impacts on forms of remembrance and identity politics. Indeed, of all the issues raised, the fact that our empathy for the victims stems from portraits made by their very murderers is not the least puzzling. Against such a backdrop, artistic remediation might well help to clarify the processes (and traps) of emotional commodification and shed light on the cultural construction of our gaze when facing such photographs.

The notion of 'genocidal images', coined by the art critic Thierry de Duve in an article discussing the exhibition *S-21* by Christian Caujolle (founder of the photo agency VU) within the framework of the 1997 Rencontres Photographiques d'Arles, proves most relevant to such discussion. De Duve argues that images produced by perpetrators are generally considered in terms of ethics and politics: they are de-aestheticised in the contexts of 'duty of memory'.[13] With the notion of 'genocidal images' he aims to open up an aesthetic perception of such pictures because 'calling the photographs the name of art ... is just one way, the clumsiest certainly, of making sure that the people on the photographs are restored to their humanity'.[14] The way such a category is reflected upon by artists who have appropriated Tuol Sleng mug shots is what this chapter analyses in relation to the following artworks: *The Texture of Memory*, by Dinh Q Lê (2000–01); *Messengers*, by Ly Daravuth (2001); *88 out of 14,000*, by Alice Miceli (2004); *In the Eclipse of Angkor: Tuol Sleng, Choeung Ek, and Khmer Temples*, by Binh Danh (2008); and *Discovering the Other: Tuol Sleng – After All Who Rewrites History Better Than You*, by Despina Meimaroglou (2008).

Genocidal images present artists and spectators with a painful challenge. Are we able to escape what Holocaust scholar Marianne Hirsch defines as 'the monocular seeing that conflates the camera with a weapon'? 'Unbearably', Hirsch argues, 'the viewer is positioned in the place identical with that of the weapon of destruction: our look, like the photographer's, is in the place of the executioner.'[15] Regaining another form of bearing witness and deconstructing the perpetrator's aesthetics and ideology, which still impregnate these images – in other words: restoring the victims' humanity – are thus core issues in the artworks concerned.

The artists resort to two kinds of strategy, often combined, to counter Hirsch's 'monocular seeing' and produce – to quote Ulrich Baer – 'corrective captions' for the mug shots. Presentational strategies that aim to modify the viewer's position, thereby making it possible 'to re-see images of victimhood from positions that break with the photographer's perspective of mastery',[16] and material strategies that reconstruct the narratives associated with the mug shots by creating 'very different embodied experiences of images and very different affective tones or theatres of consumption' through addition and medial intervention.[17] For each of the five artists, these strategies mean bringing the spectator into interaction with the image and initiating active forms of reception. Watching the mug shots is no longer a voyeuristic act framed by the perpetrator's gaze. It becomes a gesture of respect toward the victims, their memory, and toward history, too, as the spectator engages in critically viewing the images 'instead of responding to them ritualistically with fear, outrage, or pity'.[18] Dinh Q Lê's *The Texture of Memory* (the eponymous title refers to James Young's book on Holocaust monuments and memorials) is a series of portraits of Tuol Sleng prisoners. It is not the first work in which the artist remediates the mug shots. His 1998 piece *Cambodia: Splendor and Darkness* merges them with images of Angkor Wat's wall carvings through a process of photo-weaving, thereby underlining cultural connections between the Temple of Angkor and the Cambodian tragedy, the human cost of the construction of the Temple echoing Pol Pot's references to the glorious Angkor era. To manufacture *The Texture of Memory* Lê worked with women from Ho Chi Minh City. He drew sketches of several portraits; the outlines were then embroidered by the women on thick white cotton, white threads on white sheets stretched over a bamboo frame like a painting. The artist states that it is a little hard to see until you are near, then the portraits emerge. Viewers are encouraged to touch these portraits, like reading Braille: 'I hope over the years the viewers' touch will stain the embroidery and make the portraits more visible. Like the carvings at Angkor, where the more people touch, the shinier it gets and the more visible it becomes. In a way, the more people who participate, the more these memories will become alive.'[19] Blindness appears as a paradigm for traumatic memory in Lê's work. It is displayed at several levels: the blindfolded prisoners brought to the Tuol Sleng photography unit; the nature of the Khmer Rouge regime itself, secretive and conspiratorial, keeping the Cambodian population in the dark while it was watching everything ('The *Angkar* – the Organization – has the eyes of the pineapple', the infamous slogan went); and the story, mentioned by the artist, of Cambodian women survivors who resettled in Long Beach, California in 1982, who had all witnessed the execution of their husband and/or their children, and, traumatised by what they had seen, suffered from 'hysterical blindness'.[20]

Sight proves to be an unreliable, impaired and misleading sense when it comes to remembering such atrocities. It must therefore be supplemented, even replaced, by another one – that of touch. The passage from scopic to haptic as performed in *The Texture of Memory* materialises in most concrete terms Jill Bennett's notion of 'sense memory'.[21] The latter, Bennett writes, is 'not so much *speaking of* but *speaking out* of a particular memory or experience – in other words speaking from the body *sustaining sensation*'.[22] As the spectator's fingers run over the embroidered threads, the picture in turn touches 'the viewer who feels rather than simply sees the event and is drawn into the image through a process of affective contagion'.[23] It is how sense memory de-familiarises the iconic and re-affects people who have become so familiar with images that they no longer see them. The portraits forming *The Texture of Memory* are 'productive' rather than 'representational' images.

Making the act of looking a transformative memory experience is also central to the work of Binh Danh. In *In the Eclipse of Angkor: Tuol Sleng, Choeung Ek, and Khmer Temples*, the artist mingles daguerreotypes of Tuol Sleng victims with daguerreotypes of his own photographs of contemporary Buddhist monks and ancient Cambodian temples. It is not the first time, either, that Danh deals with the mug shots and develops complex photography techniques for re-presenting them. Danh has a conception similar to that of Lê regarding the active engagement of the viewer in making memories alive. In *In the Eclipse of Angkor* the spectator cannot identify the images from afar because the daguerreotypes look like framed silver mirrors. Thus, the viewer must get closer and stand in front of them so that the negative image of the daguerreotype reflects her silhouette and turns positive, visible.

In the Eclipse of Angkor fuses different kinds of image: afterimage, an image that both remains on the retina and shapes our mediated experience of traumatic memory, trace and icon.[24] Ghost-image: a remnant, a partially recorded picture. The idea of the ghost takes on further signification in the context of Buddhism. Cambodians believe that the ghosts of suffering victims still haunt places, especially where no proper burial has been conducted such as killing fields and memorials. It is this haunting presence that the image captures. Latent image: the

Fig. 2 Binh Danh, *Skulls of Choeung Ek*, 2008, daguerreotype, 45 x 60 cm, Eleanor D. Wilson Museum, Hollins University, VA, USA. Courtesy the artist.

not-yet-visible image waiting for both the artist's creative gesture (exposing the silver plate) and the viewer's movement. Afterimage, ghost image, latent image express the limits of traumatic memory: fragmented, incomplete, vanishing and shaped by the outside.

As the spectator stands in front of the daguerreotype, she is captured, merged with the victim in the same frame, the same time – neither past nor present – and the same space. The idea that viewers might literally and physically reveal the dead and that remembering means making victims 'alive' again was already an integral part of *Ancestral Altars* (2006), an earlier series of Danh's dedicated to S-21 inmates which was based on his own chlorophyll printing method:[25]

> They [the victims] all have stories to tell and are asking the same question as they peer out to the viewer: How could this happen? I wanted to give these portraits voices so they can teach us ... I hope they will be alive in us as we remember them and in return we give them life.[26]

This conception is anchored by Danh's Buddhist beliefs. There is a cycle of life in which we all take part and have to fulfill some task, which is another way to say that each of us is responsible for the memory of the victims: 'The portraits become the spectators, holding us accountable for the genocide that took place.'[27] Moreover, it is a reciprocal movement. While 'the identity recorded in the photograph is extended and enhanced, revealing a form of inner self',[28] the daguerreo-

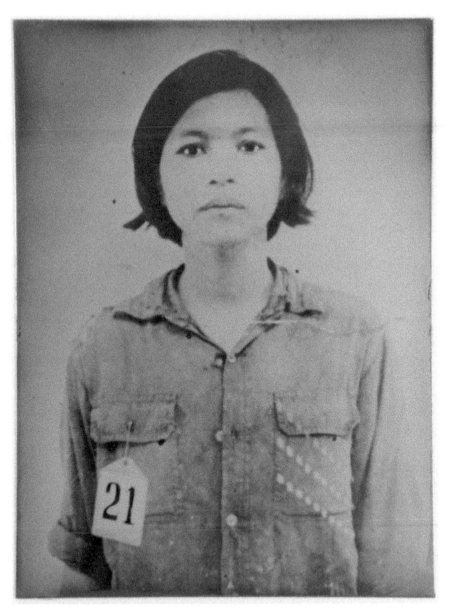

Fig. 3 Binh Danh, *Ghost of Tuol Sleng Genocide Museum # 2*, 2008, daguerreotype, 30 x 24 cm. Courtesy the artist.

type image becomes visible and another side of the viewer's identity is revealed in the process. This victim, the reflection seems to imply, could be you if you had lived in another epoch and place; in that sense the portrait is a reminder that such events might happen at any time, ensnaring those who least expect them to.

The works of Binh Danh and Dinh Q Lê deny the spectator the possibility of merely glancing at the mug shots. By integrating time and duration into the processes of both making and looking at the works, the two artists undo the gaze of the perpetrator. When Nhem En and his colleagues photographed the inmates one after another, at a fast pace, they hardly looked at them. The prisoners were mere objects, deprived of individuality. Nhem En said in an interview that within a short time he no longer felt anything when photographing incoming prisoners. As he was caught in the desensitising routine of Tuol Sleng: 'it became normal, like feeling numb'.[29] This is no surprise considering the psychological mechanisms at play in situations of mass violence. Taking pictures supplies the perpetrator with a protective shield. Victims are objectified and circumscribed within the unreality of the camera screen. In other terms, de-humanised.

According to the historian Bernd Hüppauf, such de-humanisation marks a continuity between images produced by modern technology and the scopic regime that was developed during World War II, which he describes as the

Mutation of the abstraction and emptiness of the fascist version... [T]echnology ... makes it possible for the distanced and cool gaze to watch how advanced techniques of destruction transform living beings into elements of electronically manipulated games of violence. [...] Images of dying and killing produced by advanced technology are sufficiently empty to be forgotten.[30]

The constellation formed by technology, violence and modernity (which has been analysed by Zygmunt Baumann for example)[31] explains why Lê and Danh resort to, respectively, traditional crafts (weaving) and old photographic techniques (daguerreotype) for dealing with the mug shots. Both 'neutralise' a technology that has at times served heinous objectives.

Is there a possibility of reclaiming technology against de-humanisation when it comes to genocidal images? It seems so, as *88 out of 14,000*, the video work by Brazilian artist Alice Miceli, demonstrates. In Tuol Sleng, the artist selected the portraits of inmates for whom the dates of both arrest and execution were available: 88 people. She projected the portraits onto a black space, chronologically, onto falling sand. One day of survival means one kilogram of sand, or four seconds of visibility. In her video, Miceli reverses the objectification inherent in the act of picture-taking.

Fig. 4 Alice Miceli, *88 out of 14,000*, 2004, exhibition view, Phoenix Halle

(Re)-shooting becomes a means of rescue as the artist injects life (the life of the prisoner) into the document: more than blurring the distinction between life and death, *88 out of 14,000* points out the danger that lies in looking at the mug shots as icons of death only. In doing so, Miceli emphasises the period that comes after the moment of shooting, beyond the static vision of the photograph and the photographer, because things did not stop on the chair in front of En's camera. The mug shot, although it is the last image we can see of the prisoners alive, was for the victims only a prelude to days or weeks of suffering, of being chained, starved and tortured. However fragile and near to their end, these are lives that are represented via the contracted temporality of *88 out of 14,000*: people who demand that we think about what they endured. By proposing such movement – or allusion thereof – Miceli unfreezes Tuol Sleng's 'instances of humiliation'.[32]

In *Discovering the Other: Tuol Sleng – After All Who Rewrites History Better Than You*, the Greek artist Despina Meimaroglou shows similar concerns. The installation is comprised of two parts. The first part is a replica of a cell in Tuol Sleng, realised by the film and stage designer Lorie Marks on the basis of pictures Meimaroglou had taken in the museum.

The photographs on the walls are pictures from the book she published in 2005 following her travels in Southeast Asia. Meimaroglou describes her experience in Tuol Sleng Museum, when she entered the cells as overwhelming to the point of physical pain. The idea of re-creating one of the cells in the exhibition space (the Contemporary Art Centre of Thessaloniki) was born out of her observation that 'most of my fellow travellers [visiting Tuol Sleng] refused to come along because they wanted to avoid the discomfort'.[33] With the replica, the artist wants to force the viewer to enter the room, to feel as uneasy and distressed as she felt then.

The reconstructed cell constitutes the entry point to the second part of the installation, 'Me Instead of Them', a series of five 'portraits'. Meimaroglou scanned five different people and printed each head in life-size on a paper bag. After putting the bag on her head – blindfolded as the victims were just before being photographed – the artist tries to imagine a position reflecting the facial expression of each individual and to reproduce it with her own body. By vicariously experiencing the physical visit of the museum, the spectator finds herself involved in the process of remembrance, accessing the victims through the body of the artist. In this process, the viewer is no longer a passive recipient of Meimaroglou's interpretation, but takes part in the transmission of memory. *Discovering the Other: Tuol Sleng – After All Who Rewrites History Better Than You* offers an additional approach towards the notion of 'sense memory'. In Meimaroglou's installation, the bodily experience of sustaining sensation is that of the physical

Fig. 5 Alice Miceli, *88 out of 14,000*, 2004, exhibition view, Phoenix Halle.

Fig. 6 Despina Meimaroglou, *Discovering the Other: Tuol Sleng – After All Who Rewrites History Better Than You*, 2008, multimedia, in collaboration with Lori Marks, 350 x 250 cm, National Museum of Contemporary Art of Thessaloniki, Greece. Courtesy of the artist.

encounter with the mug shots as artefact and as evidential document. In that sense, the artist opens up a reflection on the infrastructures – in this case the museum – through which the memory of the Cambodian genocide is represented and conveyed. At the same time, the installation encourages the viewer to look beyond the memorial display and think about the feelings of the inmates at the moment they were photographed. In other words, to replace the dead face of the mug shot with that of the individual, terrified but somehow alive.

The ways in which forms of mediation affect the politics of remembrance and identity politics is at the core of Ly Daravuth's work.[34] *Messengers* was presented for the first time in 2000 in Phnom Penh in a show entitled 'The Legacy of Absence: A Cambodian Story' (which he co-curated with Ingrid Muan). Ly's installation brings altogether portraits of children of present-day Cambodia and 'messengers', children who carried messages to Khmer Rouge cadres. The photographs are manipulated so that they all mimic Tuol Sleng mug shots, the more recent pictures having been deteriorated through various artificial means. Khmer Rouge songs play in the background.[35]

In *Messengers* Ly and Muan underscore that the installation questions the mechanisms at play in the interpretation of historical and evidential documents, namely, the context of their presentation. What are the preconceptions of the

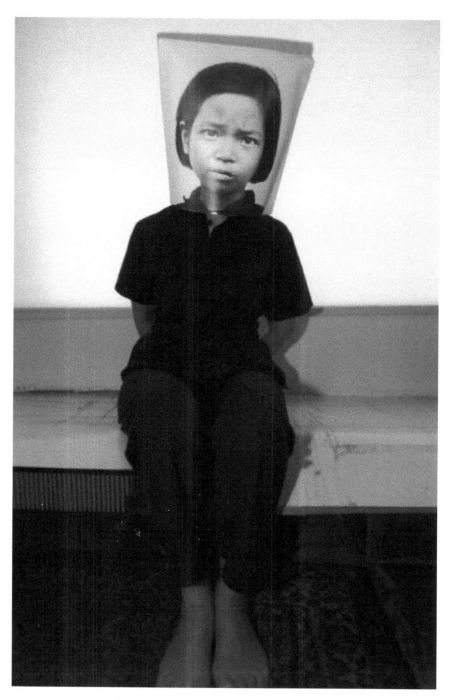

Fig. 7 Despina Meimaroglou, *Me Instead of Them*, 2008, photograph, 120 x 80 cm, National Museum of Contemporary Art of Thessaloniki, Greece. Courtesy the artist.

viewers? And what is the role of visual encoding in shaping interpretations? Ly states that

> Because of the blurred black and white format and the numbering of each child, we tend to read these photographs first as images of victims, when they are 'really' messengers and thus people who actively served the Pol Pot regime. The fact that upon seeing their faces, I immediately thought of victims, made me uneasy. My installation wishes to question what is a document? What is 'the truth'? And what is the relationship between the two?[36]

The 'immediate recognition of victimhood'[37] that Ly tries to interrupt with *Messengers* raises the issue of narrative and memory tools that have been given to Cambodians for building their post-Khmer Rouge identity, and the role that Tuol Sleng as a memorial/museum institution has played in that context.

Commenting on the museum which S-21 had become in 1980, the French journalist and researcher Serge Thion stresses that:

> the masters of the new Cambodian regime, in early 1979, commissioned some Vietnamese experts, trained in Poland, to refurbish the interrogation centre called Tuol Sleng [in order to] attract part of the sinister charisma of Auschwitz.[38]

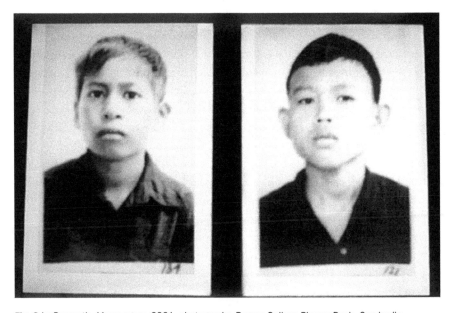

Fig. 8 Ly Daravuth, *Messengers*, 2001, photography, Reyum Gallery, Phnom Penh, Cambodia. Courtesy of the artist.

Why posit such a connection? The Vietnamese had obvious reasons for linking the Cambodian tragedy to the Holocaust, and presenting the Khmer Rouge as a fascist rather than a communist regime – a far more acceptable version of events, one which made it superfluous for Cambodians to ponder for too long the relationship between, on the one hand the 'Pol Pot and Ieng Sary' clique, and on the other the new Vietnamese-sponsored government (composed of former Khmer Rouge who had defected as late as 1978) and the Vietnamese *tout court* who had supported the Communist Party of Kampuchea for many years.

Moreover, the international community, considering the new leaders of the People's Republic of Kampuchea as nothing but a puppet government, blamed Vietnam for its occupation of Cambodia. There were both humanitarian and economic consequences (not to mention the fact the Khmer Rouge retained for years their seat at the UN as the actual representative of Cambodia!). The Vietnamese had to justify their presence in Cambodia by tugging at the heartstrings of European and American leaders and by soliciting public opinion to attract Western sympathy. Consequently, the official version of events cast the Cambodians as victims of a fascist clique that had perverted communist ideals; as a result, the forms of memory made available to Khmers in Tuol Sleng Museum were shaped by both Vietnamese ideological interpretations and Western representations of mass atrocity and mourning. Ly recounts that during the exhibition local visitors asked him whether they could make CDs from the Khmer Rouge songs playing in the background to take them home. Nostalgia? For Ly and Muan, the installation, because of its ambiguity, allowed some visitors 'to begin to care to recast themselves as, perhaps, former Khmer Rouge'.[39] *Messengers* conveys a 'grey zones'-riddled picture of Democratic Kampuchea and its poisonous legacy. By underlining the uses and abuses of memory in Cambodian society (so well epitomised by the Tuol Sleng photographs) the artist stresses the danger of collective victimhood for the Cambodians. How can there be any social healing if everyone claims to be a victim of the Khmer Rouge and escapes liability? To such a question, *Messengers* answers that the mug shots might play a significant role in reconciliation and truth finding and provide the Cambodian society with keys for self-reflection on condition that all levels of complexity making up the history of Democratic Kampuchea and its aftermath are represented.

It is a process in which contemporary art might be a chosen actor. The range of aesthetic treatments and interpretations in the works of Ly Daravuth, Dinh Q Lê, Alice Miceli, Despina Meimaroglou and Binh Danh show that genocidal images are to be assessed in a continuing process of production, exchange, usage and meaning. As Elizabeth Edwards and Janice Hart so aptly put it: photographs 'are enmeshed in, and active in, social relations, not merely passive entities in this process': changes of ownership, physical location and relationships are ascribed to photographs.[40] Genocidal images are thus reconfigured through a long chain of remediation and transformation, integrated within multiple social realms of remembrance, resounding in other contexts, signifying differently, sometimes at the expense of their original meaning. These are complex processes in which affect and understanding – emotional and epistemic regimes – combine and merge. Both sides operate together to produce 'a dynamic encounter with a structure of representation' and to put 'an outside and an inside into contact'.[41] It is through such encounters that genocidal images can reverberate at many levels (cultural, psychological, political, historical) and in widening circles: it is how they contribute as an aesthetic category to deepening knowledge of the criminal events (and their perpetrators). They clarify the role visualisation plays in the context of political terror and atrocity on the one hand; and reconciliation, healing and commemoration on the other.

And yet... In April 2009, Nhem En, the chief photographer of Tuol Sleng, announced that he was putting the camera he used in S-21 (with a pair of sandals that belonged to Pol Pot) for auction for a price of half a million dollars.[42]

NOTES

The author and editors are grateful to Rebus Journal for allowing the chapter to be re-printed

1   V. Nath (1998) *A Cambodian Prison Portrai: One Year in the Khmer Rouge's S-21*. Bangkok: White Lotus, 40.

2   See P. Williams (2004) 'Witnessing Genocide: Vigilance and Remembrance at Tuol Sleng and Choeung Ek', *Holocaust and Genocide Studies*, 18, 2, 237.

3   See D. Hawk (1989) 'The Photographic Record', in K. D. Jackson (ed.) *Cambodia 1975–1978: Rendezvous with Death*. Princeton: Princeton University Press, 210.

4   Nhem En was recruited by the Khmer Rouge at the age of nine and sent to China to study photography. Back in Phnom Penh, he was assigned to S-21. He was at that time 16. After the Vietnamese army overthrew the regime of Democratic Kampuchea, he fled with the Khmer Rouge. He defected in 1995 under governmental amnesty. Since then, he has become deputy district governor at Anlong Veng (a former Khmer Rouge stronghold). He has not been prosecuted but has testified against Duch at the Khmer Rouge trial.

5   See D. Hawk (1989) 'The Photographic Record', in K. D. Jackson (ed.) *Cambodia 1975–1978: Rendezvous with Death*. Princeton: Princeton University Press, 211.

6   Niven's and Riley's initiative was not the first of its kind. In the early 1980s David Hawk, a human rights activist, researched the Tuol Sleng archives. A few years later Cornell University was granted permission and assistance to carry out a project for the preservation of the documentation and its transfer into microfiche; see R. Hughes (2003) 'The Abject Artefacts of Memory: Photographs from Cambodia's Genocide', *Media, Culture, and Society*, 25, 1,

23–44.

7 It toured afterwards in the United States and abroad: the Ansel Adams Centre in San Francisco, Photographic Resource Centre in Boston, the Museum for Design in Zurich, Museet
for Photokunst, Odense (Denmark) and the Australian Centre for Photography in Sydney; see
L. French (2002) 'Exhibiting Terror', in M. P. Bradley and P. Petro (eds) *Truth Claims: Representation and Human Rights*. New Brunswick, NJ: Rutgers State University, 133–4.

8 Ibid., 134–5.

9 Ibid., 138–9.

10 R. Hughes (2003) 'The Abject Artefacts of Memory: Photographs from Cambodia's Genocide', *Media, Culture, and Society*, 25, 1, 24.

11 J. Wolff (2003) 'The Iconic and the Allusive: The Case of Beauty in Post-Holocaust Art', in
S. Hornstein and F. Jacobowitz (eds) *Image and Remembrance: Representation and the Holocaust*. Indiana: Indiana University Press, 165.

12 Quoted in T. de Duve (2008) 'Art in the Face of Radical Evil', *October*, 125, 11.

13 Ibid., 15–18.

14 Ibid., 23.

15 M. Hirsch (2001) 'Surviving Images: Holocaust Photograph and the Work of Post-Memory',
in B. Zelizer (ed.) *Visual Culture and the Holocaust*. London: Athlone Press, 232.

16 U. Baer (2002) *Spectral Evidence: The Photography of Trauma*. Cambridge, MA: MIT Press,
22.

17 E. Edwards and J. Hart (2004) *Photographs Objects Histories: On the Materiality of Images*.
New York: Routledge, 5.

18 U. Baer (2002) *Spectral Evidence: The Photography of Trauma*. Cambridge, MA: MIT Press,
150.

19 Email of Dinh Q Lê to Moira Roth, 11 December 2000, quoted in M. Roth (2001) 'Obdurate
History: Dinh Q. Lê, the Vietnam war, Photography, and Memory', *Art Journal*, 60, 2, 38–53.

20 See L. Boreth (2003) 'Devastated Vision(s): The Khmer Rouge Scopic Regime in Cambodia',
Art Journal, 62, 1, 67–81.

21 It is derived from the notion of 'deep memory' coined by Auschwitz survivor Charlotte Delbo
['sense memory' as affect opposes 'common memory' as representation, narrative and
communicative memory] combined with that of *imago agens* [active image: image that pos-
sesses the capacity to move the subject]. The latter refers to medieval conceptions of
(devotional) images with respect to memory processes: memory is best stimulated by visual means; memory itself is constituted by visual means; visualisation is the key to fixing
memories.

22 See J. Bennett (2005) *Empathic Vision: Affect, Trauma, and Contemporary Art*. Stanford:
Stanford University Press, 38; emphasis in original.

23 Ibid., 36.

24 See J. Young (2000) *At Memory's Edge: Afterimages of the Holocaust in Contemporary Art
and Architecture*. New Haven, CT: Yale University Press, 3–4.

25 The leaves are sandwiched with digital negatives under glass and exposed to sunlight. The
image areas that are blocked by the emulsion fade (which creates the light areas) while the
areas where photosynthesis has continued retain their dark pigment. The photosynthetic
contact prints are then pressed and blotted dry and coated with several layers of resin, after

which they are mounted and framed.

26 Quoted in R. Schultz (2009) '"Faces in the Leaves": Killing Fields, Memory, and Art', *Annual President's Forum: "Verdict(s) of History? Collective Memories of the 20th Century"*, Roanoke College, Salem, Virginia, 30 January; roanoke.edu/Documents/Schultz.pdf; accessed 14 April 2012.

27 Binh Danh, personal communication, 16 February 2010.

28 E. Edwards and J. Hart (2004) *Photographs Objects Histories: On the Materiality of Images*. New York: Routledge, 14.

29 Quoted in P. Maguire (2005) *Facing Death in Cambodia*. New York: Columbia University Press, 121.

30 B. Hüppauf (1997) 'Emptying the Gaze: Framing Violence through the Viewfinder', *New German Critique*, 72, 43–4.

31 Z. Baumann (1989) *Modernity and the Holocaust*. Ithaca: Cornell University Press.

32 U. Baer (2002) *Spectral Evidence: The Photography of Trauma*. Cambridge, MA: MIT Press, 178.

33 Despina Meimaroglou, personal communication, 4 July 2009.

34 In Cambodia, a person's surname precedes their last name. While the other Cambodian artist's referred to thus far have Westernised their names, Ly Davaruth has not. For the sake of consistency, he will be referred to by his last name from this point onward.

35 'Music, or more specifically songs and dance, were among the sites of signifying power recognised by the Khmer Rouge leaders' – T. S. Phim (1998) 'Anthropology of the Khmer Rouge, Part I. Terror and Aesthetics', Working Paper GS06, Cambodian Genocide Program, Yale University, 2–3; revolutionary songs were omnipresent: at work sites, in the communal eating hall, while packed in trucks during relocation. They were played on radio transistors, loudspeakers, or sung by workers.

36 Ly Daravuth quoted in S. Stephens (2000) 'The Legacy of Absence. Cambodian Artists Confront the Past', *Persimmon: Asian Literature, Arts, and Culture*; http://www.asianart.com/exhibitions/legacy/messengers.html; accessed 14 April 2012.

37 R. Hughes (2003) 'The Abject Artefacts of Memory: Photographs from Cambodia's Genocide', *Media, Culture, and Society*, 25, 1, 34.

38 S. Thion (1993) *Watching Cambodia: Ten Paths to Enter the Cambodian Tangle*. Bangkok: White Lotus, 181. It bears recalling that at that time the Holocaust denial positions of Serge Thion, a leftist militant involved in anti-colonial struggles throughout the 1970s, were not yet known.

39 Oliver Urbain (2008) *Music and Conflict Transformation: Harmonies and Dissonance in Geopolitics*. London: I.B. Tauris, 33–4.

40 E. Edwards and J. Hart (2004) *Photographs Objects Histories: On the Materiality of Images*. New York: Routledge, 4.

41 J. Bennett (2005) *Empathic Vision: Affect, Trauma, and Contemporary Art*. Stanford: Stanford University Press, 31.

42 See Andy Brouwer's blog, entries 20 April 2009 and 17 June 2010; http://blog.andybrouwer.co.uk; accessed 14 April 2012.

SCREENING THE 1965 VIOLENCE

Ariel Heryanto

The relationship between film and the history of the infamous 1965–66 massacres that gave rise to Indonesia's New Order regime (1966–98) is not new.[1] To a significant extent, the justification for the massacre, the silence about its occurrence and the legitimacy of the New Order's authoritarianism could be maintained for over three decades thanks to the regime's successful propaganda, of which the nearly four-and-a-half-hour-long film called *Pengkhianatan G 30 September* (1984) was a part. For at least the first ten years of its circulation, the film was either the primary or the only available source of detailed information for most Indonesians about what might have happened in September and October 1965 that marked the single most important turning point in the history of the nation since independence.[2] The film established the central and over-arching framework for any public discussion, fantasy or allusion for most of the New Order period, around and within which details can vary.

Pengkhianatan G 30 September conveys two messages. First, the Indonesian Communist Party was alleged to have masterminded a coup d'état by a group of middle-ranking military officers who called themselves the '30 September Movement'. Second, a counter attack by the army under the leadership of Major General Suharto was a spontaneous, and yet critically necessary and heroic, move to rescue the nation-state from the evil force of the communists. The film is totally silent about the killing of around one million Indonesians in the ensuing months at the instigation and with the support of the army.

For many Indonesians of the next two generations communism was and remains a taboo subject for any critical discussion, but 'Communist' became a popular swearword. In August 1985, the nation's most respected newsmagazine,

Tempo, conducted a poll. When asked what the most serious threat to Indonesia was, over one third of around 900 respondents in total gave the single most frequent answer: the potential resurgence of the communists.[3] More than half of these respondents were aged between 21 and 30. The daily *Kompas* conducted similar polls in 2002 and 2003,[4] and the results affirmed those of the *Tempo* survey. Two years into the post-New Order era, *Tempo* held another round of polls, canvassing 1,101 secondary school students from the nation's three largest cities (Jakarta, Surabaya and Medan). To the question of where they had learned the history of the 1965 events, 90 per cent responded 'film'.[5] As there was only one film on the subject, there is no ambiguity as to which film they were referring to; as many as 97 per cent said they had seen the film *Pengkhianatan G 30 September*. Asked how many times they had seen it, the largest percentage of respondents had seen it the greatest number times. The lower the frequency of viewing, the smaller the percentage of respondents.[6]

An exuberant rise in the production of short and documentary films among young and non-professional Indonesians ran high in the early 2000s.[7] The new fascination with filmmaking among young people leads us to ask to what extent, and how, the murky history of the 1965 violence has been represented in the recently produced short and documentary films. My preliminary observation suggests that until early 2010, the number of such films was very small. None has yet been able to exert the impact necessary to challenge the New Order's propaganda legacy. Thus the next question is: why and how has a decade of post-New Order rule not really undone many of the New Order's ideological constructs? Here I can only offer preliminary answers. While older people have remained largely unprepared to come to terms with the past in any reconciliatory fashion, a shrinking number of young Indonesians – who grew up in an environment engulfed by the hyper-implosion of digital messages focusing on everyday life in the present – are interested in the 1965 events.

REVISITING 1965 IN FILMS

The persistent difficulties in coming to terms with 1965 entered a new phase at the turn of the millennium with the rapid development of new media technology. Indonesia has undergone some significant changes since the fall of the New Order, but these changes cannot be wholly attributed to the New Order's fall. The development and dissemination of media technology enjoyed some autonomy.[8]

The end of the Cold War and subsequently the fall of the New Order witnessed the dramatic expansion of the media (old and new) in Indonesia. The political liberalisation following the collapse of the New Order state apparatuses of control, censorship and surveillance served to enhance the new developments. Soon after 1998 the number of print media had doubled, from nearly 300 to around 600; the number of nationwide television networks doubled from five to ten; and the first 200 local television networks sprouted across the archipelago.[9] The number of officially registered radio stations grew from 700 in 1997 to more than 1,200 a decade later.[10] The number of unregistered stations is not entirely clear but by many estimates they could amount to several hundred.

In 1998 the broadcast hours of television totaled 42,029 per year. Ten years later the figure had grown to 159,097 hours per year. During the same decade the number of households with television nearly tripled to almost 16 million. It is worth remembering that, given the communal style of television viewing in most households, the number of viewers may well be four times that figure. Mobile telephone ownership rose more than tenfold to 42 million, and private access to an internet connection increased more than eleven times to well over 14 million.[11] An estimated 65 percent of internet users were going online at one of the mushrooming internet cafés, making the actual number of internet users several times bigger than the cited number of those *owning and using* a personal computer with internet connection. According to the latest report at the time of writing (September 2011), since April 2011 Indonesians have been the world's second-largest users of the social media network Facebook, second only to the USA, and well above the UK and India.[12]

Against the background of the broad-based developments in media technology, the national film industry made an impressive revival in the number of new titles produced and in their level of commercial success. In tandem with the development of the film and television industry, and partly in unhappy reaction to it, young Indonesians discovered a new preoccupation in making short and documentary films through much of the 2000s.[13] A few striking features characterised this new trend: (a) the wide popularity of filmmaking across much of the central to western region of the archipelagic nation, especially in big cities and small towns in Java; (b) the impressive total number of titles produced, amounting to several hundred per year, although the majority of them are of poor quality;[14] (c) while a few prominent figures played a part in this new development, the demographic profile of filmmakers was predominantly secondary school students and undergraduate university students, aged in the late teens and mid-twenties; (d) the most common themes in these films were to do with everyday life in the immediate surroundings of the filmmakers; and (e) the institutional support and organisational network needed to consolidate the collective efforts of these filmmakers and their activities was sorely lacking, which led to serious problems in the dissemination of the films and hampered collective growth.

Despite these new media developments and what, at face value, appears to be a greater space for freedom of expression, there is a small number of films that have revisited the 1965 tragedy. Out of the hundred short and documentary films per year over the period of ten years, only slightly over a dozen titles were specifically dedicated to revisiting this contentious historical period.[15] Nearly all these 1965-focused films were produced by people who were older, and who had greater skills and political commitment, than the average in the field. Unfortunately, both individually and collectively, these films have had very limited impact in public, certainly too limited an impact to challenge the New Order propaganda on the issue of 1965.[16] The small number of these films and their limited impact can be easily appreciated in the light of the enormous and multi-layered difficulties in producing anything of substance on this sensitive issue. Apart from the sheer logistical difficulties and political censure, content-wise any film revisiting the 1965 violence is confronted with a set of dilemmas as a result of the complexity of the subject matter and the unpreparedness of many Indonesians to come to terms with the issue.

On the basis of their backgrounds, the makers of the few short and documentary Indonesian films about 1965 can be divided into three categories. The first is those who self-identify and are identified by others primarily as former political prisoners of the New Order, and their immediate circles. The second is the various Non-Governmental Organisations (NGOs), particularly those with a special interest in human rights issues. The third consists of individuals who have become or aspire to becoming professional filmmakers, whose interests are in filmmaking over and above other issues. As with any other categories, in reality there are several cases of overlaps, as several individuals work in, and move to and from, more than one category.

The Institute of Creative Humanity (Lembaga Kreativitas Kemanusiaan, LKK), led by poet/novelist Putu Oka Sukanta, is to date the single largest producer of documentary films (six titles) that revisit 1965 violence. Putu and several members of the LKK were political prisoners for their active membership in Institute of People's Culture (Lembaga Kebudayaan Rakyat, LEKRA), which was affiliated with the Communist Party of Indonesia (Partai Komunis Indonesia, or PKI).[17] The LKK series was most important for giving a voice to those who endured first-hand the sufferings of being political prisoners from 1965 to 1967. One main feature of these films is a large proportion of talking heads, who are mainly 1965 former political prisoners and their children or other immediate family members, plus a few historians and experts who are strongly sympathetic to the plights of these victims. One notable exception is *Seni Ditating Jaman* (2008), where a person from LEKRA's opposite camp is interviewed. Presentation techniques are not the major concern in most of these films, but one may notice the steady rise in the quality of presentation in the later titles, especially *Tjidurian 19* (2009). As the technical and aesthetic aspects of presentation have enjoyed progressively more attention, the content has become increasingly apolitical. While these films have the special value of authentic testimonies of victims of and witnesses to the 1965 events, they would have limited appeal to the young audience of contemporary Indonesians because of both the subject matter and the style of delivery. Most of the talking heads are frail-looking people in their late sixties or older. While they speak in plain Indonesian about their own concrete experience, the topics are very unfamiliar to many Indonesians, and the storytellers are not well-equipped with the necessary rhetorical devices for addressing the concerns of those outside their immediate circles.

A few other films focusing on the issue of 1965 or its aftermath have been produced by NGOs with special commitments to issues of human rights. I have managed to access five titles. Two documentaries focuses on female victims of the 1965 violence are of special interest. The first is *Kadountukibu* ('A Gift for Mother') (2004). Like the other works mentioned above, a large portion of these films present talking heads – women who were political detainees in Plentungan prison (Kendal, Central Java) due to their marriage to a Communist Party member or their membership of Gerwani, which was affiliated with the PKI. Many of the women appearing in this film are bold and rhetorically powerful in telling of their extraordinary experiences, including the sexual assaults they had to endure at the hands of their military interrogators. Despite the qualities of the personalities featured and their stories, the overall quality of this and the other two NGO films previously mentioned is not impressive.

The other documentary on female victims is remarkable in content and process of production. Entitled *Putihabu-abu: Masalaluperempuan* ('Greyish White: Women's Past) (2006), it is a compilation of six short documentary films, all produced by secondary school children (aged 15–17) from Bandung and Yogyakarta. These films are a product of their attending a filmmaking workshop hosted by Syarikat Indonesia and Komisi Nasional Perempuan in August 2006. In some of the films, fellow schoolmates as well as schoolteachers are interviewed about their views and understanding of the history of 1965. Although filmmaking workshops for students were common during these years, this specific project constitutes the single consoling practice thus far that runs counter to the general observation about the youth's lack of interest in the sensitive topic of 1965 violence. The name of the two films' co-producer, Syarikat, is an abbreviation for 'Masyarakat Santriuntuk Advokasi Rakyat' ('Pious Muslim Community for People's Advocacy'). This Yogyakarta-based NGO was founded by activists from

Indonesia's largest Muslim organisation, Nahdlatul Ulama. It represents one of the first initiatives by the Muslim communities with culpability in the 1965–66 killings to foster reconciliation with the victims and their families, and it remains the largest, best institutionalised and most radical of these initiatives to date.[18]

We get a significantly different picture when we consider the few 1965-themed films produced by those whose main interest is in filmmaking. Within this category, the three titles that are available to me vary widely in terms of their running time, their genre and the identity of the filmmakers themselves. What they all share – in contrast to the films discussed above – is their serious attention to basic techniques of filmmaking, relative to other aspects of the output.[19] The films in this last category pay maximum attention to communicating effectively and artistically with a general audience, including those who have no special interest in the history of 1965. These qualities are sometimes achieved at the expense of the background information that is required for a full appreciation of the significance of the story told. Focusing more on the impact and aftermath of the national tragedy, these more artistic films show less interest in the power struggle among the top political elite in Jakarta that precipitated the mass killings, or in the international context.

Garin Nugraha's *Puisitakterkuburkan* ('Poetry That Cannot Be Buried') (1999) was the first post-New Order Indonesian film to revisit the events surrounding the 1965 killings. Given Garin's unrivalled fame and authority among his peers, and his wide network in this domain, this is also the best-known film with that theme.[20] The film focuses on the verbal recollection of Ibrahim Kadir, a singer of an Acehnese poetry form called didong, who was taken to prison by mistake in 1965. Ibrahim, who plays himself in the film, gives his testimony as a witness to his own situation in his cell and as a forced participant in the preparation for the execution of his fellow inmates. Cinematographically, *Puisitakterkuburkan* is undoubtedly one of the best Indonesian films that focus on the 1965 theme. The dramatic suspense and pathos are intense for a large portion of this gloomy black-and-white film, with most shots confined within the space of two adjacent cells.

Two things from *Puisitakterkuburkan* stand out as unusual for anyone familiar with the comparable situations in Java and Bali as presented in the other documentaries. First, Ibrahim Kadir was released after 22 days when officials discovered his political 'innocence'. Detentions by error and deliberate detentions of the non-target population during the 1965 witch-hunt were common features in Java. To the best of my knowledge most of the innocent people held by error in Java were not released before many years of exile, torture and imprisonment without trial. Second, oddly, in *Puisitakterkuburkan* there is only one prison guard on duty for the many political prisoners, and he is extremely weak in character. Towards the end of the film, the guard appears helpless when a woman prisoner, in a confronting fashion, challenges the state-sponsored violence in the region and, more specifically, how executions are conducted in this particular prison. This kind of scene is unheard of in any other account (in film or otherwise) from the troubled period in other areas that I have studied.

In contrast, a graphic presentation of violence by the state security apparatus against a meek citizen is the focus of *Djedjakdarah: Suratteruntukadinda* ('Bloody Footsteps: Letter to the Beloved') (2004). This is short film is directed by Markus Aprisiyanto and his crew from a small Yogyakarta-based network of young filmmakers called Déjà Vu Production. In 2004 it won two awards: the Second Saraswati Award at the Bali International Film Festival and the prestigious Citra award at the Indonesian Film Festival. Comparing it with Syarikat's *Kadountukibu* discussed earlier, Barbara Hatley describes the film as

> a more ambitious work, incorporating fragments of music and sung poetry, filmic effects such as flashbacks, and subtitles in English, in representing the fictional experience of a young *ketoprak* performer, seized from his home as a suspected Communist sympathizer and brutally dragged away for 'interrogation'.[21]

The significance of the closing scene is not lost in Hatley's analysis: 'The violence with which he is treated by his captors, using graphic slow-motion shots, and the trail of blood left behind evoke strong parallels with the scenes depicting the kidnapping of the generals by the communists in the film *Pengkhianatan G30S / PKI*.'[22] In the final shot, the filmmakers leave their signature for the audience in the form of a close-up image of a pool of the protagonist's blood on the floor and the imprint in blood of an army boot (hence the title of the film). I share Hatley's view that precisely replicating the New Order framework, but turning it upside down or inside out, is one of several ways to radically confront and subvert the New Order propaganda. In the case of *Djedjakdarah*'s closing scene, by replicating the frames of scenes from *Pengkhianatan G 30 September* (depicting the blood on the floor where six generals were shot in their homes) and reversing the message, the post-New Order filmmaker directly 'writes back to the ideological constructs of New Order media'.[23]

The last film from the third category I wish to consider is Lexy Rambadeta's *Mass Grave* (2002). Produced in 2000–01 and released in 2002, it was one of the first documentary films focusing on the sensitive topic. Despite its extremely low budget,[24] the work achieves the highest standard among the post-New Order short and documentary works. What distinguishes this film from any other documentary discussed earlier is its content, namely the live recording of two events directly relevant to the topic rather than the narrative recollections of eye-witnesses as talking heads that dominate most of the other documentaries. The first of the two events shown is the exhumation of mass graves of the 1965 victims. The second is the communal reaction from local people – with some physical assaults and threats of further killings – to the intention of the families of the deceased to bury the skeletons. Having these materials, and having mastered the skills of filmmaking, Lexy also inserted highly selective archival clips from various sources, both domestic and foreign. In place of the usual talking heads these clips appear on the screen as testimonies and commentaries running through the film. The outcome is a powerful message with rich materials in terms of sound, image and action.

Lexy's *Mass Grave* also outdoes its peers for two additional reasons. First, it achieves a good balance in terms of the three dilemmas outlined above, between (a) background information relating to the past and the political confrontations of the present that should appeal to the poorly informed audience; (b) the top political elite's struggle for state power in Jakarta and the massacres in various regions; and (c) information about the global context (the Cold War) and recollections of individual victims of 1965. Secondly, the documentary is unique for having included a substantial number of original shots of anti-Communist forces (including one carrying a machete and threatening someone who was a victim of the 1965 murders) and their voices. Unlike the top military officers who reaped the benefits of the 1965 violence and its aftermath, here the local militias can in fact be further analysed as victimised in the national tragedy as the families of the political prisoners they wished to attack. Such confronting images are missing from most of the documentaries produced in the subsequent years, rendering most of these films repetitively monological.

Taken together, the films discussed above represent the small in size but nonetheless strong desire in post-New Order Indonesia to revisit the murky history of 1965 and explore alternative narratives to the official propaganda that outlived the New Order in the form of film. Indonesian art workers have produced a wide variety of products along these lines, both before and more after the fall of the New Order.[25] Some of these works refer to the bloody history of 1965 as a setting or background, while others only make a passing reference. With several exceptions, the majority of the literary works and the few cinematic works with this theme affirm rather than challenge the New Order's master narrative of communist brutality, even when they depict the plight of the 1965 victims.[26] Typical in the literary depictions (and in the film *Gie*) is the sufferings of ordinary Indonesians who were misled by the communist ideology, or who were related by marriage to those so misled. In other words, even where compassion and sympathy for innocent victims is strong in these artistic works, the blame falls squarely on the already massacred communists. What is conspicuously absent in many of these works is the role of the Indonesian military and civilian perpetrators of the 1965 killings.

Short and documentary filmmaking in Indonesia appears to have passed its initial phase as a fashionable trend. Many of the earlier filmmakers have been confronted by a wide variety of problems with resources, management, networking and distribution. Beyond the large-scale appearance of short and documentary filmmaking in Indonesia and beyond the internally divided and restless activity of filmmaking, there is no sign of any major film industry with both the interest and the capacity to produce a full feature film that would confront the nation with the long overdue challenge of coming to terms with the historical facts and moral questions of the 1965 events. The case of the aborted production of *Lastri* vividly illuminates why.

Lastri was prevented from being produced by a mob in the village of Colomadu, Karanganyar, Central Java in November 2008. The film was to be directed by the acclaimed director Eros Djarot. The much-feared Front Pembela Islam (Islam Defender Front) and Hizbullah Bulan Bintang (Moon and Crescent Party of God) were the first two social groups that protested the making of the film, alleging that the film would 'spread communism'. The protest was launched in a meeting hosted by the local police office. Although no violence was reported, the threat of forced cancellation was imminent as declared by Khoirul Rus Suparjo, Head of the Front Pembela Islam. A week later, more social groups joined the protest. According to the director, the film was meant to be a melodramatic romance between two young lovers set in the troubled years of 1965. The Indonesian Police Headquarters had issued a permit for the film production, and so had the Colomandu Sugar Factory for the shooting sites. Shooting had initially been scheduled to take place in Klaten, a neighboring town, but was cancelled due to similar threats. The incident was condemned by the Association of Independent Journalists as well as editors of the nation's major newspapers. A counter-rally took to the streets to show support for the production of *Lastri*, but the filmmakers decided not to proceed with the plan.

THE IMPOSSIBILITY OF HISTORY?

Moral imperatives often lead us, the analysts, to hold the conviction (either naively or by intent) that truth and justice must ultimately be available to victims of past gross violations of human rights. Hence the optimistic urge for taking a part, no matter how small, in the struggle to attain these goals sooner rather than later.

A cursory review of literature in Indonesia under the New Order would suffice to show the common assumption of many analysts that state repression necessarily generates either acquiescence or resentment, even if muted, among the general population. Conversely, the removal of such top-down repression supposedly opens the way for the release of voices and previously repressed emotions into the open. Such a view was strong in the discourse of 'transition to democracy' worldwide from the 1960s. Closer to Indonesia's present, the same sentiment is implicit in the title of an otherwise excellent documentary film that looks at the trauma of four victims of the 1965 violence: *40 Years of Silence: An Indonesian tragedy* (2009). As I have shown elsewhere,[27] even at the height of the New Order's authoritarian rule one could find audaciously dissenting voices from the population, as well as significant gaps, in consistencies and contradictions on the part of the state apparatuses. As suggested above, and as theorised eloquently by others,[28] there is no easy and linear progression towards self-expression in direct correlation with freedom of speech. Despite a title that can be misconstrued to imply a similar hopeful conviction, Mary Zurbuchen's *Beginning to Remember; The Past in the Indonesian Present* (2005) presents extremely important insights, precisely for problematising such conviction.[29] In her introductory chapter, she demonstrates persuasively how difficult, complex and risky the attempt to remember the violent past can be in the present.[30]

This is not a matter of time (i.e. the familiar notion that healing takes time and with the passage of time things will necessarily be easier or better), as Zurbuchen briefly contemplates.[31] Instead, as she perceptively notes elsewhere in the same chapter, those 'who have survived traumatic experiences may be unable or unwilling to express themselves',[32] even in the ideal circumstances of liberalism. One might add that there is also the possibility that these victims may prefer not to obtain either assistance to help them articulate their memory or indeed any representation to speak of their experience on their behalf. Some of the 1965 victims may have had forty years of silence; for other fellow victims, four years was enough. Other victims may opt for total silence for life. The situation is complicated further by the limited capacity of language and memory to represent the experience. Citing Edith Wyschogord, Zurbuchen considers the 'impossibility of recovering or representing the past completely' and asks 'what are the responsibilities of researching or bringing forward questions of the past, such as mass killing, if we can never really be certain of knowing what actually happened?'[33] Citing Walter Benjamin, Sarah Lincoln notes that 'to articulate the past historically does not mean to recognize it "the way it really was". It means to seize hold of a memory'; it ultimately implies 'construct[ing] a fiction of a coherence history out of the fragmentary narratives'.[34]

In an unpublished conference paper Adrian Vickers remarks, correctly I believe, on the near impossibility of engaging in a public debate on the history of 1965 and a few other related topics in present-day Indonesia with Indonesians.[35] The reason, according to Vickers, is that Indonesians are either unwilling or unable to have an 'interchange between positions' where each party 'is really listening to the other' in a sober manner. What he observes in Indonesia is the general practice of contest where 'statements are not made to persuade through logic and evidence, but to affirm absolute "truths" that are already known. Persuasion comes from actually making a statement, from its form rather than detailed content.'[36] This leads Vickers to question the merits of the various scholarly works on 'history' and 'memory' for analysis of cases in Indonesia. These are a good starting point for further enquiry, and can be explored in greater depth outside this essay. However, I beg to differ from Vickers when he makes his next argument: that the general inability or unwillingness to have a rational debate is the effect of the 'persuasive power [of] the continued workings New Order rhetoric'.[37] I wish to propose two alternative arguments on this point.

First, as I have elaborated elsewhere, underlying the power of any long-running domination in history is physical violence on a large scale and a sustained threat of its potential occurrence.[38] In the case of the New Order regime, the basis of its power was a combination of the mass killings in 1965–66, threats of the potential return of the communists, and continuing state terror with impunity. All of these provided conditions of possibility for the New Order's excessive power in various forms and genres, including rhetoric. Whatever power of rhetoric the New Order might have commanded (as alluded to by Vickers), that magic rhetoric did not simply come into existence because some clever New Order official or institution invented it. Rhetoric never occupies an autonomous space in history. Pierre Bourdieu and Jean-Claude Passeron contended that 'every power which manages to impose meanings and to impose them as legitimate by concealing the power relations which are the basis of its force, adds its own specifically symbolic force to those power relations'.[39] This is not to suggest that the 1965 violence was the sole origin and cause of all that came afterwards. Rather, in turn it can be analysed as an effect of something larger than the Cold War, but also something local and specific in the history of these people.

Second, Vickers has given the New Order more credit than is warranted. While there is no space for an adequate counter-argument here, suffice it to suggest that the New Order regime was no less subject to the 'absolutist logic' than its dissenters who adopted the same logic and rhetoric to attack the regime. This logic predated the New Order, and its genealogy deserves an examination beyond the scope of this essay. This logic was responsible for the growth of a massive sense of 'fatally belonging'[40] that severely divided the nation, with or without the instiga-tion of the state apparatuses. The actual entity to which that 'fatal belongingness' is devoted or embedded varies across time and space: nationhood in one moment, one's religion and God in another, or ethnicity or even one's sports fan club. Many aspects of the widespread sense of fatal belongingness remain in question for me, but in my provisional understanding this has something to do with a mode of living where oral communication is predominant. 'This is a world where signs and the world they represent were believed to be inseparable.'[41]

What has slightly altered the situation and captured the imagination of the mil-lions of Indonesian youths is the charms of digital technology. Unfortunately, this new development does not help much to prepare them or their elders any better to deal with the murky history of the 1965 violence. There are no homogenous ef-fects of the technology across time and space that would warrant generalisation. Social media may be instrumental in mass mobilisation leading to the overthrow of dictators in some societies. In contemporary Indonesia the affordable and user-friendly digital gadgets have not empowered youths in order to simply do what their elders have been doing, but this time only with greater speed, accuracy or ease. Rather, the new media has transformed young people into new identities in a new world that provides them with the pleasure of accessing an unprecedented speed, scale and ease with which they can record, edit, comment on and share globally their day-to-day life experience, anywhere and anytime. This is a world where everyday utterances, sighs and activities enter into a hall of mirrors on a global scale in real time.

Hence the paradox: as their network expands globally with the single press of a button, their day-to-day perspective shrinks to the size of their Facebook Wall pages or the screen of their mobile phone. While from a technical point of view mobile phones and Facebook can store, edit and transmit a lengthy and deeply contemplated string of thoughts that have been carefully crafted over many drafts and revisions, the working of this technology compels its users indiscriminately towards the opposite: incessant but short, disconnected and hasty exchanges of codes for brief moments of fragmented consciousness. This is well attested by the dominant formats and themes that appear in the majority of short and documen-tary films in contemporary Indonesia, and possibly elsewhere in Southeast Asia.

By the time the New Order regime collapsed and its repressive apparatuses weakened, the momentum for launching a counter-memory and counter-narra-tive was there. However, it dissipated very quickly, and not because the ghost of New Order returned and reigned. What impeded the potential burst of counter-narratives of 1965 violence was no longer state censorship and terror, but the layers of social events and practices that rendered 1965 increasingly irrelevant or a non-issue to many of those who dominated the public space. As many of the victims of the 1965 violence died, it was increasingly difficult for the surviving few, their descendants and their sympathisers to find the capacity to represent the victims in ways that would compel an attentive audience and sustain this audience's interest for a considerable period. An increasing number of young people not only have little or no knowledge of that past, but can also find no reason why they should.

Today, youths in Indonesia have been affected by a new global environment, which is remarkably different from that of the Cold War years. Unlike the preceding generations, who were conditioned to be conversant in romantic heroism and narratives of revolutions, most urban middle-class Indonesians today have neither the pressure nor the incentive to engage themselves passionately in any big political movements and confront the major questions that face the world, with the exception of the Islamist political movements. For the majority who are more secular minded and moderately religious, engagement with global issues has been narrowly directed towards the consumption of entertainment commodities following the global trends.

Here is the irony. Decades of the New Order's mega-investment in anti-communist propaganda had the ironic impact of keeping the counter-propaganda alive and leading the romantisation of the left among disenchanted members of the population. Those living under the military dictatorship of the New Order, with or without personally experienced victimisation, would not need special education to know and resent the regime's brutality and the sinister quality of the regime's propaganda. For every five Indonesians who might have been susceptible to the New Order's propaganda regarding 'the imminent danger of communism', there was one for whom the same propaganda would immediately imply the opposite. Each incident of censorship, ban and act of propaganda led the few critically minded citizens to imagine, investigate or suspect the reverse: what the New Order might have deliberately concealed or twisted underneath the official pronouncements, the museums, laws and films. The demise of the New Order brought with it the instigation for a counter narrative. Domination both invents and denies resistance.

NOTES

This study is part of a larger project with the generous assistance from the Australian Research Council (2009–11), with Emma Baulch as APD co-researcher, and the Australian National University as hosting institution. When collecting data in Indonesia I enjoyed the invaluable assistance and insights from Stanley Adi, Lexy Rambadeta, Otto Yulianto, Budiawan, Imam Aziz,

Dianah Karmila, Rumekso Setyadi, Astrid Reza and Markus Aprisiyanto. An earlier version of this chapter was presented at a panel in the 2010 Annual Meeting of the Asian Studies Association in Philadelphia, co-convened by Thongchai Winichakul and Mary Zurbuchen, and partially co-sponsored by Center for Southeast Asian Studies of University of Wisconsin-Madison. Jennifer Gaynor, Joshua Coene, Ramya Sreenivasan, and Roger Desforges, provided helpful comments on an earlier version of this chapter. The author thanks all of these individuals and institutions.

1   Two major books in English on the Indonesian films during the New Order (not specifically on the 1965–66 turmoil) are K. Sen (1988) *Indonesian Cinema: Framing the New Order*. London: Zed Books, and K. Heider (1991) *Indonesian Cinema: National Culture on Screen*. Honolulu: University of Hawaii Press.

2   In the first few years of its release, school students were required to pay to attend screenings at regular movie theatres during school hours. The state television network, TVRI, broadcast the film annually on 30 September. Private television stations were required to follow suit.

3   The second perceived threat to the nation for all the respondents was 'corruption' (18.42 per cent), a response amounting to slightly more than half of those who perceived communists as the most dangerous threat (33.65 per cent). Interestingly in retrospect, 'radical Islam' occupied the second to last place in the list of potential threats, with barely one per cent of the total number of answers; see *Tempo*, 'Suararakyatsetelah 40 Tahun', 25 August 1985.

4   See B. E. Satrio (2002) 'Ketakutan yang takkunjungpudar', *Kompas*, September 30, and B. E. Satrio (2003) 'Nasibkomunisme, sihantulaten', *Kompas*, August 4.

5   Respondents in this poll were invited to give more than one answer to the question. At top of the list was 'teachers and text books' (97 per cent); 'film' came second; see *Tempo*, 'Tandatanyauntuk G30S 'versiresmi'', 29, 31, 2–8 October 2000.

6   Those who had seen it once: 13 per cent; twice: 29 per cent; three times: 20 per cent, more than three times: 38 per cent.

7   See K. van Heeren (2002) 'Revolution of hope; Independent films are young, free and radical', *Inside Indonesia*, http://www.insideindonesia.org/edition-70-apr-jun-2002/revolution-of-hope-2907391; accessed 8 August 2012; and K. van Heeren (2009) 'Contemporary Indonesian film: Spirits of reform and ghosts from the past', doctoral thesis, Leiden University.

8   More than few observers have argued the reverse: that the media was one of many forces that contributed to the regime's downfall. See M. Garcia (2004) 'The Indonesian free book press', *Indonesia*, 78, 121–45; D. Hill and K. Sen (2005) *The Internet in Indonesia's New Democracy*. New York: Routledge; K. Sen and D. Hill (2000) *Media, Culture and Politics in Indonesia*. Melbourne: Oxford University Press, esp. 21–50.

9   See A. Heryanto (2008) 'Pop culture and competing identities', in A. Heryanto (ed.) *Popular Culture in Indonesia: Fluid Identities in Post-Authoritarian Politics*. New York: Routledge, 1–36; A. Heryanto and S. Adi (2002) 'Industrialized media in democratizing Indonesia', in R. H. Heng (ed.) *Media Fortunes, Changing Times: ASEAN States in Transition*. Singapore: Institute of Southeast Asian Studies, 47–82; S. Pradityo, G. W. Titiyoga and S. Khafid (2008) 'Ki

Sudrun di layarbeling', http://majalah.tempointeraktif.com/id/email/2008/06/02/MD/mbm.20080602. accessed 8 August 2012.

10 See D. Kuswandini (2009) 'Radio: A friend of yours?', *The Jakarta Post*, June 20.

11 I am indebted to the generous assistance of Hellen Katherina of AGB Nielson Media Research (private communication 2009) for the mobile phone and internet access figures as well as the figures for television broadcasts and consumption.

12 See N. Burcher (2011) 'Facebook usage figures by country – July 2008 to July 2011', <http://www.nickburcher.com/2011/07/facebook-usage-figures-by-country-july.html>, accessed 2 September 2011.

13 The term 'indie' (independent) was widely used in the early 2000s for the new trend. However, as in other places, the term progressively lost its appeal. In part, this was due to the large diversity of works that were classified within it. The term also lost its popularity following a long and unresolved series of debates in the 2000s about what exactly the ideologically loaded term should mean. Those who were initially categorised as independent filmmakers have been found at the forefront of the mainstream film industry, while others have moved to and fro between the mainstream film industry and underground and low-budget filmmaking. The term 'short and documentary films' is widely acceptable because of their largely descriptive nature, purged of the political connotations embedded in the term 'indie'.

14 When the SCTV network opened its first competition in 2002, more than one thousand titles were submitted, although only about 800 were accepted as eligible; see van Heeren (2002: 17). In the years that followed, the number of contestants in the SCTV and a few other competitions stayed around 800 plus.

15 Focusing narrowly on the post-New Order works of alternative Indonesian filmmakers (in terms of both citizenship and residence) with a thematic focus on the 1965 violence or its aftermath, this chapter will not examine several other sets of creative works that are otherwise related or relevant to the concerns of this essay. Excluded in this discussion are (i) films where the setting of 1965 remains only in the background, such as *Gie* (2005) which I have discussed elsewhere; see A. Heryanto (2008) 'Citizenship and Indonesian ethnic Chinese in post-1998 films', in A. Heryanto (ed.) *Popular Culture in Indonesia: Fluid Identities in Post-authoritarian Politics*. New York: Routledge, 70–92; (ii) films that address issues of political violence in Indonesia in other periods; (iii) a wide variety of creative works that address the 1965 issues in different media (visual arts, dance, theatre or literature) and genres (video art and animation); and (iv) foreign films with a focus on the 1965 political turmoil and its aftermath, such as *The Year of Living Dangerously* (1983), *The Shadow Play* (2001), *Terlena: Breaking of a Nation* (2004), *40 Years of Silence: An Indonesian Tragedy* (2009), and most importantly *The Act of Killing* (2012).

16 I acknowledge this assessment is open to debate. Several of the better-known filmmakers on the topic expressed separately a sense of satisfaction of the extent to which their work have been received.

17 Although the LKK can be considered an NGO, it is a special kind of NGO. Most members of an NGO can join or leave any time, subject to administrative procedure; while retaining membership they can usually, and in principle, claim an equal status. In contrast, the founding and continuously leading members in the LKK are distinguished by involuntary status as

political victims of serious crime perpetrated under the New Order.

18 See C. Olliver (2004) 'Reconciling NU and the PKI', *Inside Indonesia*, 77. For a broader context of the matter, see the detailed study by G. Fealy and K. McGregor (2010) 'Nahd-latulUlama and the killings of 1965–66; religion, politics and remembrance', *Indonesia*, 89, 37–60.

19 Fortunately, Indonesia has not seen a domestic production of films on the theme that resemble the common trend elsewhere of 'aestheticization of trauma-ridden histories and cultures by the transnational culture industry and media' – A. Kaplan and B. Wang (2008) 'From traumatic paralysis to the force field of modernity', in A. Kaplan and B. Wang (eds) *Trauma and Cinema*. Hong Kong: Hong Kong University Press, 11.

20 For a sample of a highly complimentary analysis of the film, see A. Rutherford (2006) 'Garin Nugroho: Didong, cinema and the embodiment of politics in cultural form', *Screening the past*, 20; http://www.latrobe.edu.au/screeningthepast/20/garin-nugroho.html; accessed 12 February 2010.

21 B. Hatley (2006) 'Recalling and re-presenting the 1965/1966 anti-communist violence in Indonesia', paper for the 16th Biennial Conference of the Asian Studies Association of Australia in Wollongong, 26–29 June, 6. (For a more recent publication on the topic by the same author, see B. Hatley (2010) 'Recalling and representing Cold War conflict and its aftermath in contemporary Indonesian film and theater', in T. Day and M. H. T. Liem (eds) *Cultures at War: The Cold War and Cultural Expression in Southeast Asia*. Ithaca: Southeast Asia Program, Cornell University, 265–84.)

22 Ibid.

23 Ibid., 7.

24 According to Lexy, it cost him 4 million rupiah (roughly US$400) out of his own purse (personal communication 2010).

25 These works surely deserve more serious analysis, but that lies beyond the scope of the present essay. For earlier analysis of some of these works see K. Foulcher (1990) 'Making history: Recent Indonesian literature and the events of 1965', in R. Cribb (ed.) *The Indonesian Killings 1965°1966: Studies from Java and Bali*. Clayton: Centre of Southeast Asian Studies, Monash University, 101–19.

26 One contrast can be found in the visual arts, such as the works of Dadang Christanto, or FX Harsono that challenge the master narratives on those violent years in a most direct fashion. For more discussion on Christanto's works see C. Turner (2007) 'Wounds in our Hearts: identity and social justice in the arts of Dadang Christanto', in K. Robinson (ed.) *Asian and Pacific Cosmopolitans: Self and Subject in Motion*. London: Palgrave, 77–99.

27 A. Heryanto (2006) *State Terrorism and Political Identity in Indonesia*. London: Taylor and Francis.

28 Raymond Williams noted: 'if our social and political and cultural ideas and assumptions and habits were merely the result of specific manipulation ... then the society would be very much easier to move and to change than in practice its has ever been or is' – R. Williams (1980) *Problems in Materialism and Culture*. London: Verso, 37; see also comments from Joshua Cohen and Joel Rogers on the paradoxical combination of extreme media servility and minimal state control of those media in the US – J. Cohen and J. Rogers (1991) 'Knowledge, morality and hope: The social thought of Noam Chomsky', *New Left Review*, 187, 17,

5–27.

29 M. Zurbuchen (2005) *Beginning to Remember: The Past in the Indonesian Present*. Seattle: University of Washington Press.

30 For more general discussion on the subject, see A. Kaplan and B. Wang (eds) *Trauma and Cinema*. Hong Kong: Hong Kong University Press.

31 M. Zurbuchen (2005) *Beginning to Remember: The Past in the Indonesian Present*. Seattle: University of Washington Press, 13–14.

32 Ibid., 7.

33 Ibid., 6.

34 S. Lincoln (2008) 'This is my history', in A. Kaplan and B. Wang (eds) *Trauma and cinema*. Hong Kong: Hong Kong University Press, 40.

35 See A. Vickers (2009) 'Frames and public reasoning: What do debates about the coup and killings tell us about Indonesian public culture?', paper for conference on 'The 1965–1966 Indonesian killings revisited', 17–19 June, Singapore. I am grateful to Adrian for permission to cite his work in progress.

36 Ibid., 7.

37 Ibid., 9.

38 See A. Heryanto (2006) *State Terrorism and Political Identity in Indonesia*. London: Taylor and Francis.

39 P. Bourdieu and J.-C. Passeron (1977) *Reproduction in Education, Society and Culture*, trans. R. Nice. London: Sage, 4.

40 See A. Heryanto (2006) *State Terrorism and Political Identity in Indonesia*. London: Taylor and Francis, 24–32.

41 Ibid., 32.

PERFORMING VIOLENCE

PERPETRATORS' TESTIMONY AND THE RESTORATION OF HUMANITY: *S21*, RITHY PANH

Joshua Oppenheimer

Rithy Panh (b. 1964, Cambodia) works as a film director in France, where he has lived since 1980. Following a screening in London in 2009 of his documentary film *S21: The Khmer Rouge Death Machine* (2003), Panh discussed his film with Joshua Oppenheimer.

Joshua Oppenheimer: *About the production method itself: it's extremely interesting the way you use re-enactment and the way you elicit bodily memories and the way you develop [a] pretty and accurate and precise excavation of what happened and of people's memories through a sustained filmmaking method, which culminates in bringing the survivors together with their guards. I'd like to hear in as much detail as you can give us about the whole process.*

Rithy Panh: I didn't wish the victims and the guards to meet. The encounter between Nath and Hoi happened as a result of an earlier film *Bophana* [*Bophana, une tragédie cambodgienne: Bophana A Cambodian Tragedy*, 1996, France/Cambodia]. I felt that it wasn't right to impose on the victims the difficulty of meeting their former guards. So during the interview with Hoi I asked Nath not to come while he was shooting that interview. So it rained, and he had to continue the next day so he said don't come the next day either. Nath came looking for paintbrushes and that was how he met Hoi. So what he did when he met him... he was very nervous at first so he took him by the shoulder and he led him round and showed him all the paintings that he'd made for the museum. And in front of each painting he asked, is this true or not? Nath had not seen the events that he was depicting in the painting but it had been told about them, so he wanted to verify that they were correct. And there were times when he could say 'I've really seen this scene and I've painted it like this'.

And so that convinced me that the testimony was not complete unless it was a testimony from both sides of the situation. And it's after that that I suggested to Nath to continue with this film on S21.

Now, since this film has been made it's often the case… there are several films that have been made since where they bring the victims and the guardians together. But often also against each other's will. And that gives a kind of unease when you see that kind of encounter between people. So although I understand what you mean when you use the term 're-enactment', for me it's not really that at all. It's not the right word for that. Maybe there isn't a word for it.

I met Paul, who does the re-enactment in the film, in his native village. And I understood that this man wanted very much to explain what he had done at S21. But he couldn't get round to explaining it properly, all his phrases were cut off. So at a certain moment I brought him a map of the camp. And so he said, 'oh yes, I was a guard in this part of the building'. So then he was able to explain, but in doing that he made the gestures that you see in the film, which completed the phrases he couldn't discuss. And it's then that I discovered that there was another memory, which is the bodily memory. So it may be twenty years later, but survivors would talk about pains they feel in certain areas of the body, even if it was a long time ago. But you find the same things with the former guards. Sometimes the violence is so strong that words don't suffice to describe it. And also that violence may be so strong that the words become inaudible.

So it was then that I said to the guard 'you can use gestures, you can speak, explain it in any way you wish'. And then that I had the idea of taking the guard back to S21, which is now a museum of the genocide, and because the guard said that he worked at night there, I took him there at night. I asked at the museum how the building was lit at night – it was lit only by neon – so I cut all the other lighting and just put the neon up there. I sought to create an atmosphere, which recalled the situation, which the guard was actually working in. Sometimes at night they had the radio on with revolutionary songs so that's why the radio came into it, with the revolutionary songs.

JO: *So those songs were playing during the scene or added in the sound editing?*

RP: I made him listen to the songs, but the songs were put on afterwards in the edit. It's like giving somebody a foothold to get up a mountain. He needs to have these grips as he's going up in order to get to the top, in order to achieve what he's setting out to do, which is to describe his own testimony. We found a little American munitions case, which was used as a kind of makeshift toilet in the cell, for example, one of the small bits of pieces that were in the cell which were still there. It was just placed in a corner, not knowing what the guard would actually do with it. So everything that could be found from that period – to recreate that period – was placed there at this person's disposal. Initially, they weren't put inside the cells because I didn't know exactly where they should be, so I placed them outside. But as soon as he arrived, he knew exactly where everything should go, and also put them in a particular corner that he used to. I then simply said 'so show me your work, show me how you worked'. And that's what opened up the bodily memory, if you like, in a chronological way: There is an order in which things are done; so before you put on or take off the handcuffs, you have the business with the bar as well underneath, and so there's an order in which things are done, which he followed…

When these actions were compared with the notes, which had been kept by the Khmer Rouge within the prison, it was found that this was exactly the way these things were done. So I imagine that nobody else apart from the guards and the victims would know exactly what happened in that camp. Because in that sequence everything is brought together and encapsulated, it makes it even more violent. One thing that's very important in that particular sequence is the way in which it was filmed. The moral perspective of the filmmaker at this point is very important, and it's necessary to have that moral perspective before, not while you're filming it. So you've got to be very careful that you don't topple over from the point of view of the guard to the point of view of the victim and… we're kind of captivated by the violence of the gestures. When he talks about the violence that he's meting out, he also talks about seeing the others sleeping on the floor in the cell. And if the director is excited by that violence, he'd be following it always, but happily we didn't follow the violence all the time.

So it was instinctive to stop, to hold the camera at the door, not to follow in. Otherwise we'd be walking over the prisoners, if you like. And would knock over into the side of the guards. This is something that I realised after shooting. I instinctively didn't walk over the prisoners. If I had done, 'who would I be?'

JO: *I want to ask you about the role of repetition in what comes out. I think sometimes in documentary where there's a kind of myth that the first take is the most authentic take, but, here, in a film about memory, that's often not the case.*

RP: You know, it depends, there are no cast-iron rules on this. There were times when I made just one take. Because you feel that there's no need to go beyond that; the authenticity is there in that one take. And then there are times when you come back to it time and again, and some months afterwards you ask again the same question. It's not easy to testify to these things, above all when you are a former torturer. The answer that you get most frequently is 'yes, ok I was a torturer but I was following orders; so I did wrong but I'm not responsible'. You can't advance with that, so it takes time to let people understand that for them to bear witness is also take responsibility. There's no other road. If you want to come back to humanity, then you have to testify. The worst torturer is the one who doesn't recognise his act right up until death. Because of [one's] belief in humanity, the challenge is to bring the torturers back to humanity. And that's done by the action of testifying. You have to create the most favourable conditions for those testimonies, for those witnesses' statements to be made. One principle, which I state right from the beginning, is that I am not a judge and I am not part of any group. I was against them, the torturers who were participating in the film, and it was important that they knew what side I was on. And I said also that I would accept everything that they said, and would take everything in that they said. But on one condition that I do not find proof to the contrary of what they say. If that should be the case then I would start again from the beginning. That was the deal, because not knowing what happened in their heads, in their minds, in their gestures, I had to give them the trust; I had to trust them and what they were saying. And that's the other thing – there are words in this testimony, but there were gestures also. So when you talk about destruction and reducing to dust, these are not just words, there are gestures behind these words also. So when the words are not sufficient, the image behind the words gives you the force of the gestures, of the acts.

JO: *You suggested a kind of moral dimension to what it means to help the perpetrators and help the guards testify, in the sense that you suggested that it's the only path back to humanity. And what's interesting to me there is the state that they were in when you worked with them because there's a sense in which clearly, at least in the film, we see them repeating dogma, repeating slogans, repeating propaganda... And you hear them chanting all together, 'Determined, determined, determined', and so on. And so this question of dealing essentially with the question of their conscience...*

RP: You have to look at this in its simplest form, which is that the crimes would continue to be perpetrated if the torturers were not able to understand the sense of their actions. So what can the survivors do? You can condemn them for a hundred years, but that's not interesting.

JO: *So essentially what did you find the perspective and the feelings of these characters, Po, Hoi and the others were? Did you find that they were still indoctrinated? That they were still using the dogma, the propaganda to justify what they were doing?*

RP: They were through a period of denying their actions, they were denying the acts that they committed. So the victims also had a need for those testimonies, those on the other side, from the torturers, because if not, then the victim finds him or herself cast into a kind of position of self-pity ... I am not interested in recounting what I lived through myself under the Khmer Rouge. That's not of interest. What is of interest is that that should never be done again...

Primo Levi, when he returned to Italy, had the sense that if he told the story nobody would believe it, and Nath had the same feeling himself. That's why he took one of the men by the shoulder to show him the paintings that he'd done. He needed confirmation that these things had happened.

JO: *Just to be clear, that was during the production of* Bophana, *is that right? That Nath took one of the men to show him [these paintings] – that was in the previous film. And so there was already a connection between the survivors and the guards?*

RP: It wasn't an intended thing, it wasn't something that was wished to be created...

JO: *But I think it is really fascinating and important in that the film gives us a glimpse into a contradiction between belief and knowledge, a contradiction between what the guards believe and what is helpful for them to believe, to get through their daily lives, perhaps not in a fully human state. And it's most clear to me in that moment where they talk about the interrogations. It's clear that they believe, in a way, at least they claim to believe these confessions, that they force the prisoners to say. So they force the prisoners to lie, but then the lies become somehow things that they can believe in. And that's something that I find fascinating here, and I wonder if you could talk a little about this.*

RP: I agree with you, that's what comes out of the film, but it was something I didn't know when I was making it. But it's not a definitive work. You can't explain S21. It's like explaining genocide. So I don't know how to answer. The film itself doesn't give all the answers, it can't. But it gives suggestions; it leads us into a way of examining the origins of genocide and the acts of genocide.

Joram ten Brink: *In what way can cinema advance our understanding of violence? How and in what way can cinema advance our understanding of post-trauma, and the kind of relationship between victims and perpetrators?*

RP: Frankly, I don't know. I tried to paint – I am not good at it. I tried to sing – not good; I tried to write – not good...! Cinema came by chance. Something that cinema can do which literature can't do, in the same way for example, is when you have somebody in the film, as he does, say, 'I killed', and then there's a long silence before he says, 'and I take responsibility'. This is something you cannot do as easily, as powerfully in literature. You can write, you know, 'I killed', brackets, silence, and then 'I take responsibility', but you cannot make it as powerful a statement, and as simply put as that in literature as you can in film. And how do you, for example, describe in literature the scene where he goes through the gestures of his day, or his nights' work as a guard?

JO: *I'm curious – first, going back to the two scenes where Paul is showing us the routines of his day. How, you told me earlier that you did perhaps five takes of those, and it was maybe the second that was interesting. I'm interested in how those demonstrations, those explanations of his day, how they evolved, if you remember, over the course of your successive takes?*

RP: As soon as you grasp that the witness's statement is something very difficult for him to express, you do another take to see if there's any difference in the way that he recounts his day. When you do a second take in a documentary, it's not like fiction feature film, where you do the same thing again, the second time you don't repeat exactly. When you're making a fiction film you can say, you come from here, and you cross here, and then you move to there. And after the first take you can say, come back and do it again, but not so quickly. You can't do that with a documentary. In documentary, a second take is also a unique take. You have to have a progression in each take. When there's no further progression, you stop.

JO: *When you have multiple takes in a documentary, when you're asking people to remember, are you working through different layers of resistance also? Different layers of fear, different layers of forgetting, as well. People forget. How did you find the two scenes with Po which are really fantastic scenes, and how did you feel the build-up to those worked? To that kind of precision and cohesion?*

RP: First of all you need a lot of patience. You need to be very, very patient. Also you have to know the subject very, very well. And don't forget that the whole team, the whole crew, has lived through the genocide. Po could not speak to this film crew in the way that he might be able to speak to a British journalist, for example. Because he knows that the whole crew knows the things that happened. You have this one subject, and you have to have several witnesses around that one subject, all arriving at the same point. It took three years for the registrar who noted all the names, and for Hoi himself, to acknowledge that there were children who were killed in these camps. In order to facilitate that it was necessary to find witnesses from the Khmer Rouge themselves who would say 'Yes, we saw this, we saw these children. But it didn't panic me or worry me too much.' The more I treated this subject, the more I became convinced that you cannot destroy humanity, you can't destroy a human being without leaving some trace of that human life. So it's for me to find those traces. I had to read everything, I had to look at everything that I could, to immerse myself completely in a subject that I knew at the beginning but had to know better.

JtB: *The Khmer Rouge guards photographed every victim before they interrogated them. They kept an archive of photographs. You used the photograph as another layer in the film.*

RP: I was free to use all the forms, which memorialise things. The photographs, the archives, Nath's paintings, so I was competely free to use all of these different elements. The photographs are very important, because the moment that the photograph is taken is the first step towards putting that person to death. And as soon as that photograph is taken, that person is replaced by a number, and he has lost his or her identity. To have an affective genocide machine, it's very difficult to kill a human being. But if you take away the identity of that human being, if you de-humanise that human being, it's much easier for that machine to work effectively.

The Nazis in World War II were out to exterminate the Jews. Even if it was a Jew in Siberia, they would find that person and execute him, because that person was Jewish. The Khmer Rouge were killing 'the enemy' so you had to make a dossier, to take a photograph, to prove that person as being an enemy. So you then can prove you act in destroying an enemy. It's not only a question of de-humanising the victim, but also of de-humanising the torturer, the guard. It's for this reason that they took very young boys to be indoctrinated. And that's something which is very prevalent in communist regimes, which is to rewrite, endlessly, the autobiographical confession. So [in] each version of the confession, they've been submitted to torture. And after so much torture the prisoner begins to lie. And to denounce others. So very quickly your friends become in the end your enemies.

So what had been a group of your friends suddenly becomes a network, a CIA network, or KGB. And it's not finished because then it's important that you accept and believe that. And once you've accepted that, and believed that, you can be killed. It's for that reason that I describe the crime in Cambodia as a crime of genocide. It's not recognised as such as people who prefer to say a crime against humanity.

JO: *They're fabricating these confessions, or forcing people to fabricate these confessions, and to denounce people and to conjure whole networks of enemies. At the same time of course they know that they're doing that, and at the same time the regime – inevitably this happened with the Stalin purges, and also I suppose in Cambodia – it sort of cannibalises itself, because it ends up denouncing itself.*

RP: It's important to understand why the revolution happened. In China and in the Soviet Union ... The revolution was made in the name of greater justice. But when it goes bad, the revolution goes bad – when Stalin becomes Stalin and Mao becomes Mao. Why are you killing the people who supported you? And it's for that reason that you have to start creating dossiers and have confessions fabricated. The point of a revolution is to bring justice to everyone, otherwise it's not a revolution. For that reason the Germans had no reason, in the Nazi period, to make dossiers, because it was the Jews that they were after. They were killed just because they were Jewish.

JO: *Can you talk about the impact of the film in Cambodia? I know it had an impact, and now Duch is about to go on trial.*

RP: When making the film I thought a great deal of the dead, of course. In making the film the dead were with me always ... the very fact that I am here, to a certain degree, suggests that somebody left a place for me. So my job is to transmit to the following generation what happened, but also not for them to feel guilty for what happened. Of course now the young who want to know what happened come and see the film. People are asking why certain grandparents are dead and others not, for example. If you don't explain they go around thinking that their grandparents committed a crime, and that's why they were killed. And they go around feeling guilty themselves for that. There was a young woman that I met who said she'd seen the film, which had made her suffer a lot, but at the same time it returned her dignity to her. And so that's why the film is made.

JO: *And so it had a specific effect on San Pan* [the Head of State], *didn't it?*

RP: San Pan had no need for the film to know that S21 existed, but he was able to use the film.

JO: *The film became known in part because when San Pan saw the film it forced him, in a way, or that's how it was reported, to admit the existence of the prison, which he'd never admitted before.*

RP: S21 is not a little studio in the middle of nowhere. It was a huge machine.

JO: *And so now the commander is going on trial, and you're making a film in Cambodia with some of the same people, is that right? Can you talk about that? Or do you not want to talk about it? Dutch trial starts on the 17th, right? And you're going back in two days time. So even if you don't know what you're going to do, and that's a familiar feeling…*

RP: Sometimes you have an idea and you want to make a film, which looks like your idea. It's not good. You can make a fiction film then. If you want to make a good documentary film, it's much more important to spend your time observing what happens, what people say, what people understand, what people would like to understand sometimes and what they cannot understand sometimes. That's why I don't know. Really I don't. I'm also afraid, sometimes I can't sleep at night. I spend money and no film yet…! [laughter]

JO: *Some of the relationships that we see in S21 were not intentional, you said, they began with your film* Bophana. *It'd be interesting to know more about your other relationships with the other guards?*

RP: Yes, first thing I would like to have is a Cambodian team. If I say 'kill', it's not the same meaning for you as it for me. I took five or six years to train a crew to do this film. It's very important. Everyone in the crew has the same desire. No vengeance (they're not after revenge). They want only to release something like a memory, a work on memory. That's all. So that's the first thing. The second thing is that I went to visit all the Khmer Rouge that my team could find. And I paid a visit to their village, to their homes, just to give them a signal that I know where they are now, who they are, and I will come again. I'm not afraid of them. I can come. In the first years we didn't shoot in *S21*. And I shot all over Cambodia, in different locations, but not in *S21*. And after that they respected you. They know who you are. That you speak the same language, that you can understand them. So you can start to work.

JO: *Were you specifically looking for people, Khmer Rouge, who had worked in S21, or anyone?*

RP: With the Khmer Rouge, they set up a system to produce files, many files, even on themselves. You take a file from Hoi, you have his address and you go to the village. You can find him. It's very easy. But the difficulty is if they accept or understand what you want to do.

JO: *And then you had to build the trust to bring them to...*

RP: No, to trust, it's not... Yes, we built together the trust, I cannot build it by myself alone. You know, everybody, even the perpetrators, need to speak, need to talk. Because now they have children, they have a wife. And how can you live if you don't talk about what you did? I don't know.

JtB: *The first scene of the film is with the parents of Hoi. She says to him 'you have to go through the ceremony', because he says 'I have a headache, I cannot talk.' And she says 'you have to go through a kind of ceremony to move on'. The film is a kind of 'ceremony' for the perpetrators, that them to move on...*

RP: Yes, it's really an invitation to speak.

JO: *Except that Nath says 'I can't move on and I never want to move on. I want to, until I die, struggle to understand this', near the end of the film.*

JtB: *What was the dynamic of the group of guards, during the six weeks in S21; can you talk about the relationship during the shooting between those six or seven men?*

RP: It's important to know that whilst taking the witness statements from these guards, they were done in different ways, different styles, but towards the end I decided to do a kind a collective memory. It's difficult, when you are face to face with one another; it is difficult to lie. Even if the junior guards still look up to Hoi because he was the chief. There's very little use of a throat microphone, or body mic in the film. On the one or two occasions that it was used, Hoi at one point forgot that he had a mic on. It was when he was away from the camera that he told the others 'say no more, because if you tell him any more he'll know what other things have been happening' and so on... That was accidental because he didn't know he had a mic on.

JO: *So what did you do? Did you do anything? Did you tell Hoi that you heard him telling them, did you intervene there?*

RP: No, sometimes I shouted a lot... When someone continues to lie, I shout. Because I'm a human being like him. Sometimes people living around S21 heard me [laughs], because I shouted, yes. I shouted. I told Hoi not to try to hide things from me. You know, one time I was in the countryside, I rode with a group of the Khmer Rouge. The first day I went to this village, I found everyone. Who the killer was, who the guard was. There was only one survivor, who still lives in the same village. But this guy didn't want to talk to me, but each time he saw a Khmer Rouge coming, he spoke very, very softly. Next day I came to the village, nobody wanted to talk to me. So I know that one of the guys who is today a policeman ordered everybody to keep silent. And when I saw him, I said 'I know you ordered everyone not to speak to me.' And everybody came with machetes to surround us; you have to face that situation. But if you show your fear, you will lose control. Never show them that. Of course sometimes I'm afraid, like you. But you have to cut sometimes when you are making a film! I have 1,200 hours of rushes... At the end, over the last year, I concentrated the shooting on S21 for one reason: the Khmer Rouge continued to say that S21 did not exist. And maybe in 25 years somebody will be able to say that the genocide did not exist. You cannot say that it didn't exist when the S21 is inside the city, inside the Khmer Rouge organisation. You can't deny S21. It's inside your machine.

JO: *One thing that strikes me about this film, and from what I know of your other work, is that you're dealing with places that are of such deep human significance that I want to say almost sacred. The locations themselves bear witness to so much that they become a kind of character in your film. Here it seems to be true in even* The Burnt Theatre *[France/Cambodia, 2005]. There are these locations that bear witness to something and what's really fascinating to me is how you use the location. You don't set up, you don't try to use the location to depict what happened, to make it look like it looked, but you bring in certain elements like the lights, as you said before, or a few props, or debris...*

RP: When you want to make a film about location, or a film about human beings, It's very simple. If you want to make a film about dignity, about memory, you stay very close to people. You don't need to show it's a wide shot... Memory is like a territory and the surprise, with regards to Nath finding the pen on the floor in S21 building, is more than a coincidence after what you were filming. So the buildings, the location is part of the human story because it contains the memory.

JO: *The film is made within a very difficult coexistence between people who are clearly victims, people who are guards and we invariably wonder – what are they thinking, why are they going through this? And you framed the film in a very precise way to say that we need this testimony, we need to show, to see what happened. What are the guards doing in being so cooperative with you, are they still indoctrinated and just showing you what they did because they want to, or are they...*

PR: They cannot refuse to cooperate. Because I am here.

JO: *In what sense?*

RP: I was in Cambodia.

JO: *But they could say, I don't want to talk about it, I'm not coming to...*

RP: I'm still here. It was their responsibility to cooperate. How can you refuse? I don't know how. I'm back again. I know you. Maybe I will not make a film with you, but I know who you are. And until you die I know who you are. You cannot refuse. No way for you to get out. I know where you are, who you are. They have no other way to get out, the only one way to get out for them is through testimony. To testify. To cooperate. I am not a judge. But they have to cooperate.

JO: *Did they feel intimidated?*

RP: No. Why? They intimidate me with the machete. I have only a camera and microphone. No gun. Very simple, when I talk with them I look straight into their eyes, and explain what I want to do. There's no trap, nothing like that. One of the victim's sisters wanted to see Prakun, the torturer. I asked him if he agreed or not. He said 'ok', and after the confrontation, he asked me not to do it again. I respected it. I don't impose. 'You don't want to see her any more, ok. We stop there.'

Audience member: *I'm curious about what your thoughts are on the forthcoming trials?*

RP: I think justice cannot resolve the problem, only a small part of the problem. People have waited a long time for this tribunal to bring them a solution. But they will be disappointed. Because a tribunal cannot bring a solution to their questions. But we need it because a tribunal can recognise who is the victim and who the perpetrator, like the film does. At the beginning of the film, Nath says 'If they [the guards] are also victims, who is a victim? Who are we?' It's very important to recognise who the victim is and who the perpetrator is. In this way you can start to mourn. You can start to talk. It's also important for the tribunal. I support that, because I think that if you want to build democracy, it's not only economics that you need. You need also a state of love. If people who killed millions do not face justice, how can you put a guy who steals a bicycle in jail?

THE KILLER'S SEARCH FOR ABSOLUTION:
Z32, AVI MOGRABI

Joram ten Brink

Avi Mograbi, a documentary film director, lives and works in Tel Aviv, Israel. *Z32* was produced in 2009 as a French/Israeli co-production.

Joram ten Brink: *Can we start by discussing the use of a digital mask in Z32 to conceal the identity of the soldier?*

Avi Mograbi: This was done in response to his demands, that his identity would not be exposed. He wanted to travel to London and not be arrested in Heathrow. He was fearful because he participated in a revenge operation. You can understand, although it almost never happens – in his mind he also can become a subject for revenge. Somebody might take revenge on him. And so he doesn't want to be exposed so that the son of the person he killed will not have ideas about how to 'bring back' his father by killing someone else. His demand has brought up many issues but, of course, I kept my promise and I concealed his identity. It was a very elaborate and economically painful operation. At the beginning you start working on the film and then you come up with the idea of the mask, and when it works, you say, 'oi-va-voi' it works! I'm concealing a murderer in my film! I'm giving shelter to a murderer! Of course, it's a problem for the filmmaker, but basically it's a problem for the society. We are a 'defense shield' for many murders that are done in our name. We talk about wanting to have a high moral society but we send our kids to do terrible things and then we give them shelter.

JtB: *But then your responsibility as a filmmaker is not to betray your subject. You* *'play the game', and you do shield him. Because he says 'I won't participate in the film if you reveal my identity.'*

AM: My responsibility is more complex. It's not just as a filmmaker. Before a filmmaker, I'm a human being, and a moral human being, and a citizen, or someone who cares about his society and communicates his ideas etc. Let's say, that if this was a Nazi officer, I would not be condemned for having lied to him, after I have promised that I will conceal his identity, and then exposed him. On the contrary, you would say that I have done the right thing.

JtB: *Here you chose to shield him and not to betray him, because you promised him not to reveal...*

AM: Yes, but also I chose to deal with those questions, which have become actually the main subject of the film. It's more important, I think, to present to the society here, to my community, those questions of sheltering our own assassins, then to expose one soldier who was really the last person in this huge chain of command. He was the person who pressed the button, but he was only the person who pressed the button. He had no power and of course the big guys are not in danger. So for me it's more important to bring it into discussion the whole issue rather than to expose one person. I found his testimony in the archive of [the group] *Shovrim Shtikah* ['Breaking the Silence'], which I'm part of. One of the things I do with the group [of soldiers] is to listen to testimonies and log them. Later they are transcribed, edited and published. In *Shovrim Shtikak*, one of the first things that they are very clear about is that if you break the rule once i.e. of exposing somebody, you lose the rest. As there will never be anyone who will be prepared to step forward again. Never. By now, *Shovrim Shtikah* include four hundred, five hundred soldiers, reserve and soldiers in active service, who have already testified during a period of five years. Now, after the Gaza war, there have been more than thirty or so soldiers who came forward to testify. There is a booklet out of their testimonies. It's absolutely clear that if a person is exposed, you know that this is the last soldier that you have seen coming forward. And the question is, what is more important? The publication of testimonies right after the events, as it's not so easy, as the press and public are reluctant to deal with our own doings, or, to have a 'victory' of one person being sent to jail. Mind you, he wouldn't go to jail either after all.

JtB: *What you also create is a very strong filmic presence through the use of the mask.*

AM: Yes, of course, but again, this was not the intention, but as we moved along we realised that giving him a mask created something that was not planned: the fact that he is both himself, and not himself, that he is one person but he also becomes many persons. In one of the screenings of the film in Tel Aviv a friend of mine came to me after the screening and said that he saw him in the crowd, watching the film. But he wasn't there, I didn't allow this to happen – that he would be identified. But the fact that this guy started looking at possible candidates in the audience for being Z32, this has made Z32 more than one person. It became more an abstract idea and a very interesting reflection on making the film. Of course it also reflects on Greek theatre, not only because of the masks, but because of the music, the songs that I sing, which become like a Greek chorus, or it reflects on Brechtian theatre etc. But I think it's mainly that you get a very strong sensation when you watch it: sometimes, you think it is a real person, because it's done in such a way that it's very hard for you to say that this is a person with a digital mask, but then he smokes, and he brings his hand under the mask, and the smoke comes out of his eyeholes and the illusion collapses immediately. So it becomes a very strong cinematic and viewing experience.

JtB: *And there's also of course the issue of the truth, because one speaks of evidence in documentary. So does he stop being 'evidence'? Is he 'evidence' in the traditional sense?*

AM: Yes, it reflects on those questions of testimony. Confession used to be in British law 'the mother of all testimonies'. Now it is not so any more, but in Israel it is still the case. If I confess to having done something terrible, then you will say: look, unless you think I'm a psychopath, a normal person would not say such terrible things about himself, unless they were true. It is such a big risk for the person to confess. We have learned that this is our intuitive response to self-incriminating testimonies, but we know that a lot of times people have said things that have never happened. I made a film called *The Reconstruction* fifteen years ago, about five Palestinians who confessed to killing a child, Danny Katz from Haifa, and they are still in jail, but it's absolutely not clear that they're the killers, and if you ask me, I think that they are absolutely innocent. Although you see them in front of the camera saying that they have done it. They confessed to the camera.

JtB: *Can we speak a moment about the music, before we go back to the image. How did you decide on the music and its style?*

AM: It was Noam's [the composer] idea. It's in Eisler's style. It was Noam's idea to take it to a Brecht-ish concept. When I started talking to him there was not even an idea of what this film would be like. There were two basic ideas: one was to make a very, very simple film with the person talking to the camera, and telling his story. I heard his story on an audiotape, during my *Shovrim Shtikah* voluntary work. I thought it was very strong and impressive and I thought that it will be even more impressive on video. I thought to make a very, very simple film, not an 'Avi Mograbi' film. This is why I resisted making this film. I didn't want to make it. I thought it should be made, but not by me, because it didn't fit the way I make films. The other idea was very, very different from that – it was to turn his text into a libretto for an opera. Because I thought his story is a tragic story, he is, you could say, a tragic figure; I wouldn't say a hero, but a tragic figure, someone who had the opportunity to make the right decision, yet he made the wrong decision, and he will have to live with this decision for the rest of his life. There's no 'correction' possible. And if you understand that you made the wrong decision – and he does understand it – and because there are millions like him that don't understand it and they make the wrong decisions but they don't even give it a thought. But he will never be able to get rid of this burden, because he, at a certain point, understood that what he has done was wrong and that he could have taken a different choice. So I thought, this sounds like an operatic protagonist. But the opera idea died very early; we very quickly understood that it was too big for us as I spoke with Noam Inbar, the composer, about the opera. I gave him the audio recording of the testimony, and he then tried to do some kind of an audio experimental piece. Anyway, nothing came about. Then I approached the Z32 person, and proposed to make a film. He immediately said yes, with a 'but'. And the 'but' started the real film: 'Okay, no problem, but you cannot expose my identity.' And so from being a very, very simple film about someone talking to the camera, it became a very complicated film of how to make a film with a person speaking to the camera for ninety minutes, and you don't see his face, or his facial expressions. How is this different from a radio show, and what will keep you watching it? There is a film called *Massaker* [2005] by a German director, Monica Borgmann, and a Lebanese director, Lokman Slim, interviewing three Phalangists who participated in the Sabra and Shatila massacre. You cannot see their faces as they are completely darkened, and thus there are many compensations for the lack of expression and identity. First of all, it's shot inside the destroyed building, with many coloured lights on the walls. You see parts of bodies, and sometimes they are topless – everything to get you interested. I didn't want to do a *Massaker* film. I wanted to do something that would be cinematic. It took months to come to this mask solution…

JtB: *So, back to the music...*

AM: The music came back once I realised that it is going to be an Avi Mograbi film after all, because the making of the film raised a lot of questions, a lot of dilemmas. I decided I will address those dilemmas in the film, and not ignore them, or deal with them outside of the film. And thus I started thinking about my presence in the film, or how to present those dilemmas in the film. Having done this and that in previous films, which I didn't want to repeat, at a certain point, without really understanding what the impact of it will be, and whether I can sing at all, because there was no record of me singing without people leaving...

JtB: *The film itself is such a radical shift from your initial idea, as you said. What you achieved here is a much more complex structure which actually gets us to a much more accurate understanding of the state of mind of a killer. Four 'characters' tell the story: the songs, the soldier, the girlfriend, and the film, as a film. There are four attempts to look at the story through different characters and protagonists. Although the girlfriend is in essence the protagonist of the film, we'll come back to her later...*

AM: She's the most important. Without her...

JtB: *Without her there's no film.*

AM: Yes. And it wasn't my idea to put her in the film.

JtB: *She's the audience. She is 'me', the viewer.*

AM: Yes, yes. She's you, but not the obvious you. Not the 'Israeli'. Most Israelis don't identify with her. They identify with him. But yes, she's definitely the audience, definitely the listener; the listener who asks difficult questions.

JtB: *In the last shot, she brings the film back to me when she turns to the camera and looks at me.*

AM: Yes. She looks at the millions watching her at home.

JtB: *She hears the story and she cannot make sense of it. She refuses up until the last moment to forgive him and you don't know if she will ever forgive him. She doesn't say anything.*

AM: She looks at the camera…

JtB: *She looks at the camera, and says, 'What do you think? Now you've seen the film; I presented it to you for the past ninety minutes, now what do you think? You, the viewer.'*

AM: I think she also looks at the camera as a kind of enemy because she's trapped by the camera. If the film starts with some kind of embarrassment with the presence of the camera – people are embarrassed because they are dealing with an intimate story and they're not ready for the exposure – at the end, she looks at the camera as a kind of enemy. The camera has done much more than just be present in a private or intimate moment. The camera has stimulated some kind of penetration to places she didn't really acknowledge that she would go to.

JtB: *But she wanted to go there…*

AM: Yes, but…

JtB: *That's why she confronts her boyfriend? She wanted to go there and, in a sense, the camera helped her in her mission?*

AM: I'm not sure. I think that in the end she feels, even if she wanted to do it, that the camera somehow is an enemy, she doesn't want it there any more. She wants to be away from it. But it's a question of interpretation of what you see in that look of her at the end.

JtB: *Does the camera help her to discover the truth about the murder?*

AM: No, because she knows the truth. She's heard it tens of times. She has, like most people, found ways to inhibit the story, although she heard it many, many times, and even on video she hears it, and yet she doesn't remember it. Again and again. She inhibits it completely. She finds a way to repress it. Not to know it. She feels inhibited, unlike for instance, others who inhibit because they identify with the event. It is burning material for her; it's too dangerous stuff. Once she deals with it, she has to deal with who he is. She doesn't want to deal with it … he's her lover.

JtB: *In some situations she pushes him to go on; in some situations he is the one that pushes her to go on.*

AM: She inhibits it from outside of the film. But in the film you see the traces of it. Because when the film starts, it's not the first time she hears this story. When the film starts, at the first conversation on the bed in India, they mentioned previous times when talking about it, it created tension between them. And so she heard it many times, and knowing him, I know that he tells it all the time. If he sits with you for fifteen minutes and trusts you, you will hear this story.

JtB: *So you found the right person, as a filmmaker.*

AM: I think I made the right choice. Because there was another person who did the same thing on the same night in a different location, and he wasn't the right person for the film. Unlike Z32, he really wants to find absolution. He's now working with the lawyer representing the families of the victims in a civil law suit, to help them to get compensation. Z32 was asked to do the same thing and he declined.

JtB: *Why?*

AM: Because I don't believe he is sincere. I don't think he's very sincere. I think one of his reasons for making the film is that he thought the film would absolve him. And this will be the end of it. He will not need to ask for forgiveness again. Apparently it's not so easy, more complex than that. But he's less serious.

JtB: *So the film actually has two functions; the cinema is a tool that helps us to uncover and recover acts of violence, but also a tool to help us to find redemption.*

AM: Of course, I use him and he uses me. I use him for two purposes. One, the one you mentioned, and the other one is to be even more famous, for my own career... I also try to deal with it in the film, with who gains from all this, or what comes out from all this. For him it is some kind of absolution or forgiveness or temporary forgiveness. He hopes to feel better at the end of it. He definitely uses me to get there, and doesn't go where one would go. Many people have asked: Why ask forgiveness from his girlfriend? How is she connected to the event? How can she forgive? Nothing was done to her. Of course, psychologically one understands it. He is not really asking for forgiveness. When he says 'Do you forgive me?', he actually asks 'Can you still love me? Will you stay with me?' It's not real forgiveness, it's a sort of forgiveness within an image of what you expect your spouse to be. He asks for *acceptance*, not *forgiveness* for the act of violence.

He uses forgiveness, but if he really looks for forgiveness he could have done a lot of other things. Like the other soldier does…

JtB: *Through the film one understands how violence operates…*

AM: This film came after my film *Avenge But One of My Two Eyes*.[1] In the last scene of *Avenge…* I shouted at the soldiers at the checkpoint: 'We don't let the children cross.' This was shot at the end of 2003. In 2004, the group *Shovrim Shtikah* was formed. Miki Kratsman, the photographer who works with Gideon Levy, the human rights journalist, and the guys who formed *Shovrim Shtikah* wanted to create an exhibition of their own photographs taken during their military service in the city of Hebron. They approached Miki and asked him to curate the show. They said that they may want to do some video testimonies, and he asked me to join and produce the video testimonials. It was a very interesting exhibition and very well attended.

JtB: *Were the soldiers speaking to the camera, without hiding their faces?*

AM: We blurred all their faces. The first testimonies that came in were mostly concerned with the activities of the Jewish settlers of Hebron. My contribution was to distract them from the Jewish settlers and lead them to their own conduct. So I became involved in *Shovrim Shtikah* and listened to a lot of testimonies and edited their video testimonies etc. This was 2004. In 2005, my elder son refused to serve in the military and was jailed. And so I found myself, again, but eventually, in retrospect, I realised that I was very much into thinking about what it means to be a soldier, what it means to become a soldier, what makes a good kid…

JtB: *Which was never a question you asked yourself when you were his age?*

AM: Not in this way. I didn't want to go to the military, but my mother … it wasn't so much an ideological thing, but my mother told me that if my father will hear that I am planning not to go to the military he will kill me, so I decided to live. [Laughs] And I did my military service, but eventually in '83 I refused to serve in Lebanon and was jailed for that. I was a founding member of *Yesh Gvul* ['There's a Limit'], one of the first 'refuseniks' [to serve in the army] movement in Israel. So in retrospect my interest in the soldier in the Z32 film is how you become a soldier and what makes a good kid soldier, which in turns, is a bad human. It's supposed to be obvious but it's not so obvious. I was more interested in those questions, not only for dramatic reasons, but also for my own reasons. That is why in the first third of *Z32*, we don't talk about the 'story' but we talk about his training; how he has developed as a soldier; how he arrived to the moment when he was told to do the revenge operation, and kill people who, as far as he knew, were innocent. In retrospect we all know that they were also unarmed and elderly. This is why the *Z32* film starts with the pre-production part, a pre-production to the event, and so I use in it in the film as a pre-production for the development of the mask and a pre-production for the development of the singing.

JtB: *Back to the girlfriend in the film...*

AM: I knew about his girlfriend who wasn't very happy about what he had done. He told me himself.

JtB: *It bothered him?*

AM: Yes, but I didn't know how bad it was. It developed in such a way that I didn't think of having her in the film. At that early stage I had a very different concept – I still wanted to have a second soldier [involved in the killing] in the film. I was looking to find a way to conceal him, not just with a digital mask but I looked also at an option of finding someone to play his role. I wanted him to find the person to play himself. I proposed to do auditions for young men, without me being there. The idea was that he will tell them the story, they will repeat it in the way they see it, and hopefully – because he would perhaps pick people with a similar history and upbringing like his – maybe they will have their own stories as well to tell in the course of the audition. At a certain point I thought of sending Z68 to this audition, the other soldier who did the same thing on the same night. So they went together. But they had very similar stories, and I thought that perhaps they will exchange stories and in the film we'll find ourselves with two gladiators with masks each telling the story of the other. He did a couple of these auditions and they weren't very interesting. At a certain point, after one of the interviews when I filmed him quite a few times, he said that he wasn't very happy with how he was talking to the camera during the interview. He explained that the night before he would rehearse the interview at home and he would think of saying things differently and yet when it came to *the* interview, he didn't say what he was hoping to say. So I gave him a camera, and sent him home to do his own interview, without my interference, and without my presence. Which he did. And there were some interesting things there.

JtB: *As a video diary?*

AM: Well … a self-confession kind of thing. When I watched the first batch of tapes, he was in India with his girlfriend. The second Lebanon War started and he was afraid that he would be called to serve in the war. They brought the trip to India forward and left a day or two after the war started, so I watched his tapes when they were already in India. I thought they were interesting, and maybe I'll ask him to film one testimony in India too, because India is a place of symbolic value for Israeli soldiers. They go there after the military service to 'take off', or get rid of whatever they have to get rid of, and some even go deeper into 'purify' themselves after the military service through different methods. I thought maybe this will add something to the film, and also they were planning to go to Varanasi, the death city, where they burn the bodies on the river… It was a long shot. He took a camera in Delhi and did his own 'diary'. He then started talking to his girlfriend. And from then on…

JtB: *So when they came back you continued to work with both of them…*

AM: No, I was never there. I met her only for the rough-cut viewing of the film, I felt I was obliged to. I never asked her, why she did it. Maybe she thought that he wants her to do it as she knew it was bothering him. Maybe she thought she should collaborate to help him. I don't know what she thought.

JtB: *She doesn't just try to help him, she also tries to help herself. She needs to find answers for herself, and in the last shot of the film, she really needs to find out. She becomes more and more disturbed throughout the film and that's why the last shot is so strong, because she says 'I don't know anymore; what am I sup-posed to say to you now? I don't know what to do with you now? Am I going to kick you out?'*

AM: I'm not sure all of this was part of her incentive. I think that this is where she found herself. She found herself in a situation where her own dealing with the story of murder had to change because of this 'staged' moment that they ar-rived at.

JtB: *Because of the presence of the camera…*

AM: Yes. But truthfully, I'm not really interested in what her psychological process was. Now I know that her view of this event, both morally and politically, is very radical. And *very* different from the way he sees it. And that this was obviously an obstacle in their relationship. But I don't know.

JtB: *And the film was shown in Israel on television?*

AM: It was screened in the Cinematheques, it was broadcast on Channel 8 on cable. And you can find it in one or two video libraries.

JtB: *And the reviews in Israel?*

AM: Were very good.

JtB: *But the film didn't generate a public discussion?*

AM: Nothing, because it was broadcast just at the end of Operation Cast Lead [in Gaza]...

JtB: *Did you arrange a special screening for the soldiers in Shovrim Shtikah?*

AM: Yes. It was very strong. Actually we had a screening in my place, about twenty of them, some came with their girlfriends, and it was a very, very strong screening and discussion. They discussed whether they are at all different from him.

JtB: *What was Z32's response?*

AM: His first reaction was that he felt that I could have made a more complex character out of him. He felt that it was too superficial. He was shocked when he saw in the film some conversations that were later forgotten. Suddenly it's on screen – she says 'it was a murder, and you are a murderer', it suddenly becomes a statement with a 'full stop'. To his credit, he understood very well that it's my film. It was his story, but now it's my film. The only contract we had was about his concealment, not the 'art' of his concealment but only about the fact that he has to remain concealed. When the film came out and he showed it to his friends and family, little by little he realised that what he thought was the portrayal of a very superficial one-sided character was actually different. He even realised, that I also felt, that many people can actually identify with him, and not only condemn him. She liked it from the first instance. From the first viewing.

JtB: *Once a film about violence is made in a very detailed and considerate way – our soldier begins to have questions or doubts for example – there is a point perhaps when the audience might begin to empathise with the guy. 'After all he's* *not so bad ... so he did something terrible, but he's like you and me; he's reason-able, not a monster, he's an articulate, sensitive guy, talking about his fears and doubts.' Perhaps at the end of the day the audience will walk out and say – he's quite sympathetic character.*

AM: It's possible and it happens sometimes but this is the risk you take. If you want to do a very clear, one-sided film – that's okay. You might like it or not, but I thought it was very important to make him a rounded character. It could have been very easy to show him as a monster. It wouldn't be interesting; the film would have lost much more than it gained.

NOTE

1   See the interview with Avi Mograbi about the film in this volume.

IMPUNITY

Benedict Anderson

There is a jolting moment in Jean Rouch's famous 'anthropological' film *Moi, Un Noir* (1958), about a small, attractive group of young males from then French colonial Niger trying to find work in the more prosperous, but still French co-lonial, Côte d'Ivoire. We see them periodically at work, but most of the film shows them at leisure, drinking, joking and hooking up with women, so that the atmosphere is generally lively and cheerful. But toward the end, we find the main character, who calls himself Edward G. Robinson (parallel to a friend who names himself Lemmy Caution), walking with a sidekick and an invisible Rouch along a riverside levee. Quite suddenly he starts to re-enact for the camera an ugly scene from his real or imagined past. He was among the many francophone Africans who were sent as colonial cannon-fodder to fight for France against the Ho Chi Minh-led Viet Minh – before the fall of Dien Bien Phu. He seems to enjoy replay-ing his bloody killing of captured Vietnamese. His sidekick pays no attention, making us realise that he has seen this shtick many times and knows it by heart. So the brief show is meant for Rouch and for us. Once the scene is over, and the cheerful tone resumes, the viewer is immediately assaulted by the obvious doubts and questions. Why did Rouch include this short scene in an otherwise friendly film? Did Oumarou Ganda, aka Edward G. Robinson, who was Rouch's main collaborator, insist upon it? Why did the African perform this way, quite sud-denly? Did he really do what he re-enacted? Why the sudden turn from jokes to horror – and back? Did Rouch intend to situate the Niger boys of that generation within the larger framework of the ferocious decline and fall of France's empire? Was Ganda releasing a kind of frustration about his life, and resentment of the French, perhaps even of his patron and friend, the famous Rouch?

When I watched the film, some years ago, it occurred to me that the crucial motif to think about was simply impunity. Like everyone else involved in France's huge, disastrous military endeavour to recover colonial Indochina between 1946 and 1954, the young African soldier could not be punished for 'acts of war', no matter how sadistic and in contravention of the Geneva Convention. He would always be a hero of a very small sort thanks to this impunity. At the same time, impunity is nothing without repetitive, boastful demonstration to different audiences. Drifting, poor, irregularly employed, Ganda takes on the menacing 'Don't mess with me, motherfucker!' persona of Edward G. Robinson, the master actor of gangsters in the Hollywood of that era – who usually dies at the end of each film, but comes back as saturninely alive as ever in the next. But *Moi, Un Noir* goes on to show the local hollowness of the impunity. In French Côte d'Ivoire, the colonial auhorities put one of Ganda's comrades in jail, and clearly would not hesitate to nab the hero of Vietnam, if he broke the local laws. At the end he is beaten up by a large drunken Portuguese sailor in a quarrel over a prostitute.

Always somewhere in the back of my mind, this episode tentatively offers me a way to think about Rouch-fan Joshua Oppenheimer's extraordinary films about the massacres of communists in Indonesia in 1965–66, and their next-century re-enactment before the camera. One of these films – *Snake River* (2013) – shows (to me at least) a connection between the situations of Rouch and Oppenheimer, as well as deep differences. The grisly re-enactment of the torture and murder of doomed communists on the bank of this river, half a century after they happened, is also about impunity and boastfulness. The two starring elderly brutes take the young man from anti-comunist USA as more or less on their side, just as Edward G. Robinson took Rouch as a sympathic anticolonial Frenchman. But they also evince a kind of 'Don't mess with me, motherfucker!' attitude which they regularly practice for various other local audiences. They are not suspicious of Oppenheimer's motives, and Oppenheimer gets his own immunity from this guilelessness and also from inviting them and other killers to participate as they wish in the filmwork, not merely as actors, but also as, up to a point, filmmakers. Another tie between the films is, as we shall see later on, the collaborators' fascination with Hollywood. This time not Edward G. Robinson, outlaw, but Rambo and the Duke, patriots.

Yet Oppenheimer's performing killers do not have their exact counterparts – so I think – in other parts of Indonesia, for example, East and Central Java, as well as Bali, provinces where the numbers of those barbarously tortured and murdered were far higher than in North Sumatra where the serpentine river flows. The question is why? In what follows I will try to offer a historical explanation that deals with the national-level and official version of 1965 and its commemorative aftermath, and at the same time contrast North Sumatra with East Java, which can be thought of as the most striking opposites.

1 OCTOBER 1965

In the wee hours of that Jakarta morning, six important generals were murdered by soldiers and NCOs belonging to President Sukarno's elite guards, the Tjakrabirawa Regiment. At 7am a military group calling itself the September 30th Movement announced over national radio that it had taken action to forestall a coup meant to overthrow Sukarno four days later, on Armed Forces Day. The deaths of the generals were not mentioned. A few hours later, two key announcements followed. One declared that in place of the existing cabinet, a large Revolutionary Council would temporarily take power for protection of the president. Its membership was a weird mixture of left- and right-wing civilians and military men, but also included the leadership of the September 30th Movement: one general, one colonel, one lieutenant-colonel, and two or three lower down. The second announcement was even stranger. The Movement said that lower military ranks were enraged by the corruption and sexual license within the military high command, which also neglected the poverty of the soldiery. Therefore, all ranks above that of lieutenant-colonel were abolished, while all supporters of the Movement would be promoted two ranks. A spectacular mutiny, in effect, creating a crisis-solidarity among clique-ridden generals and colonels. The Movement did not last long. After 3pm it went off the air, to be replaced at 7pm by proclamations in the name of General Suharto, commander of the army's elite Strategic Forces, who, curiously enough, was not a target of the Movement. By midnight, the mutiny had been crushed, and its leaders scattered and on the hopeless run. The capital's newspapers, except those of the military, were closed down the next morning, and national TV, along with national radio, fell into Suharto's hands.

THE COMMUNISTS

The Communist Party of Indonesia (Partai Komunis Indonesia, or PKI), Asia's oldest, had made the fateful decision – once Indonesian Independence had been recognised by the Dutch colonialists and the rest of the world at the end of 1949 – to take the parliamentary road to power, shutting down a few small guerrilla bands left over from the Revolution of 1945–49. In the first national elections (1955), it was already the fourth of the four huge parties that dominated Parliament. When provincial elections were held two years later in the densely populated and impoverished island of Java, it secured the largest number of voters, but still less than 25 per cent. After that, elections were not held again. The primary reason for this was the government's decision, in the spring of 1957 to declare nationwide martial law in the face of warlordism, regional discontent and rising, fanatical anti-communism in the so-called Outer Islands, most significantly in Sumatra and Sulawesi. The situation deteriorated until the point in February 1958 when a civil war broke out between the now military-dominated government in Jakarta and its Sumatran competition, the PRRI, or Revolutionary Government of the Republic, led by a mixture of national-level 'modernist' Muslim politicians, regional warlords and many of the local inhabitants. A sister-rebellion in Sulawesi soon joined the Sumatrans. The uprising, in spite of being heavily supported by the CIA, was rather quickly crushed by mostly Javanese troops loyal to the High Command, ironically with help from both the Pentagon and Moscow.[1] By the time President Sukarno repealed Martial Law in May 1963, the army had entrenched itself in national power and refused to tolerate any further nationwide elections on grounds of 'national security'. But, protected by Sukarno, who used it to counterbalance the dangerous anti-communist Army leadership, the PKI rapidly expanded its popular support by putting its energies into its mass organisations rather than the parliamentary Party. By early 1965, it was the largest communist party in the world outside the Communist bloc, with over three million members, and perhaps eighteen million followers in its mass organisations: for women, students, intellectuals, peasants, agricultural labourers, workers, fisherfolk, youths, artists and so on. (It was far better organised and disciplined than its political-party competitors). The shift had momentous consequences. Electoral politics are punctuated in time from this election to the next; but mass organisation politics are tensely ceaseless, day in day out, especially when no elections are foreseeable.

In the early 1960s Indonesia became increasingly polarised between right and left. A major factor was economic decline and an inflation that eventually became beyond control. People on fixed salaries and pensions, mostly civil servants, tried to maintain their standards of living by corruption, embezzlement and investing in farm land. This last not only put pressure on land-hungry small farmers, tenants and rural labourers, but clashed with the PKI's attempts to enforce a weak land reform law, fiercely resisted by landowners old and new. Where such landowners were respected *ulamas* and rich *hajis*, resistance was often couched in terms of religion versus atheism. Many of them shrewdly donated surplus hectares to mosques as unalienable *wakaf* property, and sat on the boards administering these gifts. Now religious, no longer personal private properties they were difficult for the PKI to seek to redistribute, since even poor and land-hungry Muslims would come militantly to their mosques' defence. Generally speaking, the collapse of the currency helped to create a pervasive atmosphere of fear, uncertainty and anger. These tendencies help to explain why the largest and worst massacres took place in the country's villages, where land was most seriously contested and the big-party mass organisations were most active.

The fatal weakness of the PKI emerged from its decision to take the parliamentary road. It was not an irrational decision, given the vast extent of the archipelagic country and its huge ethno-religious diversity, as well as the Party's commitment to 'national integrity', and the menacing proximity of America's armadas and air power. But it meant that the Party was mostly above-ground, its members well-known nationally and locally, and it had no armed power of its own at all. The PKI attempted to substitute for this weakness an increasingly harsh rhetoric, which did not add to its real power and frightened its every-day enemies. Meantime, the anti-communist army leadership increasingly backed, openly and surreptitiously, right-wing social, political, religious and intellectual organisations. Membership of any political party was banned within its own ranks as a way of keeping the communists out.

ORIGINS OF THE SLAUGHTER

Army leaders, helped by advice and half-concealed support from both the Pentagon and the CIA – then reeling under heavy reverses in Vietnam – had long been looking for a justification for a mass destruction of the Party. Now the September 30th Movement and the murder of the six generals provided the opening they awaited. Almost immediately the army-controlled media started a lurid and successful campaign to convince the citizens that the Movement was simply a tool, manipulated behind the scenes by the Party, and that it was absolutely not an internal military mutiny. The communists were said to have been planning a vast extension of the murders to the civilian population all over the country. The army's campaign began on 3 October, when the bodies of three of the generals were exhumed from a dry well in a remote part of the Air Force's Jakarta base. (They had not been killed at home, but kidnapped to this area and then shot dead.) The media, using blurred and retouched photos of the bodies, claimed that the victims had had their eyes gouged out and their genitals sliced off by sex-crazed communist women. (Many years later, thanks to military carelessness, the post-mortems written up on 3 October by experienced forensic doctors, and directed personally to Suharto that same day, came to light. No missing eyeballs or genitals, just the lethal wounds caused by military guns.)[2]

In a move that would have pleased Goebbels, the Movement's full name was deleted in favour of Gestapu (GErakan September TigA PUluh). (No one noticed that the word order here is impossible in the Indonesian language, but is syntactically perfect in English. Very few Indonesian generals then had perfect English.) On top of the hyperinflation, this cunning Big Lie propaganda had the desired effect: massive anti-communist hysteria.

The coolly-considered plan of Suharto and his henchmen for the physical and organisational destruction of the Party was based on the huge numbers of its members, affiliates and supporters. To accomplish this mission as rapidly as possible, army personnel were not enough; civilians had to be involved on a large scale, with half-concealed military direction, financing, intelligence, transportation and even the supply of weapons. As secretive corporate bodies notionally devoted to external defence against foreign enemies, armies almost never boast about mass murder (see the mendacious handling of the Rape of Nanking by the Japanese military and the near-genocide of Armenians by the Turkish army). International scandal was to be avoided as much as possible. National armies are not supposed to slaughter their fellow-citizens, especially, as in the case of the PKI, if they are unarmed and put up very little resistance.

Who were the primary collaborators? The two provinces with the highest number of victims, Muslim East Java and Hindu 'Paradise Island' Bali are exemplary. Both provinces were densely populated, ethnically quite homogeneous, and with strong, conservative, traditionalist leaderships. The key thing to bear in mind (when we come to consider North Sumatra) is that they were longstanding strongholds of the two well-rooted legal, 'national' political parties, other than the PKI, both with very large organisational and popular bases. In East Java it was the traditionalist, orthodox Muslim Nahdlatul Ulama, with its militant youthful-male affiliate Ansor. In Bali, it was the PNI (National Party) led locally by landowners, Hindu priests and members of the two upper castes of Satrias and Brahmins. Small Catholic and Protestant parties with their affiliates were also used in places where these religious minorities were influential. (The large 'modernist' Muslim party, Masjumi, fiercely anti-communist, was organisationally unavailable, since it been banned and disbanded in 1959 for its role in the civil war of 1958–59, of which more later.)

These civilians were not professional killers. Once the massacres were over, they 'returned to ordinary life', while the military went on killing large numbers of people in East Timor, Aceh and Papua over the final two decades of the Suharto dictatorship. Many of them, in an atmosphere of media-generated hysteria, genuinely believed that 'they will kill us if we don't kill them first'.*

Needless to say, the military had no interest in punishing any of those involved, but their immunity was also guaranteed in part by the national institutions to which they were affiliated.

Aftermaths? During his brief presidency (October 1999–July 2001) Abdurrah-man Wahid, the charismatic, 'progressive' and politically astute Nahdlatul Ulama leader, decided to ask forgiveness from surviving ex-communists. He did so, how-ever, not for individual killers, but for Ansor in particular and the NU in general. (No other national-level politician has followed his example.) More striking is the fact that over the past decade many young members of Ansor, born well after 1965, began systematically to help communists who had managed to survive the massacres and very many years of brutal imprisonment. Fairly recently a recon-ciliation meeting was held in Jogjakarta between NU and ex-communist women. Everything went well, until an elderly communist described in detail how she had been raped and tortured by Ansor members. As she spoke a young Muslim girl stood up, ashen-faced, and then fainted. Among the rapists and torturers she recognised her own father. It is interesting to note that, quite early on, stories cir-culated widely that 'amateur' killers had mental breakdowns, went mad, or were were haunted by terrifying dreams and fears of karmic retribution. Otherwise, silence. Nothing to boast about in public or on TV, one might say.**

MEDAN AND NORTH SUMATRA: LOCAL HISTORY[3]

Oppenheimer's city of Medan in North Sumatra was and is very different. The strange, dull name of the city already tells one something. It simply means 'field' or 'open space'. It was the last major city begotten by Dutch colonialism – beginning to rise only in the 1870s and 1880s, when the colonial authorities realised that the surrounding fertile and near-empty flatlands were perfect for the development of large-scale agribusiness – tobacco, rubber, palm-oil and coffee plantations. One of the earliest oil-fields in the colony was also discovered there just in time for the automotive revolution. The area was thinly inhabited by Malays, related to the Malays across the narrow Straits of Malacca in today's Malaysia. In so far as there were any rulers at all, these were very small-scale and without much armed power, even if some called themselves 'Sultan'. For their own reasons, the Dutch protected these petty rulers and allowed them to share in the profits of the expanding economy; but the 'Sultans' had to do what they were told.

Medan was created in the era when the Dutch colonial regime abandoned monopolistic mercantilism and adopted British-enforced economic liberalism and open markets. Hence a motley crowd of investors – Dutch, British, German, Austrian, American and eventually Chinese and Japanese – poured in. From the start there was the huge problem of creating a submissive labour force. The local Malays were too few and anyway not interested, and the large numbers of young Chinese imported from Southeast China and Malaya-Singapore soon proved too refractory and mobile to be long usable. The answer came with the recruitment of indentured labourers from poverty-stricken, overpopulated Java. It was a kind of modern slavery. Labourers were not only pitilessly exploited, but had to sign contracts preventing them from quitting and making sure that their 'debts' to the companies that transferred them to Sumatra could rarely be repaid – thanks largely to company stores. Thus, at least until the onset of the Great Depression, Medan was a bit like a Gold Rush town.

Non-indentured Javanese moved in too, serving as small and medium merchants, lawyers, newspapermen, teachers, foremen, accountants, nationalist activists and civil servants. 'The Field' was thus far more variegated than any other Indonesian city, including even the capital Batavia (Jakarta today): Europeans of various kinds, Chinese, Americans, Indians, Japanese, Arabs, Minangkabau, Bataks of many sorts, Acehnese, Javanese and so on. None formed a dominant majority. As a consequence, religious variegation too: Protestant British, Dutch, Americans, Germans and Toba Bataks, Catholic Dutch and Austrians, Confucian and Buddhist Chinese, Hindu and Muslim Indians, strong Muslims like the Minangkabau and Acehnese, and syncretic Hindu-Islamic Javanese. Of course, there was always a stable racial hierarchy, with Whites and 'honorary-white' Japanese at the top, Chinese, Arabs and Indians in the middle, and natives mostly at the bottom. 'The Field' also was notorious for its Wild West social mores – gambling and prostitution were widespread, and handled mainly by mainly Chinese *tokés* and an ethnically diverse assortment of thugs. (To get a nice picture of Medan at that time, one can profitably read the final, confessional chapter of Mangaradja Onggang Parlindungan's weird masterpiece, *Tuanku Rao*.) Opium was a state monopoly.

In early 1942, the Japanese military, having disposed of the British in Malaya and Singapore, took over the Dutch East Indies in a few weeks. Sumatran and Bornean oil was the military's main interest, but the plantation economy also fell into Japanese hands. However, effective Allied bombing of Japanese shipping soon made the export-oriented agribusiness economy collapse, leaving in place only domestic demand and the military's local needs. In North Sumatra, the indenture system broke down to make way for smallholder producers of foodstuffs like rice, vegetables, tea and coffee, as well as castor oil. To make this new wartime economy work the Japanese authorities opened the door to 'illegal' occupiers of agribusiness lands, including a huge wave of Protestant Toba Bataks from the interior.

After the American atom-bombing of Hiroshima and Nagasaki, the Japanese state surrendered unconditionally, but several months passed before the British and Dutch could bring colonial military power back to the Indies, and in this vacuum the Republic of Indonesia was born on 17 August 1945. In the exhilarating, chaotic first year of the Revolution (1945–46), there were a number of regions in Sumatra and Java which experienced vengeful revolutionary onslaughts on 'collaborators' with Japanese and Dutch, semi-feudal local aristocracies, abusive civil servants, and so on. The most chaotic and bloodthirsty of these occurred – unsurprisingly – in North Sumatra. The local petty sultanates were overthrown with ease; many of the Malay 'aristocrats' were murdered and their wealth stolen or confiscated. Indonesia's greatest poet, Amir Hamzah, was among the victims. Toba Bataks, Acehnese, Simalungun Bataks and Javanese seized Japanese guns, and fought each other for the spoils without being able to establish any coherent political order. The Republic's Socialist-dominated government was appalled by all this, knowing that it would blacken the country's name overseas, enrage colonial-era investors wanting their properties back, and alienate possible diplomatic allies. Gradually, with military help, some kind of order was established, after which the Dutch succeeded in reoccupying Medan's plantation belt. But not for long.

In December 1949, after four years of intermittent war and negotiations, the Netherlands signed over sovereignty of the old colony to a 'Federal Republic of Indonesia', one of whose components was North Sumatra (then still called East Sumatra), headed by surviving local aristocrats. But within a year federalism disappeared, the aristocrats succumbed, and today's Unitary Republic was established. The central condition of this transfer of sovereignty, insisted on by the rapacious Americans, was that all Dutch (and British and American) pre-war properties be returned to their colonial-era owners. The situation was particularly volatile in the surroundings of Medan. Even in the last two decades of colonial rule, 'the Field' had become a hotbed of anticolonial nationalism. This trend accelerated in the last year of Japanese rule and after the Declaration of Independence. The radical language of 'Revolution' made a deep impression too, mostly for the good. But revolution also allowed hardened criminal elements to operate under its aegis, sometimes with half-genuine revolutionary commitment.

North Sumatra was a natural zone for successful recruiting by a reborn PKI, which had been suppressed by the Dutch after the failed uprisings of 1926–27 and later by the Japanese military. In the 1950s, the single most militant organisation there was the Sarekat Buruh Perkebunan Indonesia, or Sarbupri, a huge union for plantation labourers, whose mass base lay in the once indentured Javanese labour force, combined with leadership mostly provided by educated Javanese and Protestant Batak activists. It is useful to note that the PKI Politburo, headed from 1951 on by D. N. Aidit, had real trouble with Sarbupri's militancy, since the Party, having chosen to join the parliamentary system (at the national and local levels) was worried by unauthorised local revolutionary activities which could damage its cautious political strategy. A number of Sarbupri leaders were demoted, expelled or disciplined. Sarbupri also got political support from the smallholder migrants of the Japanese occupation whom the returning white planters were eager to kick out or subdue. Strikes in Tandjung Morawa, in the plantation belt, only 14 kilometers from Medan's city centre, even brought down one of the early constitutional-era cabinets.***

Medan proved an especially difficult city to handle from Jakarta because there was no 'traditional' social order to work with, and no ethnic, party-political or religious group in a dominant position. It contained, proportionately, the highest number of 'foreign Asian' inhabitants. Situated close to Singapore, it was also notorious for its talented smugglers. In addition, the fractious local military often created additional problems.

When the Revolution of 1945 broke out, the national army was formed in a very unusual way. The core of its middle- and upper-echelon leaders had been low-level NCOs and junior officers in Japanese-created auxiliary forces trained to help the Imperial armies, if and when the Allies landed, in local guerilla warfare. Since Sumatra and Java were controlled by different Japanese armies not subordinated one to the other, the Peta in Java and the much smaller Giyugun in Sumatra had no organic connection. Almost all recruits to the new national army were in their twenties, no matter what posts they held, so that it was usual for commmanders to be chosen by their own men, rather than by any higher authorities. In the 1950s therefore, the High Command in Jakarta had great difficulties in controlling local, and locally popular, military officers, who frequently refused to carry out orders and sometimes acted like warlords. Medan was a striking case. The Protestant Toba Batak commander for the years between 1950 and 1957 was Colonel Simbolon, who controlled large-scale smuggling operations through Medan's port, and refused to be transferred. But when he joined the anti-Jakarta coalition which in February 1958 started the PRRI rebellion, he was quickly toppled by a counter-coalition of the High Command, leftist local Javanese juniors and the clique of his successor, Lieut. Colonel Djamin Gintings, a Karo Batak who claimed to speak for Karos oppressed by their distant Toba cousins. Once installed, Ginting turned on the leftist Javanese officers. Many Islamic organisations, mostly controlled by Minangkabau, who also supported the PRRI, were crippled by its defeat and the ban on the Masjumi modernist Islamic party.[4]

The other crucial development came from the mess created by President Sukarno's rash decision in December 1957 to nationalise all Dutch enterprises in retaliation for The Hague's constant refusal to settle diplomatically the conflict over Western Papua, which was supposed to have been solved early in the 1950s. Takeovers were initiated by unions affiliated with the PKI's secular rival, the PNI, but the communists quickly joined in. Not for long. The Army High Command used its emergency powers to take control of all the nationalised enterprises, claiming that they were vital assets for the nation. For the first time in its history the military obtained vast economic and financial resources, especially plantations, mines, trading companies, utilities, banks, and so forth. Needless to say, strikes were forbidden in all these sectors. Since these sectors, owned hitherto by foreigners, were those where leftist and nationalist unions had had the greatest freedom, the military had to develop an effective corporatist counterforce. In partial imitation of the PKI's SOBSI, a nationwide federation of its affiliated unions, the army created SOKSI. Its name indicated the intentions of its creators. K stood for *karyawan*, a corporatist neologism for 'functionary', a term that covered everyone – management, office staff and white-collar workers, as well as labour. One could think of SOKSI as an agglomeration of 'company' unions. Thus the B in SOBSI, standing for *buruh* (labour), was to be eliminated.

In the Medan area, and in the face of SOBSI's well-established presence, the military needed substantial manpower outside its own active ranks to impose its will on the huge plantation belt. It so happened that an instrument was at hand. In 1952, the Army Chief of Staff, the Mandailing Batak A. H. Nasution, was suspended for his role in a failed mini-coup in Jakarta. Still young and ambitious, he decided to form an electoral organisation of his own, which he called IPKI, Ikatan Pendukung Kemerdekaan Indonesia, or League of Supporters of Indonesian Independence, described as a movement opposed to the existing major parties, especially the PKI.[5]

In the 1955 elections, it won only four seats, but it was evident that the strongest of its bases lay in Medan. In that year, Nasution was reinstated as Army Chief of Staff by Prime Minister Burhanuddin Harahap, scion of a clan of Southern Bataks (Angkola) well-comnnected to the Nasution clan – but he kept control of IPKI. After the crushing of the PRRI, but with Martial Law in solid place, IPKI developed a 'youth wing', parallel to those of the major legal parties, which came to be called Pemuda Pantjasila (PP), nominally composed of retired soldiers and civilian veterans of the Revolution. The key figure in this Pemuda Pantjasila was another Mandailing Batak, a serious Medan gangster and ex-boxer called Effendy Nasution. These gangsters had had their own clashes with the PKI youth organisation, Pemuda Rakjat, over 'turf' as well as ideology, and were ferociously anti-Communist. But as members of a 'national organisation', sponsored by the top Army officer, they had excellent protection, also for their protection rackets. In the years between 1959 and 1965 the military and the Medan gangsters collaborated more and more closely with each other. The PP significantly helped SOKSI to control the plantation belt against formidable SOBSI/Sarbupri resistance. Thus when Suharto decided to inaugurate the massacre of communists, the Medan underworld, dressed up as Pemuda Pantjasila, was ready to 'help' and accustomed to carry out 'confidential' Army directives.

The contrast with the East Java plantation belt is striking. We have seen how in this zone the army could rely on the Nahdlatul Ulama's huge, and legal, mass-organisations, as well as the authority of the mainly Javanese territorial civilian bureaucracy, manned heavily by conservative elements in the PNI. In Medan, the NU presence was minimal, the PNI was factionalised, while the once-powerful modernist Muslim party Masjumi had been banned in 1959. No united civil bureaucracy existed in such an ethnically complex melting pot. This is why, when the massacres drew to an end, NU and Ansor members in Java generally returned to 'normal' religious life (and soon came into conflict with the military), while Medan's gangsters returned to another 'normal life', of extortion, blackmail, 'protection', gambling dens, brothels and so on, while staying close to the military. But with new patrons, as time passed. General Nasution, now retired, gradually faded away. Eventually, in 1980, the PP's leadership went to Yapto Soerjosoemarno, the Eurasian son of a Surakartan aristocrat and general, and a Jewish-Dutch mother.

Yapto, ice-cold mercenary killer and big-game hunter, had long been close to the Medan gangsters, but was also a relative of Mrs. Suharto. Officially, PP was an independent organisation, but it always supported Suharto and his policies, and helped to enforce the steady series of electoral victories by Golkar, the regime's nonparty party-of-the-regime. It remained loyal to its patron right up to his abdication. (Since then, it has found no steady patron, and its power and unity have visibly declined.) Meanwhile, the NU, a national party, tried its best to compete with Golkar in elections, and for a time was the most significant component of the largely impotent legal opposition.

PETRUS

It is instructive to note what happened when Suharto decided, in 1983, to liquidate substantial numbers of petty gangsters. (In the press the killers were initially termed *penembak-penembak misterieus* i.e. mysterious shooters, quickly and sardonically given the acronym Petrus, i.e. Saint Peter, since the operational mastermind was Catholic, Eurasian Lieutenant-General Benny Murdani.) In Java several thousand people were brutally murdered, in the dead of night, by Army commandos in mufti. In Medan their opposite numbers went untouched. The reason for the difference is clear. In 1980, Central Java was unexpectedly rocked by a coordinated wave of violence against local Chinese, in which petty gangsters played a visible role. Many of these people had worked as electoral enforcers for Suharto's *éminence grise*, Major-General Ali Murtopo, who also headed Suharto's private political intelligence apparatus, Opsus. For an always-suspicious tyrant, it looked as if his once-trusted accomplice might be flexing his own political muscles, to show what his shady apparatus might do before and during the next elections. The unexpected and unauthorised anti-Chinese violence hit Suharto's nerves in another way. Twentieth-century Java had a long history of popular Sinophobic movements, which could spread alarmingly fast if the circumstances were suitable. Furthermore, the successes of Suharto's New Order 'development' economy depended heavily on the energies of the country's Chinese, whose safety and prosperity were excellent signs of stability in the eyes of foreign investors. Thus the liquidation of Murtopo's gangster network can be understood both as reassurance to the Chinese, and as depriving Murtopo himself of any independent political power. Not long afterward, he was exiled as Ambassador in Kuala Lumpur where he succumbed to a heart attack. Nothing like this happened in distant Medan, since the gangsters were reliable allies of the local military, not dangerous minions of a key figure in Suharto's own Jakarta entourage. If, as periodically happened, they were behind anti-Chinese violence, the main motive was not Sinophobia but a raising of the level of protection payments. It is instructive, one may note in passing, that in his bizarre semi-ghosted memoir, *Otobiografi: Pikiran, Ucapan dan Tindakan Saya* ('Autobiography: My Thoughts, Statements and Actions') Suharto boastfully took responsibility for these extrajudicial killings, in the following dishonest manner:

> The press has been busy writing about the mysterious deaths of a number of people, referring to the shooting of thugs as 'mysterious shootings' or 'mysterious marksmen', or in short form 'Petrus,' etc. A number of politicians and a group of intellectuals have spoken or written about all this. The public too has been busy discussing it. [...] There is nothing mysterious about what happened. The reality is that before these events, the People were already terrified. They experienced threats from evildoers, robbers, murderers, and so on. [...] The actions of these criminals overstepped the bounds of human decency. For example, an elderly person was not only robbed of some of his property, but was also killed. Isn't that beyond the bounds of human decency? If you want to rob someone, well go ahead, but don't kill your victim. Then there was the case of a woman who was robbed of her belongings, and was then raped by these thugs, right in front of her husband. That's too much! Could one simply ignore what was happening? Obviously we [all of us, *kita*] had to

provide a *treatment*, and take decisive action. But what kind of decisive action? Well, it had to be violent. But this violence did not mean just shooting, dor! Dor! [an Indonesian onomatopoeia for gunshots] Not at all! But where the thugs resisted, well, willy-nilly they had to be shot. They were killed because they resisted.

Their bodies then were left where they died. This was to be *shock therapy*, a real shock. In this way the public would realise that there were still forces that could take action against, and suppress, criminal activity. [Emphasis in original]

But the dictator never boasted about his masterminding the massacres of 1965.

With this comparative background in mind, it becomes easier to understand the peculiar impunity flaunted by Oppenheimer's collaborators in his films *Snake River* and *The Act of Killing* (2012). They had been professional criminals all their adult lives, and if some of the leaders had political ambitions these were essentially local or provincial, aiming little higher than the governorship of North Sumatra, and far removed from Jakarta. In power, they pursued traditional gangsters' interests, money, respect (fear), immunity from the law, and some political positions. They were not associated with any nationally important political or religious organisations beyond Suharto's own Golkar, which they served obediently. They had worked with the military from well before the massacres, and carried out the killings of communists with savage efficiency. They did not organise substantial Sinophobic murders after 1966, nor did they put the squeeze on local foreign investors. One could say that, in an odd way, they even regarded themselves as a sort of half-hidden left hand of the New Order Leviathan: uncivil servants.[6] Best of all, when Suharto turned on gangsters in Java, the Medan 'boys' were left untouched. Not surprisingly, there was no question of Abdurrahman Wahid's plea for forgiveness.

Nonetheless, we can surmise that they had their disappointments. One of these must have been lack of national-level recognition for their role in the massacres, the one moment in their otherwise humdrum criminal lives where they could imagine themselves as among the saviors of their country. The problem lay with 'Jakarta', where Suharto and his henchmen handled the annual commemoration of 1965 by concentrating mainly on 1 October's first victims. Every town had streets named after these generals, and in Jakarta a special museum was created in their heroic honour. A state-sponsored film – for which annual viewings were compulsory in all schools and colleges – consisted entirely of mourning for the generals, and execration of the diabolical PKI. But in Medan, no general, or indeed any military officer, had been killed.

Furthermore, the basic official account of the last three months of 1965 depended on a rhetoric of popular fury at PKI bestiality. American journalists at the time liked to explain, in colonial-speak, that the primitive population had run *amok*. The military's propagandists employed this idea, describing the Army's role as curbing and calming down this wave of 'spontaneous' popular violence. (In fact, there is overwhelming evidence that the masssacres in Central Java started with the arrival of the red-beret commandos in mid-October, and in East Java one month later when these professional killers moved east.)

Thus, there were no heroic slaughterers honoured by the Suharto regime. The most notorious red-beret officers never made it up to the top levels of the military. Finally, the euphemistic official language of the regime precluded heroism. Thus communists arrested by the military, then executed or imprisoned for years without trial, were said to have been *di-amankan*, which can be translated as 'secured', for the sake of *keamanan* or 'public security'. In later years, when generals got the itch to write their memoirs, they used the same euphemisms. They had 'secured' communists, not least to protect them from 'the anger of the people'. The regime never boasted about the massacres and never announced any figures of the number who had died. This entire propaganda strategy, also aimed at foreign audiences, left no national place for the 'heroic killers' in Medan's imagery. But hadn't the gangsters helped to save the country? So, they set up their own monument to themselves, a 30-feet-high chrome '66' next to the city's railway station.

Furthermore, had these old-timers been adequately rewarded in practical terms? If one looks at the two killers featured in *Snake River*, one can see that they are actually nobodies. Elderly men, with decaying muscles and petty bourgeois clothes and homes, few visible signs of prestige, no medals, only local fear. To be sure, the top gangsters have acquired splashy mansions, luxurious cars, expensive kitschy jewelry and wristwatches, and some important but local official posts. But these emoluments were not, primarily, immediate rewards for yesterday's 'heroism', nor were they much then publicised, but rather evolved incrementally over mundane decades of dictatorship and criminality. They are not 'in national history', in a country where national history is very important, and national heroes abundant.

This condition helps to explain some of the peculiarities of the figures we can see in Oppenheimer's films. His camera offers them the possibility of commemoration, and transcendence of age, routine and death. When the more ghastly of the two killers in *Snake River* is shown in his petty bourgeois home with his wife and family, he is re-narrating some of the most terrible tortures and murders that he inflicted. The family is used to this endless domestic reenactment. His plump wife giggles to keep him happy, and the children pay no attention at all. (Compare this with the indifference of Edward G. Robinson's friend to the creepy reenactment on the levee). He boasts of his magical powers, saying that the widows of communists come to him for healing. True? Maybe, but their arrival at his house is merely a sign that forty years later they are still afraid of him. His invisible medal is this abiding terror. A kind of dim hierarchy is still visible, when the two veterans have to decide who will play communist and who killer.

They have a commemorative idea about film, actually Hollywood films which they loved from their teens. The Lone Ranger, Batman, Patton, Shane, Samson, MacArthur and Rambo – all real or imaginary men – are figures of immortality for killers who are heroic patriots, not grand gangsters. This 'cosmopolitan' idolising does not mean that the Medan 'boys' do not live within local cultures – supernaturalism, Gothic horror comics, kitschy melodrama. Oppenheimer thus comes to them as a kind of providential 'Hollywood' ally. They will die soon, but maybe he will make them immortal.

Yet they are stuck. They do not have available to them anything that can represent the communists. While Suharto was still dictator, his regime could issue must-watch films showing the bestiality of the PKI, and mourning the murdered generals. But such films have gone out of circulation since his fall fifteen years go. The 'Medan boys' have nothing like this, and the local history of events over 45 years ago is gradually headed for oblivion or myth. Thus some of the 'boys' have to act the communists themselves, sometimes even in drag. As nationalist gangsters, however, they have no place in a national history into which the Indonesian Army as a corporate institution with an 'honorable' patriotic record can be inserted. Their gangsterism is filmable only in terms of costume, body language and kitschy imaginative success. (This attitude resembles the outlook of American Cosa Nostra people, who, journalists report, love going to gangster movies and identify with the FBI!)

At the same time, these old men realise that they are also within a market of industrial fantasies, access to which comes through the American, who is young enough to be their son. This is a market, which, over the years, has increasingly blurred the boundaries between the established genres of heroic war films, gangster films and horror films, at the expense of the former and to the advantage of the latter. (This condition makes it imaginable to have *Apocalypse Now* replace *Bataan*.) But it also allows for fantasies not available in 1965. We can take Anwar Congo (the main character in *The Act of Killing*) as exemplary. He proudly shows himself as a sadistic murderer, yet he is haunted, or so he plays it, by the ghosts of his victims; but then he congratulates himself on helping to send his prey straight to Heaven, as if in a 'black mass' retroversion of jihad theology. He displays his authority by making his favourite, large, overweight henchman Herman dress up as a communist woman. 'She' appears with the depressing glitzy outfit of a well-off, middle-aged transvestite in a TV competition. A real communist woman, a gaunt, shrivelled, terrified widow in her seventies would never do. Actually there are no limits (let's see what we can do!) except that only he and his boys can appear in the film. There is a kind of despair at work.

This despair is actuated by Oppenheimer. The gangsters re-enact whatever they wish and can imagine, but they cannot control what 'their' film will be like in the end. Oppenheimer is a conundrum. He is there, like Rouch, beyond the camera's reach, an unseen interrogator, pal, witness, kid, judge, motherfucker. They have no idea how to control him, because they are his actors and there is no final script that they master. He is not part of their film but they are part of his. There are no famous Hollywood films with invisible interrogating Joshua Oppenheimer's in them. This is a source of anxiety. (Oppenheimer has written to me that while many of these people trust him almost completely, others are becoming suspicious that he may be betraying them.)

The inevitable response is a strange mixture of motivations. Excess first: 'Beat this, motherfucker! I sent them all to Heaven and they should grateful to me.' Second, recourse to the filmic super-natural: 'That bastard Ramli was so magically invulnerable that it us took ages to kill him, and we had to cut off his dick first!' Third, pride: Today, so many years after 1965, 'They are still terrified of us.' Fourth is hope: 'We'll be famous around the world, even after we die, no matter if young Indonesians don't want to think about us, and the government will never give us the monuments we deserve.'****

Fifth: Truthfulness: 'There was no *amok*, and we loyally carried out the instructions of the national army.' Last: the smugness of impunity. 'Kid, we can re-enact anything at all, and there is nothing anyone, including you, can do to us.' All the same, they are, like every one else, under sentence of death from the day they were born. They know they will soon be buried, and nobody will give a damn. There is no one who can send them straight to Heaven.

NOTES

1   In the late 1950s, the US government was giving official military aid to the Indonesian armed forces in order to encourage the military to become increasingly hostile to the PKI. Because the PKI was sympathetic to the People's Republic of China, the USSR was also supporting the Indonesian military, to encourage the army to become increasingly hostile to the Chinese. At the same time, the US government's assessment was that the risk of Indonesia becoming communist (through the electoral process) was high enough that the US should also arm, fund and fly bombing sorties for anti-communist rebellions on the outer islands (which is where Indonesia's valuable natural resources lay, and where most foreign-owned plantation, mining and oil companies had their operations). Thus did the ironic situation

emerge where the CIA was participating in a civil war against an army receiving significant US aid (training, weapons and money). It cannot be said, however, that US strategy was incoherent, contradictory, or even that the US was supporting two genuinely opposing sides (both sides were anti-PKI, after all). The outer island rebellions created a pretext by which the army could force Sukarno to declare martial law, and thereby stop the electoral process through which the Communist Party would have come to parliamentary power. So in fact the US's two seemingly contradictory anti-communist strategies complemented each other rather nicely: it helped put an end to Indonesian democracy, it thereby blocked the PKI's path to power, and it ensured the army was pro-US when there finally was a chance to move against the communists.

2   See B. Anderson (1987) 'How Did the Generals Die?', *Indonesia*, 43 (April), 109–134, which includes the original documents in Indonesian and their English translations.

3   The most relevant English-language sources on North Sumatra in the late colonial and post-independence periods are: A. Stoler (1985) *Capitalism and Confrontation in Sumatra's Plantation Belt*. Princeton: Princeton University Press; A. Reid (1979) *Blood of the People: Revolution and the End of Traditional Rule in Northern Sumatra*. Kuala Lumpur: Oxford University Press; M. van Langenberg (1976) 'National Revolution in North Sumatra, Sumatra Timur, and Tapanuli, 1942–1950', Ph.D. dissertation, University of Sydney; M. Steedly (1995) *Hanging Without a Rope: Narrative Experience in Colonial and Postcolonial Karoland*. Princeton: Princeton University Press; and L. Ryter (2002) 'Youth, Gangs and the State of Indonesia', Ph.D. dissertation, University of Washington.

4   A masterly analysis of North Sumatra's military chaos can be found in J. R. W. Smail (1968) 'The Military Politics of North Sumatra, December 1956–October 1957', *Indonesia*, 6 (October), 128–87.

5   See D. Lev (1966) *The Transition to Guided Democracy: Indonesian Politics, 1957–59*. Ithaca: Cornell Modern Indonesia Project, which covers Nasution and IPKI's foundation in the larger context of the disintegration of parliamentary, constitutional democracy in Indonesia; see also Ryter 2002 for the later development of IPKI.

6   In the mid-1980s, I was contacted by a lady lawyer in Germany, asking me to provide professional testimony for a youngish Indonesian pleading for sanctuary. In written correspondence, the man said he had fled to Germany on the advice and with the help of his father, a middle-ranking officer in the Army's military police. He had been a member of a gang, mostly of sons of military officers, which made its living by 'guarding' bars, discos, nightclubs. The gang strongly supported the Suharto government and helped to make every election a 'success'. Then, out of the blue, came Petrus and he had to run for his life. I told him that since it was well known that Petrus was aimed solely at gangsters, the only way to get the German court to believe that they should grant him sanctuary was to admit that he was a gangster. The curious thing is that he could not bring himself to do so, insisting that he had always been loyal to the regime, and where required carried out its policies. This is a perfect example of left-hand bureaucratic consciousness.

* **Comment from Joshua Oppenheimer:** Here I think my experience in Sumatra has taught me something different. All of the killers I have met *knew* that it was *not* 'a kill or be killed' situation, but could make themselves *believe* otherwise, both at the time and in the decades

afterwards. This contradiction between what people believe and what people know is one of the things I have come to understand makes killing possible. The perpetrators I've worked with will go through extraordinary intellectual contortions to justify and celebrate what they did, no matter what they *knew* to be facts. For example, Amir Hasan (who appears in *Snake River*) killed his teachers' college friend, Subandi, the religious instructor from the mosque and the man who sang the call to prayer. He knew Subandi to be the most religious man in the village, but he was also in the PKI. Hasan rarely bothered with the mosque, but when he did he would without fail meet Subandi there. Still, Hasan could kill Subandi because Subandi was 'anti-god'. I do not think Hasan believed, at the time anyway, that Subandi's religiosity was just a guise. He knew Subandi was religious, but he was whipped up, and whipped himself up, into *believing* the contrary. People are ready to disregard knowledge – especially when it serves their interest, when they stand to gain money, power, their victim's land or wife or livestock. They can believe things they know are false, and with just as much conviction or passion as they might feel toward beliefs that they know are true.

** **Comment from JO:** I'm not convinced that this boasting is unique to Medan. In 1998, the flamboyant Brigadier General Herman Sarens Soediro said 'Like in the old days, when only seven communists kidnapped [army generals] and wanted to change Pancasila, I ran over a hundred men with a tank. I was protected by the imperative to ensure the survival of the state's sovereignty and protection of the population. Why should I be scared? I don't care.' (AKSI, 2, 100, 13–19 October 1998; translated by J. Oppenheimer).

*** **Comment from JO:** One might also mention some of Sarbupri's successes. During the hyperinflation of the early 1960s, Sarbupri was famous for securing its workers payment in the basic essentials ('*tjatuh*' in Sumatran plantation lingo). These included high quality rice, salted fish, milk powder, sugar, salt, eggs, oil, kerosene, clothing, etc. They also brought cultural activities even to remote plantations, including film screenings and theatre performances. These achievements are summed up with derision in the 1967 NBC special report, *Indonesia: The Troubled Victory*: 'Indonesia has a fabulous potential wealth in natural resources, and the New Order wants it exploited.' Cut to a Goodyear plantation near Tebing Tinggi, North Sumatra. 'The communists still work the rubber, but now they are prisoners, and they work at gunpoint. The New Order wants Goodyear to come back. And Goodyear and other capitalists are anxious to return, but not all their findings are happy. When the communists ran the plantations, they built schools, raised salaries, but productivity didn't rise, and profits went out the window.' The communists never ran the plantations, and NBC doesn't acknowledge the possibility that the primary purpose of a public sector company might be something other than making profits for the owners, and instead to provide jobs and lift people out of poverty.

**** **Comment from JO:** So they build their own monuments, like the '66' monument by the train station in Medan, and the obelisk in the village of Kampung Kolam, celebrating the massacre of the villagers, and inventing their own savagely tortured and killed Pemuda Pancasila members to parallel the national fantasy of generals mutilated by sex-crazed communists in Jakarta.

SHOW OF FORCE: A CINEMA-SÉANCE OF POWER AND VIOLENCE IN SUMATRA'S PLANTATION BELT

Joshua Oppenheimer & Michael Uwemedimo

The evening breeze was gentle. The crescent moon crept behind the clouds like a thief terrified of being caught. The air grew colder, unaware of our burning spirits. Our sweat ran hot, our faces flush. We had asked Dormin to drive us to the execution site. [...] The car sped to Sialangbuah to pick up our quota. Who knows why, but we feared nothing. Dormin was a real James Bond, racing down the potholed road. Perhaps he was daydreaming, imagining Japanese beheading allied soldiers like in some old WWII movie, and not looking at the road in front of him. We walked the last hundred yards, making our way through undergrowth and oil palm. Under the gleam of flashlights, we arrived at an old well. One by one, Karlub, Uyung and Simin beheaded the five goats.

– *Embun Berdarah* ('Dew of Blood'), Amir Hasan Nasution[1]

HISTORY: SCENE AND OBSCENE

On the night of 30 September 1965, six of Indonesia's top army generals were abducted and murdered in an abortive coup attempt. Who was ultimately behind this operation, and their final objectives, remains unclear.[2] In a response that appears to have been remarkably well rehearsed, General Suharto seized control of the armed forces and instigated a series of nationwide purges to consolidate his power. Suharto engineered and set in motion a killing machine whose chain of command reached into every region and every village, murdering alleged communists, trade unionists, organised peasants, members of the women's movement and anybody else the army considered a threat.[3]

The campaign was deliberately organised so as to implicate the 'masses' (or *massa*, the term used by Indonesian officials when reference to the massacres is unavoidable): much of the killing, although under the supervision of the army, was actually carried out by paramilitary branches of political groups opposed to the Communist Party of Indonesia (Partai Komunis Indonesia, or PKI) and affiliated groups. As the pro-Suharto American diplomat Paul F. Gardner observes, Surharto 'did not wish to involve the army directly ... he preferred instead [quoting Surharto], "to assist the people to protect themselves and to cleanse their individual areas of this evil seed [the PKI]."'[4] This 'cleansing' cleared the political stage for the creation of the 'New Order' military dictatorship.

The massacres that swept the archipelago in the months after October 1965 were one of the most systematic genocides of the twentieth century. To the extent that the genocidaires remain largely in power, its national (and to a significant degree, international) account has been given by its victors.

The rendering of this account, however, has not been a project of straightforward revisionist erasure. While there have been no memorials for genocide victims, and no trials for their killers, the official histories of the New Order do not simply deny its constitutive violence: ever since the killings, the Indonesian government has worn the face of that violence, as administrators and agents of genocide were promoted through the ranks of military and government.[5] The violence of the massacres continued, and those who instigated it still seek to conjure its force in ways that we will analyse here.

Yet the official history (and this is no surprise) refuses to recollect the systematic nature of the terror within a judicial, ethical or forensic frame. The deliberate nature of the massacres is *obscene* to an official history, which casts the extermination programme as the spontaneous uprising of a people united in a heroic struggle against the 'evil seed' of atheist communism.[6] Wherever this historical scenario is rehearsed – in the official history books or statue books; in classrooms or national parades; in propaganda films or the rallies of paramilitary groups; in the management and labour structures of the plantations or, until recently, the stipulations determining the status of identity cards – its obscenity operates, insinuating terror, haunting the available spaces of social interaction.

The apparatus, activities and artefacts of movie-making provide the means and methods of research for the project upon which this chapter reflects. As cinema has been both a means of research and an object of it, a rehearsal of the New Order history that bears particular mention here is the four-hour propaganda film *The Treachery of the September 30th Movement of the Indonesian Communist Party* [*Pengkhianatan G 30 S/PKI*] (dir. Noer, 1984). The film was mandatory viewing every year for twenty-four years on Indonesian television and in all cinemas until Suharto resigned in 1998. Schools would visit the cinema, and families were compelled to watch the film on TV. These thousands of screenings surely constitute the most potent performance of the official history of 1965–66. As such, *G30S* is marked by (or marks) the generic imperatives, stylistic tendencies and performative routines and effects of the New Order history. It is precisely these imperatives, tendencies and effects that this chapter focuses on.[7]

The film restages the night of 30 September 1965 as a curious blend of documentary exposé, political thriller and slasher movie. It opens and closes as sensational reportage (black-and-white archival footage and photographs; shots of documents and newspaper clippings; a mastering narration over dramatic music) while the requirements of a thriller narrative are fulfilled through a plot performed by shadowy enemies of state, here played by treasonous PKI villains. The slasher aesthetic renders the graphic murder of the six generals at the hands of a communist mob, their genitals mutilated in a sadomasochistic orgy perpetrated by members of the PKI-affiliated Gerwani (Women's Movement), burnt with cigarettes, slashed with razor blades, stabbed with bayonets, beaten with rifle butts, all to the accompaniment of wild chanting and drums.

The exposé and the slasher are both forms predicated on an explicit and excessive visibility. In the exposé this takes the form of an insistence on the self-evidence of its images ('it is plain to see how things really were and this is plainly how things were'). The excess of the slasher, insists that we see everything, revelling in the generic gore of a projected PKI sadism. This grotesque excess operates in interesting ways. It is not merely designed to elicit a common outrage for the PKI, but to create a scene of sacrificial and ritual participation. And, as spectacle, the violence fascinates. Thus are spectators bound and incorporated by an enthrallment with their projected enemy. In as much as the PKI violence is clearly displaced (and projected) state violence, should one identify sympathetically with the massacres' victims, that violence would immediately become a threat.

These genres serve the New Order 'historiography' well, staging the PKI as both self-evidently and explicitly sadistic, while, as the political thriller's necessarily shadowy villains, also threateningly spectral (and spectral not least because, by the time of the film's production, the PKI had been exterminated). For all its excessively visible violence, the film *withholds* from view the true force of the violence which it performs – that of the massacres.

The film is so potent because it serves to justify a massacre that remains obscene, or inadmissible, within the framework of the narrative. The film *generically* rehearses the killing of six generals, a general's daughter, and the same general's adjutant. The rehearsal is generic not only because of its respect for cinematic codes and conventions, but also its faithfulness to a twenty-year-old official history that those codes serve. That is to say this scene, the murder of the generals, is received as *the* legitimating metonym for the massacres that followed.

The subsequent murder of at least half a million people goes unmentioned, and yet it is this unspoken terror that provides the film with a certain mystique, a *frisson* and fascination.[8] For the massacres hardly fail to haunt *G30S*, because the film exists almost wholly to justify the massacres and the regime founded upon them. The film's generic rehearsals derive their conventionality precisely from their social and political context – a context constituted by genocide; the film is able to perform the genocide without directly citing it, then, because the genocide is the violence that continues to constitute the film's iterative condition. Thus the film conjures a violence as *spectre* – the extermination of the entire PKI (a group itself rendered spectral) – by not mentioning it explicitly. It is in this way that *G30S* is a *performative* instrument of terror – it does violence. *G30S* was, perhaps more than any other piece of propaganda, the basis for the second half of Suharto's rule.

The film graphically demonstrates the way in which New Order history at once conjures the PKI as a spectral power and condenses that power in spectacular images of violence, so as to claim that power for the shadowy techniques of state terror. The spectral subsists in the spectacle. Obscene to the staging of national history, the systematic nature of the violence nevertheless *sets the scene*, lurking in the wings and constantly threatening a spectacular (re)appearance. It is a haunting presence that might flare up again in a show of force through which the nation has been compelled to imagine and perform itself.

Researchers of New Order histories will find a generic coherence to its scripts and performances (such as one finds in *G30S* – no transgressive formal experiments there), but clearly the aim of these 'historiographic' conventions is not historical coherence as such since they are not concerned with adequacy to actual events. New Order historiography is not a history in the realist register. It is not recounted in order to refer; rather, it is rehearsed in order to *exercise a power*. It is a history in the performative register: history as a histrionics of terror.

Michael Taussig, writing of the economy of violence in the Amazonian rubber boom of the late nineteenth century, describes '*the mediation of terror through narration*, and the problem that raises for effective counter-representations'.[9] This chapter and the film project it reflects upon attempt to make headway in analysing this problematic even as it re-casts its epistemology.

Eschewing an epistemology of representation, we avoid considering historical narration as mediation of a past that can be made coherently and fully present; instead we consider historical narrative as a performance whose staging produces effects. It is these historical and contemporary effects that are our primary concern here. We analyse how the elaborations and ellipses of the ceaselessly rehearsed histories of the period conjure terror and interact with the conjurations of previous acts – whether acts of historical account (speech acts) or historical acts (the events that constitute the past).[10] It is less a matter of producing effective counter-*representations* than intervening with counter-*performances*, that is, interventions capable of countering the spectral powers of history as terror.

This chapter sketches out some critical moments from the early stages of a film project that intervenes into Indonesia's history of terror to re-stage its performance for the camera, to re-frame it in a way different from its repeated rehearsals in schools, on national television, on days of official memorial.[11] The aim is, in the first instance, to perform it in such a way that the operations of its obscenity can be grasped, so that the spectres it produces can enter the scene in a way that allows them to be addressed, acknowledged and contended. Whereas *G30S* exists to justify a massacre it does not name and thereby conjures as spectral, this project seeks to stage a series of 'perverse' performances of official history that will name it and give it substance. It thus sets out to frame performances that contravene the generic imperatives of official history while nevertheless acting in its name and acting out its routines.

Here we focus on the performances of perpetrators. By giving perpetrators free reign to declaim their pasts for our camera, in invariably generic terms (in 'testimonial' interviews, re-enactments and even musicals), we have sought to deconstruct the ways in which generic and political imperatives always already shaped not only the victor's history (including such scenes as we filmed), but also the violence of the genocide itself. By making these codes, conventions and scripts manifest, by marking the ways in which the historical accounts and enactments of the New Order are elements of a performative apparatus of terror, the project attempts to make these insights – as well as previously repressed historical detail – available to a political and historical imagination that can draw the process of national- and self-imagining from under the shadow and sway of catastrophe.

What follows is a critical reflection on an early moment of the project: the filmed encounter between two aging genocidaires at an execution site by a river in North Sumatra. From the many hundreds of hours of footage that followed the filmed encounter, this project is now resolving itself into three film works. Here we focus on just a few of those hours.

SNAKE RIVER: A ROUTINE ENCOUNTER

At the National Security Archive in Washington D.C. there is an anonymous and untitled folio of notes recording some of what little is publicly known of the

1965–66 Indonesian genocide. A Sumatran massacre of 10,500 people is record-ed in a typical entry as follows:

CARD NO: 20 143
DATE: NO DATE
INDIVIDUAL: N. Sumatra
ITEM: From North Sumatra came a report of the slaying of 10,500 prisoners, who had been arrested for PKI activities. Their bodies were thrown into the Sungai Ular.

The Sungai Ular, or Snake River, is distinguished only by its size and relatively swift flow. It was for this reason that it was chosen as an execution site – unlike slower smaller rivers, the Snake River could be relied upon to carry the dead out to sea. Before the river meets the sea, it passes under the trans-Sumatran highway at Perbaungan, about thirty miles southeast of Medan, North Sumatra's capital city. Within sight of a bridge where the highway spans the river is one of the clearings in the plantation belt where the Snake River was loaded with its nightly freight of bodies.

Fig. 1 On 22 January 1966, Amir Hasan's first five victims were dumped in a disused well at Batang Kepayang, Teluk Mengkudu, North Sumatra. This illustration introduces a chapter in *Embun Berdarah* (1997) in which their ghosts narrate the massacres that follow.

It is here, 38 years later, that we brought Amir Hasan Nasution and Inong Syah. Amir was com-mander of the Komando Aksi death squads for the Teluk Mengkudu district, where he killed, by his own account, 32 people at this clearing on Snake River. During the 1960s he was an art teacher and a primary school governor. After the killings, he was asked by the plantation management to found the management-and-military-dominated union that replaced the progressive union that he exterminated. He was later promoted to school inspector, and then regional head of the govern-ment's Department of Education and Culture. Af-ter retiring, he was appointed head of his district's KPU (Komisi Pemilihan Umum, or Public Elec-tion Commission). His duties were to ensure that general elections are 'fair and clean' – an ironic reward for a man who was earlier responsible for exterminating the largest political party in the same district.

Now the elections are passed and he has time on his hands. An avid writer and painter, he has already produced a lavishly illustrated book about his life; it is titled *Embun Berdarah* ('Dew of Blood').

Inong Syah was a carpenter for the British rubber plantation, Harrison-Crossfield (now London-Sumatra). He was the youngest member in a death squad of nine. At the Sungai Ular, his role was to bring victims to the river and drag them to be killed.

Although they participated in the massacres during the same period, and were surely on occasion at the river on the same nights, Amir and Inong were in different death squads and did not meet until, decades later, they enthusiastically agreed to give an account for the camera of their role in the killings.

The two former death squad members stand on the roadside where a dirt path leads towards the river, down a steep bank, through the trees to a clearing by the water. They take this path, addressing the camera directly as they go. Each takes it in turns to play victim and executioner. Despite their age they go at it with gusto, assuming all the necessary positions for their demonstration: squatting with hands bound behind back; lying with legs raised while dragged by the ankles; pulling, pushing forcefully with feet in a wide stance to take the strain; bowed forward, nape of the neck exposed for decapitation.

From the unloading of bound and blindfolded prisoners to a demonstration of decapitation at the site of dispatch, they go through the motions of what was their nightly routine.

The fact that the performance does indeed make the process *seem routine* has two somewhat contradictory effects. On the one hand, it allows us to understand the killings as *routine*, as *mass* killings, as systematic and thus scripted, rehearsed and generic. On the other hand, this scripted quality leads one to doubt the footage's evidentiary value for any *particular* killing. In this respect Amir and Inong's performance is wholly typical of the perpetrators' accounts this project has gathered.[12] Even the performances that seem most graphic appear not to be rendered as singular explications of specific events, but rather (as we shall explore in some detail below), as rehearsals of *genres* whose register is the graphic.

A PROPER PERFORMANCE: THE TV PRESENTER'S LIVE SPECTACULAR

As Amir drags imaginary naked victims along the ground, beats them senseless *en route* to execution, perhaps the most unnerving thing is his relentless smile. It is a smile appropriate to the type of performance for which the camera seems to offer Amir an opportunity: that of the TV presenter.

Not only does Amir never stop grinning, he provides a seamless, present-tense narration of everything they are doing. As he shows the camera how they would drag victims on the final stage to the river, lines such as this are typical of his continuous commentary: 'So now I am demonstrating how we drag him to the riverbank.' The lines seem appropriate to an on-location reporter providing a blow-by-blow account of a shoot out between police and some bank robbers caught in the act (*Cops*-style reality crime shows are a regular feature of Indonesian national TV programming), or perhaps even a sports caster providing play-by-play narration for a football match in which the national team is trouncing the traditional opponents.

Amir holds forth as if from a *live* event. His re-enactment of course *is* live, though as re-enactment it seems to gesture to the past. In as much as this past threatens to return, the re-enactment is a *preview*. Thus his presentation is strangely tensed, he seems neither to be referring to a particular past, nor to an actual present (we shall return to the future in a moment): not so much, 'this is what we did' nor 'this is what we are doing', as '*this is what is done*'.

In the observance of 'what is done' there is a peculiar formality to Amir's presentation. Like anybody boasting on camera, Amir is camera-conscious, and in this decorous self-consciousness, his performance becomes more intensely, explicitly theatrical. And so, focused through the camera's lens, two senses of performativity converge: there is the performative in J. L. Austin's sense on the one hand (and just what, in the performative sense, this act *does* we shall consider in a moment), and performative as in 'theatrical', on the other.[13]

Perhaps these two senses of performativity, despite Austin's proscription of the theatrical, are already implicated in a 'general iterability'.[14] As we shall see, this general iterability conditioned the staging of the massacres themselves, and therefore it conditions Amir and Inong's performance both 'then' and 'now'. This is not to claim that there were no originary acts that constituted the genocide. If only this were so. Rather it is to recognise that these fatal acts reveal the threat of repetition as a constitutive element of the performance of terror: not merely, 'this is what is done', but 'this is what *will* be done'.

It is this theatricality, conditioned by a general iterability, that makes visible the imprint of the generic – the performance of a script that appears to be well-rehearsed. Amir becomes a smiling presenter, and whenever he finishes a certain explanation, he pauses, refreshes his already gleaming smile, and gives the camera alternatively an enthusiastic thumbs-up or a 'V' for victory.

In his Playboy shades, pausing at the end of his demonstration to pose for a snapshot at the murder site, his is the same pose struck by those leering American soldiers in Abu Ghraib.

The perverse *tableaux vivants* staged by Amir and Inong during their demonstration are re-enactments in an obvious sense, but just as those of Abu Ghraib, they are also rehearsals of 'standard operating procedures'[15] (and certainly in the case of the latter, these procedures were codified in legal directives and described in detailed official interrogation manuals, all now in the public domain).[16] That is to say, the gestures of murder and torture are and were already re-enactments, just as these smiling snapshot clichés are pulled from a repertory of stock poses and therefore already and always repetitions. What Rebecca Schneider notes of the Abu Ghraib photographs also holds for the pose Amir assumes for his souvenir photo: there is a 'citational logic' in the staged triumphalism of these gestures – these are poses struck precisely to be repeated, not only through the rehearsal of the torture scene in other such institutions (in the case of Abu Ghraib) or the threatened return of anti-communist massacres (at Snake River), but also through the circulation of the images at viewings that are yet to come. Facing the camera, and looking deliberately toward a future spectator, the ostentatious theatricality amplifies the effect of the performance as show-of-force.[17]

Here, in the future, looking back at Amir posing for his souvenir by the river where four decades previous he had struggled so tirelessly, we can ask how our camera is implicated in this staging. Indeed, in response to this image, we went on to explore the ways in which a filmmaking method that re-stages particular events and typical routines ('standard operating procedures') in a deliberately theatrical mode might insightfully frame the genocide's operations as performances (that is, as oriented towards a spectatorship that was both contemporaneous and anticipated). These explorations lead to further questions: if re-enactment is scripted into terror's performance and its staging as spectacle, what role might re-enactment play in a critical and interventionist historiography; and how might such critical re-stagings and re-framings, in turn, render legible

Fig. 2 Amir Hasan supervises the electrocution and torture of trade unionist Mohammed Yusuf in the machine room of the Matapao oil palm refinery; from *Embun Berdarah*

the scripts of such performances, describing their mises-en-scène, and revealing the ways in which the operations of the genocide were generic – that is, both routine and conditioned by genre?

Responses to these questions emerge from a more detailed consideration of Amir and Inong's walk to the river.

GENOCIDE AND GENRE: HEROIC ROMANCE

At the start of his walk to the Snake River, Amir goes to great lengths to set the scene, wistfully referring to the 'romance of their work' (*romantisme pekerjaan*), describing the 'fearsome night' (*malam takutkan*) with the crescent moon hanging over the dark oil palm plantation. Amir even attempts to freeze the moon in its romantic crescent, as on an opera stage, suggesting that the moon was always a crescent, as if, during the time of the killings, the lunar phases froze to create the right *suasana* (ambience) for the bloodshed. In his remarkable memoir of the killings, *Embun Berdarah*, incredibly *written in the first person from the perspective of the ghost of his victims,* and illustrated with his own graphic paintings of the murders, Amir goes to even greater lengths to tell his story in an idiom faithful to a genre of romantic heroism.

Amir 's clichés include: 'A great nation is one that knows her history'; 'It was a matter of kill or be killed'; 'A man who doesn't know his history is a small man who accepts whatever comes his way'; 'It was a time of revolution'; and the trauma and violence were all part of 'the romance of life on this mortal earth' (this last one, certainly, is self-invented).

Clichéd invocations of massacre as 'heroic' and 'historic' frame the killing as part of an epochal battle against an enemy of mythic proportion. This is a central trope in both Amir's memoir and his and Inong's performance at the Sungai Ular: set in a gothic landscape of ghosts, crescent moons and a watchful animal kingdom (frogs, monkeys and birds are invariably mentioned as the witnesses of Amir's atrocities), the PKI is performed as a supernatural threat to be overcome. Amir empowers his victim as a mythic power to be conquered, allowing him and Inong to claim that power at the moment of slaughter, transforming themselves into heroes rather than people who committed the cowardly deed of executing those with no power to resist.

There is a tension between that which is *well-rehearsed* about Amir and Inong's performance and the fact that this is their first visit to the Snake River since the killings, and certainly their first time together. The scripted-ness of the encounter derives, surely, from the generic conventions conditioning all public discourse about the killings. For example, 'the generation of '66' (*angkatan 66*) has been celebrated as heroes, and so they easily slip into a well-rehearsed performance as heroic patriots who would stop at nothing to defend the nation.[18] Yet there is a grim misfit between their claim to be heroes and the events they perform. First, they must overcome the abject powerlessness of the victims, and this forces them into a supernatural register, conjuring magic powers of resistance. In *Embun Berdarah*, Amir's narrative strategy is to blame any obstacles faced by Komando Aksi on the mischievous ghosts of those already killed; thus, only posthumously do the PKI victims summon the resistance required to constitute their killers as heroes. Having established the epic struggle between killer and PKI members, the stage is now set for another genre, quite unlike that of patriotic heroic struggle: slasher or shock-horror.

GENOCIDE AND GENRE: SLASHER AND *SADIS*

Indeed, it comes as a real shock when, smiling as ever, Amir holds the stick he is using as a sword over his mouth and says, 'Sometimes the executioner would drink the blood like this.' Drinking blood is one of many grisly details unabashedly recounted. Others include how water, not blood, would flow from the amputated breasts of Gerwani members, how victims would urinate at the moment of death, how human corpses smell, how the *kebal* (those imbued with the power of invin-

cibility) were forced to eat and then defecate to overcome their magic powers, and how Komando Aksi rigged the bodies to float rather than sink so as to terrorise people living down stream.[19] These stories recount details that are routinely, to the point of cliché, called *sadis* (an Indonesian appropriation of 'sadist'); indeed, these stories are told in the register of *sadis*. The enthusiastic recounting of the *sadis* conjures, for the killer, an ultimate, metaphysical and magical power over death. It is a power to be relished, savoured, by rehearsing again and again the grisly details. Thus, through the genre of *sadis*, may killers perform themselves not just as victors and appropriators of the PKI's projected powers, but as men of preternatural strength with an *ilmu* (or magical knowledge) far greater than that of their victims.

Demonstrating in this way their own magical power over life and death is important, because it makes the killers (and sometimes when they at-

Fig. 3 An illustration of the killings at Snake River; from *Embun Berdarah*

tach names to their victims, the killings, too) *specific*, locating the power of death in the actual individuals who finally carried out the murders. (Here, as we shall see, is where Amir and Inong contravene the conventions of the official history, not least by identifying a locus of culpability, albeit one focused on instruments of murder, rather than its institution).

If the routine they performed seemed predicated merely on efficiency rather than theatricality, if they spoke only in statistical terms, performing themselves as no more than killing machines in the service of the army, it would be apparent that the true spectral power of death was located in those who assigned their 'quotas' (*jatah*, the term used to describe their allotment of victims). When Amir and Inong highlight the singular and inevitably lurid moment of slaughter, by speaking the language of *sadis*, Amir and Inong take for themselves, as individuals, the power of death otherwise vested in the institutions that commanded them.

Sadis, given its prominence on Indonesian TV networks like Trans TV, may be described as a non-fiction sub-genre of shock-horror. Violence is always explicit. Grisly and shocking details are told with pride and smiles, by respectable citizens – a school governor, in Amir's case. *Sadis* is presented as public fact. But despite the fact that *sadis* is so self-consciously explicit, almost pornographically so, despite all the detail – or perhaps because of it – one cannot help but feel the loss of the actual event, its eclipse by its symbolic and generic performance. And because the grisly detail is rehearsed as a boasting, one cannot help but feel the performer's *interest*, his *investment* in claiming power through the performance.

Perhaps it is this way in which the *sadis* always conjures something as *held back* that Inong alludes to when describing how *dukuns* (or shamans) always hold back the lion's share of their knowledge from their students so that, if a *dukun* must fight his student, he will know the key to overcoming the student's power, but not the other way round.

This provides an allegory for the *gesture of withholding*, a gesture that structures that most explicit of genres – the *sadis*, the shock-horror. For this withholding, this *secret* that one must always conjure as an excess or supplement even to the most luridly graphic story, also constitutes a certain *ilmu*, a mystique, a non-transferable power claimed by the performer who refuses to give away the whole game. As we have noted, the film *G30S* is analogously structured, and we are suggesting that structured into Amir, Inong and other killers' performance of *sadis* is the same withholding, so that in a double movement, they can at once claim the godly power over life and death from their superiors, while at the same time locate this power beyond that which they reveal, in a mystique conjured as a supplemental spectre, encrypted as the *obscene* to their performance – a performance whose explicitness, as we shall see, is itself already the obscene to the official history.

Amir and Inong's performance exemplifies this replenishment of spectral power through storytelling, through performances that seem well-rehearsed, even scripted. Inong in particular tells a lot of graphic stories. In his own community,

Inong's stories, whether true or merely 'empty talk' (*omong kosong*), disseminated far and wide via Inong's 'big mouth' (*mulutnya sampai ke mana mana*), have acquired for him the reputation of being an *algojo*, or executioner, a word often used generically – and *sotto voce* – for anybody rumoured to have participated in the killing. This reputation makes Inong feared, anticipated as one with sufficient ties to the terrifying Indonesian state to be instructed to kill, and then be protected. There is a tense relationship to an unstable logic of anticipation, as Inong acquires a force precisely because his spectral violence threatens to suddenly explode into the spectacular. As such, this constitutes a real social power for Inong in his community – one constituted through stories, through his big mouth.

UNDER THE SPELL OF STORIES

These stories are performatives (in Austin's sense). It is not enough to drink blood or cut off heads; one must also tell about it, rehearse it again in whispered performances and repeated gestures, if one wants to conjure the spectral power claimed during the massacre, and manifest it as a social force. The performances of killers as they rehearse these stories are what accomplish this conjuration.

In her essay on gender constitution, Judith Butler argues that the constitutive performatives of gender are 'objects of belief'.[20] However, the 'conjurative' performances of those such as Amir and Inong need not be correspondingly charged with credulity. That is, they need neither themselves believe all they say, nor need their audience, for the conjuration to be effective, any more than they need believe in the propaganda about a murderous PKI to act *as if* they believed it.

Acting 'as if' the PKI posed an overwhelming threat was a moment in the appropriation of that threat's projected power, moreover one needs to be *recognised* as a killer in rumour and whispered gossip. For this reason, establishing yourself as a killer – or potential killer – in the eyes of the community may be more important than participating in the killing itself. The killers, or would be killers, act out of the fascination of their own terrorising fiction. Thus may people brag of things they never did or exaggerate their role. This attests to the *power of narrative* – of rumour, stories and performance.

Taussig writes about how such terror can lead those under its spell to themselves do terrible things. Writing about the Amazonian rubber boom, Taussig describes the reaction of colonists to the spectral terror of the imaginary Indian threat:

> The managers lived obsessed with death, Romulo Paredes tells us. They saw danger everywhere. They thought solely of the fact that they lived surrounded by vipers,

tigers, and cannibals. It was these ideas of death, he wrote, that constantly struck their imagination, making them terrified and capable of any action. Like children, they had nightmares of witches, evil spirits, death, treason, and blood. The only way they could live in such a terrifying world, he observed, was *to inspire terror themselves.*[21]

The nature of this 'terrifying world' needs real thought. Does it mean that the colonists actually *believed* they were surrounded by cannibals? Taussig does not quite say so. In the case of 1965, would it mean that Amir and Inong actually believed the PKI kept secret death lists with their names on them, and were poised to massacre anybody who believed in God – despite the fact that PKI members prayed in the mosque as much as everybody else? If they did believe it, what is the nature of such belief? Or, perhaps the colonists described by Taussig were obsessed by cannibals without having actually to believe that they were surrounded by them. Perhaps they lived 'in such a terrifying world' because they were told, and were telling each other, terrifying stories about their world. But that does not mean they actually believed the stories. What matters is the genre of story, how it is repeated, how it is insinuated as rumour into the subtext of daily life, its context of circulation. A ghost story can terrify without one believing that it is true. Narrative has the power to conjure terror, and somehow, as with ghost stories, this power is attractive; we *want* to hear stories, even, or perhaps especially, terrifying ones; we voluntarily place ourselves under the spell of the terrifying effects of stories.

This is not a unique observation about our susceptibility to narrative; we merely suggest that this dynamic of narrative can have very real and terrible political consequences. Just as we need not discuss belief to account for the spectral effects of ghost stories, we need not when we describe the effects of anti-PKI propaganda, or stories about Indian savagery. In order to kill, and to kill so many, Inong and Amir may indeed have been *under the spell* of this narrative terror. But when we say Amir and Inong were under the spell of terror, we do not say anything about what they *believed*. Rather, we mean that they were attracted by the spectral power of terror invested in the phantasmatic PKI by all the stories about them then in circulation, and they availed themselves of the opportunity to appropriate some of this power by participating in the killing. It does not follow that in order to be under the spell of terror they had to believe the stories that conjured it in the first place. This is a terrifying and terrible actuality: that one could commit genocide under the spell of stories – stories of heroism, horrors, ghosts.

These stories haunt, yet are themselves haunted. What haunts these stories of *sadis* is the real. These displays of excessive visibility, by eclipsing with their generic gore the terrible singularity of each murder, make visible the relationship between obscenity (in the everyday sense) and its own obscene – the historical real itself. And in this evocation of the historical real, what is made real is the *absence* of the victims – that is, their death.

SHORT CIRCUITS: CAMERA AS LURE, FILM AS INTERVENTION

If the haunting persistence of the massacres remains the source of Amir and In-ong's conjured power, we will be able to see now how it is also their undoing. For they have done more here than merely provide us with an opportunity to analyse the narrative and generic imperatives of their recount.

We have suggested that Amir perceives the filming as a rather unusual public relations opportunity – to claim, rather than deny, the killings and so too to claim the spectral power that attends them. Yet Amir's bid for publicity is fraught with contradictions. As he writes in his memoir, *Embun Berdarah*, and repeats for our camera when he first presents the book to Inong, 'This is for people who wish to know more about our struggle, so that what we did will never be forgotten.' He makes photocopies of the book, but then tells us the book is full of national secrets and should not be made public. He changes all the names in the book, but then on the final page provides a key so the reader can know the names of the actual people upon whom the characters are based.

Following the walk to the river, he suggests a collaboration to adapt his book into a musical film, and enthuses about the project to his friends. When his friends try to warn him off the project, suggesting the film might be too explicit (and thereby violate the national taboo around publicly discussing the massacres), he changes all the names in the screenplay and sets it on another planet, leaving the story intact. He is, after all, reluctant to give up the enterprise. Whole segments of his own community are already in the grip of his power – that is, they are afraid of him – and he hopes that the film he would make might enlarge the compass of that power, drawing others into his fold, manifesting publicly that which has hitherto been made explicit only on the unread and moldy pages of his own memoir, written yet secret.

If he does see the film as somehow condensing his claim to spectral power, in what fora of presentation or circuits of distribution does he see his power emerg-ing? That is, who is Amir's imagined audience? Given how worried he is about 'revealing secrets', despite his vigorous boasting, it is probable that he has no *par-ticular* audience in mind. For as soon as Amir imagines any *particular* audience, he becomes aware of *risk*. It is only when he imagines actual and singular hu-man beings viewing his filmed performances does he realise that he is providing substantive and singular information. That is, only when he imagines a specific audience does he realise that his performance substantiates so much that had previously been unsaid, condensing the audience's reception of his image into the transaction of a secret. Here is where he imagines danger, and suggests changing names.

At other times, for instance with Inong at the Snake River, rather than imagining any particular audience, it is as if he is performing for an anonymous and, like spectrality itself, miasmic public defined and interpellated by an equally generic 'media'. Or perhaps he does not even imagine the public, but only the system of images that constitute 'media'. Perhaps it is the rather impressive technology of filmmaking itself that enables Amir to avoid thinking about how his performative project, in his mind, *lacks* an audience. That is, perhaps the spectacle of filmmaking functions like a fetish, a substantive *metonym* for the missing audience, as well as a concrete *metaphor* for the abstract apparatus of television and media as system of images. Thus does the camera entice Amir to forget, momentarily, the absurdity of the fact that he has authored and starred in performances for nobody.

Fig. 4 Original and Fictional Names from the memoir, *Embun Berdarah*. The right column is victims, the left perpetrators and their supporters.

The film Amir has set out to make is self-consciously influenced by *Pengkhianatan G30S PKI*. (In an unrecorded discussion about how to transform his novel into a heroic musical, he said that the model for him would be *G30S*.) By conjuring a PKI opponent roughly consistent with that conjured in *G30S*, he would claim some of the latter film's force: as we have seen, *G30S* has also been an instrument of terror, the film itself is part of the *ilmu* used to conduct the séance of Indonesian state terror, attempting to conjure the spectral power of the PKI, condense it in the film, and claim it for the state.

He hoped to use the film to close the circuit of spectral power's passage from them PKI to himself, and to amplify the strength of this power with the dissemination of his image through his generically imagined audience. But rather than complete it, the film *shorts* this circuit of acquiring spectral power. That is, once Amir and Inong make a spectacle of their spectrality, they undermine their own power, because their power was established precisely as that spectrality conjured by that which was *obscene*, unspoken and unsubstantiated (and ideally, for the architects of genocide, unsubstantiatable).

By publicly performing the well-rehearsed but *obscene* scripts that constitute the massacres' systematicity, Amir and Inong reveal that they were instruments of a system rather than its masters – they show themselves to be culpable functionaries. And so, in their attempt to use film to complete the circuit of acquiring spectral power, and to manifest spectral power as actual power, they reveal that the power was never theirs in the first place. Amir was ordered to kill by his brother-in-law, an army major. The killers were under army orders. They were killing only those whom they were authorised to kill. Lured by the opportunity they perceive, Amir and Inong get sloppy and fail to meet the terms of their own genre. They name names, including their own and, worse still, their superiors. They stumble and make precisely the kind of public admissions that have been proscribed.

Particularly, by naming names and describing the killing machine in such detail, the footage confirms what had long been suspected, or substantiates that which had been spectral. Tellingly, after our first visit, Amir would never perform another 're-enactment' (*peragakan*) as such. However, the route to the historical scene through *fiction*, no matter how transparently direct, remained open.

Originally, Amir had asked to produce an explicit adaptation – albeit a musical, heroic one – of his memoir. After talking (bragging?) about this with friends in the regional government as well as veterans of his Komando Aksi group, including a member of the Badan Inteligen Negara (National Intelligence Body, Indonesian equivalent to the CIA), he was told that this might not be such a good idea. He was warned against doing any more filming about 1965–66.[22] He was crestfallen, until he came up with his strategy of interplanetary displacement.[23]

He considers this within the sacrosanct realm of 'art', and thus somehow no longer about his experiences, but continues to make the same blunder of making explicit that which had been obscene. The disguise of changed names and the relocation of events to an imaginary cosmos already structured by the well-rehearsed genres of patriotic heroism that code films like *Star Wars*, a model for Amir's adaptation, is fragile. Not only do we know all the names already, Amir is repeatedly *arrested* and *possessed* by the singularity of his own experience and repeatedly interjects tellingly specific detail. He even wants to shoot his film in more or less the historical locations, with original costumes and weaponry, along the muddy rivers of Sumatra's oil palm belt, despite its purported interplanetary setting.

Amir's use of historical performance as a performative bid for power, and his veiling of that performance, even from himself, in the name of 'art', is repeatedly troubled by the tension between the spectral and the substantial. The meaning, force and consequence of circulating substantiated stories with named killers and victims is vastly different from that circulating unsubstantiated and spectral rumours. Moreover he does so on record. Not only do they substantiate their stories before the eye of the camera, their self-conscious histrionics make all-too-evident the generic imperatives that have constituted so many thousands of similar historical performances that remained unrecorded, always and again *live*. As a living threat, these performances are moments in the spectral circulation of terror; as *material artifacts*, they can be analysed critically, decoded, rendered evidential – that is, their own theatricality, borne of their eager attempt to seize the filmmaking as *opportunity*, produces a kind of over-acting that makes obvious the fact that their performance is scripted. These previously inadmissible scripts, thus revealed through the obviously generic qualities of their histrionic performance, lose the obscenity from which they derived their power.

It is through cinema that Amir and Inong's power dissolves at the moment that their performance is condensed onto tape and taken away from them, beyond their control. They have revealed at once the details of their own role and the generic imperatives of a broader chain of command. Above all, they transformed rumour into evidentiary account. Rendering the spectral explicit allows it to be critically reframed, and this process opens on to the potentially redemptive and retributive possibilities of this project. Once captured on film, these performances can be given over to those very subjects that the performance of the massacres was and is intended to physically and symbolically annihilate – survivors of the terror and those still under its sway.

ARCHAEOLOGICAL PERFORMANCE

This moment of restaging the perpetrator's performance *in ways that allow survivors to imaginatively respond* to a history bent on their destruction is beyond the scope of such a brief essay, one which has focused on just four hours of footage from an archive of many hundreds of hours, and one which has focused on only the first moment of a production and research method that can be thought of as an *archaeological performance*.[24]

This method of archaeological performance entails successively working with and through the gestures, routines and rituals that were the motor of the massacres, as well as the genres and grammars of its historical recount, typically moving from interview and re-enactment with the historical actors, such as that of Amir and Inong on the Snake River, to increasingly elaborate re-stagings of the events related in the interviews. Between a buried historical event and its restaging with historical actors this method opens a process of simultaneous *historical excavation* (working down through strata), and *histrionic reconstruction* (adding layers of stylised performance and recounting).

So, to close, let us briefly look at one of those moments of histrionic reconstruction with Amir Hasan.

ON CECIL B. DEMILLE AT LAKE TOBA

In his study of the psychology of denial in perpetrators of atrocity, Stanley Cohen argues that 'Participants glibly appeal to "history" for vindication. A Serb soldier in 1999 talks about the Battle of Kosovo as if it happened the week before.'[25] The power of the victims in the past, be it actual or mythic, is used to figure the victims not as victims but as powerful adversaries to be overcome in heroic defence of the nation. Amir and other perpetrators' repeated appeals to the propagandistic commonplaces of PKI treachery at the 1948 Madiun rebellion and 1965 'Gestapu' coup – even if both are ultimately spectral conjurations in their own right – perform this same role.[26] So does Amir's clichéd claim that 'they would have killed us if we didn't kill them first'.

But Cohen continues, referencing Michael Ignatieff's 1997 study of ethnic cleansing in the Balkans:

> This nationalism, Ignatieff points out, is supremely sentimental: *kitsch is the natural aesthetic of an ethnic cleanser.* This is like a Verdi opera – killers on both sides pause between firing to recite nostalgic and epic texts. Their violence has been authorized by the state (or something like a state); they have the comforts of belonging and being possessed by a love far greater than reason: 'Such a love assists the belief that it is fate, however tragic, which obliges you to kill.' This is your destiny.[27]

In the case of Amir Hasan, Cohen's description of the Verdi opera proves to be more than just a metaphor. In a still-in-progress part of the film practice Amir has been working with us to film a musical adaptation of his memoir, *Embun Berdarah*. Amir himself has assumed the role of 'film director' for this musical film-within-our-film. To this end, he has recruited a university choir to create the music. He then wrote a series of poems and speeches, and recited them 'amidst the beautiful nature of Indonesia' in North Sumatra's crater lake, Danau Toba, a well established tourist destination. Basing these speeches on Cecil B. De Mille's introduction to *The Ten Commandments* (1956), which we had showed him as one of many possible models for his production, passages include:

Why make this film? Because this is my creation, the fruits of my own imagination, expressing the history of my own life.

Let me tell you something you should know: [Quoting directly from *Embun Berdarah*] *The red sunlight shines down upon the earth. Red, green, blue and other colours struggle to dominate the heavens. Banners emblazoned with writing seek to discredit everybody else. But storm clouds are gathering, and they cannot hold back the rain of blood that will fall upon our mother, the Earth. This is the fight between good and evil.*

This is the romance of life [romantika kehidupan] *in our mortal world.*

Amir directly addresses the audience from this picaresque scene, pausing to wave and shout, 'ahoy!', to a lake-tour boat that passes behind him. Paraphrasing De Mille, he declares, 'By watching this film, you will have made a pilgrimage to the actual land sanctified by blood in the patriotic battle to save our nation.' Under a soundtrack of choral music, Amir Hasan delivers his speech before a shifting background of clumsy tourists learning traditional Indonesian dances, sipping multi-coloured cocktails, and bemusedly enjoying Amir's poetry amid the tropical paradise.

NOTES

An earlier version appeared in *Critical Quarterly*, 51, 1, 2009, 84–110. This version has been revised and updated.

1   A. H. Nasution (1997) *Embun Berdarah*. Unpublished memoir.

2   The most compelling analysis, and a useful survey of other accounts, would be J. Roosa (2006) *Pretext for Mass-Murder: The September 30th Movement and Suharto's Coup d'Etat in Indonesia*. Madison, WI: University of Wisconsin Press; see also B. Anderson and R. McVey (1971) *A Preliminary Analysis of the October 1, 1965 Coup in Indonesia*. Ithaca, NY: Cornell University Press; C. Budiardjo (1991) 'Indonesia: Mass extermination and the consolidation of authoritarian power', in A. George (ed.) *Western State Terrorism*. Cambridge: Polity Press, 180–212; C. Budiardjo (2002) 'Soeharto and the Grand Scheme of Things', *The Jakarta Post*, 2nd June; J. Hughes (2002) *The End of Sukarno – A Coup that Misfired; A Purge that Ran Wild*. Singapore: Archipelago Press; D. S. Lev (1966) 'Indonesia 1965: The Year of the Coup', *Asian Survey*, 6, 2, 103–10; and P. D. Scott (1985) 'The United States and the Overthrow of Sukarno, 1965–1967', *Pacific Affairs*, 58, Summer, 239–64. See also Benedict Anderson's contribution this volume.

3   This campaign was not without its international enthusiasts. The CIA provided radio equipment and arms, MI6 provided 'black propaganda' (propaganda whose imputed source is the enemy), the US military provided training and cash, the US state department provided death lists, and the Agency for International Development provided support for 'youth groups' that

were groomed to become death squads. The campaign was presented in the West as 'good news' (see NBC Special Report (1967) *Indonesia: The Troubled Victory*. Broadcast 19 February 1967 and J. Reston (1966) 'A Gleam of Light in Asia', *The New York Times*, IV, 4, 19 June). For background on the United States' role, see P. D. Scott (1985) 'The United States and the Overthrow of Sukarno, 1965–1967', *Pacific Affairs*, 58, Summer, 239–64; for the CIA, State Department and US Defense Department's roles, see especially FRUS (Foreign Relations of the United States 1964–1968) (2001) Volume XXVI, Indonesia; Malaysia-Singapore; Philippines. Documents 100–205. Washington: The Office of the Historian, U.S. Department of State, and K. Kadane (1990) 'U.S. Officials' Lists Aided Indonesian Bloodbath in '60s', *The Washington Post*, 21 May; for the UK's role, see M. Curtis (1996) 'British Role in Slaughter of 500,000', *The Observer*, 28 July; M. Curtis (2003) *Web of Deceit: Britain's Real Role in the World*. New York: Vintage; M. Curtis (2004) 'Britain's Real Foreign Policy and the Failure of British Academia', *International Relations*, 18, 3, 275–87; W. A. Hulami (2000) 'MI6 Overthrew Sukarno', *Malaysia General News*, 18 April, P. Lashmar and J. Oliver (1998) 'How we destroyed Sukarno: Foreign Office "dirty tricks" helped overthrow Indonesia's President Sukarno in 1966. Over the next 30 years, half a million people died', *The Independent*, 1 December, P. Lashmar and J. Oliver (2000) 'MI6 Spread Lies to Put Killer in Power; Revealed: Healey Admits Role in British Dirty Tricks Campaign to Overthrow Indonesia's President Sukarno', *The Independent*, 16 April, and E. McCann (2002) 'West has Played a Major Role', *Belfast Telegraph*, 17 October.

4   P. F. Gardner (1997) *Shared Hopes, Separate Fears: Fifty Years of U.S.-Indonesian Relations*. Boulder, CO: Westview Press, 229.

5   An account of the pervasiveness of perpetrators in positions of state power is well beyond the scope of a footnote, or even a brief essay. Executioners were promoted, offered scholarships and given seats in the Indonesian legislature. Commander of the strategic reserve in North Sumatra, General Kemal Idris, was promoted to commander of the Indonesian Strategic Reserve (Kostrad), the position occupied by Suharto immediately before he became president. Indonesia's current president, Susilo Bambang Yudhoyono, is the son-in-law of the former head of the Indonesian special forces, Colonel Sarwo Edhie Wibowo, who claimed in a deathbed confession that he killed three million people; see B. Anderson (2000) 'Petrus Dadi Ratu', *New Left Review*, 3, May–June, 1–7.

6   A particularly absurd condensation of the official history may be found at Jakarta's Museum of PKI Treason; see also Sekretariat Negara Republik Indonesia (1975) *30 Tahun Indonesia Merdeka: Jilid 3 (1965–1973)* ['30 Years of Indonesian Independence: Volume 3 (1965–1973)'].

7   See also Ariel Heryanto's contribution to this volume.

8   The exact number of dead is unknown, but historians' estimates range from 500,000 to 2.5 million people killed – plantation workers, landless farmers, ethnic Chinese, intellectuals and other alleged 'leftists' – in under six months.

9   M. Taussig (1987) *Shamanism, Colonialism and the Wild Man: A Study in Terror and Healing*. Chicago: University of Chicago Press, 127; emphasis added.

10 Of course, history in normal usage has several simultaneous meanings, referring to past events, to the narratives that claim representational adequacy to those events, and to a discipline that seeks to narrate and interpret the past and define protocols for that process. For the purpose of this essay, we will refer to the past not as history but as the past, or events, or, occasionally, the historical real, a term used to explicitly contrast with historical narrative, the ungraspable and therefore also spectral actuality of the past itself. This project does not seek to take events and create new histories, but rather to talk about history-making, and

to intervene in the spectral fields of power that are both constituted and claimed during the process of history-making.

11 Joshua Oppenheimer began his filmic excavation of the 1965–66 Indonesian genocide in collaboration with Christine Cynn, Michael Uwemedimo and Andrea Zimmerman in 2004. This project culminated in the documentary films *The Act of Killing* (2012) and *Snake River* (2013). This chapter focuses on key moments from the shooting in January–August 2004 (that is, the earliest stages of the project).

12 Each successive interview or re-enactment generated histrionic performance after histrionic performance that were ill-suited to a historiography that strives to representational adequacy and coherence. Interviewees would say their lines, rehearse a script, plot out a carefully staged mise-en-scène, re-staged for the camera in a mode not of remembrance but of *performing ideology* (though of course memory stages its own show). Althusser's notion of the ideological is useful here; see L. Althusser (2001) *Lenin and Philosophy and Other Essays*. New York: Monthly Review Press. For Althusser the domain of ideology, which mediates 'the imaginary relationship of individuals to their real conditions of existence' (2001: 109), is not so much the realm of theory, but rather of practice, that is to say, of performance: ritual re-production, an endless going through the motions, rehearsing the gestures – giving salutes, bowing in deference, genuflecting, drawing machetes, tying up bodies, shaping words.

13 See J. L. Austin (1975) *How to Do Things With Words,* second edition. Cambridge, MA: Harvard University Press. While Austin excludes the later from the former, perhaps they are always already implicated. He argues that performative speech consists of utterances that actually *effect* something, with prime examples being wedding vows and other promises, such as bets. See also, J. Butler (1993) *Bodies that Matter: On the Discursive Limits of 'Sex'.* New York: Routledge, and J. Butler (2004) *Precarious Life: The Powers of Mourning and Violence.* New York: Verso: Butler expands Austin's theory, arguing that 'reality' is always already constituted by the performative effects of discourse; in J. Butler (1990) 'Performative Acts and Gender Constitution: An Essay in Phenomenology and Feminist Theory', in S.-E. Case (ed.) *Performing Feminisms: Feminist Critical Theory and Theatre.* Baltimore: Johns Hopkins University Press, she builds on Foucault's understanding of discourse as constituting the objects it names and describes, arguing that reality is not a given but is continually created 'through language, gesture, and all manner of symbolic social sign' (1990: 270). As she explains, 'Within [Austin's] speech act theory, a performative is that discursive practice that enacts or produces that which it names' (1993: 13). A speech act can produce that which it names, however, only by *iterating* a previously established discourse. Any speech act is therefore always a citation of a previous discursive formation. Butler also cites Derrida who indicates performative utterances' dependence on the iterability of discourse: 'Could a performative utterance succeed if its formulation did not repeat a "coded" or iterable utterance, or in other words, if the formula I pronounce in order to open a meeting, launch a ship or a marriage were not identifiable as conforming with an iterable model, if it were not then identifiable in some way as a "citation"?' – J. Derrida, J. (1988) 'Signature, Event, Context', in G. Graff (ed.) *Limited, Inc.* Evanston, IL: Northwestern University Press, 61–2. Butler expands both speech act theory and Foucauldian accounts of discourse by tracing the ways in which discourses *perform* social reality in precisely the same way as speech acts. By continually *rehearsing* the conventions and ideologies of the social world around us, we enact – or manifest and conjure – that reality. Thus does Butler argue that 'performativity must be understood not as a singular or deliberate "act", but, rather, as the reiterative and citational practice by which discourse produces the effects that it names' (1993: 2). She goes on to suggest how performative citations of existing discourses can either, on the one

hand, reinscribe and reify existing discursive formations, or else trouble them by citing them out of context, constituting a de-naturalisation, an interruption which she terms "subversive resignification" (see 1993: 226–7).

14 'Performative utterance will, for example, be in a peculiar way hollow or void if said by an actor on the stage' – J. L. Austin (1975) *How to Do Things With Words*, second edition. Cambridge, MA: Harvard University Press, 22.

15 See also Joshua Oppenheimer's contribution to this volume on Errol Morris.

16 See also John Yoo's 'Torture Memos'. Penned while working at the Office of Legal Counsel, these memos make clear that the 'abuses' at Abu Ghrib, Bagram, Guantanamo, or the archipelago of CIA 'Black Sites' and client torture centres were of course not aberrations, precisely not 'scandals', but part of a systematic regime at a prison/torture network instituted with the active complicity of the very highest levels of the US administration. The torture techniques were not born of the crazed imaginations a few low-level individuals, but 'scientifically' detailed procedures designed with the support of psychologists, physicians, lawyers and 'skilled interrogators'. From 'Phoenix' (Vietnam) to 'Condor' (Latin America), the systematic nature of US-executed or supported terror is well documented. See, for instance, 'Kubark Counterintelligence Interrogation' (1963) http://www.gwu.edu/~nsarchiv/NSAEBB/NSAEBB27/01-01.htm; accessed 14 April 2012, and 'Human Resource Exploitation Training Manual – 1983' (1983) http://www.gwu.edu/~nsarchiv/NSAEBB/NSAEBB27/02-01.htm. It should be noted that the Indonesian genocide was carried out with significant US (and UK) support (see footnote 3, above). Though the *systematic* terror of the massacres was downplayed for an international public, that very terror was deliberately conjured by the CIA six years later, when, going after Allende, they sent key figures on the left and the ultra-conservative right alike, cards, each day for a month, reading 'Djakarta se acera.' – Jakarta is coming. See . D. Scott (1985) 'The United States and the Overthrow of Sukarno, 1965–1967', *Pacific Affairs*, 58, Summer, 239–64, and D. Freed and F. S. Landis (1980) *Death in Washington*. Westport, CT: Lawrence Hill, 104–5. Here, the CIA invokes that which it did and denied as a spectre; or rather, as a spectral *refractor*, through which left and right are rendered as spectral but lethal threats to each other. The massacres are deliberately produced as spectral the better to serve as an instrument of terror. And thus word of the systematic terror must be excluded from official history, but kept in alive in a liminal, or covert, circuit of discourse. Thus terror is produced as spectre. See also L. Mira (1985) 'The G30s/PKI symbol is the major obstacle to democracy', *Tapol Bulletin*, 71, September.

17 See R. Schneider (2005) 'Still Living: Performance, Photography, Reenactment' paper delivered at Roehampton University, 28 February, 17–18.

18 Publicly, perpetrators of the massacres are of course not celebrated for their role in killing people, but rather for their participation in a generic struggle to save the nation from communism.

19 All these claims are made in recorded interviews with Inong Syah and Amir Hasan, or can be found in Amir Hasan's memoir.

20 J. Butler (1990) 'Performative Acts and Gender Constitution: An Essay in Phenomenology and Feminist Theory', in S.-E. Case (ed.) *Performing Feminisms: Feminist Critical Theory and Theatre*. Baltimore: Johns Hopkins University Press, 271.

21 M. Taussig (1987) *Shamanism, Colonialism and the Wild Man: A Study in Terror and Healing*. Chicago: University of Chicago Press, 122; emphasis added.

22 When Amir described his film project to the *bupati* (district head), he was told that he should not adapt *Embun Berdarah* into a film because another film, *Pengkhianatan G30S PKI*, can no longer be screened now that Suharto is not in power. This is an interesting and perhaps

disingenuous response, because *G30S PKI* certainly *can* be screened; it simply is no longer mandatory viewing.

23 There are many hours of footage documenting the workshops wherein Amir makes these adaptations.

24 The disciplinary encounter is wholly figurative, and not like the literal exchange of 'theatre/ archaeology'.

25 S. Cohen (2001) *States of Denial: Knowing about Atrocities and Suffering*. Cambridge: Polity Press, 96–7.

26 The PKI joined the nationalist revolution, Indonesia's war of independence from the Dutch, from 1945–49, but its fortunes changed dramatically during the so-called Madiun Rebellion of 1948. No matter what one's interpretation the events at Madiun, the PKI was brutally crushed by the Indonesian military, with the summary execution of eleven PKI leaders, including Musso, and the imprisonment of 36,000 PKI members and 'sympathizers'; G. J. Pauker (1967) *Indonesia in 1966: The Year of Transition*. Rand Corporation report number P-3525. Santa Monica, CA: Rand Corporation. The movement behind the failed coup attempt of 1965 was originally known as Gestok (or Gerakan Satu Oktober, or October 1st Movement), but its name was quickly changed by Suharto to Gestapu (or Gerakan September 30) to evoke the spectre of the Nazi Gestapo. Officers leading the campaign against the PKI at Madiun included General Haris Nasution and Kemal Idris, both of whom took leading roles in the 1965–66 genocide and invoked Madiun as proof of PKI treachery: 'Nasution ... called for the total extinction of the PKI, "down to its very roots so there will be no third Madiun"' – P. D. Scott (1985) 'The United States and the Overthrow of Sukarno, 1965–1967', *Pacific Affairs*, 58, Summer, 247.

27 S. Cohen (2001) *States of Denial: Knowing about Atrocities and Suffering*. Cambridge: Polity Press, 91; emphasis added. See also M. Ignatieff (1997) *The Warrior's Honor: Ethnic War and the Modern Conscience*. New York: Henry Holt/Metropolitan Books.

MISUNDERSTANDING IMAGES:
STANDARD OPERATING PROCEDURE, ERROL MORRIS

Joshua Oppenheimer

Errol Morris, a documentary film director, lives and works in Cambridge, Massachusetts. *Standard Operating Procedure* was produced in 2008 in the USA.

Errol Morris: Part of the problem with talking about images, photographic images in particular, and violence, is that people really don't understand photography to begin with. They don't understand the effect that images have on us, how we deal with images, how we often make inappropriate inferences from images. Probably because when our brains were put together by natural selection, sight was given this privileged place among the senses. We think that having seen something – even if it's in a photograph – that we've seen some piece of reality that we know what we're looking at, and we can make inferences from it accordingly. My movie *Standard Operating Procedure* is about how we can't make those kinds of inferences. That there are all kinds of hidden assumptions in photographs – and in the process of looking at photographs. I'm sure that you've read about so-called 'selection effects', where we think that having seen a part of the whole, that we're seeing everything. And the Abu Ghraib photographs are a perfect example of that sort of thing. Because we think we've seen Abu Ghraib, and we think that we've seen the crimes that were committed at Abu Ghraib, when in fact what we've seen is a couple of hundred images which were taken during a very restricted period of time on Tier 1A of the prison during the fall of 2003. And the real story of Abu Ghraib is in no way contained in those images. Nor do those images contain the worst of the violence. Nor do those images tell you the role of the Defense Department and the White House and the policies with respect to 'detainees' carried out at Abu Ghraib. None of the above. And I would have these endless discussions with Philip Gourevitch – we put out this book together, based on the transcripts of the interviews for the film.[1] His fascination with the ocular proof – the demand made by Othello to Iago – 'Give me the ocular proof' – and the irony here, of course, is that Othello gets what he considers to be the 'ocular proof' but it's no proof at all. In fact, he makes the incorrect inference from it, namely the inference that Desdemona is unfaithful, and kills her. So, I have a different attitude about photography and images and war that comes from a very, very different place to, say someone like Susan Sontag, who is concerned about the relationship between distancing, empathy and violence.

Joshua Oppenheimer: *I think that your work has dealt for a very long time with the way images, cinema, movie images, television, photography as well, are implicated in how we see ourselves, in the stories we tell about violence, and how we respond socially, politically, judicially, to violence. I was thinking about this interview, going back twenty years to* The Thin Blue Line [1988], *and I was thinking of Emily Miller's love of detective movies. And what your film reveals is that the detective movies that Emily Miller watched seem to have conditioned what she thinks she saw. She probably thought she saw the things that she thought she saw because she somehow had seized Randall Adams' trial as an opportunity to project herself, or somehow to stage herself, or transform herself into the star witness that she'd always wanted to be. And I felt also, thinking about this, Doctor Grigson. Doctor Grigson also has his own habits of misinterpretation, that seem probably very sound to him, but that are probably based on very generic ways of imagining, very generic ways of seeing, that leave him also blind to the specificities of virtually every case, or many of the cases, that he examines.*

EM: I think that's absolutely true.

JO: *And I had this feeling that in a way, as a series of moving images, in a series – that these ingrained habits of seeing that your characters in that film have – had very, very serious consequences. Indeed, they were going to cause Randall Adams to be killed. And as a series of moving images,* The Thin Blue Line *somehow intervenes in what was really a moment of violence that was about to – an imminent moment of violence – to prevent the killing, and to do so by somehow assembling testimony and then also what I for lack of a better word will call 'dramatisation', but I think it somehow assembles these things in such a way as to reveal that something else might have happened, that the characters were unable and unwilling to see, because of ingrained habits of seeing, fantasies, prejudices, projections* *that had left these people blind to so much of the picture. And even in the case of Emily Miller, she turns out to have vision problems. She sees – she imagines that she saw things that she couldn't have seen, or at least she enjoys saying that.*

EM: She, like all of us, confabulates – conflates reality with other things. This is a general problem, which I believe is exacerbated, not caused, but just exacerbated, by the proliferation of all kinds of media. My view on this is that when natural selection put our brains together, it didn't have a set of pigeonholes, where you can say 'This came from Fox News', 'This came from reality', 'This came from the *New York Times*', 'This came from the *Weekly World News*' or the '*National Enquirer*' – 'This came from *The Sun*' – whatever. We are, you know, in a sea of information. And, you know the story that I always like to tell is a story about Ross McElwee's *Six O'clock News*. I was directing a commercial on the beach in Santa Monica, and I was with the producer from the agency – Iddo Patt, who was Ross's student at Harvard. And so I'm talking to him and I said, 'You know, it's strange, the last time I was on this pier, I was watching them film *Baywatch*.' And he said to me, 'No you weren't. You were watching Ross's film where he shows them filming *Baywatch*.' And I realized, Oh my god, he's absolutely right.

I mean, we're all in that position, but some people – like Emily Miller – are more susceptible to confabulation and confusion than others. You know, is it easier for some people to believe complete nonsense than others. If there were the choice, for example, between Emily Miller and Bertrand Russell, I would say Emily Miller was more likely to become utterly confused about her experiences, but, nevertheless, it happens to all of us. It's a problem, which can infect anybody, and how they see the world. It's unavoidable.

JO: *In* Standard Operating Procedure *I have this feeling that you've done something that is quite profoundly similar, but also different than* The Thin Blue Line *in that it's we, the public, who are the people who have misperceived the evidence. And that misperception of the Abu Ghraib photographs, which was encouraged by the government, has led us to misperceive ourselves and our own complicity or involvement or engagement in what happened, and what was continuing to happen when the film was released.*

EM: One thing that's absolutely clear to me is that the photographs worked to the advantage of the administration, and you would say, well, how could this possibly be? Wasn't this one of the worst scandals in American history? The answer is, yes it was, but in the end, it focused attention, I believe inappropriately, on a very small group of people who were responsible for little or nothing, and directed attention away from people who were far more complicit in what happened in that prison. And that's what I mean by a selection effect – very specifically – is that you look at the photographs and you think that's all there is – and you make inferences from that collection of photographs. Well if you see in the photographs the same soldiers appearing again and again and again – by the way, because they were the ones who took the pictures – then you make the inference that all of the crimes really came from them, and that every picture that you see is a picture of a crime. And all of those are inappropriate inferences. I mean it's one of the things that truly fascinates me; how a seeming disaster – a public relations disaster – for the Bush administration (not that they consciously did this – I think that they just fell into it), they were able to manipulate it to their advantage, and it became a different kind of issue. Photographs can be responsible for incredible misperceptions. And not because of what these newspapers are all afraid of; they're all afraid of Photoshop, or in a digital manipulation of one kind or another – I'm prone to pointing out that all you have to do to change a photograph is change the caption. And you don't even have to do that, because we all come to photographs with a certain set of expectations and beliefs that determine what we see, or at the very least, can influence what we see, and prevent further investigation.

JO: *The irony here is that we tend to think of photographs as revealing rather than concealing, but the opposite turns out to be the case. Because they make visible only fragments, contingent on a frame, a moment in time, a point of view, and between each photograph in a series of snapshots there is a blindspot, just as there is between shots in a film. We make sense of these gaps. We make up stories to fill these gaps, these blindspots, and these stories are shaped by our storytelling traditions, conventions, our habits of viewing, our inclination to identify good guys and bad guys, simplistic and generic ways of imagining. In the case of the Abu Ghraib photographs, top administration personnel concocted and promulgated the 'bad apple narrative' to help us fill in the gaps between and around each photo, and thereby transforming photographic evidence of what in fact was a vast, premeditated and institutionally sanctioned crime (a criminal standard operating procedure) into a tool in the cover up of that same crime. The irony is that photographic evidence of a crime became tools in a cover-up, allegories for the visible become mechanisms of blindness.*

EM: That's correct.

JO: *Subjected to the wrong interpretive framework, the photos themselves slip into the blindspots that lie between them. And part of your work as a detective in*

Standard Operating Procedure *was to gather other evidence – Sabrina's diaries, the photographs' metadata, and so on – to show that the bad apple story couldn't really be true. In this sense, then, the film was as much an exposé about the misuse of photography as the criminal torture and detention policy.*

EM: I'm reminded of Mark Twain's *King Leopold's Soliloquy*, which is based on the atrocities in the Congo – the same atrocities that are at the heart of Conrad's *Heart of Darkness*, by the way. At one point, Twain gives King Leopold the line, 'Ah, Kodak: the only witness I have been unable to bribe.' And I always thought, well yes, it's the only witness you were unable to bribe, but it's still a witness. And when the witness takes the stand you don't know what they is going to say.

JO: *There's something about the misleading visibility of photographs, as if somehow through their graphicness or their explicitness we become passive or dazzled by the image itself and suspend any critical judgement. We accept whatever story they seem to support. It's as though the visibility deflects any attention from what remains invisible, that which is around the frame, or after, before or after the shutter was clicked. I think that goes back to the question of how the government was able to use the Abu Ghraib photos in the way they did. These photos are not taken from afar, with a telephoto lens, providing some kind of an objective document of a crime from without, as it were. Instead they are artifacts from the crime, they are part of the crime, or at least they appear to be.*

EM: And in many cases the photographs, which appear to be of crimes, are not of crimes.

JO: *Like Al Jamadi's body.*

EM: Well, that's a crime, but not a crime committed by the MPs who were on the Tier that night: not by Fredrick, Graner, or Sabrina Harman, it was a crime committed by the CIA. And the Navy Seals.

There are other instances where it's not at all well known that there were crazy people housed in the prison, and housed on these tiers as well. One of them, a character nicknamed 'Shitboy', who covered himself with shit at every opportunity. And they were charged with his management as well. He also had the habit of banging his head against the wall. So you see these various videos of Shitboy, and you see this video of him banging his head against the wall, and the inference of course is that the MPs were responsible for this, or did nothing to try to stop it. And both are incorrect inferences in my opinion.

JO: *The thing about the photographs that's also disturbing is this sort of ambiguity about what they actually are.*

EM: I think it's important to remember that there is an inherent ambiguity in almost every photograph. Those photographs, I would say, are particularly ambiguous in this sense: I can remember more or less when I first saw them, and think 'What in God's name am I looking at here?' 'What is going on?' 'What is this?' The pictures seemed so weird, so nightmarish, that they begged all kinds of questions. That doesn't mean that when we look at a seemingly innocuous image, that we aren't doing something very much the same.

JO: *The strange thing about the Abu Ghraib photos is partly that they're staged as snapshots, or they appear to be. And to be seen and looked at and enjoyed by the reminiscing photographers and their friends afterwards. And they appear to be oriented towards a specific audience, which is themselves, and their friends, who might enjoy them later.*

EM: I don't think that's true in all cases, and I think it's another idea about the Abu Ghraib photographs that persists. When the photographs were first brought to the attention of the public by Sy Hersh and by *Sixty Minutes*, Susan Sontag wrote a piece that appeared in the *New York Times Magazine*, one of the best pieces that she has written on photography, in my opinion. And she decried what she thought was the most unspeakable aspect of the images, namely that they seem to be celebratory, or that they were these snapshots that soldiers took of themselves in order to remember their good times at Abu Ghraib. Again, this is a fiction that is not entirely true.

I think everybody wants some kind of simple explanation that tells you everything that you need to know about a story. Another example is Sabrina Harman. If you really believe that this was thrill-seeking, that this was even more craven because people were taking pictures of their own war crimes without even realising the moral content, or the immoral content, of what they were doing, it's belied by the letters that Sabrina wrote back to her girlfriend, Kelley, in the United States. Now here's what's interesting to me: when the letters were shown to people in the movie – I would have rough-cut screenings, show the letters, and talk about the letters, etc – people would say, 'Those letters are fake, they were probably sent after the fact', 'They were written for an audience that would eventually see them and could serve to exonerate her.' Well, for what it's worth, I just think that's far-fetched, *recherché* explanation. The letters themselves contain too much bad stuff to be seen as merely self-serving. And I truly believe they were written at the time. And they talk about Sabrina's desire to use the photographs as evidence. I have never spoken to Graner. Graner remains in deep lock-up in Leavenworth to this day. My guess is that part of the reason the photographs were taken in ordered series – because that seems very odd and neurotic way to take snapshots – to provide evidence of what they were being asked to do.

JO: *She says that very directly in your film, does she not?*

EM: She does indeed.

JO: *It's the smiles in the photographs that allows her and the other soldiers to seem celebratory, and that becomes then the lynchpin of the government's bad apple argument, which is essentially a denial of what was standard operating procedure. And then the smile – you wrote about it once, you were so fascinated by it that you analysed whether the smile was in fact a genuine smile. But the other question, the other fascinating thing, is if Graner and the others were with her on this, that's one thing, but her smile may have been directed more towards her colleagues at the time, and the photographs may not have been intended as memorabilia at all, but rather as a kind of, as she says, as a way of exposing what they were being asked to do.*

EM: Or both! The two are not mutually exclusive.

JO: *In a way her smile must have been genuine at moments. As you know, I've spent the past few years filming seemingly unrepentant and boastful death squad leaders, corrupt men in positions of great power. I have won their confidence and let them tell their stories, suspending at times my own judgements in order to help them dramatise their memories of killing, as well as their fears of revenge, their nightmares – whatever traces I could find of a conscience. I became very close to them throughout the process, and it's that closeness that the audience must feel, too. I would smile with them, laugh with them, and although I never lost sight, I think, of the moral purpose to which this work was put, the goal of exposé – not merely of the crime itself but of the nature of the regime and society and particular forms of evil built upon that crime – I certainly experienced moments of genuine pleasure with these men. In a way, this even was a way of protecting myself – as it may have been for them, too – from the worst of the horrors being described, or in Sabrina's case, being photographed.*

EM: What you're saying, I believe is correct.

JO: *And here I'd like to come back to Sontag. I think that whatever Sabrina's intention or feelings, Sontag's conclusions remain totally relevant. Fundamentally, Sontag argued that this celebratory staging of snapshots to be browsed through fondly again and again betrays an amorality and alienation in the broader culture. Even if the photographs may be, as I think your film reveals, artefacts of Sabrina Harman's effort at exposé, an act of disobedience, the mere fact that Sabrina might imagine her gloating smile and 'thumbs up' to be a plausible cover for her undercover project reveals something very nasty indeed about the culture of the guards at Abu Ghraib. And that in turn reveals something even more frightening about our society as well – the same frightful thing, I think, that motivated Sontag's essay. That is, whether or not the celebration is genuine, whether or not Sabrina's smile is sincere, the very thing Sontag laments in her essay is indeed apparent in the photographs: namely that we inhabit and are products of a culture in which such photographs are plausible mnemonics for happy memories.*

EM: The intention behind Sabrina's smile is a red herring, and it's a red herring because what we're trying to say here is not whether or not she was enjoying herself – say she was, for the sake of argument, enjoying herself – isn't the issue still, 'Who killed the guy? Who was responsible for this man's death? Who, and if it was a murder, who was the murderer?' That's the issue. The photograph, of course, provides no context. The photograph tells you nothing about what happened before or after … there's just a group of photographs.

And one of the things that I became obsessed with is the question of whether one can read the intention of the photographer from the photograph and, by extension, can one read the intentions of the people who were in the photograph from the photograph itself?

Because the Abu Ghraib photographs are digital, they have these hidden files, EXIS files, that contain all this information. We can take all the photographs of Al Jamadi that night in the shower room, including the two trips to the shower room that Sabrina made, one with Chip Frederick, one with Chuck Graner, and we can order the photographs within a fraction of a second. It's a straightforward process, and one of the things that I noticed about the photographs is that, if you have a pile of photographs on a desk in front of you, you can order them, and you can tell which camera took which photograph – there were three cameras involved – and you can, on the basis of that order, try to imagine certain things about the nature of what the people were thinking. Now, could I be wrong about it? Absolutely, I could be wrong. But I am taking my inferences about what they were thinking, not from some imagined order, but from real order that is represented by those hidden digital files that are extracted, the EXIS files. And it's interesting to note that the first photographs are of Sabrina with her thumb in the air, followed by a photograph of Chuck Graner with his thumb in the air. You can imagine them joking. It has the feeling of, you know, we're in the shower room with a corpse, let's take this picture. Over the course of the night, the photographs change, and they change from these wider shots to more and more specific shots, until the last shot was taken of Al Jamadi's eye with the band aid pulled off of his eye. Now, I interviewed Sabrina at length about these photographs. I couldn't interview Frederick, he was in prison, and he still will not talk to me, and Graner is in prison and can't talk to me. But I interviewed Sabrina, and her view was that they went in there, and she gradually became more and more interested in the corpse, in the sense of a forensic interest, that she suspected that a crime had been committed – she had been told by her commanding officer that this guy had died of a heart attack. And Sabrina said, 'If you took one look at him you knew that this was a lie. This man had not died of a heart attack, this man had been horribly, horribly, horribly beaten; maybe he suffered a heart attack as a result of being beaten, but he had been horribly beaten.' And she took these photographs, the last photograph is the photograph of the eye, and what is so interesting is – this doesn't come up in any of the statements – Sabrina's explanation for this is that the C.I.D. Interrogators wanted to stay as far away from this as they possibly could. And so initially she had been charged with tampering with evidence – by removing the bandage. And she jokes in the movie, she said, 'They put the bandage on his eye so that they could tamper with evidence! ... So I was being accused of tampering with evidence that they had already tampered with.'

JO: *Tampering with the tampering.*

EM: By un-tampering it, or whatever! And she is amused by that fact. Yeah, what a tortured, tangled, screwed-up story.

JO: *The irony there of course is that she was, in fact, tampering with evidence – evidence of the thing that the film, and a closer look at the photographs, starts to reveal – which was that there was something much more systematic which was going on that was actually terrifying. And it sort of implicates all of us in a very different way. This is what was going on between those frames. This raises two very interesting questions. One is about the scope of your film, because just as the film is kind of a critique of, or kind of an exploration of, the limits to any single photograph in any single photo album, at the same time you've very rigorously limited the scope of your film to those same people who, you are, pointing out,* *won't supply the smoking gun. And I actually think that's a kind of brilliant turn in the film, and I wonder if you could talk about that.*

EM: Well, it might not have been a brilliant turn, I'll never know really. But many of the other Iraq documentaries took a completely uncritical look at the photographs. Those filmmakers were interested in simply decrying the policies of the Bush administration so just took an uncritical look at all of these kinds of things; they were just simply illustrations of torturing, nothing more. And the fact that I was willing to look at these photographs in a different way – some people suggested that I was an apologist for torture, or I approved of the policies of the Bush administration, which is just crazy talk.

JO: *But yes, if you look at the photographs simply as a documentation of torture, then they must be seen for what they appear to be, which is on the surface, at first glance, as Susan Sontag wrote, these celebratory memorabilia, and doesn't that feed into the whole 'bad apple' denial, which then allowed the scope of the investigations to be limited?*

EM: At its heart, Abu Ghraib is a story about photographs, misdirection and war crimes. But it's a different story than people really want to see. It's complex, and it's nuanced. The movie was longer at one point, and had many more photographs, and maybe I wish that I had left it that way. I cut it because, you know, movies, if they get to be too long, no one's going to go see them. There's always the hope that people will actually see them. The other interesting phenomenon I wanted to talk about is Zimbardo, who became entangled in all of the defense arguments, or many of the defense arguments made on behalf of the bad apples. And one of the things I find really deeply uninteresting are attempts to link Abu Ghraib with the Milgram experiment and the Stanford prison experiment. I find it to be really, really close to nonsense, for a number of reasons.

To start with, Milgram's experiments were done with civilians in New Haven, Connecticut, in a very controlled laboratory situation. The Stanford prison experiment was done with members of the Stanford community at Palo Alto. Some students, some just local citizens. You don't use an experiment like that to show why people obey authority in the military. Correct me if I'm wrong, but the entire military is based on obedience – it's given, it's part of what you're trained to do! So having to bring up some of social science experiment in order to explain why people follow orders in the military … that's really stupid. And yet no one seems to ever say this. And yet I see it again and again and again. But what is interesting is that the taking of the photographs, and I will say this, I believe this is true in many instances, by Chuck Graner, and by Sabrina Harman, was *disobedience* to authority, not obedience to authority. The photography was an act of freedom and disobedience.

JO: *Disobedience under the cover of a smile and a thumbs up.*

EM: People think they need to explain these people, because everyone assumes they're bad. Doesn't matter whether you're left or you're right, they're bad, bad, bad, bad. If you're on the right, you think that they're bad in and of themselves. Self-directed, evil incarnate.

If you're on the left, you think they're bad, just as bad as the people on the right think, but you think that their badness was engendered by the evil Troika of Rumsfeld, Cheney and Bush. And no one ever considers the fact that they might not be totally evil, that they might be people like you and me, with complex emotions and reasons, and that these social science experiments, far from explaining any of it, obscure it, just in the same way that the photographs obscure looking more deeply into what happened there, and the motivations of these soldiers.

JO: *I kind of constructed the story of the MPs in my head from the photographs and video you gave to me. I had this image that Sabrina Harman was trying to do something good, at least certainly partially good, that she was essentially a whistle-blower. I kind of perceived her as a sort of taker of snapshots, of souvenir photos, of torture, but I interpreted that as sort of a cover, as if she was almost, kind of, infiltrating these moments and I took the fact that that might be a work-able cover for a whistle-blower to speak volumes about this sort of amorality of the entire workplace. The amorality of something large and systemic. But I didn't see Graner that way, maybe because I've not met him and we didn't see him in the film... But, I definitely didn't see Sabrina as bad after the film, I saw her as terribly, terribly wronged and hung out to dry. Perhaps I too am too eager to make sense of things by telling myself a simplistic, Manichean story.*

EM: About Graner, I've never been able to speak to, so I sort of remain agnostic. I think that there were monstrous aspects of his behavior, but again, you know, I would love to talk to all of these people, obviously I've invested a lot of time in thinking about the whole story. I mean, it's interesting that in order to deal with history, and it probably goes well beyond photography, we have to de-contextualise it, we have to simplify it, we have to put it into some narrative form where we can understand it, because the complexities of history are just unfathomable otherwise. McNamara is yet another perfect example. You can't really talk about him without people accusing you – and you in this particular instance means me – accusing me of being an apologist for a war criminal, for letting him off the hook, excusing his behavior, etc. I mean, often we don't want explanations because we want to condemn, we don't want to excuse. We don't want to see a story as being grey. We want to see it as being black and white; we prefer to leave it that way, because it offers answers to our social concerns. And history, of course, falls victim to that kind of thinking, history becomes a kind of cartoon, a gross simplification of what is really happening, or what really happened. And photography helps us to simplify, and to lie to ourselves about the world.

JO: *Do you think that there's something in what you were saying also about understanding, and the role of empathy, trying to understand the way people make choices and to get into their heads? Certainly one thing that you do is you bring us incredibly close to the characters. I saw* Standard Operating Procedure *in a very big cinema, and as is my habit, I sat in the front row.*

EM: That is overwhelming.

JO: *Well especially Lynndie England, with those jawbones that she has…*

EM: I saw it at the Berlinale in 2008. And it was in this theatre, and Lynndie England seemed like she was forty feet high. I felt like screaming, I felt like crawling under the seat and hiding. It was so oppressive. It was so much of the stuff of nightmare. I thought, 'what the hell were you thinking?'

JO: *To bring us so close to these faces seems to be almost like an expression, and effort, almost like an antidote to seeing Lynndie England in all these photographs. Here we're forced to see her and encounter her in a completely different way. Maybe it felt oppressive to you, but it certainly breaks through all the preconceptions we have about her. These close-ups not only make Lynndie England strange. They make her human, almost mythically so. The 'bad apple' narrative tries to cast her as a monster, qualitatively different from the rest of us, but of course there are no real monsters in life. You introduce us to the characters already at the size we expect to meet them – huge, looming over the whole case, without 'humanising' them in the false and cliché way that a medium-shot would. Is it possible that these close-ups do both of these contradictory things at same time? Perhaps it's the contradiction itself that disorients us, and opens us up to reinterpreting the whole story, which is what the film's really trying to do.*

EM: Yes, it is. I think that they're all really, really interesting characters, and you know the job of documentary, if there is a job, the job as I see it is to capture; you can't ever be successful at doing this, so the futility of the attempt is also of interest, but it's to try to the best of your abilities to capture the complexity of reality. Of incorporating something of the real world, and its complexity, that informs the story. And if you do that, that's a noble enterprise. Simplifying things crudely to some ordinary kind of narrative doesn't particularly interest me, because then it doesn't really do anything different than the expected. Particularly with the narratives that spill out, or the expected narratives, the thought after narratives, the narratives that will be the least controversial, and the most easily taken in. You know one of the amazing things about Abu Ghraib is that not only did we have to identify the villains, and again, this is true of those on the political left and the right, is we have to identify villains. We also have to identify heroes.

And Zimbardo, in his book *The Lucifer Effect*[2] spends an inordinate number of pages on what it considers to be the flipside: how we need not just to explain villains using the Stanford prison experiment, we also need to explain heroes as well, and then he takes as the central hero of Abu Ghraib, Joseph Darby. Now, I took Darby out to the movies, and I did it for a whole number of reasons; I had this extraordinary number of interviews with Darby, I could go on and on and on, I could make a film about Darby. But to me, Darby is no hero. I truly believe that Sabrina Harman is no villain; I would say that Darby is closer to a villain. And so it becomes odd, this need to project, and this Manichean worldview, onto this set of images. Who is Darby? Darby is the guy who turned the images into C.I.D. Now many people think that Darby is responsible for these images getting to Sy Hersh, and to *Sixty Minutes*. Well, wrong. All the army did with those images was suppress them. They had no interest in making them public. Sy Hersh and *Sixty Minutes* got them from a completely different source. That's one of the ironies that no one knows about. And, supposedly Rumsfeld outed Darby by accident. He didn't out him by accident; that was no accident, it was because he needed a hero, we needed a hero from Abu Ghraib, the guy had the courage to go to his commanding officers and tell them that this stuff was going on.

You know, I went with Robert S. McNamara to the international criminal court in The Hague, and we showed the movie *The Fog of War* [2003] to the International Court – I was there with Samantha Power and Robert McNamara. And McNamara went in and talked to one of the officials of the court and they were talking about current statues about war crimes, and McNamara said something to the effect, 'Well I wish those kinds of statutes had been in place when I was Secretary of Defense.' And the guy looked at him and said, 'But Sir, they were.' And it was such a surreal moment.

NOTES

1   P. Gourevitch and E. Morris (2008) *Standard Operating Procedure: A War Story*. New York: Penguin Press HC.
2   P. Zimbardo (2007) *The Lucifer Effect*. London: Rider.

INDEX

Lightning Source UK Ltd.
Milton Keynes UK
UKHW011846110621
385358UK00003B/122